COMPARATIVE PUBLIC BUDGETING

COMPARATIVE PUBLIC BUDGETING

GLOBAL PERSPECTIVES ON TAXING AND SPENDING

GEORGE M. GUESS
AND
LANCE T. LELOUP

Published by State University of New York Press, Albany

For information, contact State University of New York Press, Albany, NY
www.sunypress.edu

Production by Robert Puchalik
Marketing by Michael Campochiaro

Library of Congress Cataloging-in-Publication Data

Guess, George M.
  Comparative public budgeting : global perspectives on taxing and spending / George M.
Guess and Lance T. LeLoup.
      p. cm.
  Includes bibliographical references and index.
  ISBN 978-1-4384-3309-7 (hardcover : alk. paper) 1. Budget. 2. Finance, Public.
I. LeLoup, Lance T. II. Title.
HJ2005.G85 2010
352.4'8—dc22

                              2010005122

10 9 8 7 6 5 4 3 2 1

DEDICATION

This book is dedicated to my co-author, Lance T. LeLoup. I learned of Lance shortly after I began teaching public budgeting courses in 1977. In a state of panic, I needed to know quickly about American budgetary systems and politics (Schick and Wildavsky alone wouldn't do it!). A small paperback with a dollar sign on the cover caught my eye at Georgetown University bookstore. That, of course, was *Budgetary Politics* (first edition, King's Court Press, 1977), and I vowed one day to thank him for saving me from disaster in my first semester of graduate teaching. Like many in our discipline, I got to really know Lance over the decades through participation with him on professional panels and informal chats at conferences. It soon developed that we shared a common interest in comparative public budgeting and institutional politics, especially those of Central and Eastern Europe. Both of us had been faculty at Central European University in Budapest—he in 1998–99 and me in 2004–07. His interest in the fantastic city of Budapest preceded mine as he had been a Fulbright Scholar there in 1995 at Corvinus University. It was during dinner at one conference that we conspired to write a book on comparative public budgeting. He would bring his deep knowledge of American budgetary politics and those of Central Europe, Europe, and the EU. This would mesh nicely with my experience with Latin America, the Former Soviet Union, the Balkans, and Commonwealth countries. Off we went. We worked together from great distances—he from Washington State University in Pullman and me from Budapest and later from here at American University. Through the magic of e-mail and phone, we would work together until the book was out and then have a hearty celebration. It was not to be. In spring of this year, Lance told me about the severity of his cancer, and I knew that there would be no such celebration. Since we had both finished our assigned parts, the project was in that sense at least successful. His wife Pam knows better than I what an effort all this must have been for Lance. I want to thank him for his wry sense of humor and for his refreshingly absurdist commentary in a profession known for its self-importance and sobriety. I am honored to have known and worked with someone of Lance's stature, dedication and warmth. Like many, I will miss him.

CONTENTS

ILLUSTRATIONS

TABLES

FIGURES

PREFACE

Facing the multiple challenges of a major global economic contraction and ongoing collapse of both the financial-banking and nonfinancial sectors, government financial policymakers have been called upon as never before to respond effectively. Super-expansionary fiscal policies have been enacted in the United States, Germany, and elsewhere. These include direct spending for infrastructure, social safety net benefits, and asset purchases/loan guarantees of banking and finance institutions. The multiple purposes are to stimulate lending, borrowing, overall macroeconomic demand, and to provide job security. Whether and how well they will work is still an open question. Policymakers are devising strategies and revising them almost by the month in an effort to trial and error their way to success on all fronts. For one of the first times in the history of many economic crises, public sector finance officials can point elsewhere for the causes—to the failures by private firms to apply known creditworthiness standards to mortgages and property loans and to ideological deregulation of fiscal controls These changed the rules of the game and allowed commonly used innovative financial instruments, such as derivatives and credit swaps, to quickly contaminate the economy Long-practiced public sector requirements that reveal financial risks and unsustainable conditions were not followed by the private sector. Instead, banking and finance analysts failed to notice or report that the underlying collateral for most of the complex securities were worthless—based as they were on high-risk loans that in many cases never should have been originated. Regardless of the causes, the current capability of governments to respond to this serious crisis depends largely on the degree of their fiscal management prudence during past boom times—their propensity to save funds that can now be invested in expensive stimulus programs. Economic history provides some policy guidance. For most governments, however, the lessons of good public budgeting and financing need to be relearned or acquired from comparative examples in other regions (often from their own region and countries). This book examines the major tools, systems, and practices from five geographic regions or fiscal clusters of the world. It is hoped that our efforts will add to ongoing applied work in comparative budgeting and that it will ultimately stimulate new research methods, budget practices, and fiscal theories.

Both authors would like to thank Mike Rinella and Gary Dunham at SUNY Press for their support on this project. George Guess wishes to acknowledge the substantial research efforts of Mr. Marvin Ward, Assistant Director of the Center for Public Finance Research and doctoral student in public affairs at American University. In addition, he would like to thank Vassia Stoilov, doctoral candidate in public affairs at American University, for her assistance on manuscript preparation. He wishes to thank his students at the University of Fribourg, Switzerland, and in the AU-Central Bank of Haiti International Public Policy and Finance program at Port-au-Prince, Haiti, for their critical feedback on the draft manuscript of this book used for their courses in 2009–10. He would also like to thank those colleagues from whom he has learned most during work with them in the field on applied comparative public budgeting issues at the local and national government levels: Jorge Martinez Vazquez of Georgia State University; Bill Allan and Jack Diamond of IMF; Bob Ebel, David Shand, and Malcolm Holmes of the World Bank; and Mark Gallagher of DAI. He also wishes to thank his wife Regula for her patience and understanding of his peculiar behavior during this and many previous projects. Lance LeLoup wishes to acknowledge the invaluable help of his graduate assistant Ingrid Bevo for her research on key parts of several chapters— particularly the European chapter. He would also like to thank his many colleagues in the United States and around the world over the years who have contributed to his understanding of public budgeting. In particular he wishes to acknowledge his dear colleagues at Corvinus University in Hungary (formerly Budapest University of Economics); George Jenei and Mihaly Hogye; and Bogomil Fereila at the University of Ljubljana. Finally, he wants to thank his wonderful wife Pam for all her love and support for this project and others.

GEORGE M. GUESS, Washington, D.C., 2009
LANCE T. LELOUP, Pullman Washington, 2009

1

COMPARATIVE BUDGETING

INTRODUCTION

Budgeting has come of age in the twenty-first century. As globalization progresses, more information is available about budget processes and practices of nations around the world. Budgeting continues to be recognized as one of the most critical policymaking processes, reflecting national priorities and previous policy choices. Nearly a generation after the fall of the Berlin wall and the collapse of the Soviet Union, we have seen the creation of new economic and political institutions across a range of transitional democracies. The European Union has grown to twenty-seven nations and contemplates further expansion. Its budget processes and decisions become more important to member nations every year. Rapid globalization has not only affected commerce, it has also increased the degree that innovations in budgetary practices are recognized across international borders. Nations continue to attempt to learn from the successes and failures of others. International reform efforts have been launched to give poor countries better systems and outcomes. But budget reform targets rich countries as well: budget deficits, government guaranteed pensions, and health care costs challenge budget makers around the globe. This book attempts the massive task of comparing budget systems around the globe. The first chapter attempts to develop a comparative framework that can provide global perspectives on government taxing and spending.

A budget tells much about a nation: its health, wealth, problems, and priorities. It reveals the size of the public sector compared with the private sector and the degree of government control of the economy. It indicates the share of national wealth devoted to military spending versus social programs. It reveals a set of policy choices made over a long period of time. A budget is an accounting of revenues and expenditures and can variously be a planning document, a proposal, a guide to operations, or a record of what was collected and spent. National budgets serve several purposes simultaneously and in various nations; budgeting has evolved to encompass new and different objectives. In a democratic political

1

system, the budget process usually involves the preparation of proposals by an executive, review by a parliament, and execution by a bureaucracy.

Budgeting is an important component of governance. What does it say about a political system if it is incapable of rectifying fiscal imbalances, for example? Budgeting is also a critical component of policymaking. Comparative budgeting is premised on the fact that the allocation of public resources affects policy results. Progress in solving public policy problems is linked to how resources are allocated within and between sectors. While some policy failures are linked to disputes about the desirability of certain goals or the means to achieve them, other failures can be traced to weak management controls, underfunding, improperly designed projects, or institutional disincentives for proper performance.

Developing a comparative framework to analyze budgeting around the world is challenging for many reasons. What are the relevant variables? What are the consequences of whether a country is rich or poor, developed or developing, democratic or democratizing, transparent or secretive, centralized or fragmented? What is the appropriate level of detail or generality? The challenge for an effective comparative analysis is to develop meaningful categories that recognize both important differences and commonalities, recognizing interesting details without being swallowed up in budget trivia. What is the role of normative judgments? Much of the comparative budgeting literature is normatively based, focusing on the application of practices in advanced countries. But how transferable are knowledge and budget practices from one political system and political culture to the next? These are some of the questions that we will try to answer.

In this first chapter, we present a framework for comparing budgeting across a range of political systems, from the United States and Europe, to democratizing and developing nations around the world. First, we explore the dimensions of the political and economic environment that create a context for national budgeting. Second, different levels of budgeting—microbudgeting versus macrobudgeting—are considered. Third, we consider how constitutional structure and political institutions affect budgeting. Fourth, we consider budget institutions and processes and identify the stages of budgeting that are commonly found. Fifth, we take up the question of reform and the transferability of practices from one country to another and the international institutions that are pursuing reform agendas. Finally, we look at the policy context and policy challenges facing budget makers as well the constraints that often limit maneuverability.

THE CONTEXT OF BUDGETING

Wealth and Economic Strength

Work on comparative budgeting going back to the 1970s (Caiden and Wildavsky 1974; Wildavsky 1975) focused on the relative wealth or poverty of a country as a predictor of their budget processes. While Aaron Wildavsky had popularized the theory of budgetary incrementalism in the United States (Wildavsky 1964), he recognized that budgeting was not stable from year to year in poorer countries. He hypothesized that the wealthier countries would have more predictable budget outcomes, while poorer ones would be unstable and characterized by repetitive budgeting—the need to frequently revisit or revise previously made budget decisions. He wrote:

> Wealth and predictability control all other variables. Poverty homogenizes behavior. When nations are extremely poor and woefully uncertain, the consequences are so pervasive and profound as to determine almost all budgetary behavior. The rulers, so long as they are in power, may decide who gets what the government has to give, but the formal budget is unlikely to be a very good guide to what will happen. . . . Rich and certain environments lead to incremental budgeting; poverty and predictability generate revenue budgeting; unpredictability combined with poverty generates repetitive budgeting; and riches plus uncertainty produce alternating incremental and repetitive budgeting. (1975, 11–12)

In the twenty-first century, the link between economic conditions and budgeting still are very important. The poorest nations of the world often have poorly functioning political institutions and public financial management systems. Clearly, the level of economic development and national wealth has a tremendous impact on public budgeting. In nations such as Malawi, with a per capita Gross Domestic Product (GDP) of $140 per year, governments are limited in what they can tax and spend compared to Luxembourg, with per capita GDP of $53,000. The structure of the economy (agrarian, industrial, postindustrial), the rate of economic growth, and the possession of natural resources are all significant as well. Table 1.1 examines per capita GDP for the wealthiest and poorest nations. Clearly, governments cannot tax and spend what citizens do not have.

Size of the Public Sector

One important comparison among nations concerns the size of the budget relative to GDP and the degree to which GDP is composed of private versus government spending. Before the end of the cold war, the economies of the Soviet Union and Eastern bloc nations were government-run, using centralized planning rather than a market system. In many of these nations a large underground or "gray" economy existed. With the democratization in the 1990s, many such nations began to privatize their economies, some gradually, some rapidly using "shock therapy." Today, with the exceptions of a few holdouts such as North Korea, most national economies have significant elements of market capitalism.

Rank	Country	GDP Per Capita	Rank	Country	GDP Per Capita
Highest GDP Per Capita					
1	Luxembourg	$52,990.0	36	Puerto Rico	$17,420.0
2	Norway	$49,080.0	37	Israel	$17,220.0
3	Switzerland	$44,460.0	38	Kuwait	$16,700.0
4	Denmark	$39,330.0	39	Bahamas	$16,590.0
5	Ireland	$38,430.0	40	Greece	$15,650.0
6	United States	$37,240.0	41	Martinique	$15,560.0
7	Iceland	$36,960.0	42	Cyprus	$14,790.0
8	Bermuda	$35,940.0	43	Portugal	$14,640.0
9	Sweden	$33,890.0	44	French Polynesia	$14,190.0
10	Japan	$33,680.0	45	Slovenia	$14,130.0
11	Netherlands	$31,770.0	46	South Korea	$12,690.0
12	Austria	$31,410.0	47	Taiwan	$12,670.0
13	Finland	$31,070.0	48	Malta	$12,160.0
14	Cayman Islands	$30,950.0	49	New Caledonia	$11,920.0
15	United Kingdom	$30,280.0	50	Netherlands Antilles	$11,140.0
16	France	$29,240.0	51	Bahrain	$10,790.0
17	Belgium	$29,170.0	52	Barbados	$9,690.0
18	Germany	$29,130.0	53	Saudi Arabia	$8,870.0
19	Qatar	$27,990.0	54	Czech Republic	$8,790.0
20	Canada	$27,190.0	55	Hungary	$8,360.0
21	Australia	$26,520.0	56	Trinidad & Tobago	$8,010.0
22	Italy	$25,580.0	57	Guadeloupe	$7,950.0
23	United Arab Emirates	$23,650.0	58	Oman	$7,480.0
24	Hong Kong	$22,380.0	59	Estonia	$6,990.0
25	Virgin Islands	$22,320.0	60	Croatia	$6,540.0
26	Faroe Islands	$21,600.0	61	Mexico	$6,050.0
27	Singapore	$21,490.0	62	Slovakia	$6,040.0
28	New Zealand	$20,400.0	63	Equatorial Guinea	$5,900.0
28	Spain	$20,400.0	64	Reunion	$5,750.0
30	Guam	$19,750.0	65	Poland	$5,430.0
31	Greenland	$19,640.0	66	Lithuania	$5,360.0
32	Aruba	$18,940.0	67	Lebanon	$5,040.0
33	Andorra	$18,790.0	68	Latvia	$4,770.0
34	Brunei	$18,290.0	69	Chile	$4,590.0
35	Macau	$17,790.0	70	Gabon	$4,510.0
Lowest GDP Per Capita					
1	Burundi	90	11	Mozambique	230
1	Ethiopia	90	11	Nepal	230
3	Congo	110	11	Niger	230

TABLE 1.1. (continued)

Rank	Country	GDP Per Capita	Rank	Country	GDP Per Capita
4	Liberia	130	14	Uganda	240
5	Malawi	140	15	Tajikistan	250
6	Guinea-Bissau	160	16	Gambia	280
6	Sierra Leone	160	16	Tanzania	280
8	Eritrea	180	18	Bhutan	300
9	Rwanda	190	18	Cambodia	300
10	Afghanistan	200	18	Chad	300

Source: The Economist, *Pocket World in Figures* (London: The Economist Ltd, 2006), 28.

Even China, which retains a one-party communist political system, has allowed extensive growth of a market economy and has become a major player in the global economic system. One indication of the size of a nation's public sector is the amount of GDP that is collected by the government. Figure 1.1 compares tax revenue as a percentage of GDP for OECD countries (Organization for Economic and Development—a group of wealthier, more developed countries). On the low end are Mexico, Japan, Korea, and the United States, taxing 25 percent or less of GDP. On the high end are Scandinavian countries such as Sweden, Denmark, and Finland that provide extensive "cradle to grave" social welfare systems and tax nearly one-half of GDP.

Governments do not necessarily raise money using the same kinds of taxes. Some nations, such as the United States, raise the majority of revenues by taxing income and profits. Most other nations depend much more heavily on taxes on consumption of goods and services. For example, taxes on goods and services in the United States averages less than 5 percent of GDP compared to 16 percent in Iceland.

Economic factors are a crucial element of the budgeting environment. Irene Rubin suggests that the level of resources influences the degree of centralization or decentralization in budgeting (Rubin 1990, 24). Under conditions of scarcity, budget processes are more likely to be centralized than under conditions of abundance where decision makers can afford to be more decentralized in responding to the demands of interest groups. We will discuss this further when political and budgetary institutions are examined.

Public Debt and Social Contracts

Taxing citizens is the main way governments pay for programs and investments, but borrowing is another source of funds, particularly in wartime. When governments spend more than they collect in revenue, they run budget deficits and

FIGURE 1.1. Total Tax Revenue as a Percentage of GDP, 2003

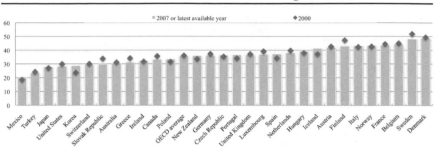

Source: Organization for Economic and Development, *OECD Factbook 2006*, 193.

borrow the difference. The sum of all deficits in history minus any budget surpluses equals a nation's debt or financial liabilities. In the case of extremely poor nations, debt relief is sometimes granted, but most nations must meet their financial obligations. Extensive government borrowing is dangerous, and most nations try to maintain relative balance between revenues and expenditures. This is often politically difficult because of public demands for programs and benefits. However, large amounts of accumulated debt make budgeting more challenging because it reduces decision makers' degrees of freedom and straps the budget with debt service payments—interest on past borrowing. Figure 1.2 shows the changes in public debt levels of OECD countries in the decade between 1995 and 2004. In the early 1990s, debt was rising in most countries. Since the mid-1990s, as the world economy performed well, debt began to decline in many countries but with some notable exceptions. Debt ratios rose rapidly in France, Germany, and Greece. Countries such as Luxembourg and Korea have maintained relatively low levels of debt, while Italy and Japan have accumulated significant amounts of debt. Japan's debt in 2005 was more than one and one-half times the size of its entire GDP. The United States was about average with its $8 trillion debt equal to about 60 percent of GDP. After having surplus budgets for three years between 1999 and 2001, U.S. deficits surged to record levels and the level of debt began to increase again. Because of the recessionary effects on GDP and expansion of public expenditures for the stimulus program and aid to the financial and banking sectors, U.S. new public debt will reach an estimated 98 percent of GDP in 2009 (Economist 2009). As we will see in chapter 3, the European Union has rules concerning how large budget deficits can be but have had difficulty enforcing them.

In addition to accumulated debt, other past budget decisions are a critical dimension of the environment for national budgeting. Nations that commit to comprehensive social welfare programs—a social contract with citizens—limit the

FIGURE 1.2. Comparing National Debt 1995, 2004

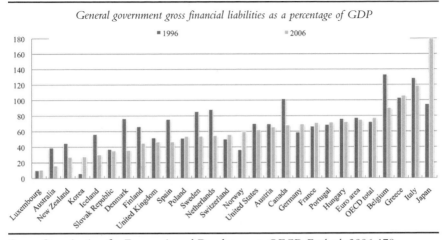

General government gross financial liabilities as a percentage of GDP

Source: Organization for Economic and Development, *OECD Factbook 2006*, 179.

FIGURE 1.3. Public Social Expenditure as a Percentage of GDP, 2001

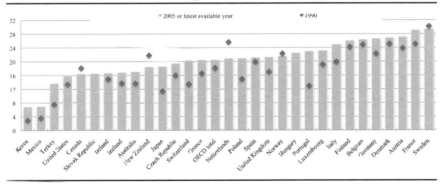

Source: Organization for Economic and Development, *OECD Factbook 2006*, 63.

degrees of freedom of subsequent decisions. Figure 1.3 takes an overview of social spending in OECD countries. On average, OECD countries spend 21 percent of GDP on social spending, but the range is from 5 percent in Mexico to nearly 30 percent in Norway and Sweden. The United States is below average at just under 15 percent of GDP. The kinds of budget choices made in the past have significant constraining effects on budget choices in the future.

Budgeting is increasingly reliant on estimations and projections of economic performance, revenue collections, and social spending. Budget estimates are based on a set of assumptions derived from econometric models, themselves contingent on a set of assumptions. Projections are often wrong. If the economy under-performs, cyclical deficits are created. In the United States' case, an increase in unemployment of 1 percent over projection can increase the budget deficit by $40 billion by reducing revenues received and increasing social spending (such as unemployment compensation). Conversely, an improvement in real growth of 1 percent over projection can reduce the deficit by more than $100 billion in a few years. Because many nations run deficits and have accumulated debt, budgets are also sensitive to changes in interest rates.

POLITICAL CULTURE AND BUDGETING: FRENCH-, U.S.-, IBERIAN-, BRITISH-, AND SOVIET UNION–INFLUENCED SYSTEMS

Political culture is also a key contextual element in comparative budgeting. Fol-lowing the fall of the Berlin wall in 1989 and collapse of the Soviet Union in the early 1990s, many nations of Central and Eastern Europe underwent dramatic political and economic transitions. Political culture consists of values and attitudes that affect political behavior. For example, an authoritarian setting driven by brutal police state tactics for more than forty years discouraged personal trust, individual risk taking, and adoption of new political ideas, management systems, and production methods. Mass publics and elites living under generations of com-munism with centralized resource allocation, artificially low prices, and few taxes on individuals have made it difficult to adopt new budget processes and policies. Writing about budget reform in Hungary, Jeffrey Straussman warned that "pre-scriptions need to accommodate the realities of history, particularly after more than four decades of experience with a command economy" (1996, 93). How can the relevant features of political culture be identified in comparing budgeting around the world?

In comparing budgetary systems and considering the transfer of practices from one country to another, one must account for local values, attitudes, and customs. Political culture can be viewed in several ways, either emphasizing atti-tudes and values (sociological/ anthropological) or political and economic insti-tutions. Viewed as a response to political and economic institutional forces, political culture can be useful in explaining budgetary practices such as the lack of program analysis, resistance to devolution of authority, and centralization of power in developing and democratizing countries. Some centralized cultures have highly formalistic, top-down relationships, where managers exercise authority in peremptory fashion. Underlings are berated in public or even flogged for minor errors. In Nepal, a process of endless movement of documents for signature ensures delay and allows senior officials to maintain control over all but the most minor decisions (Somali, 1992, 6). In some Latin American and Eastern European countries, middle managers may not make even minor transfers between budgetary funds without approval from superiors. From the perspective of budget reform, the degree of mutability of a political culture is critical. There is evidence from Central and Eastern Europe during the 1990s that budget practices can change quite rapidly (Thurmaier 84; LeLoup et al. 1998). Observers such as Harrison (2006, 97) believe that political cultures can be roughly classified a "change-prone" and "change resistant." In their view, cultures are independent variables that influence individual and institutional behavior and affect how societies evolve. For purposes of comparative budgeting improvements, all cultures are not of equal worth and can operate as major constraining influences. From sustainable economic success stories such as Chile, Botswana, and the Novgorod region of Russia, they argue that cultures are variables not constants. Politics can change culture (2006, 97). These can be incremental cultural changes produced by marginal technical reforms. For example, when the MOF introduced a mechanism to increase expenditure reporting and control in exchange for devolution of increased budget management authority to line officials in ministries, Ecuador developed an improved culture of budget reporting (Guess 1992).

How do political cultures influence budgetary behavior? It can be surmised that the effects of political culture and institutional history will influence efforts to change official and institutional behavior relevant to public budgeting. What is relevant for budgeting is that more advanced political cultures are compatible (encourage) institutions that transcend individuals, families, and clans. Budgetary institutions in such cultural contexts are more transparent allocations take place more transparently. Conversely, less advanced or backward cultures encourage opaque allocations according to individual or family discretion. Institutions in such cultural contexts do not function systematically and according to transparent rules. They are more arbitrary and less predictable than in advanced cultures. It can be suggested that cultural and historical factors will likely have greater influence over broader policy changes (e.g., elimination of state enterprise or SOE subsidies from the budget for improved macroeconomic stability) than over narrower technical changes (e.g., change local government or LGU budget and accounting codes for improved reporting). Thus, for broader policy changes (e.g., devolution and delegation of functions) one may expect political culture to exert positive and negative influences. In order to cover the widest number of countries, it may be helpful to examine those core systems that had significant influences over other countries (Guess, Loehr, and Martinez-Vazquez 1997, 45). For explanatory purposes, institutional historical generalizations from former colonial blocs can be useful in thinking about models of budget culture: (1) French, (2) Iberian, (3) U.S., (4) British, and (5) Former Soviet Union.

French Systems

ASSIGNMENT OF AUTHORITY

The French context is that of a state-created nation with strong treasury influence over central and local fiscal and policy direction. States under the historical influence of the French system (Africa, and Eastern European states with French-speaking elites such as Bulgaria and Albania) often function consistently with principles behind this institutional model. The French model of strong central state has influenced several states to deconcentrate their services rather than devolve control of them to local units; or to retain control at the center.

FINANCIAL MANAGEMENT PROCESS

The French financial management system is based on two principles: strong financial control and a central treasury (Premchand 1983, 133). Fiscal controls are exercised by cadre of ministry comptrollers, public accountants, and powerful financial inspectors. The treasury functions as a cashier and a banker. Control and treasury functions are devolved to subnational units so that local authorities are integrated into the national system. Of late, to achieve fiscal decentralization efficiencies, greater authority has been devolved to local units.

LEGAL BASIS OF PUBLIC MANAGEMENT

The French legal system (the Napoleonic civil code tradition) attempts to codify public decisions and tends to work against the U.S. tradition of managerial autonomy. The French legal system is similar in management function to the Spanish code—both operate to some extent as constraints to increases in public sector productivity by increasing the perceived risk of making an erroneous and possibly illegal decision.

Iberian Systems

ASSIGNMENT OF AUTHORITY

The Iberian-Spanish influence over Latin American governmental structures and processes remains strong. The Spanish centralist tradition created governments throughout Latin America with central government control over the country. Intermediate administrative layers represented arms of the central government rather than autonomous tiers of government in a federal system. The centralist tradition produced either unitary-style systems or strong reactions to authoritarian centralism as exemplified by the "laissez-faire" decentralization in Brazil. In the Brazilian federal system, central influence over local priorities is limited. By contrast, in Mexico, which is also a federal system, the influence of the central government is very strong (Shah 1994, 6).

The Iberian centralist tradition can be reversed or mitigated by changes in colonial masters or evidence of economic benefits outweighing political costs. In the Philippines, the U.S. colonial system restored the local role in government that had been eliminated under the rigidly centralized political authority of Spanish influence (Miller 1996, 6). Centralist controls can be mitigated by institutional quid pro quos without encountering major cultural constraints. For example, to speed up budget releases the Ecuadorian MOF reduced multiple steps for pay order approvals in 1989 in exchange for greater post-audit reporting requirements. The experience of learning and performing novel but narrower technical tasks can change routines incrementally, which leads to cultural adaptation and change (Guess 1992). Many Latin American local governments still lack the discretion to decide which programs to apply funds, (i.e., devolution). But since the mid-1990s, Latin American states have delegated many functions to municipalities to serve as agents for the central government in program administration (Lopez Murphy 1995, 31). Of late, Spain has adopted a highly decentralized system, devolving expenditure and taxing powers to two regions. Although Spain still has a unitary system of government, many of its features are similar to those in federal systems.

FINANCIAL MANAGEMENT PROCESS

Latin American budgetary systems have evolved from Iberian influence partly from their own administrative experiences. The major features of Latin American budgetary systems have been: extensive earmarking of funds and deconcentration of government activities into autonomous agencies (Premchand 1983, 134). Budgets are narrow in coverage, meaning that fiscal deficits may not measure operations of the consolidated public sector. This has inhibited central macroeconomic planning and expenditure monitoring and control, and explains some of the more serious fiscal policy problems with which Latin American states have had to grapple.

LEGAL BASIS OF PUBLIC MANAGEMENT

Institutional change and assumption of management responsibilities have been inhibited by the formalistic tradition of the legal codes that attempt to codify public decision making. The tendency of management to await specific orders from higher authority before taking action is a direct product of this legal tradition (and is similar to the legal environment faced for years by socialist officials). Where a tight vertical command structure governs official action at the expense of program efficiencies, risk taking and innovation are inhibited.

United States Systems

ASSIGNMENT OF AUTHORITY

Governmental structure consists of constitutionally based delegations of substantial authority to states. States delegate authority to local governments. States can choose their own tax structures so long as they do not violate the Constitution, which prohibits levies that interfere with interstate commerce or that discriminate against subgroups in the population. Each tier of government has its own budget. But budgets are related through networks of intergovernmental transfers. State and local recurrent budgets must be balanced. Borrowing is officially allowed for capital purposes only. The U.S. government receives most of its revenues from income taxation; the states from sales and income taxes; and municipalities from property taxes and state transfers (Bahl 1995, 77). The level of budgetary autonomy and taxing powers of LGUs in the United States are for the most part unmatched in the world. This makes the United States a special case.

FINANCIAL MANAGEMENT PROCESS

The U.S. local government budgeting model is heavily oriented toward management discretion and away from legal restrictions on operations. Budgets are prepared and approved according to matches between revenue authority and expenditure needs. Budget items are not legally coded; accounting and budget codes can be changed for purposes of improved management without legal decisions; expenditure authority is granted by the council and exercised by managers subject only to internal and external controls. Emphasis is also on post facto responsibility for expenditures through audits rather than pre-control of each transaction (as is common in Latin America) by ministry accountants that can delay service delivery and drive up costs of investment projects.

LEGAL BASIS OF PUBLIC MANAGEMENT

U.S. LGU managers have considerable discretion based upon broad grants of legal authority. LGU units formulate budgets without specific reference to legal codes. Formats and budget structures can change within the context of potentially adverse judgments by financial markets and auditors on transparency criteria. Accounting codes can be changed within the same broad framework. Managers implement budgets within council-approved budget limits and are subject to discipline depending upon budget resolution language on overspending items and totals. Reasonableness of managerial discretion can be the subject of cases brought before independent administrative law tribunals.

British Systems

ASSIGNMENT OF AUTHORITY

In the British model, delegation of power has evolved over the years in a way that has blurred accountability. The Westminster model consists of a very centralized unitary state, a vague constitution that is very adaptable but can easily be manipulated, an executive that dominates Parliament, and an ethos of Treasury dominance of the Whitehall bureaucracy (Whiteley 1996, 945). Emphasis on the cabinet-parliament form of government within the framework of common law has influenced the design and functioning of "Commonwealth" nations across continents from Australia, to Central America (Belize) and Africa (Ghana). In this context, local governments are integrated into the central government structure and are provided with substantial levels of transfers to cover local constituent needs. This balances treasury preferences for expenditure control with local authority preferences for autonomy.

FINANCIAL MANAGEMENT PROCESS

The budget law establishes a central consolidated fund through which all revenues and expenditures flow. In the UK model, budgeting focuses mainly on the expenditure side and spending agencies are subject to different degrees of control during budget execution (Premchand 1983, 133). Cash limits were introduced in the 1970s as an instrument of budget control and they indicate in advance the maximum amounts to be spent by line agencies on blocks of services. Cash limits incorporate prespecified amounts for inflation and indicate that some purchases are to be cut if prices exceed the limits. The cash limits extended to fiscal transfers to local governments. In the UK, about 80 percent of local government revenues flow from the central government in grants. Even though local governments provide only 20 percent of their own revenue, the UK is considered decentralized by many observers. Because of substantial revenues from transfers (which eliminate most of the vertical imbalance), UK local governments spend the second highest share of total public sector expenditures among OECD countries (World Bank 1995, 38).

The UK budget model uses a multiyear expenditure planning and control framework. The Public Expenditure Survey (PES) of the 1970s created a framework for: analysis of expenditures within functional groups, provision of revenue and expenditure estimates on a constant basis (ensuring that agencies and local governments would be funded in real terms), and budgeting through annual budgets made part of rolling multiyear plans. High inflation weakened this framework and cash limits replaced the PES in the 1980s (Axelrod 1988, 279).

Soviet Union–Based Systems

This is the largest of centrally planned systems in transition. External assistance programs have had to account for the extraordinary political and ethnic diversity of the Russian Federation. The challenge is to build effective institutions for intergovernmental relations, budgetary management, and economic stabilization within the historical context of a society that lacks a civil society tradition (Hoffman 1996, A1).

The system of intergovernmental relations in the Former Soviet Union (FSU) had a profound effect on the financing systems that emerged with its breakup. For many years during the transition, the Russian Federation continued to use the same fiscal framework and approaches that were used in the Soviet Union. This was also the case with most of the former Soviet Republics including Ukraine and Kazakhstan. The only break with the old system took place in the Baltic countries (Martinez–Vazquez and Boex 1995b).

The Soviet system of intergovernmental finance was de jure a highly decentralized system. But de facto the system operated more like a centralized unitarian system than a decentralized federal system.

ASSIGNMENT OF AUTHORITY

The legal framework provided each level of government with significant freedom to formulate their budget and even raise their own revenues. In practice, all decisions were made at the center. The only agency with ultimate decision power was Gosplan (The Ministry of Planning and Economy). Even the role of the ministry of finance (MOF) was secondary. The system was pervaded by "dual subordination" which meant that LGU officials at the republic, regional (oblast), and local (*rayon* and city) levels had to respond not only to their government but also all the way to the top in Moscow.

However, because of the vastness and diversity of the system, it was hard for the center to exert close-range control of subnational government activities. The authority of the central authorities was based more on legal instructions on the use of thousands of budgetary items for public expenditures, than on the ability to control or receive information from subordinate units. This lack of control was evidenced by the fact that what ultimately led to the breakdown of the FSU was the refusal of the republic governments to transfer up tax revenues that supposedly belonged to the Federation.

FINANCIAL MANAGEMENT PROCESS

The main feature of the budgeting process under the Soviet Union was a model of the "nested" budgets that had been associated with the image of Matrushka dolls, a popular folklore item in Russia. Like dolls hiding smaller dolls within, the budget of the Federation contained all consolidated budgets of the republics. The latter in turn contained the consolidated budgets of the regions (*oblasts*). And the budgets of the regions contained the budgets of the lowest tier of government, *rayons*, which are similar to counties, and the *gorads* (or cities). The budget process was informed by a fairly detailed assignment of expenditure responsibilities for the four tiers of government and by an extremely detailed set of budgetary "norms" or physical standards on how public services at each level should be provided (e.g., roubles/meal/type of hospital/type of patient). The assignment of expenditure responsibilities was roughly consistent with the general principles of expenditure assignment reflecting benefit areas and the possibility of economies of scale in production. However, this assignment was not linked with any significant degree of budgetary autonomy. Budgets were formed according to a vertically hierarchical process and had to be based on centrally set budget norms. Even though the norms were supposed to represent minimum standards of service, they in fact represented budget ceilings (Martinez-Vazquez 1994b).

The assignment of revenue sources and the determinations of transfers (or subventions) took considerable effort and negotiation through successive interactions among the four tiers of government. But in reality the only purpose of these negotiations was to provide enough funding to cover the minimum expenditure budget determined through application of the norms. Thus, the negotiated budget process was about the size of the minimum expenditure budget. These negotiations always took place in the hierarchical fashion implied by the "nested" budgets. For example, rayon and city officials negotiated only with regional or oblast officials and after the federation, republican, and oblast budgets were already approved.

Even though all levels of government had been assigned their own sources, the most important source of funding was the sharing of national taxes. The sharing rates were "regulated" and adjusted on a customized basis so that funding would not exceed the minimum required expenditure budget set by the norms. In those cases where even total sharing of taxes was insufficient to cover the minimum expenditure budgets, republics, oblasts, or rayons received a subvention or block grant. The end result of this financial management process was a crazy quilt of different sharing rules and subventions in a negotiated process that favored officials with more power and access. The distribution of public resources however, was only partially determined by the budget. Considerable levels of public services (from kindergartens and health clinics to roads and heating plants) were provided outside the budget by state enterprises. The location and resources of each enterprise were determined by Gosplan.

This financial management process is still largely operational in most of the former Soviet republics. In some of the former republics, improvements and innovations have been introduced. For example, in Russia revenue-sharing rates between the federation and the regions are now uniform and part of the equalization transfers are implemented through a formula. However, the basic concept of determining a minimum expenditure budget and filling the funding gap with revenue sharing and subventions still persists. In Russia, intergovernmental relations between the eighty-nine regions and the local governments within each region still replicate the old Soviet model. This is also the case for most of the Central Asian republics and those in the Caucasus, Ukraine, and Belarus.

Why, then, is political culture important to budgeting? One reason is to avoid application of culture-specific concepts to reform programs. Analysis of cultural constraints can avoid wasting funds, and wasting policy capital on reforms that might have succeeded if designed with such sensitivities in mind. For example, as we examine in chapter 7, budget reform is often equated with performance-type budgeting systems. But the concept of "performance" itself is relative and culture-specific—it could mean rule compliance, obedience, protection of resources, cooperation/overt conflict avoidance, etc., where these are the dominant local goals (Schiavo-Campo and Tommasi 1999, 11).

This section has identified some important contextual factors to consider in comparing budgeting across a range of countries: wealth and economic strength, government spending as a proportion of GDP, previous budget choices such as debt accumulated from running budget deficits and past choices in terms of promises of social programs for citizens, and the political culture in which budget choices are made. Next we distinguish decisions on the parts of the budget versus the whole budget.

MACROBUDGETING VERSUS MICROBUDGETING

A key development in budget theory in recent years has been the differentiation between microbudgeting and macrobudgeting and the dynamic between them (LeLoup 1978, 1988). Macrobudgetary decision includes choices on broad-based budget totals, the size of the public sector, deficits and debt, relative budget shares of military, social, and other spending categories that are influenced by aggregate economic trends and external constraints. These are decisions about the budget as a whole more than its many detailed parts. Macrobudgeting represents more centralized, top-down processes and decisions made by higher-level officials. Microbudgetary decisions include lower-level choices on programs, agency and ministry budgets, influenced by specialized interests and constituencies. Decision making tends to be more fragmented and decentralized, more bottom-up, and focused on middle- and lower-level officials and MPs. It tends to represent the parts of the budget rather than the whole. The tension between macrobudgeting and microbudgeting can be thought of as the tension between the whole and the parts of a budget. It has been shown that in times of fiscal stress, nations turn more frequently to macrobudgeting procedures to restore fiscal order and reduce deficits. Table 1.2 compares microbudgeting to macrobudgeting.

Microbudgeting and macrobudgeting can be compared across a number of dimensions. In terms of executive branch actors, microbudgeting involves agencies, ministries, and bureaus encompassing the full range of what governments do and the services they provide. Their interest and perspective is on their own program, their part of the total budget. Ministers and U.S. department heads are often assertive advocates for their ministries and departments, and they are often backed up by influential interest groups, from pensioners to public employees to veterans. Macrobudgeting, on the other hand, describes the perspective and deci-

TABLE 1.2. **Microbudgeting versus Macrobudgeting**

	Microbudgeting	*Macrobudgeting*
Executive Actors	agencies, bureaus, ministries, and interest group allies	president, prime minister, finance minister, budget director
Parliamentary Actors	specialized committees, individual taxing and spending bills, individual MPs responding to constituents	committees that take overview, budget committee, rules committee, party leaders, government ministers
Policy Actions	specific taxing and spending legislation, funds individual ministries and programs, line items	overall budget legislation shaping budget totals, budget resolutions, deficits, debt levels
Process Characteristics	bottom-up, fragmented, decentralized	centralized, top-down
Reforms	expenditure management, cost-benefit analysis, audit and financial control	all budget process reforms, spending limits, treasury systems, unified budgets, external limits on deficits (EU)

Source: Authors.

sions of those responsible for the budget as a whole: the prime minister or president, the finance minister, the officer in charge of the national budget. They are responsible for the overall totals, the deficit or surplus, and the fiscal policy consequences of the budget. They are often oriented to resisting spending pressures, imposing limits or caps on expenditures.

Similar distinctions can be made in the legislative arena. Few national parliaments are as powerful as the U.S. Congress, which reformed its budget process in 1974 (LeLoup 2005, 32–37). It created a budget resolution that would set binding totals to limit the actions of the other standing committees, which were often oriented to increasing spending in their own areas. It also created House and Senate budget committees to draw up the budget resolutions and enforce them. This system was superimposed on the old fragmented authorization/appropriation system very much oriented to microbudgeting (Fenno 1965). In parliamentary systems, different macrobudgetary institutions serve as restraints on spending. In a country such as Slovenia, the finance ministry is generally powerful enough to enforce spending limits. In other systems, the parliament may be prohibited from increasing spending over levels requested in the government's budget requests. In strong parliamentary systems with single party majority, the government is very powerful in its ability to impose discipline or to make substantial changes in budget policy.

The kind of legislation or policy action is different in macrobudgeting and microbudgeting. Macrobudgeting is characterized by laws that set overall budget totals, cap spending, or otherwise set parameters for other policy actions. In the United States, the president's budget and the congressional budget resolution are such documents, as contrasted to individual spending bills, tax changes, or individual programs. The processes of microbudgeting and macrobudgeting are different as well. Microbudgeting tends to be bottom-up. Agencies make requests to departments or ministries, ministries compile requests together and submit them to the finance minister or budget director. The basis for recent expansion of microbudgetary requests in regions such as Latin America and Eastern Europe are populist pressures from parties and groups outside the formal budget process for more social spending. Macrobudgeting, conversely, is more top-down and centralized. The president, prime minister, or finance minister may have to make hard decisions, cut back on spending, raise taxes to balance the budget, or take other such decisions.

Finally, microbudgeting and macrobudgeting encompass distinct sets of reforms. Microbudgeting tends to focus on discrete issues, procedures to gain greater expenditure control, better accounting, and more professional expenditure management. Macrobudgeting reforms tend to be much broader, aimed at deficit reduction or limiting the growth of surging program expenses in health care or pensions. In the U.S. Congress, they have involved strengthening enforcement mechanisms or trying to force spending cuts if deficit targets were not met. The Maastricht treaty gave the European Union a set of "convergence" criteria to both constrain the macrobudgetary policies of its member states and to provide targets for countries that wished accession into the EU (Annett and Jaeger 2004). In comparing budgeting around the world, the macro-micro distinction is very useful in explaining why some nations seem to have stronger, more disciplined budget systems and others are weak in response to spending pressures from interests.

Other analysts have used similar frameworks to demonstrate the tension between macrobudgeting/microbudgeting. Anthony and Young (1984), for example, distinguish three levels of organization: strategic, management, and operations. The World Bank has long used a distinction between strategic-policy, allocation/ sector, and management/operations (1998). Anthony and Young focused on the tensions and relationships within particular state and nonprofit organizations. The Bank has applied the framework to budget systems and issues, for instance, failure to budget for operations and maintenance at the operations level that affects policy results at the strategic level and allocation of funds to particular sectors such as health or education. Thus, our framework is consistent with earlier efforts but focused more on analysis of the tensions to encourage valid and reliable comparison of financial management functions and systems cross-nationally.

CONSTITUTIONAL SYSTEMS AND
POLITICAL INSTITUTIONS

The relative balance in a nation between macrobudgeting and microbudgeting often is a function of the constitution and political system in a nation. In terms of comparative budgeting, countries differ in their ability to make decisions in a timely fashion, to keep revenues and spending in balance, or to make difficult decisions that impose losses on powerful interests. Interest in the link between constitutional systems and governing capacity goes back to Woodrow Wilson and before. In particular, in the 1980s, critics blamed large U.S. budget deficits on the system of separation of powers and divided government. In the 1990s, the nations of Central and Eastern Europe (CEE) went through a period of rapid political and economic transition, usually writing new constitutions. It provided an opportunity to examine links between political system characteristics and budgeting (see LeLoup 1998). In particular, we are interested in the degree to which decisions are centralized, are subject to multiple veto points, and the extent to which political leaders share a set of common values (Weaver and Rockman 1993, 7).

One of the main distinctions to be made in comparing democratic political systems is that of parliamentary versus presidential systems (Lijphart 1992). Scholars generally find that parliamentary systems, where executive and legislative powers are fused, provide greater capacity to make decisions than presidential systems, where legislative and executive functions are separated. Weaver and Rockman (1993, 11) argue that parliamentary systems usually display greater party discipline, a cabinet of ministers largely taken from the parliament, centralization of power in the cabinet, and greater accountability to voters. Other key differences stem from the nature of electoral systems. Single-member districts tend to produce majoritarian legislatures with fewer numbers of parties represented. Proportional representation systems tend to produce a representational legislature often with multiparty governing coalitions and a larger number of parties represented. Parliamentary governments with majoritarian legislatures tend to provide governments the greatest capacity to perform policy tasks, including budgeting.

As with the influences on budget systems discussed earlier, the distribution of constitutional systems around the world is related to various cultural influences: American, British, European, Iberian, Soviet, and others. In general, the American constitutional model reflects a separation of powers system that often produces divided government; the British model encompasses a strong parliamentary system that often produces single-party majoritarian governments; and the Western European model reflects a proportional representation system that often produces multiparty coalition governments. Table 1.2 is adapted from the work of G. Bingham Powell Jr. and shows how these and several other models have influenced a number of other countries. In the 1990s, Central and Eastern European countries rewrote their constitutions and largely followed the cultural influence of Western Europe. This was their model in terms of representational legislatures and parliamentary systems, although some (such as Hungary) developed hybrid electoral systems that included both proportional representation and single-member districts.

The main difference between constitutional types has to do with the relationship between the executive and legislative branches. But there are important differences within presidential and parliamentary systems. Weaver and Rockman (1993, 21) identify three parliamentary regime types: multiparty coalition, majority party government, and single-party dominant. Electoral systems with single-member districts disproportionately reward one party, discourage the formation of third parties, and allow factions to exist within major parties without splitting off. Proportional representation systems can provide elections results that make it difficult to form a governing coalition or lead to instability and frequent elections, as in the case of post–World War II Italy and Fourth Republic France. Within these three types, different kinds of governments can and do occur and often depend on the rules and norms surrounding government formation and no-confidence votes.

Scholars have suggested that the ideological distance between coalition partners affects budgeting and fiscal performance. Alesina and Perotti (1995) suggest that coalition governments with greater ideological differences would be less capable of agreeing on fiscal consolidations. Mark Hallerberg (2004) suggests that under an ideologically more united government, it is possible to delegate power to a strong finance minister and maintain greater fiscal discipline. An example of this is the United Kingdom, with two major political parties, or France, where the governing parties are relatively close to each other. He cites Finland and the Netherlands as opposite cases where ideological distance among parties in the governing coalition does not allow delegation. Instead, fiscal discipline depends on negotiated agreements or budget rules accepted by the parties. We will examine these hypotheses more closely in chapter 4 on budgeting in Europe.

Within presidential systems with separation of powers, party control of the two branches is an important variable. The differences in performance between divided and unified party control has been the subject of much recent research. In the 1980s, several writers linked the record high budget deficits to the continued pattern of divided government (Cutler 1989, 391; McCubbins 1991). The assumption that unified party government produced greater policymaking capacity was challenged by David Mayhew with his 1991 book *Divided We Govern.* Subsequent research, however, has challenged Mayhew's approach and conclusions by noting that more major legislation fails to pass (Edwards, Barrett, and Peake 1997) during divided government. Binder (2003) suggests that if the national policy agenda is measured, unified government is able to enact a higher proportion of those policies than divided government. A recent study of the congres-

TABLE 1.3. Models of Constitutional Arrangements and their Cultural Influence

Cultural influence	Predominate constitution type	Countries fitting type	Exceptions or mixed
American or American-dominated	presidential executive and majoritarian legislature	USA Philippines	West Germany Japan
British or British-dominated or educated	parliamentary and majoritarian legislature	UK Australia Canada Ceylon India Jamaica New Zealand	Ireland
Continental Western Europe and Scandinavia	parliamentary and representational legislature	Austria Belgium Denmark Finland Israel Italy Netherlands Norway Sweden	France Switzerland
Latin America	presidential executive and representational legislature	Chile Costa Rica Urugway Venezuela	pre-1967 Uruguay
Other	parliamentary and representational legislature	Greece Turkey	

Source: G. Bingham Powell Jr., "Contemporary Democracies: Participation, Stability, and Violence," in *Parliamentary Versus Presidential Government*, ed. Arend Lijphart (Oxford: Oxford University Press, 1992), 230.

sional budget process and divided government has shown that divided government affects budgeting in several important ways: it leads to significant delays in meeting deadlines, it increases the probability of a government shutdown, it constrains the policy options that can be considered in deficit reduction plans, increases the use of omnibus appropriations over individual bills, and increases the likelihood of some kind of extraordinary means of resolving budget issues such as a budget summit or bipartisan commission (LeLoup 2005, 214–20).

In comparing budgeting around the world, cultural, constitutional, and political variables are linked to budget processes and outcomes, but we cannot always specify those links with precision. In addition to these factors, more specific differences in budget systems and processes are also significant.

BUDGETARY SYSTEMS AND PROCESSES

Nations differ in manner of budget systems and budgetary institutions that they adopt. Much of the analysis in subsequent chapters will focus on comparing those systems. At the same time, it is possible to identify some common institutions, processes, and stages in budgeting. In making comparisons, several key questions need to be asked. Is the system relatively centralized or decentralized? Is the budget "unified" or is it fragmented and approved in various pieces? Does a nation have a Treasury system where all revenues are centrally collected and disbursed? Does a country have a federal system and what kind of financial relationships exist between national and subnational governments?

Defining the "Budget"

One of the challenges of comparative budgeting is that of definition and measurement. In many places around the world, no single national budget exists. Instead, there may be several budgets and different budget processes. The United States did not even have an executive budget until 1921 with the passage of the Budget and Accounting Act. Before that, limited government activities were financed through individual appropriation acts emerging from Congress. After 1921, the president was given the responsibility to coordinate all the requests for money coming from the government in a budget (the beginning of macrobudgeting in the United States).

Defining budgets requires some common characteristics. The Government Finance Officer's Association identified four elements of budgeting (Miller 1984):

- The budget should be a **policy document** that describes and articulates policy changes and their impacts.
- The budget should be an **operational guide** that provides data for comparison with past operations, measures of performance that clarifies the relationship between capital and operating outlays.
- The budget should be a **financial plan** that consolidates operations and financing, including extrabudgetary funds.
- The budget should be a **communications device** that is comprehensible to citizens that outlines key choices and decisions with supporting fiscal data.

One of the major reforms in U.S. budgeting took place in 1968 when the federal budget was "unified," bringing together the operating budget with social security and other trust fund budgets that raise revenues from payroll taxes. Even in the United States, the unified budget has sometimes been challenged. In 1990, for example, in the massive deficit reduction package negotiated between the first President Bush and the Democratic Congress, social security was technically taken "off-budget" to protect it from cuts. However, exceptions to the concept of unified accounting and control are still possible. From 2003–06, about $120 billion in outlays for the Iraq war were made largely off-budget. This was made possible by use of "emergency spending bills" to keep war costs out of the federal budget process (Reuters 2006) More recently, U.S. Treasury assumption and guarantee of about $5 trillion for the mortgage lending losses of the Federal National Mortgage Association (FNMA) and Freddie Mac (*Washington Post* 2008) are commitments that will add to the national debt but not the current (FY 2009) cash deficit. FNMA and FMAC are effectively off-budget government-sponsored enterprises—though some characterize them as neither on nor off-budget! (Mikesell 2007, 103). Similarly, recent bank recapitalization expenditures of about (L50 billion) $87 billion in the UK by the Treasury are off-budget, will not add to the deficit, but will push the debt up to about 50 percent of GDP. Growing macrobudgetary pressures in the UK have caused the fiscal and budgetary framework there to become "frayed" (*Economist* 2008, 65).

Hungary in the 1990s, immediately after the democratic transition, is an example of a budget system that was extremely fragmented and lacked a standardized accounting and budgetary information system. Hungary did not have a unified national budget but rather four major budget subsystems:

- *Central Government Budget* made up of activities concerning general administration, defense, education, and some social benefits.
- *Chapters and Ministries* made up of separately funded bureaus (chapters) and ministries, each created by an act of parliament, which collect and control their own revenue sources.
- *Social Security Budget* encompassing an obligatory insurance system, financed by payroll taxes on employers and employees, that is self-governing and independent but must be approved by parliament.
- *Local Government Budget* consisting of a mix of national revenue and own-source revenue, the most independent and autonomous subsystem.

This level of fragmentation made it difficult to get a handle on macrobudgetary totals. One observer concluded that the financial flows between the different budgetary funds and entities are "almost innumerable, making accounting accurately for totals extremely difficult (Semjen 1994). Despite the fact the Hungary was running deficits, certain independent ministries and budget entities were engaging in for-profit activities and running surpluses. While Hungary has subsequently modernized its budget system and adopted a Treasury system, there still exists a number of countries without a completely unified budget and a number of important "off-budget" entities.

In general, a national budget provides comprehensive coverage of financial operations, specifies the deficit and any needed public borrowing, accounts for extrabudgetary funds, provides for budget execution, and presents the annual budget within a macroeconomic framework (Allan 1994).

Federalism

Federalism is an important element in comparative budgeting. In federal systems, state and local governments are often autonomous and independent, although usually they are supported by some kind of subsidy or revenue sharing from national government. In the United States, where states enjoy a measure of con-stitutional power, they are still highly dependent on the federal government. In the late 1970s, state and local government received as much as 27 percent of their revenues from the federal government (U.S. Advisory Commission on Intergov-ernmental Relations 1983). It began to decline after that and was below 20 per-cent by 1990. Revenue transfers from national to subnational governments can take many forms, ranging from categorical grants, with very specific guidelines for use, to general revenue sharing, with few strings attached. Decentralized federal systems often result in varying levels of fiscal health for subnational governments. In the United States, several cities have gone into bankruptcy and some states have chronic revenue shortfalls while others consistently run surpluses. In Hun-gary, there is dramatic variation in the financial health of cities and the level of taxation and services delivered (Straussman and Fabian 1995). For other regions, such as Eastern Europe and the Former Soviet Union where the central govern-ment still provides much of the revenues for local government, the types and pur-poses of fiscal transfers vary more widely. Ebel and Peteri (2006, 5) distinguish transfers that: (1) provide incentives to promote efficient local service provision/ stimulate spending on local public goods (expenditure side) and promote own-source revenue raising (revenue side), (2) guarantee a minimum level of services through devices such as conditions, assurance of citizen access to basic services, and differentiation between unit costs of services (expenditure side) and grants that equalize differences in revenue-raising capacity, and (3) reduce regional eco-nomic disparities by providing grants based on needs, workloads, and revenue base differences.

Budget Formulation

Whether they are referred to as advocates and guardians or claimants and conservers, it has long been recognized in budgeting that certain actors base their behaviors on gaining more resources and other sets of actors base their strategies on constraining excessive resource demands. This is true during the executive formulation stage and the legislative approval stage of budgeting. Advocates or claimants are generally engaged in microbudgeting, budgeting from the bottom-up, summing up all the needs and desires for resources. Guardians or conservers are generally engaged in macrobudgeting, putting constraints and limits on total spending and cutting back budget requests where possible. Wildavsky (1986) argued for strong guardian and spender institutional roles to produce optimum budget and policy results. Where one or both are missing from the arena, problems arise. An excessively strong guardian role can control expenditures but can discourage useful analysis and local needs policies (e.g., occasional IMF austerity programs for particular African countries); a stronger advocacy set of roles can lead to overallocations (e.g., honey and sugar cane subsidies); and where both roles are weak and funds are plentiful, the results may be both inefficient and ineffective (e.g., special purpose district to abate mosquitoes).

These relationships become important in comparing budget formulation around the world. Formulation generally takes place in the executive branch. In parliamentary systems, where legislative power is concentrated in the cabinet or "government," budget formulation usually takes place in the finance ministry or exchequer. Generally, finance ministries have some kind of budget office and deputy minister in charge of the budget. In the United States, the Bureau of the Budget was reorganized as the Office of Management and Budget by the Nixon administration in 1970. The OMB director (or budget director) reports directly to the president. OMB, finance ministries, and central budget offices are guardians in the budget process—they are looking at the budget as a whole. How effective they are differs widely by country and depending on the institutional arrangements, prevailing culture, and, sometimes, the will of the current government.

The budget formulation process involves estimates of budgetary needs of hundreds and thousands of bureaus, agencies, ministries, and other entities. In Hungary, for example, a single ministry, the Ministry of Culture and Education, encompassed more than 1,400 separate entities ranging from universities to the state opera. Agencies and ministries generally act as advocates for greater funding, although some agencies are assertive, seeking large increases, while others are more satisfied with the status quo. Agencies and ministries are often supported by various clientele groups in society and use that political support to help them in budgeting. Agencies and ministries do not have unlimited degrees of freedom in how much they ask for in the next budget. Governments often place caps or guidelines to limit growth. Budget formulation is an extremely political process where heads of departments or ministers lobby within the upper levels of government for the programs in their portfolio.

Agencies, bureaus, and ministries act strategically in most cases to maintain or to expand their funding base. Faced with budget cuts, these entities will develop strategies to try to minimize the damage, portraying their programs and activities as more vital to the nation than other activities. Although the specifics may vary considerably, many strategies by claimants can be observed across nations. One device is to mobilize supporters or organize demonstrations against cuts or in favor of increases. Taking budget disputes to the streets is a common characteristic of French politics and budgeting. Agencies, interest groups, and other claimants often tie their goals to popular causes, from antiterrorism to combating climate change. The U.S. National Parks Service's suggestion that they would close the Washington Monument if their budget was cut exemplifies that strategy of threatening to cut the popular program. Agencies and ministry officials around the world may try to use highly technical, bureaucratic jargon to obfuscate the discussion and to protect budgets. Another tactic in budgeting by agencies and ministries is to propose small-scale initiatives with low start-up costs. One U.S. member of Congress once complained during a budget hearing that "this is the camel's nose. These things never get out of a budget. They manage to stay and grow." (Committee on Appropriations 1976, 144). One of the most common tactics is the "end run" where agencies and ministries to try to circumvent the budget.

Agencies and ministries may share the general orientation to protect and increase their funding base, but they can differ significantly in terms of how assertive they are in pursuing their own budget goals. Agencies staffed with younger, more activist employees, in an environment of strong public support and reasonable economic growth might be willing to challenge limits imposed by central budget offices in proposing larger than average increases. In times of retrenchment, they may be more willing to try end runs and mobilization of constituent groups. Old-line bureaus, with less glamorous activities and weaker constituent group support, would be less likely to push hard for budget increases.

The central budget office and president or prime minister play critical roles in budget formulation as well. One of the key variables in comparative budgeting is the strength of the central budget office—whether they have the ability to impose cuts on powerful ministries. The role of the president or prime minister is the archetype of macrobudgeting. He or she is involved at the highest level, setting broad priorities, articulating an overall vision rather than being involved in details. The top leader's impact can vary depending on their institutional strength and the nature of their government. In the United States, a lame duck president late in his term, or a president with low approval ratings will have less clout and is more likely to have his budget priorities challenged by Congress. In a parliamentary system, a prime minister with a single majority party is more likely to get difficult budget choices adopted. In Hungary in the mid-1990s, Prime Minister Horn was able to impose significant unpopular cutbacks because of his party's majority status in parliament. In Slovenia at the same time, taming rising pension costs was much more difficult because the Slovenian Pensioners party was part of the multiparty coalition running the country.

Budget Adoption

The adoption of a national budget is most often associated with the legislative branch in political democracies. However, significant differences exist between presidential, separation of powers systems, and parliamentary systems where legislative and executive powers are merged. For the most part, parliaments have limited powers in making changes to the budget proposal formulated by the cabinet or government. Great Britain, with the Westminster model and single majority party, is an example of a system where the House of Commons has very limited ability to change what the government proposes. Yet even here, parliament can have some occasional impact and the budgetary power of the government is not unlimited. MPs can initiate investigations or hold committee hearings on certain provisions in the budget. While they are unlikely to be able to defeat the government on a vote in parliament, they can attract media attention and stimulate activities by interest groups that can lead the government to withdraw or modify a proposal. Parliaments have influence on the budget in several ways:

- Through the regular parliamentary budget process, which often involves approving an overall plan for the budget and then approving specific taxing and spending bills.
- Through proposing changes in parliamentary rules by which the budget is approved to enhance their influence.
- Through the committee process, which involves holding hearings on specific parts of the budget and testimony by interested parties.
- By increasing the number of parliamentary staff that can provide backbenchers and committees with independent sources of budget information allowing them to challenge government assumptions and claims.
- By proposing amendments on the floor to alter the government's budget, although in strong parliamentary systems this is rarely an effective strategy unless the proposal has majority support within parliament. If it does, it is more likely to initiate intraparty negotiations than a successful floor vote.

- Through the plenary debate on the government's budget, where they can make a public record and gain publicity through the media for certain positions in opposition to the government's budget.
- Through informal, behind the scenes negotiations within the party factions during formulation and while the budget is being approved. Governments often do modify proposals during the approval process based on these negotiations and this is often the most effective way for MPs to have influence.

All in all, despite the limitations of parliamentary ability to significantly alter the government's proposed budget, the role of parliament remains significant. In a democracy, parliamentary approval is a critical if often symbolic stage. In many parliaments, budget rules limit influence, such as a rule that all proposed amendments must be deficit-neutral or that spending increases must be offset by cuts in other program. Parliamentary committees can focus attention on controversial aspects of the government's budget, leading to media coverage. Most importantly, strong parliamentary support for a change can force the government to respond to backbenchers and may lead to intraparty negotiations that can change budget proposals.

In the United States and other presidential systems, Congress has a stronger, more independent role but it also varies significantly across time. In the United States, the power of the purse is constitutionally guaranteed to the legislative branch, but beginning in the early twentieth century, much power began to shift toward the presidency. In 1974, Congress enacted legislation to restructure its own budget process, for the first time engaging in macrobudgeting to enable it to compete with the president. It also created its own budget office (Congressional Budget Office—CBO) to provide independent information during the budget process. We will look at the congressional budget process in more depth in chapter 2. Congress has the power to approve or reject administration budget proposals, but most of the budget is not controversial and is routinely approved. Attention focuses on the overall size of the budget and the deficit, major new spending initiatives, and major changes in tax law. Despite the independent power of Congress, presidents are more likely than not to be successful. President Clinton succeeded in getting a very unpopular deficit reduction plan adopted in 1993 despite including significant tax increases. President George W. Bush had an easier time convincing the Republican Congress to cut taxes in 2001 and 2003, although in both cases, he received fewer tax cuts than he initially wanted. In the U.S. and other systems, the existence of unified or divided party control of government has a significant outcome on budget approval and outcomes. (LeLoup 2005, 214–20). We will see in the subsequent chapters that there are many variations in the process of approving budget proposals within these general patterns.

Implementing the Budget

Budgeting does not end with the approval of the budget by the legislative body. Budgeting then shifts to the execution stage where the decisions are carried out, revenues are collected, and money is spent. The operation of programs involves a host of decisions that take place during the year. Within the constraints imposed by macrobudgetary decisions, agencies and ministries often retain latitude for considerable discretion. Budget management is a dimension of comparative budgeting that shows a great deal of variation and is a topic of many reform proposals. Budgeting implementation is constrained by certain control mechanisms: cash management, pre-audit systems, allotment and apportionment rules, and transfer authority (Axelrod 1988, 170) Accounting and performance reports provide data needed to ensure deficit control, cash management, and maximization of funding for service delivery. The strength of budget management systems determine how effective budgeting is for policy and financial planning purposes. Some of the most important aspects of budget implementation that we will compare include:

- *Monitoring Budget Execution.* Are monies going to the purpose that they were intended for? Do managers have the tools to monitor execution and take corrective action if necessary?
- *Line-Item Controls.* Most governments focus on specific line items to control implementation of salaries, maintenance, supplies, investments, and so forth. Sometimes these controls can create an overly rigid system that is not adaptable to changing needs. Some nations have attempted to provide managers more flexibility for implementing budgets without losing capable oversight.
- *Budget Modification.* Because of revenue shortfalls or unforeseen expenditures, such as for national disasters, budget adjustments become necessary. This may take the form of transfer of funds within or between categories, reprogramming between larger units, or shifting funds to different programs altogether. Again, we will see that countries differ in how they handle budget modifications during the year, and how centralized or decentralized is control over implementation.
- *Budget Reserves.* Reserve funds provide a cushion against unexpected changes in the economy and can mitigate the need to borrow additional funds to finance short-term operations. These "rainy day" or "fiscal stabilization" funds provide flexibility as well as predictability during budget implementation. We will examine how these reserve funds are used around the world.
- *Treasury Management.* Treasuries play an important role in budget implementation from cash management to actual execution of the budget. Systems without treasury systems, such as Hungary in the years

after the transition in the 1990s, face daunting problems during the implementation stage of budgeting. They may not know what assets ministries control or how much is being spent. Effective treasury systems help control aggregate spending, minimize borrowing costs, and help ensure that monies go for what they were intended. There are three main treasury functions: accounting-reporting, cash and debt management, and budget execution and financial planning.

- *Monitoring and Evaluation.* Another dimension for comparison is monitoring and evaluating the effectiveness of program spending, including both fiscal and physical performance indicators. Monitoring can involve progress reports, surveys, or simply looking at complaints received. Program evaluation is more systematic, designed to study and compare program results.
- *Budget Compliance and Control.* Nations have a number of institutions designed to ensure compliance and control during budget implementation. In Ukraine, for example, five sets of institutions perform this function (see chapter 7).
- *Audits.* Audits are also an important part of budget implementation, including internal audits and external post-audits. Internal audits are designed to determine that funds are being spent properly. In the United States, inspectors general are assigned to take an independent look at what agencies and departments are doing. In some cases, excessive audits can become a legal control function that requires multiple steps. This has been common in Latin America and often leads to the kind of corruption that it is designed to prevent. External post-audits are *lookbacks* to ensure the legality of expenditures. Legislative audits typically focus on year-end reports of budgetary accounts. Performance audits are increasingly seen as a way to maximize program effectiveness.

Implementation of budgets is where the rubber meets the road in terms of government spending reaching its intended purposes. It is also one of the main targets of budget reform in countries around the world.

THE POLICY AGENDA AND CONTEXT FOR BUDGETING

For all our attention to conceptualizing budgeting, distinguishing macro- from microbudgeting, examining the stages and cycles of budgeting, one of the most important elements of comparison is the kind of policy choices that nations confront. In a sense, budgeting creates its own agenda. Because of path dependency, choices and commitments made by a nation in the past create expectations for effective decision making today (Pierson 2000, 251–67). Once appropriations create budgetary bases, they typically develop political support that may be hard to confront for program modification or especially elimination. Budgets in most political systems become "sunk costs" in areas such as entitlements and defense. Before the advent of social security and national old-age pension systems, nations could budget without worrying about funding programs to take care of the elderly. After the leadership of political leaders such as Bismarck and Roosevelt changed policies in their respective countries, leaders today in the United States and Germany face pressures to adequately fund pension systems. Today, one of the most pressing budgetary problems confronting developed countries is funding pension systems as demographic trends push up the number of retirees while reducing the percentage of contributing workers. There are many examples and very different budget paths that shape current budget choices. Scandinavian countries have opted for more comprehensive social service networks, which requires much higher levels of general taxation to pay for them. Nations such as the United States, Mexico, and Japan have opted for less generous social welfare systems with more gaps in coverage that allow lower levels of taxation. Even with these differences, there are many similarities in terms of the policy issues and policy contexts that influence budget choices. The following are some of the key policy issues that challenge budget makers around the world and shape their choices.

- *Maintaining support for social security and pension systems as the baby boom generation reaches retirement age.* This issue challenges most of the developed and postcommunist nations that maintain social security systems in Asia, North America, and Europe. Because long-term trends show many pension systems becoming insolvent over the next two decades, one of the tests of national budget systems will be whether they can impose losses on some stakeholders in order to put those systems into solvency. Those losses could be assessed on younger workers who are forced to pay higher payroll and other taxes, or they could be borne by retirees getting lower benefits and related services.
- *Controlling health care costs while keeping up with new medical technologies and treatments.* The growing cost of health care is not just a problem in the United States with its largely private system, but also a huge problem in Commonwealth countries, Europe, and Asia. In recent decades, health care costs have outstripped general price inflation by three and four times, creating budgetary problems. The cost of Medicare and Medicaid in the United States are the fastest growing budget outlays, the first hitting the national government, the second impacting the states particularly hard. If not changed, current Medicare and Medicaid expenditure policies will grow from 4.6 percent of GDP in 2009 to 12 percent of GDP in 2050. In countries with national health care

systems, cost increases have led to delays in service and the development of a fledgling private system, creating a two-tiered system of care. How nations deal with health care policy and costs is a critical budgetary comparison.

• *Decisions on national defense and military preparedness.* While this is a problem primarily for the United States, which outspends all other countries by a large margin, it is also an issue for many other countries. Even developing nations in Africa and South America face classic guns versus butter choices in the budget process.

• *Decisions on energy, natural resources, and climate change.* Significant differences are found in comparative budgeting depending on the resource wealth or resource dependency of nations. As the majority of nations are net resource importers, decisions on energy policy, whether to produce nuclear power, and many other choices, influence the national budget a great deal. The nations of the Middle East and other net energy exporters depend heavily on natural resources as a source of energy.

• *Decisions on levels of taxation, the tax structure, and tax incidence.* Related to questions of how much government social services to provide is the question of how to pay for those services. There are sharp differences in the tax structures of countries around the world. Europe depends more heavily on consumption taxes such as the value-added tax, which can run in the range of 20–25 percent. The United States depends more on income taxes for general government spending and payroll taxes for entitlement programs. These decisions have implications for many complex elements of policy including economic growth. In the 1960s, Great Britain had very high levels of progressive taxation, leading to the Beatles' famous song "Taxman" complaining about the 95 percent top rate on the income tax at that time. A generation later, radical changes in tax policy led to much more favorable policies for business and a revival of the British economy. Decisions on taxes affect a vast array of other policies by encouraging or discouraging certain behavior.

• *Government ownership, privatization, and intervention in the economy.* Budgeting also involves what assets or industries the government owns. Even laissez-fare capitalist nations such as the United States own huge amounts of assets and government corporations. Privatization versus continued government ownership has been a vital issue for Russia and the former eastern bloc nations. These questions are also important among developing nations and can have significant effects on national economic growth.

• *Agriculture policy and trade restrictions.* Farming, fishing, and the raising of animals for food are important elements of the economies of virtually every nation, developed or developing. Budget decisions to support or to subsidize agriculture are key elements of budgeting but also major bones of contention among nations in terms of trade. The Common Agriculture policy of the European Union which highly subsidizes inefficient farmers (French and otherwise) is highly controversial both within and without the EU. U.S. agricultural subsidies are also substantial and controversial. Budget decisions on agriculture are also a major controversy between developed and developing countries who believe that subsidies in wealthy countries stifle their struggling agriculture industries.

Ultimately, budgeting is important because of the policy choices that it produces, continues, and embodies. While policies may not change every year, decisions to fund those prior and future decisions are a critical dimension of comparative budgeting.

CONCLUSION

Comparing the budget systems of the more than 230 recognized nations in the world is indeed a daunting task. One could easily get lost in the minutia and detail of budgeting in the literally thousands of differences between even two countries. In this first chapter we have attempted to develop a framework for comparison, occasionally noting detailed differences, but focusing on middle to high levels of comparisons. It began with comparing the economic environment for budgeting, a nation's wealth, its historical commitment to a certain level of spending and taxing. We examined political culture and its historical roots in identifying the influence of French, American, Spanish, British, and Soviet cultures on the budget systems of nations once under their influence. We next examined constitutional and political differences, and compared the main constitutional models, noting that constitutional systems matter in governance of which budgeting is a crucial part. To better understand different kinds of budget decisions, we distinguished between macrobudgeting and microbudgeting, and made comparisons between actors, policy actions, processes, and reforms. Next, we considered budgetary systems and processes, including the stages of budgeting that are identifiable in most countries. Within those stages, considerable variation exists depending on parliamentary or presidential system. For the execution stage, we further identified a number of key elements that have particularly been important in normative critiques of budgeting. Finally, we examined the policy agenda and context for budgeting—key challenges that confront many nations around the world and shape budget choices.

In the subsequent chapters, we will look at specific countries and regions. We begin with the United States in chapter 2 where major transformations in budgeting have taken place in recent decades. We will include the successful effort to balance the budget in the 1990s followed by a rapid return to deficits in the twenty-first century. A. Premchand (1999, 84) argues that the U.S. budgetary system has had a pervasive influence on the rest of the world. He makes the case based on five factors:

- A number of countries were at one stage in their history under the administrative management of the United States.
- Many countries received technical assistance from the United States in setting up their budgetary systems.
- Budgetary innovations since the early 1950s (performance budgeting, zero-based budgeting, etc.) all emanated from the United States.
- Many countries that became democracies after 1990 were influenced by U.S. institutions and experiences.
- In countries where there has been no explicit adaptation of practices from the United States, such as Commonwealth countries, academic theories developed in the United States have influenced practices. (Premchand 1999, 84–85)

While taking care that the book not be overly U.S.-centric, it is important to recognize the United States' influence on budgeting around the world. Next, we examine Commonwealth countries in chapter 3 including Great Britain, Canada, Australia, and New Zealand, whose political systems make for interesting comparisons with the United States, and where a number of important budgeting innovations and "new public management" reforms have emerged. Chapter 4 examines budgeting in Europe and the EU. As European integration continues, standardization across budgeting is increasing but far from complete. We compare individual countries such as France and Slovenia, as well as the European Union and its influence on member-nation budgeting. Chapter 5 examines Central and Eastern Europe and the former Soviet Union. Even though Hungary, Poland, Czech Republic, and others are now part of the EU, we consider them in this chapter because of their illustrative budgetary transformations since 1990. In the length that is available for the book, it is not possible to do justice to budgeting in all the parts of the world. Chapter 6 reviews international budget problems and practices in Latin America. In the conclusion, we concentrate on two elements of comparative budgeting. First, is it possible to move toward any kind of general theory of budgeting or are differences between countries too great? Second, in this global age, to what extent can innovation and reform in one country be transferred to another country? We conclude with these challenges and some speculation about future directions and the dissemination of budgeting innovations.[1]

2

BUDGETING IN THE UNITED STATES

INTRODUCTION

The United States finds itself at the beginning of the twenty-first century as the world's dominant economic and military power. Even though the war in Iraq has shown the limits of U.S. military might and the U.S. economy is increasingly less dominant in the world, American influence remains strong. The United States is influential in budgeting just as it is in entertainment and culture. A. Premchand asserts that in budgeting, "U.S. institutions, systems, and intellectual debates have had and continue to have a pervasive influence, in one form or another, on the rest of the world" (1999, 83). That influence, he argues, is a function of direct U.S. administration, technical assistance, first implementation of innovations in budgeting such as Planning Programming budgeting (PPB), influence on new and emerging democracies, and the dominance of the academic literature on budgeting. We will examine Premchand's assertion and begin our comparisons with the United States, but not with the intention of setting up U.S. practices as models to be emulated. While the United States may be influential in comparative budgeting, its constitutional system and budget institutions are considerably different than most parliamentary democracies.

The United States' system of separation of legislative and executive branches often results in divided party control, which can make budgeting more difficult. Federalism and extensive devolution of fiscal autonomy to subnational governments are other key structural characteristics of the U.S. system. Fragmentation and the division of control between national and subnational governments can make governing harder in some cases. Conversely, federalism can be a source of innovation in budgetary practices. The United States differs in other important ways as well. It is at the low end of levels of taxation and share of GDP allocated to government, but spends proportionately more on national defense than the vast majority of nations. Its tax structure relies more on payroll and income taxes than

35

on consumption taxes that dominate so many national tax systems. It has a larger private sector component in health care than most other nations. The United States has also shown volatility in fiscal balances, moving from a position of large and projected surpluses in 2000, to significantly high and persistent deficits in a matter of a few short years. We begin by looking at the economic and political context for budgeting in the United States.

POLITICAL CULTURE AND THE ECONOMIC CONTEXT FOR BUDGETING IN THE UNITED STATES

The United States still maintains the largest economy in the world, with a GDP in 2008 of $14.5 trillion (CBO 2007). It is among the top six countries in the world in per capita GDP (*Economist* 2006). Throughout its history, however, the United States has a political tradition of limited government, which extends into the realm of public budgeting. It might be accurate to say that Americans have a love/hate relationship with government. While many depend on government benefits and programs, tax cutting is usually much more popular than social spending, excepting Social Security and Medicare.

While Europe was shaped by a rigid class system that defined an individual's opportunities at birth, the United States had a more fluid class structure. The European notion of "noblesse oblige," that the wealthy had an obligation to take care of the poor, was less present in the United States. Individuals, including the poor, were seen as responsible for their own condition. Partially as a result, social welfare programs emerged later in the United States than in Europe and, to this day, less extensively. In the United States, cultural beliefs surrounding the idea of individualism, values supporting private property and individual liberty helped shape the political and economic system, and subsequent budget choices. As we saw in chapter 1, the United States has a smaller public sector than all but a handful of developed nations. Federal spending composes around 20 percent of GDP, state and local spending another 10 percent or so, for a total "size" of government of less than one-third of the economy. This compares with 45–55 percent for many European nations today with more extensive social service networks. The low U.S. ranking on public social expenditure on a comparative basis must be understood in the context of the long-standing preference of Americans for private rather than public solutions. In terms of health care, for example, because most of the system is private, the United States actually spends more per capita on healthcare than any other nation in the world.

Although there were periods when budget surpluses were suspect in American history, for the most part a balanced budget has been seen in the American context as highly desirable (Wallace 1960, 10). This is true not only in economic terms, but in moral terms: in Ben Franklin's enduring value system, to live beyond one's means is a sin. Nonetheless, the United States has often run national budgets with deficits, accumulating national debt. Running massive budget deficits was critical to winning the World War II, and since that time, the United States has run a budget deficit most years. Despite the fact that American politicians love to rail against budget deficits, only in a few instances have deficits really been high on the public's list of pressing national problems (LeLoup et al. 1987).

In American politics during the twentieth century, Republicans were originally seen as the party of fiscal conservatism, favoring less government spending and balanced budgets. In the 1930s, influenced by the ideas of economist John Maynard Keynes, President Franklin D. Roosevelt helped lead a paradigm shift in American public policy and budgeting in terms of government services and the use of deficit spending to stimulate the economy (Fusfeld 1982, 91) Thereafter, Democrats were seen as more "liberal" in the American sense meaning more willing to borrow and spend money on government programs to achieve desired ends. That positioning of the two political parties on deficits lasted until the Ronald Reagan presidency, when under the influence of supply-side economics, he pressed for major tax cuts regardless of their consequences on deficits. Reagan believed privately that large deficits would force Congress to cut spending (Stockman 1986). The result was record levels of deficits during the 1980s, including a deficit equal to 6.2 percent of GDP in 1982. President George W. Bush also successfully proposed massive tax cuts after the 2000 election and saw U.S. fiscal balances once again move into the red. In a few years, the United States moved from a position of record surpluses to deficits that were records in nominal dollars, about $1.4 trillion or around 8 percent of GDP in 2009. The size of the U.S. government deficit will depend on how much of the $1.6 trillion planned for economic stimulus and bank recapitalization actually convert into cash outlays and how the $212 billion tax cuts affect the balance (Montgomery and Eggen 2008; Montgomery 2009).

Figure 2.1 shows the total deficit or surplus in the United States as a percentage of GDP from 1966 projected through 2016. The figure shows the rapid growth of deficits in the early 1980s, the achievement of a balanced budget and surpluses in the late 1990s, and the rapid return to deficit spending after 2001. This was a function of the September 11 attacks and resulting economic downturn, increased military spending, Bush tax cuts, and fiscal policy responses to the economic meltdown beginning in 2006.

The national debt is the sum total of all budget deficits in history minus all surpluses. Again, politicians like to dramatize how large the national debt of the United States is by noting how a pile of dollar bills equal to the debt would reach the moon and other similar illusions. The most accurate way to assess the size of a nation's debt is to measure it as a percentage of the national economy. Using this

FIGURE 2.1. The Total Deficit or Surplus as a Share of GDP, 1970 to 2019

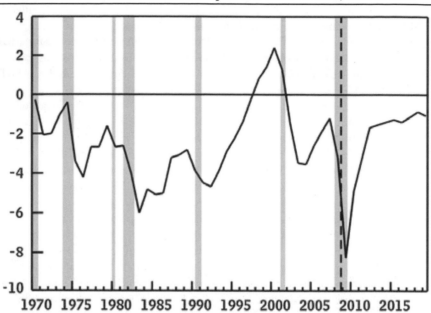

Sources: Congressional Bufget Office, Department of Commerce, Bureau of Economic Analysis.

measure, Figure 2.2 shows the national debt of the United States as a percentage of GDP since 1940. The massive borrowing for World War II was followed by a gradual decline in the size of the debt in real terms through the mid-1970s. After that, the debt piles up again, rising to around 55 percent of GDP in 2012. Looking back at Figure 1.2 in the previous chapter, one can see that the United States is around average for countries in the world for debt and deficits, despite the large absolute size of the debt. The differences in percentages shown in the two figures is a function of using debt held by the public and additional debt that is held within the government by agencies such as the Social Security Administration.

In short, the United States is one of the world's wealthier countries but with a tradition of limited government. The size of the public sector expanded rapidly in the twentieth century but not to the level of European democracies. Its overall fiscal balances show that deficits have been an issue over recent decades, but were largely overcome by fiscal discipline and increasing public sector accountability. Good budgeting consistent with fiscal sustainability principles ensured reasonable and manageable levels of structural and cyclical deficits. While these deficits were not particularly severe compared to other

FIGURE 2.2. Debt Held by the Public as a Percentage of GDP

Note: All figures after 2008 are projections.
Sources: Congressional Bufget Office, Office of Management and Budget.

countries, the 2006–07 collapse of financial and banking sectors around the globe have taxed fiscal policymakers in the United States as well as in Latin America, Eastern Europe, Asia, and European regions. Budget makers now face macrobudgetary and microbudgetary challenges as never before. From the macro perspective, global imbalances in savings (current account surpluses in China and deficits in the United States) produced a "savings glut" in search of higher returns from more advanced financial sectors. The macroeconomic forces that drove the capital flows were hard to reverse (*Economist* 2009a, 75). Nevertheless, lax controls and passive regulation over lending origination and sale of loans by the financial sector (especially for $6 trillion in subprime mortgage debt), produced a massive failure of trust in financial institutions and innovative credit instruments (2009a 73). This failure of trust has contaminated the global financial sector and the pipes of credit plumbing (*Economist* 2008a, 73) have seized up. Coupled with the economic recession that preceded these events in 2006, the task of responding and providing the right fiscal and regulatory incentives has largely fallen to the U.S. Treasury and U.S. Government. The 2009 stimulus program (infrastructure projects and fiscal transfers to maintain state and local services and jobs) and the Troubled Asset Relief Program (TARP) for the financial sector are attempts to target the funds properly to encourage lending and growth. The targets are firms, individuals, and sectors. Those countries with the best record of fiscal discipline (largely in Asia, some in Eastern Europe

such as Estonia, and some in Latin America such as Chile), which increased savings during the period of economic growth, now have more reserves and fiscal
space to try and respond effectively to the crisis. What is significant here for the
study of public budgeting in action is that U.S. policymakers are vigorously
using all available fiscal tools to respond to the crisis: loan guarantees, direct
expenditures, targeted subsidies, purchases of assets, tax cuts, and nationalization
of affected organizations. The public sector response to what is effectively a private sector crisis is producing the highest growth in the fiscal deficit in history.
But as the vaudeville character said, right now "that's another story."

In the next sections, we will examine the particular political and budgetary
institutions in the United States, and examine innovations in budget processes and
systems that have been influential on other countries.

CONSTITUTIONAL AND POLITICAL INSTITUTIONS

The United States has one of the oldest functioning democracies in the world
and is considered to have the oldest written constitution still in use. Thousands
and thousands of volumes have been written on the U.S. constitutional system
and its evolution and we will only spend a little time here on the subject. The
most important structural feature of the Constitution is the feature of separation
of powers. With their distrust of individual power holders in government, James
Madison led the other founders to create a system of separation of powers into
legislative, executive, and judicial branches, dividing and overlapping powers
among the branches to create a system of checks and balances. (Fisher 1978, 11)
As noted by Lijphart (1992) in chapter 1, this is a key distinction between presidential and parliamentary systems. In the United States, the president and members of Congress are elected separately. In parliamentary systems, the prime
minister is usually elected as a member of parliament, and selected to form a government as the leader of the majority or largest party. As we noted in chapter 1,
parliamentary systems are generally considered to have fewer veto points and be
less prone to stalemate than presidential systems with separation of powers. That,
of course, depends a great deal on the nature of party systems and election results
that determine the composition of the legislative body.

In parliamentary systems with two or relatively few parties, where one party
often wins an absolute majority, strong party discipline can make the government quite powerful and able to implement sweeping budget and policy
changes. In parliamentary systems with proportional representation systems and a
tradition of multiparty systems, party blocs in parliament can be quite fragmented, leaving the resulting coalition government less powerful and more constrained. In the United States, party control of the executive and legislature is

also a critical variable in explaining budget outcomes. When both branches are under control of one party, fairly dramatic budget changes can be made. This occurred in the 1930s under FDR with the creation of Social Security, in the 1960s under President Lyndon Johnson with the creation of Medicare, and in the 2000s under President Bush with a series of large tax cuts. When government is divided, stalemate is not necessarily the result. Other political factors, such as the president's popularity, can strengthen the hand of either the president or Congress. In 1981, President Reagan was also able to enact massive tax cuts despite the existence of one house of Congress under Democratic Party control. In comparing budgeting in the United States to other nations in the world, we will look more carefully below at research on the impact of divided or unified control of government on budgeting.

Another key structural feature of the U.S. system is federalism. In trying to create a stronger central government during constitutional deliberations in 1787, the founders had to confront the reality of thirteen largely independent and autonomous states. As a result, many powers were reserved to the states, including a number dealing with public budgets. While many have argued that, over the years, the national government has aggrandized power from the states, state and local governments remain a critical element of budgeting today. In the nineteenth century, the national government and states tended to operate in their own separate spheres (Grodzins 1966). In the twentieth century, as the scope of government expanded, the roles of state and national government became more entwined. The Social Security Act of 1936, which retains huge budgetary importance today, created programs such as welfare and unemployment compensation that were shared between state and national governments. Particularly since the 1960s, state and local governments have become increasingly dependent on federal government grants-in-aid, creating what some call "fiscal federalism." With those monies came strings giving the federal government more control over state policy.

On the other side, state and local governments still account for about one-third of public taxing and spending in the United States. Governors and other state officials are powerful political forces in lobbying certain national budget issues. The Medicaid system, health care for the poor, is closely intertwined between the two levels of government and federal budget makers are highly sensitive to the consequences of their policy decisions on states. The states have also influenced federal budgeting as a source of innovation in both process and policy. Comprehensive welfare reform, enacted under President Bill Clinton and a Republican-controlled Congress in 1996, was shaped in part by approaches taken by states in the decade before. Zero-based budgeting (ZBB) was implemented in states such as Georgia before President Jimmy Carter mandated ZBB for the entire federal government in 1977.

THE EVOLUTION OF BUDGETING AND
BUDGET INSTITUTIONS IN THE UNITED STATES

The Creation of a National Budget

The U.S. Constitution granted Congress the power of the purse: the sole authority to raise revenues and appropriate monies. Over the years, Congress developed a committee structure, and an important component of it was the committees that dealt with money. The House Ways and Means Committee has existed since the early 1800s and later, House and Senate appropriations committees were created. Despite clear constitutional authority in budgeting, Congress long recognized the need to allow some executive branch discretion in spending. Throughout history, Congress fluctuated between very specific line-item appropriations and broader grants of money. (Fisher 1975, 59–63) The president also was granted the veto power subject to the limitation of an override by two-thirds vote of both houses. Over the years, the president has used this power to force Congress to enact policies to his liking. It is a blunt instrument, however, because the president lacks a line-item veto that many state governors possess. Therefore, if a president does not like a bill because of something that is included or excluded, he must veto the entire bill.

In fact, the modern idea of a "budget" in the terms that we mean today did not emerge until the end of the nineteenth century. Part of the Progressive movement, budgeting as a more detailed public accounting of government revenues and expenditures, was a reform designed to promote good government and better control over officials and the monies they controlled. Previously, individual agencies went directly to Congress with spending requests. Congress passed separate legislation to raise taxes, distinct from spending decisions. Spending was approved in a very fragmented fashion, by passing a series of separate appropriations bills. That system, in modified form, continues to this day.

The movement for a national budget picked up steam in the early twentieth century and culminated with the passage of the Budget and Accounting Act of 1921 (Berman 1979). This was a critical law in the development of the institutional presidency, since for the first time, Congress delegated significant power to the presidency in the area of budgeting (Ferrier 2004). It created the concept of the president's budget—a compilation of all the budget requests from the executive branch to submit to Congress in a single document. This is the first example of macrobudgeting discussed in chapter 1—the president and budget director became the actors in the process who took an overview of all the activities of the budget and how expenditures and revenues matched. To help the president prepare this document, the law created the Bureau of the Budget (BOB) located in the Treasury. The primary purpose of creating a national budget was control of expenditures (Schick 1966). Implicit in the 1921 legislation is the notion that the presidency is more "responsible" than Congress in terms of spending discipline. However, Congress did not intend to abrogate all responsibility and tried to adopt a more comprehensive treatment of the budget within its own processes. The vested interests reflected in the powerful, independent standing committees made this impossible and so the gain in influence went to the president.

The true magnitude of that delegation did not become totally apparent until the administration of Franklin D. Roosevelt. FDR revolutionized the U.S. presidency and radically expanded the scope of government and public policy in the United States. When he took office in 1933, there were around six hundred thousand federal employees. When he died in April 1945, there were nearly four million federal employees (U.S. Census Bureau 1976). The budget of the United States similarly expanded during this time from outlays of $4.5 billion in 1933 to $92 billion in 1945. To help him manage the expanded presidency, initially for programs to combat the Depression and later to win World War II, FDR moved the BOB from Treasury to the Executive Office of the Presidency (EOP).

Executive Branch Reforms to Improve Budget Planning and Management

From the beginning, budgeting was political. Alexander Hamilton had called money the "mother's milk of politics." Members of Congress were elected to take care of their constituents as well as make national policy, so "porkbarrel" spending—specific state or district projects—were part of budgeting from the start. This aspect of taxing and spending was often disparaged by presidents and other executive branch officials. There was a desire to find some formula for knowing how most effectively to decide which projects should be funded and which should not (Key 1940). Economists in particular were interested in extending analysis of marginal returns and other economic concepts to budgeting. This led to a reform developed by the Rand Corporation in the 1950s called Planning Programming Budgeting (PPB) (Lyden and Miller 1972). PPB was a system based on identifying goals to be achieved rather than on dollars to be spent. Agencies were required to work from a program budget rather than a line-item budget. After goals were defined, alternative means of achieving the goals were to be examined. Next, cost-benefit analysis was applied to the various alternatives to choose the most effective alternative. Throughout the process, analysis was to be used extensively.

This system captured the imagination of many in government in the 1960s. It represented a system to make budgeting more rational, more objective, less political. In 1961, new Secretary of Defense Robert McNamara adopted PPB for the Defense Department. Despite mixed results in DOD, in 1965, President Lyndon B. Johnson mandated the use of PPB for the entire U.S. federal government. PPB promised much and seemed logical on the surface, but had difficulty penetrating the ingrained routines of federal budgeting. By 1971, the more formal requirements for PPB had simply been abandoned. It did not respond to the needs of individual agencies, many of whom had programs to administer that were not conducive to quantitative analysis. The BOB lacked commitment to PPB and continued to produce the more familiar line-item budgets. Congress was also not enthusiastic about PPB and demanded that in addition to any program budgets, agencies submit a line-item budget. Despite the setbacks, the appeal of more rational budgeting remained strong.

PPB was followed by several derivative budget systems along the same lines. Management by Objective (MBO) was also developed in the private sector and applied to government. More flexible than PPB, MBO emphasized comparing policy alternatives based on management objectives and making decisions accordingly. Perhaps the most successful was Zero-Based Budgeting (ZBB). ZBB's underlying goal was to take away the assumption that once a dollar was in the budget, it was there forever. In other words, ZBB aspired to start, if not truly from base zero, by not assuming that all spending projects would be continued. Instead, projects would be compared at the margins, and the more effective ones selected over less effective ones. Also a private sector innovation, ZBB had been applied to the state of Georgia by Governor Jimmy Carter. Happy with the results, Carter imposed ZBB on the entire federal government when he became president in 1977. It too, ran into problems, had difficulty penetrating the routines of budgeting, and ultimately died out.

Despite these seeming failures, the allure of more rational budget systems has not gone away. PPB, MBO, and ZBB, although met by a raft of skepticism and cynicism, left their mark in terms of increasing the amount of cost-benefit and other quantitative analyses associated with federal budgeting. Around the United States at different levels of government, reforms to make budgeting more effective for planning and management have continued to make an appearance. In the state of Washington in the early 2000s, for example, Governor Gary Locke introduced a system called the "priorities of government" that reflected elements of the earlier reforms by comparing spending decisions on the margins. These reform efforts in the United States had spinoff effects around the world.

Several reforms to improve budgeting in the late twentieth century stuck. In the 1960s, the U.S. federal budget had become fragmented, with many separate parts. In 1969, the government merged federal funds budgets with trust funds creating the "unified" budget. This was an important change since in one document a more realistic perspective on U.S. taxing and spending commitments could be gained. Although efforts have been made for various political reasons to put some items "off-budget" (such as Social Security), for the most part the United States retains a comprehensive budget that reflects the vast majority of federal activities.

In 1970, President Richard Nixon reorganized the BOB into the Office of Management and Budget (OMB). Nixon did it partly for management reasons and partly for political reasons. Mistrustful of the federal bureaucracy including the BOB, he wanted a central budget office that was more responsive to the president and less to the Congress and the bureaucracy. In that way, the change was actually designed to weaken OMB by moving its policy responsibilities to the newly created Domestic Council. However, even renamed, OMB remained a powerful actor in the federal budget process, as we will see in the next section.

Microbudgeting, Macrobudgeting, and Budget Reforms

The microbudgeting/macrobudgeting dichotomy introduced in chapter 1 is useful for analyzing the budget processes across nations. Those actors with responsibility for the entire budget, totals for revenues and outlays, whether there is a deficit or surplus, and how much is spent relative to domestic or defense needs, are the macrobudgeters. They tend to be a force for spending restraint in the process, trying to limit competing claims for resources that exceed available funds. Conversely, those actors with a relatively narrow focus and defined set of budget goals, such as federal agencies or programs, are the microbudgeters in the process. These actors tend to develop strategies to increase their own funding, largely unconcerned with the totals that are the responsibility of others.

Before the Budget Act of 1921, when federal agencies submitted requests directly to the Congress, the system was bottom-up, dominated by microbudgeting. After 1921, the president and the BOB took on macrobudgetary roles that served to control federal spending. From the 1920s until the 1970s, the system worked fairly well despite continued fragmentation and an emphasis on the parts rather than the whole. By the 1970s, however, federal spending seemed out of control and Congress unable to stop it. That resulted in a series of budget reforms in Congress that dramatically changed the budget process.

THE U.S. FEDERAL BUDGET PROCESS

The Annual Budget Cycle

In addition to being the product of top-down, macrolevel forces and bottom-up, microlevel forces, national budgets are also a repeated series of steps, or a cycle. In the cycle, the U.S. budget process is extremely fragmented. Many groups, officials, and participants have a hand in the final result. Figure 2.3 shows an overview of the budget cycle. Tables 2.1, 2.3, and 2.4 below detail the main steps, the participants, and the timing.

FIGURE 2.3. The Budget Cycle

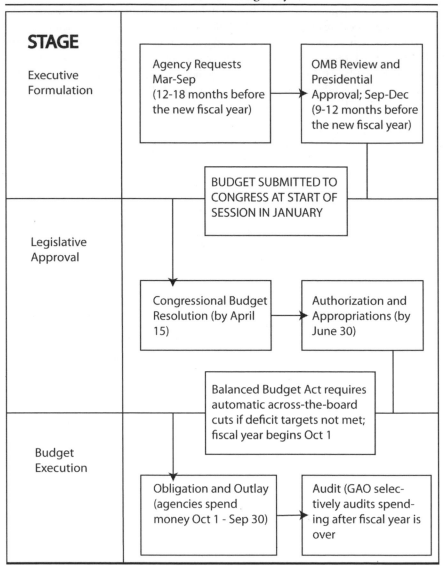

The U.S. government operates on a fiscal year (FY) that runs from October 1 through September 30. The accounting period begins three months before the calendar year. For example, on October 1, 2009, FY 2010 will begin. The entire budget cycle takes more than three years from the time agencies first begin to put together their requests until the Government Accountability Office (GAO) completes its selected audits.

The budget process is initiated in the offices of agency officials who begin to assemble their requests up to a year and a half before the start of the fiscal year. The president submits the budget in January, a few weeks after Congress starts its session. Congress has nine months to do its part with the budget and tries to get everything completed by late September. If it fails to do that, emergency funding legislation must be approved to prevent the government from shutting down. Once a budget has been enacted, the OMB, the Treasury Department, and the agencies work together in the process of spending the money—writing the checks and paying the government's bills. After the fiscal year has been completed and another budget has taken effect, the GAO chooses certain key agency programs to audit to ensure that money is spent legally and efficiently.

The cycle of budgeting is one of the most regularized patterns of national policymaking. But the budget is more than routine annual decisions. Many choices involve the commitment of funds for multiyear periods. It takes many years, for example, to build a nuclear aircraft carrier. Another example, the Social Security legislation passed in 1983 made commitments that extended through the twenty-first century. On the revenue side, the Tax Reform Act of 1986 affected revenue totals for decades. Budgeting is a combination of decisions that commit spending and tax policies for one year and for many years.

Budgeting in the Executive Branch

Participants in the budgetary process adopt certain roles defined by their self-interest and responsibilities. Agencies are generally advocates trying to get more money for their programs. The OMB, in contrast, is a guardian—the budget cutter of the executive branch. Its job is to say no in order to keep spending down. The president stage-manages the whole process, trying to establish priorities as well as to protect or enhance his personal political record.

AGENCY STRATEGIES

Agencies love to spend money because their employees believe in the programs they deliver, but they find many potential budget cutters in their path. One of the first things an agency has to decide is how much to ask for. Is a 50 percent increase too much? Is a 5 percent increase too small? For the most part, agencies act assertively: they request increases as large as they think they can justify. Behavior varies with the age, mission, and general personality of the agency. If it wants to achieve even modest growth an agency must request increases. This behavior is observable in virtually all budgets around the world. Of course, agencies in the United States and elsewhere are not free actors in the process. They are subject to instructions from the department, the OMB, and the White House and to over-sight by Congress. Yet they are not without their own friends, allies, and power. To succeed in budgeting, an agency must be imaginative as well as aggressive.

The budgeting environment is different for each agency. The Department of Health and Human Services, for example, despite its large budget, is relatively "poor" in terms of discretionary funds. It administers programs that largely involve cash transfers, and although it does a lot of check writing, it has little direct control over the money. Budgets seem to grow in phases. Early in their history, agencies usually experience a period of rapid expenditure growth, which then levels off or declines. At all phases of their existence, they are strategic partic-ipants in quest of dollars. The most successful agencies are often the most politi-cally astute, sensitive to the changing political winds in Washington. The national and international environment can influence budgeting, particularly with choices concerning national defense and domestic spending, the classic "guns versus butter" dilemma. The Reagan presidency was a difficult time for domestic agen-cies, as top-down cuts made serious inroads in agency operations. The 1990s under the Clinton administration proved to be difficult for the defense establish-ment, as officials sought a "peace dividend" by paring military spending. In the 2000s, during Bush's two terms, the situation completely reversed. Following the September 11 attacks, the United States entered into wars in Afghanistan and Iraq and spent billions more on homeland security as well as defense.

The OMB and the Budget

The Office of Management and Budget has the reputation of being one of the most powerful agencies in Washington. Its relatively small size (six hundred employees) belies its influence over budgeting and policymaking. In addition to assembling the massive budget documents, the OMB monitors agencies through-out the year and helps formulate national policy. The complexity of government makes the OMB and its analytical tools invaluable to the president and the White House staff. Table 2.1 shows the major steps in the budget formulation stage in the United States.

The budget process begins with the spring planning guidance, where the OMB requires agencies to review their broad goals, programs, and activities. At the beginning of the summer, the OMB sends out instructions to the agencies about the submission of their requests. Agencies sometimes do not strictly follow these instructions, but they must be prepared to justify contrary requests. By the end of the summer, agencies are required to submit formal requests to the OMB. Budget season really starts with the fall review, where the OMB takes a careful look at the budget requests and almost routinely cuts back what the agencies have asked for.

The Office of Management and Budget works within the broad guidelines established by the president, but many specific decisions are left to the OMB. By

TABLE 2.1. Major Steps in the Formulation Phase

What Happens?	When?
OMB issues Spring planning guidance to Executive Branch agencies for the upcoming budget. The OMB Director issues a letter to the head of each agency providing policy guidance for the agency's budget request. Absent more specific guidance, the outyear estimates included in the previous budget serve as a starting point for the next budget. This begins the process of formulating the budget the President will submit the following February.	Spring
OMB and the Executive Branch agencies discuss budget issues and options. OMB works with the agencies to: identify major issues for the upcoming budget; develop and analyze options for the upcoming Fall review; and plan for the analysis of issues that will need decisions in the future.	Spring and Summer
OMB issues Circular No. A-11 to all Federal agencies. This Circular provides detailed instructions for submitting budget data and materials. July Executive Branch agencies (except those not subject to Executive Branch review) make budget submissions. See section 25.	September★
Fiscal year begins. The just completed budget cycle focused on this fiscal year. It was the "budget year" in that cycle and is the "current year" in this cycle.	October 1
OMB conducts its Fall review. OMB staff analyzes agency budget proposals in light of Presidential priorities, program performance, and budget constraints. They raise issues and present options to the Director and other OMB policy officials for their decisions.	October–November
OMB briefs the President and senior advisors on budget policies. The OMB Director recommends a complete set of budget proposals to the president after OMB has reviewed all agency requests and considered overall budget policies.	Late November
Passback. OMB usually informs all Executive Branch agencies at the same time about the decisions on their budget requests.	Late November
All agencies, including Legislative and Judicial Branch agencies, enter MAX computer data and submit print materials and additional data. This process begins immediately after passback and continues until OMB must "lock" agencies out of the database in order to meet the printing deadline.	Late November to early January★
Executive Branch agencies may appeal to OMB and the President. An agency head may ask OMB to reverse or modify certain decisions. In most cases, OMB and the agency head resolve such issues and, if not, work together to present them to the President for a decision.	December★
Agencies prepare and OMB reviews congressional budget justification materials. Agencies prepare the budget justification materials they need to explain their budget requests to the responsible congressional subcommittees.	January
President transmits the budget to the Congress.	First Monday in February

★OMB provides specific deadlines for this activity.
Sources: OMB Circular A-11.

TABLE 2.2. Major Steps in the Execution Phase

What Happens?	When?
Fiscal year begins	October 1
OMB apportions funds made available in the budget process and other available funds. Agencies submit apportionment requests to OMB for each budget account by August 21 or within 10 calendar days after the approval of the appropriation, whichever is later. OMB approves or modifies the apportionment specifying the amount of funds agencies may use by time period, program, project, or activity.	September 10 (or within 30 days after approval of a spending bill)
Agencies incur obligations and make outlays to carry out the funded programs, projects, and activities. Agencies hire people, enter into contracts, enter into grant agreements, etc. in order to carry out their programs, projects, and activities.	Throughout the fiscal year
Agencies record obligations and outlays pursuant to administrative control of funds procedure.	Throughout the fiscal year
Fiscal year ends	September 30

Source: OMB Circular A-11.

November, the director's review takes place. The OMB director meets with the cabinet secretaries and budget officers to go over the specific amounts that will appear in the president's budget. Conflict is often heated and intense when the budget director confronts powerful cabinet secretaries. Under David Stockman in the 1980s, the OMB was more aggressive about imposing top-down cuts on agencies in the early 1980s. Agency officials claimed that their input was completely ignored in the budget process as the administration used a "meat-ax" approach to pare agency requests.

The budget must be completed by January in time to go to the printer. Because of estimation error, changing economic assumptions, or late decisions by the White House, some of the totals are left open until the last possible minute. The OMB has a difficult job, attempting to be both objective and loyal to the president, and it is not particularly popular with other agencies or with Congress. OMB's role does not end with the submission of the budget to Congress or the final enactment of the budget. It is also involved with the execution phase of the budget—spending the money requested by the president and approved by Congress, Table 2.2 examines the major steps in budget execution.

THE PRESIDENT'S ROLE

Because the budget is submitted in the president's name, many people assume the president is deeply involved with budgeting. Such is not always the case. The budget process presents a president with political opportunities, but is also creates some difficult political problems.

What are the problems of presidential budgeting? All presidents talk like prudent budgeters but the public likes action, progress, *and* low taxes, and these cost money. Public expectations are fickle: People want limited government and lower spending as long as their favorite programs are not cut. The government's response is often a heavy dose of public relations, trying to make the budget all things to all people. If the president wants to cut back, he may emphasize his role as fiscal conservative and note that sacrifice is necessary. If the president wants to increase spending, he is likely to emphasize public necessity and innovative leadership. If he wants to cut taxes without compensatory spending cuts, he emphasizes the benefits of economic growth and minimizes the problems associated with growing deficits.

The White House is subject to tremendous pressure from the interest groups and agencies to increase spending, but even relatively free-spending presidents, such as Lyndon Johnson, have to say no to many requests. Perhaps the biggest problem of presidential budgeting is the creation of high expectations and the inevitability of disappointing certain groups and interests. Presidents must focus on macrolevel choices. But a major constraint on the president is the inflexibility of budget outlays, limiting the potential of top-down budgeting. A president simply cannot turn the government around that quickly. It takes years of consistent effort to make changes in the composition of the budget.

What direct role does the president actually play? Although the budget is a critical part of presidential policymaking, presidential involvement with the details of the budget is extremely limited. The president sets the broad outlines under which others work, and the OMB puts the budget together. At certain times, the budget has been prepared virtually without the president, as during the months that Nixon was preoccupied by Watergate. When the president is inactive, authority drifts downward to the OMB officials and the White House staff. Yet as President Reagan showed, effective delegation to a powerful budget director but setting clear priorities can produce results. Presidents also set the broad themes of budgeting. President Clinton's emphasis on protecting Social Security and Medicare before touching the surplus had a big impact on the budget debate in his second term. President George W. Bush's tax cuts in the first term and the war in Iraq had tremendous budgetary consequences and will continue to do so for many years.

In addition to overseeing the preparation of the annual budget, the president has several opportunities to affect taxing and spending. Although impoundment is no longer legal, the president can request a *deferral* (a proposal that the funds not be spent that year) or a *rescission* (a proposal that the funds be returned to the Treasury). Deferrals are automatically accepted unless Congress passes a motion to the contrary; rescissions must be approved by a vote of Congress. Second, the president can also veto appropriation bills. Although Congress passes its budget in the form of budget resolutions, which do not need the signature of the president, these do not create spending authority. The resolutions are binding only on the congressional committees that create spending authority through appropriations bills, and these bills are subject to presidential veto. Third, the president can propose emergency spending legislation as President Bush Sr. did in 1990 to support the fledgling democracies in Panama and Nicaragua. A huge proportion of monies spent on Iraq and Afghanistan have come through emergency appropriations outside of the regular process.

The first year of the Reagan administration was a model of presidential management of the budget process to achieve political and economic objectives. Reagan succeeded for several reasons. First, the administration was well organized and got its proposals to Congress extremely quickly. Mr. Stockman had already outlined cuts in agencies' budgets before many department heads had even been named. The timing worked to the administration's advantage. Second, the president was able to dominate the policy agenda by focusing attention on a few crucial taxing and spending proposals. President Reagan did not swamp Congress with his complete "wish list" based on campaign promises. Third, the administration was innovative in its use of procedures. The use of reconciliation, a previously little used procedure, was the best example. Finally, the president waged an effective lobbying and public relations campaign. Capitalizing on his first-year popularity, his effective use of television, and a professional congressional liaison operation, he was able to change budget trends.

Presidential budgeting took on a new dimension during the Clinton administration. In his first year, Clinton made deficit reduction the highest priority of government. It took a bruising battle with Congress to enact an unpopular program of spending cuts and tax increases. He prevailed by a single vote in the Senate, but his budget victory may have cost the Democrats control of the Congress. In the 1994 elections, Republicans swept to office for the first time in forty years. But despite an assertive Congress, Clinton held his ground, and in 1995, a budget stalemate resulted in several government shutdowns. The pattern of confrontation and the effective use and threat of a veto allowed Clinton to influence the shape of budget policy even without a Congress sympathetic to his views. Congress and the President worked together in reaching a historic balanced budget agreement in 1997.

The first year of the Bush administration in 2001 had parallels to Reagan twenty years earlier. President Bush was able to convince Congress to enact a massive package of tax cuts despite having a narrow majority in both houses, and one could argue, without the economic conditions of a high tax burden that could warrant the cuts. The situation changed dramatically after 9/11, but President Bush continued to have success with compliant Republican majorities in getting his budget priorities adopted concerning taxes, defense, and national security. That was not the case in 2005 concerning Social Security following his election to a second term. Despite a vigorous national campaign and intensive lobbying of Congress, the administration was unable to get Congress to seriously consider a major restructuring of Social Security that would allow individuals to hold private accounts. After the Democrats took control of Congress in the 2006 elections, Bush had much more trouble with his budget proposals than in the first six years.

Budgeting in the executive branch takes place in the agencies, the OMB, and the White House. When observers talk about the "president's budget" they are only partly correct. The chief executive has final responsibility, but his influence over the budget is limited in a number of ways. Still, despite the budget inflexibility created by mandatory entitlements such as Social Security, the sensitivity of the budget to inflation, interest rates, and other economic changes and general spending pressure, the president can effectively use the budget as a vehicle for setting national priorities.

BUDGETING IN CONGRESS

Congressional Budget Decisions

Unhappy with their inability to control deficits and disturbed by President Nixon's impoundments, Congress passed a major revamping of their budget process in 1974 (LeLoup 2005). The Budget and Impoundment Control Act for the first time gave Congress the capacity for macrobudgeting, creating institutions that were responsible for budget totals and multiyear budgets. The act created separate House and Senate budget committees, and a budget resolution that would spell out the congressional budget. To help them with budgetary information, the act created the Congressional Budget Office (CBO). Well into a new century, the budget process is still in place despite having been modified and amended many times.

Congressional budgeting is a series of separate taxing and spending decisions that are only loosely linked. Table 2.3 summarizes the five categories of decisions that Congress makes on the budget. Macrobudgeting takes place by establishing budget *totals*. The House and Senate approve overall spending and revenue totals through *budget resolutions* prepared by the House and Senate budget committees. Resolutions are based on economic and budget projections made by the CBO. *Authorizations* are the legislative authority for a program and must be passed before money can be appropriated. The standing committees in both houses (except the budget and appropriations committees) report authorizations. *Appropriations* are the way Congress actually creates the spending authority that allows the executive branch to operate. Working primarily in highly specialized subcommittees, the House and Senate appropriations committees are responsible for this traditional exercise of the power of the purse. *Revenue decisions* are under the purview of the tax-writing committees: the House Ways and Means Committee

TABLE 2.3. Congressional Budget Decisions

Types of Congressional Budget Decisions	Key Participants in Congress	Type of Action by Congress
Budget Totals	CBO, Budget Committees, and Party Leaders	Concurrent Resolutions on the Budget
Authorizations	Authorizing Committees	Authorizations, Entitlements
Appropriations	Appropriations Committees	Individual Appropriations Bills
Revenues	Ways and Means, and Finance Committees	Tax Bills
Oversight and Review	Appropriations and Authorizing Committees; CBO and GAO	Hearings and Investigations; Special Studies, and Audits

Sources: OMB Circular A-11.

and the Senate Finance Committee. They consider tax bills separate from spending legislation. As conflict between the legislative and executive branches over the budget escalated in the 1980s, Congress was frequently forced to enact budget resolutions, authorization appropriations, and revenue bills in a single massive omnibus bill. A variety of congressional efforts to see that money is effectively spent come under the category of *oversight and review.*

Authorizations and Appropriations

Authorizations are statues that establish the authority for an agency or a program to exist and may set limits on the amount of money that may be appropriated for that purpose. There are three kinds of authorizations. Annual authorizations, for such agencies as NASA, the Atomic Energy Commission, and the National Science Foundation, require reapproval every year. *Annual authorizations* offer the most through oversight and program review but are often duplicative and cumbersome because agencies must appear before four committees each year. *Multi-year authorizations* allow a program to exist for a fixed period of time, usually between two and five years. An example was revenue sharing, authorized for four years. The third type of authorization is a *permanent authorization,* which establishes indefinite authority for a program and for funds to be appropriated for it. An example is Medicare. More than 60 percent of authorizations are permanent, 25 percent are multiyear, and only around 15 percent are annual.

Authorizing committees—the standing committees of Congress—play an important role in taxing and spending. Authorizations set boundaries for the appropriations committees. During the 1960s and 1970s, the authorizing commit-

TABLE 2.4. Major Steps in the Congressional Phase

What Happens?	*When?*
Congressional Budget Office (CBO) reports to Budget Committees on the economic and budget outlook.	January
CBO reestimates the President's Budget based on their economic and technical assumptions.	February
Other committees submit "views and estimates" to House and Senate Budget Committees. Committees indicate their preferences regarding budgetary matters for which they are responsible.	Within 6 weeks of budget transmittal
The Congress completes action on the concurrent resolution on the budget. The Congress commits itself to broad spending and revenue levels by passing a budget resolution.	April 15
The Congress needs to complete action on appropriations bills for the upcoming fiscal year or provides a "continuing resolution" (a stop-gap appropriation law).	September 30

Source: OMB Circular A-11.

tees tried to get around the stingy appropriations committees (which were not approving enough money to suit them) by creating "backdoor spending"—entitlements, loan guarantees, and other devices to circumvent the normal process of review. The Budget Act of 1974 attempted to curtail backdoor spending.

Appropriations are the actual means by which the Congress creates budget authority. It is a process that occurs every year, and much of the work is done by the House and the Senate appropriations committees and their subcommittees, which hold extensive hearings into the agencies' activities. As "guardian of the public purse," the House and Senate appropriations committees were among the most powerful and influential panels in Congress. Commenting on the way the committees fulfilled their trust, appropriations expert Richard Fenno (1964, 143) noted:

> The action verbs most commonly used are "cut," "carve," "slice," "prune," "whittle," "squeeze," "wring," "trim," "lop," "chop," "slash," "pare," "shave," "whack," and "fry." The tools of the trade are appropriately referred to as "knife," "blade," "meat axe," "scalpel," "wringer," and "fine tooth comb." . . . Budgets are praised when they are "cut to the bone."

By the end of the 1960s, it was clear the appropriations committees were behaving less like guardians and more like advocates of particular programs. The authorization-appropriations process was deteriorating. Spending bills were not passed in time, and some were not passed at all. But rather than eliminate the old system, congressional reformers superimposed a new system on top of it.

The Congressional Budget Process

The Budget and Impoundment Control Act of 1974 established a new congressional budget process and gave legislators a macrobudgeting perspective for the first time. The original timetable was followed for a decade before it was revised by the Gramm-Rudman-Hollings mandatory deficit reduction law (Balanced Budget Act) in 1985. The major steps in the congressional budget process are shown in Table 2.4.

The budget process is supposed to work as follows. When the president's budget is transmitted to Capitol Hill, the House and Senate budget committees begin to hold hearings, taking testimony from administration officials, the Congressional Budget Office, and outside experts. The authorizing and appropriations committees are required to submit "views and estimates" to the budget committees. These reports project the committees' taxing and spending plans for the coming year. The budget committees in both the House and the Senate each draw up the congressional budget resolution that specifies (1) the total revenues, (2) the total spending, (3) the size of the deficit, (4) the total national debt, and (5) a breakdown of outlays by functional category. Key economic and budget assumptions are developed by the CBO, which issues a series of annual reports containing five-year projections. Congress is required to pass the budget resolution in late spring and it becomes the framework for subsequent decisions by the spending committees.

While the budget committees and party leaders are shaping the budget totals, the authorizing and appropriations committees are working at the same time on the specific parts of the budget. The president's requests are divided into thirteen separate appropriations bills, each considered by a subcommittee. Appropriations bills are supposed to be reported by early summer but are often late. Differences in the spending bills and the budget resolutions are resolved by a process called *reconciliation*. Originally designed to be used at the end of the process in September, reconciliation since the mid-1980s has been used at the beginning of the process and has become a powerful tool for party leaders. Reconciliation rules evolved in a way that could protect major budget legislation from perhaps its greatest legislative threat—the Senate filibuster. The process worked poorly under divided government, on several occasions resulting in the shutdown of large portions of the federal government. High deficits and frustration with conflict between the Republican president and Democratic Congress led to the passage of a controversial reform in 1985.

The Balanced Budget Act

On December 11, 1985, Congress enacted the Balanced Budget and Emergency Deficit Control Act, more commonly known from its co-sponsors' names as

Gramm-Rudman-Hollings. This reform revised the congressional budget process and set deficit targets for five years. If the annual target was not reached, across-the-board cuts would be imposed. One half of the cuts would come from defense programs, the other half from domestic programs. The theory behind this approach was that the cuts would be so onerous that Congress and the president would be forced to put together their own package to meet the targets. To help Congress reach the deficit limits, Gramm-Rudman-Hollings enhanced macrobudgeting in Congress, beefing up enforcement procedures and strengthening the ability of party leaders to quash "budget-busting" bills from the authorizing and appropriations committees.

Automatic cuts, called sequesters, were to be ordered through a complicated process involving the Office of Management and Budget, the Congressional Budget Office, and the General Accounting Office. The Supreme Court struck down the provisions for automatic cuts as a violation of separation of powers. In 1987, Gramm-Rudman-Hollings was revised to repair the constitutional flaw and to change the deficit targets, which had quickly proved unworkable.

Congressional Budgeting Under Bush, Clinton, and Bush

Deficit problems continued in the Bush Sr. administration, again resulting in major changes in budget priorities and the budget process itself. Using a summit between the legislative and executive branch, a $500 billion deficit reduction package was finally enacted, the largest in history in real terms. Also enacted were further process reforms such as spending caps for defense, domestic, and international programs and "pay as you go" rules (PAYGO), meaning that any changes that lost revenue or increased spending had to be offset. The 1990 budget agreement also strengthened enforcement mechanisms within Congress, making it more difficult to approve any changes that would increase the deficit.

Bill Clinton and the Democrats took control of the presidency for the first time in twelve years in the 1992 elections and narrowly managed to enact a major budget package in 1993. It was controversial because nearly one-half of the savings were the result of tax increases. Not a single Republican voted for the package. Nonetheless, along with the 1990 deficit reduction package, it provided the policy changes necessary to reach a balanced budget by 1997. With Republicans taking control of both houses of Congress in 1994, the balanced budget agreement of 1997 was a bipartisan compromise made easier by a vigorous U.S. economy. Beginning 1998, the federal budget showed several years of large surpluses after decades of deficits. Those surpluses faded quickly after 9/11 and the downturn of the U.S. economy.

Clinton faced a Republican Congress for six of his eight years in office. During those years of divided government, the Republican majorities showed remarkably high party discipline and an inclination to use its power to impose its will on the president. With George W. Bush in the White House, the Republicans proved just as partisan, but much more deferential to the president. Other problems had emerged with the congressional process under the Republicans. Although the budget process still served as a key set of institutions supporting majority rule in the legislative process, it had become less of a tool for fiscal restraint under unified Republican control in the 2000s. During the 1990s, under both presidents Bush and Clinton, budget procedures were critical in enacting major deficit reduction legislation. Once the budget was in surplus under George W. Bush, Republicans appeared less interested in fiscal restraint. Congressional appropriators were under less constraint from the budget resolution, and earmarks for special state and local projects exploded. Republicans failed to extend some of the rules that had made it possible to balance the budget in the 1990s. Pay-as-you-go (PAYGO) rules that require offsets for tax cuts or spending increases were allowed to expire in 2002 (but reinstated under President Obama in 2010).

Emergency provisions were used more frequently after 2001 as well. Billions and billions of dollars for the wars in Iraq and Afghanistan and the war on terror were passed under emergency provisions outside of the constraints of the budget process. Republican majorities created a new prescription drug entitlement program in hopes of attracting support from senior citizens. Critics within the party despaired about their party's budget record and said there was no longer even an attempt to disguise its record of expanding big government. Federal spending increased by 46.5 percent between 2001 and 2007 (OMB 2008). Receipts over the same period (2001–07) increased by 29 percent. The taste for bold conservative budgets, so apparent in 1995, seemed long gone.

The transition of budgeting to macrolevel negotiations between Congress and the president to achieve top-down control has altered the nature of the budgetary politics in the United States. Partisanship, legislative–executive conflict, and the uncertainty of budget estimates make meeting deadlines difficult. Congressional actions in terms of authorizations, appropriations, and budget resolutions are overlapping and repetitive. The process remains vulnerable to special interest amendments that can quickly unglue a tenuous compromise package. Budget totals are increasingly sensitive to the economy. They are also highly influenced by party alignments in the Congress and the presidency.

Divided Government and Budgeting in the United States

Although David Mayhew's study (1991) in the early 1990s asserted that just as much legislation is passed in the United States under divided government as under unified party control, subsequent research has suggested divided government is critical in a number of ways (Binder 2003). Divided or unified control of government affects budgeting in a number of ways (LeLoup 2005, 214–20). First, divided government is much more likely to produce delays in the timetable and result in government shutdowns. The government has never shut down because of a budget impasse under unified control but shut down eleven times under divided government. Second, Congress is less likely to enact appropriations bills on time under divided government and more likely to wrap appropriations in an omnibus bill. Third, extraordinary means of resolving stalemates such as budget summits, bipartisan commissions, or mandatory deficit-reduction schemes such as Gramm-Rudman-Hollings take place almost exclusively under divided government. Fourth, budget policy outcomes differ significantly under divided versus unified control. The only time that tax increases made up as much as half of deficit reduction was under Democratic unified control.

Divided control in budgeting in the United States is comparable to coalition government in parliamentary systems. Institutions such as budget summits have emerged to enable the two parties to work out some compromise, just as members of a coalition government do. Divided government does not preclude agreement, but it clearly changes both the process and the nature of the policy decisions.

Republicans controlled both houses of Congress for twelve years,[1] until the 2006 elections swept the Democrats back into power. Significant changes occurred during this era. Three Republican congresses (104th, 105th, and 106th) worked under conditions of divided government, the last three (107th, 108th, 109th) primarily under unified Republican control of government. In 1995 and 1996, House Speaker Newt Gingrich and the Republicans tried to use the budget process to force their priorities on a defensive President Clinton. A dozen years later, at the end of unified Republican control, Congress could not enact a budget resolution to guide appropriators, could not agree on restoring pay-as-you-go rules (PAYGO), could not pass eleven of thirteen appropriations bills, and in the end, could not even enact an omnibus appropriations bill to fund agencies through the rest of the year. In the 1990s, Republican congresses confronting a Democratic president were able to balance the budget. In the 2000s, Republican congresses working with a Republican president saw fiscal discipline decline, earmarks and supplemental appropriations grow exponentially and the deficits balloon.

The budget process and budget politics in the United States have changed dramatically over the past four decades. Today, U.S. budgeting takes place on several levels. Most visible is presidential-congressional bargaining over high-level totals, tax packages, and entitlement reform. The patterns of bargaining vary significantly depending on party control of the two branches. Second, budgeting takes place at a lower level over program authorizations and appropriations. More important here are agency officials, committee and subcommittee members, and interest groups. At a third level is budgeting in state and local governments.

Practices and financial conditions vary widely between states. For example, even in good economic times, California struggles to make resources match commitments while in Alaska, oil revenues permit low taxes and the payment of an annual "dividend" to every citizen of the state. States are relatively autonomous, but as fiscal federalism has evolved, state and local budgets are heavily influenced by national decisions.

MAJOR BUDGET ISSUES FACING THE UNITED STATES

What are the major budget issues confronting the United States in the coming decades? The challenges are quite similar to other industrialized democracies, particularly in terms of pensions and social security and rising health care costs, but are somewhat different in terms of military spending.

Defense

The United States is in a unique position in the world in terms of its military spending and commitments. Between 2002 and 2007 U.S. military spending rose over 50 percent to $522 billion, many times more than any other country in the world (CBO, Options 2007, 7). Part of the increase was a result of wars pursued in Afghanistan and Iraq. The greatest determinant of military spending in recent history could have been affected by the result of the 2008 presidential election. All of the Democratic candidates urged disengagement from Iraq and scaling back military commitments; Republican candidates pushed for a long presence in Iraq even as troop levels were to be drawn down. President Obama and the Democratic Congress in fact instituted an increase or "new surge" of transfer of troops to Afghanistan to stop field reverses there against the Taliban.

The United States faces a number of other budget issues in defense based on what type of military confrontations are most likely in the future and what kind of weapons systems are most appropriate. Certainly, serious reevaluation of force structure and weapons will take place as a result of the unsatisfactory results in Iraq. Other decisions will surround weapons such as space and laser weapons and the type of aircraft to procure for the future. The National Aeronautic and Space Administration (NASA) has chosen to retire the space shuttle program in 2010 and embark on its Vision for Space Exploration (VSE) which will have significant costs associated with it. New budget makers in the coming decade may have alternate plans or wish to scrap VSE.

Agricultural Subsidies

One budget issue that the United States shares in particular with Europe is the question of agricultural subsidies. Although not as heavily subsidized as European farmers, U.S. farmers and growers received over $28 billion in subsidies in 2007. Payments come through direct subsidies, crop insurance, countercyclical payments, and loans. The issue of agricultural subsidies is also an important foreign policy question. Underdeveloped nations around the world have been highly critical of high subsidization of U.S. farmers, which serves to cut many poor nations from breaking into lucrative American markets. Agricultural subsidies are very difficult for budgeters around the world to cut. Farmers have political power disproportionate to their relatively small number and it is hard for governments to impose losses on them. Because of their high costs and questionable economic effects, they remain a target.

Health Care Costs and Coverage

The United States spends more per capita on health care than any other country in the world, yet nearly 50 million residents have no health insurance. One of the most critical budget issues in the coming decades in the United States is extending insurance coverage and containment of spiraling costs. Despite the fact that the United States largely relies on a system of private insurance, the U.S. government spends a great deal on health care for the poor (Medicaid) and the elderly (Medicare). They are the fastest rising costs in the federal budget with Medicaid growing around 8 percent annually in 2007–08 and Medicare growing at 9 percent per year for the same period (CBO *Options* 2007, 165). In 2007, the United States spent $215 billion on Medicaid and $370 billion on Medicare. Under current law, the Medicare financial system will not be able to keep up with the expenses in less than a decade. In terms of the uninsured, universal health care coverage remains supported by the American public but its costs are a huge political stumbling block. The effect of the Clinton administration's ill-fated attempt to enact universal coverage in 1994 still has a chilling effect on reform efforts.

Budget makers will have a number of options for expanding coverage and containing health care costs. The leading options for expanding coverage include expanding Medicaid to cover families at higher percentages of the poverty line. Covering families up to 300 percent of the poverty line would cost an additional $72 billion over ten years (CBO *Options* 2007, 155). Medicare costs could be reduced by gradually raising the eligibility age. For example, if the age for eligibility for Medicare benefits (currently sixty-six) were to be raised two months per year until it reached seventy years of age, the United States would spend 10 percent less on Medicare over the next generation. Other cost-saving options are to increase co-payments and deductibles and to reduce physician and hospital reimbursements. Each of these faced harsh political opposition in a system that has many veto points.

Social Security and Pensions

One of the most pervasive budget issues facing the developed world concerns financing government-funded pension systems such as Social Security. In some countries of the world, Slovenia for example, the number of retirees already exceeds the number of workers paying into state pensions systems. In many other countries in the Americas, Europe, and Asia, the ratio of workers to retirees continues to drop in an unfavorable direction, putting more financial pressure on the system. Despite all the political rhetoric, the U.S. Social Security system is in better short-term financial condition than many other nations. In the future, however, some combination of benefit reduction or tax increase will be needed to keep the program solvent. The United States spent $615.3 billion on Social Security payments in FY 09.

Those options could take many forms. In 2005, President Bush launched his second term with a drive to allow some private accounts within the system for younger workers. Despite weeks of using the "bully pulpit" of the presidency, the proposals simply grew more and more unpopular with the public and never even came close to reaching a vote in Congress. Policy alternatives designed to reduce the growth in benefits include increasing the age of retirement, similar to the Medicare option. The justification is that life expectancy is much greater today than when the program was started but the age of retirement has barely advanced. Raising the retirement age to seventy, for example, would save $86 billion over ten years (CBO *Options* 2007, 218). Benefits could also be reduced by increasing the computational period that benefits are based on. Significant savings could be realized if current law was changed to limit the increases in initial Social Security benefits so that the real value of the benefit doesn't increase over time. This could save $141 billion over ten years, but the value of the benefits would be significantly less in real terms than they are projected to be currently. Of course, all these proposals are sure to be sharply opposed by senior citizen groups, the demographic with the highest rate of voter turnout. Social Security has been called the "third rail" of American politics—touch it and you die (politically). That is what makes social security and pension reform so difficult in the United States and around the world.

Revenues and Tax Policy

With recurring deficits, fiscal conservatives look either to cutting spending or increasing revenues to solve the problem. As we noted earlier, despite the strong anti-tax sentiment in the United States, taxes are generally lower than in other developed nations. The U.S. tax system at the federal level depends more on income and payroll taxes and less on consumption taxes, such as sales tax or value-added tax, than most other developed nations. From time to time, proposals to switch from income to consumption taxes are forwarded, but they are also a very difficult sell to the public and the Congress. The main issues concerning national government revenues in the coming years in the United States will surround the extension of the Bush tax cuts enacted in 2001 and 2003. In order to take advantage of the reconciliation rules of the budget process that protects major tax and spending bills from amendment and filibusters, the Bush tax cuts could only extend out for ten years. Republicans want to make them permanent; Democrats want to take a hard look at them in terms of the nation's fiscal balances. Extending the Bush tax cuts for another ten years would cost $2.26 trillion over ten years, or conversely, to not extend them would raise taxes by that amount over ten years (JCT 2008; CBO 2009).

Other tax issues concern the alternative minimum tax, originally targeted to only the wealthiest taxpayers, but that now hits many middle-class taxpayers. Other possible revenue increases could come from reducing or eliminating the home mortgage deduction ($418 billion in additional revenues over ten years), the deductibility of state and local taxes ($694 billion in additional revenues over ten years), or to limit itemized deductions to 15 percent of gross income ($1 trillion in additional revenues over ten years) (CBO *Options* 2007, 253). Of course, these are extremely popular, entrenched tax provisions that are very unlikely to be eliminated except under extreme circumstances.

Economic and Financial Stimulus

As indicated, the global seizure of the banking and financial sector, to some extent originated in the United States by irresponsible mortgage lending and securitization into opaque credit instruments, is the major current fiscal challenge for the U.S. government. Since the credit instruments were marketed abroad and severely damaged banking balance sheets around the globe, most governments devised workable fiscal and regulatory policies in response. The United States is the largest by far at 12.8 percent of GDP (5.8 percent for the fiscal stimulus and 7 percent for the financial rescue). This includes use of the full range of fiscal tools, from infrastructure investment, tax cuts, loan guarantees, asset purchases, liquidity provision, and nationalization (*Economist* 2009b, 79). Massive projected deficits and debts, including staggering increases in entitlements burdens (pensions, health, social security), have become almost secondary to the issue of how to target sufficient funds to generate economic growth in the real or nonfinancial sector. In contrast with previous fiscal crises, in this case economic weakness in the financial and banking sector led to the deficits—not the other way around (see Guess and Koford 1984). As one Latin American finance minister put it, "Thank God! At least this time it isn't our fault!" (*Economist*

2008b). Economic stimulus via infrastructure investments can help in countries such as the United States that need new bridges, roads, railroads, water-sewerage systems, and mass transit systems. The infrastructure investment is a surer way to boost aggregate demand than tax cuts for firms and consumers, as they are more likely to save the funds than investment them in a climate of extreme uncertainty (2009b, 80). It should be noted that the net costs of the financial rescue will be far less than the gross costs of 7 percent GDP. The Treasury could recoup from 50 to 90 percent of the investments based on comparative experience of Sweden in 1992 (2009b, 80).

In the long term however, structural reforms are needed that include: paring entitlements burdens, reducing health care costs, covering unfunded social security liabilities (e.g., $43 trillion or 5 percent of future wages), reducing dependence on foreign oil by raising the federal gasoline tax 10 cents/gallon, strengthening the accountability and transparency of the U.S. budget process, developing a U.S. capital planning and budgeting process that allocates funds to the highest economic priority projects (not for just short-term jobs or politically favored projects), and reducing the overall burden of massive annual defense expenditures that are critical for fiscal sustainability. As of 2009, CBO predicted that the debt burden will grow to 400 percent of GDP by 2058, which is clearly unsustainable (Conrad and Gregg 2009). Basic and structural reforms are essential.

CONCLUSION

We opened the chapter with the proposition that the United States has had pervasive influence on the development of public budgeting around the world. While it would be difficult to find another country that has had a greater influence on budgeting, this chapter also reveals that the United States is unusual in many respects, and more different than similar to most countries in terms of constitutional structure and budgetary institutions. Certainly the United States is distinct in that Congress is capable of having more independent influence on budget outcomes than virtually any other legislative body in the world. Differences in budgeting under divided and unified government are comparable to parliamentary systems budgeting under coalition or single majority party government.

In terms of the evaluative criteria introduced in chapter 1, how does the United States stack up? First, the U.S. federal budget is clearly a policy document—it details past choices and the consequences for taxing and spending for years to come. That feature is highlighted in the United States because of separation of powers and separate budget agencies to forecast the economy and project budget trends. Between OMB and CBO there is a great deal of policy analysis surrounding the budget. Second, in terms of an operational guide, the U.S. budget with its multiple volumes and thousands of pages may seem to be highly detailed, but in many ways leaves agencies and departments considerable discretion over their programs. Congressional oversight is inconsistent—it can be extremely tight in some instances and relatively light in others. Influenced by reforms such as PPB, MBO, and ZBB, agencies use performance data to make decisions but this is not consistent across the bureaucracy. Third, is the federal budget a financial plan? The unified federal budget ranks relatively high concerning its comprehensiveness compared to many nations around the world. But there are also numerous off-budget entities that generate loan guarantees, and other federal obligations which are not regularly included in the budget.

Finally, how effective is the U.S. budget as a communication device? For those who are interested, a great deal of information is available for scholars, journalists, and interested citizens. OMB and CBO Web sites offer historical data and current analyses. However, as in most countries, the vast majority of the public has only a hazy idea of the federal budget. They occasionally become engaged as a result of extensive media coverage or governing strategies by the president and legislators. Examples include the Bush tax cuts, the balanced budget agreement in 1997, and other select macrobudgetary issues. Public engagement is no guarantee of political success however, as the Bush effort to add a private component to Social Security in 2005 showed. In general, the United States scores well on the criteria for successful budgeting, but improvements are needed that will require new and different reforms.

3

COMMONWEALTH COUNTRIES

INTRODUCTION

In this chapter, we examine the budgetary behavior of the former countries of the British Empire known as "Commonwealth" countries. The Commonwealth system uses a similar set of public financial management system rules and offers a unique opportunity to observe the performance of a similar system in many countries of the world, such as Canada, Australia, New Zealand, and the U.K. itself. The question is how our five-variable Comparative Budgetary Framework explains the purposes and results of this system? How does it explain the strengths and weaknesses of that system? Can it assist in policy decisions on which of its elements might be transferable to other regions of the world?

There are many issues of budgetary behavior that need explaining in particular country and regional systems and it would be improbable that one framework could explain all of them. For example, familiar challenges such as: (1) the propensity to engage in major reforms, (2) proper budget composition (i.e., are funds directed to pro-poor programs?), (3) gauging budget program performance, (4) ensuring effectiveness of control (e.g., debt and deficit targets), and (5) providing sufficient managerial capacity to achieve budget objectives (i.e., management autonomy) are faced by most countries. Each problem will have different solutions and face local constraints. In this chapter, it will be argued that focusing on particular variables of our model—context, political culture, and institutions—can explain a great deal of the Commonwealth propensity to implement performance or output-based budgeting and the *new public management* reforms.

Overall, Commonwealth budgetary behavior is remarkably similar in that it demonstrates an "abiding concern" for (1) "consistency between policies and expenditures" and (2) "efficiency in the use of resources" (Petrei 1998, 82). The Commonwealth budget model, if it could be oversimplified, is strong on multiyear expenditure planning, weak on parliamentary analysis and approval, strong on implementation accounting, auditing control, and strong on value for money post-evaluation of expenditures. The influence of Commonwealth budget systems on developing and transitional countries was noted in chapter 1. Institutional transfer followed colonial influence. For example, Tanzania inherited many of the features of the British Commonwealth systems: (1) a legal framework emphasizing accountability, (2) a cabinet of ministers with strong budget-making powers, (3) a parliament with very limited budget powers, (4) budget execution decentralized to individual ministries, and (5) accounting officers responsible to a parliamentary accounts committee (Lienert 2007). While many countries claim they have the same fiscal concerns, and make occasional efforts to reform, only in this region does behavior consistently match expressed intent. Why is that? This chapter will offer an explanation from our framework, review major reform efforts of Commonwealth countries in budgeting and public management, point to some remaining issues that need attention, and provide some cautionary advice on transfer of lessons from this region to others of the world.

FISCAL CRISES IN COMMONWEALTH STATES

Countries implement minor methodological and major systemic budget reforms for various reasons, ranging from international donor and consultant pressure, vendor sales of new software products, technical recommendations from ministries of finance, and examples provided by similar countries. These have all been important. Political leaders rarely make budget reform a platform issue because it is considered over-technical, invisible, or process-oriented, and generally a vote loser. The Hungarian Prime Minister Ferenc Gyurcsany recently announced in a closed session that he hid the need for fiscal reform from voters in order to get reelected (Gyurcsany 2006). He hid the facts because he knew that the same people burning cars in front of government buildings in Budapest in 2006 would burn cars later if he cut the size of the state, raised university tuitions and health, and raised taxes on wealthier groups to try and trim the budget deficit within limits required by the EU Stability and Growth Pact (3 percent of GDP). He knew well that most voters are bored by discussions of the public finances unless it affects them directly, such as income and property taxes. The only exception to this is when there is a genuine fiscal crisis that will affect services and programs. In such cases, fiscal reform is a way out for most political leaders and they become more receptive to the recommendations of their technical advisors. This is not to say that political leadership in any country has to respond to fiscal crisis properly or at all. Some regimes simply engage in denial in the hope that printing money will work in the short term, and later that a kind international donor will bail them out. It is only to say that most Commonwealth countries are no exception to this pattern of crisis-driven fiscal reform.

TABLE 3.1. Projected Fiscal Deficits and Debt 2009

Country	Total Expenditure (Billions, Home Currency)	Total Expenditure ($B)	GDP (Billions, Home Currency)	Total Expenditure as a % of GDP
Hungary	12666.2	53.9	25419.2	49.83%
United Kingdom	622.0	892.7	1401.0	44.39%
United States	5129.1	5129.1	13741.6	37.33%

Sources: Economist (2009), IBP (2009)

Currently, Commonwealth countries, like the United States and governments in the rest of the world, face a serious fiscal crisis. The crisis did not begin in the public finances in most cases. But the public policy responses to recession, growing entitlements burdens, and the collapse of the finance and banking sectors will greatly increase estimated fiscal deficits and public debt for the foreseeable future. While the U.S. fiscal deficit was only 2.5 percent of GDP in 2006 and the U.K deficit was 3.2 percent of GDP (slightly exceeding the EU Stability Pact limit of 3 percent), as indicated in Table 3.1 by the end of 2009 they will climb to: 12.0 percent and 98.0 percent for the United States and 8.0 and 48 percent in the UK respectively. These are conservative estimates, as the tab for banking rescues and stimulus programs increases almost weekly. Should Treasury decide to classify recapitalization of banks as control of corporate policy, the commitments would be direct expenditures, increasing debt to more than 100 percent of GDP (*Economist* 2008b, 65). What we are witnessing in Commonwealth countries and the United States is the largest and fastest growth of fiscal deficits and debt in history. The severity of the fiscal crisis now depends on the relative health of the public finances in each country. Those that controlled deficits and debt to sustainable levels, and that engaged in macroeconomic reforms, now have more "fiscal space" to finance stimulus and rescue programs with deficit financing. For example, Canada and Australia both had budget surpluses of 0.6 percent and 1.5 percent of GDP respectively (*Economist* 2008a, 110). As noted in Table 3.1, these will shift to deficit balances of 2.2 percent and 2.9 percent of GDP respectively. Both levels are entirely sustainable but depend on the responsiveness of the financial and non-financial (or real) economy to respond to fiscal policies.

To summarize the current fiscal situation in 2009, because of the external shocks of: world record high oil prices/barrel, the meltdown of financial sectors in the wake of revenue losses from the subprime mortgage crisis, and growing social insurance/unemployment obligations as the economy slows, revenue losses and stabilizer increases in all Commonwealth countries have returned them to fiscal deficits. Budget processes can provide analytically sound options and, if implemented as policies by political institutions, these crises can be managed properly. What we must relearn, it seems, is the requirement that budget systems be disciplined, manage programs efficiently and effectively, and plan for future revenue losses and expenditure increases should be in force in good times as well as bad.

Among Commonwealth countries, Canada has continuously attempted to rein in spending to cut its budget deficit, reduce its debt burden, and efficiently allocate resources. Note in Table 3.1 that of the Commonwealth countries, it has the lowest projected 2010 fiscal deficit (2.2 percent GDP) of all countries except New Zealand. Historically, to achieve this sound fiscal position it has borrowed all or parts of the fiscal system reforms used in other countries, such as the United States (e.g., program budgeting), France (e.g., redistribution of institutional fiscal powers within the Cabinet), Australia (e.g., management incentives) and the UK (e.g., performance measurement and expenditure programming). Each of these reforms has contributed to improvements in its budget processes and systems. Canada has never faced a major fiscal crisis, and this has permitted it to adopt its reforms piecemeal, in a reasoned atmosphere. Until recently, Canada was the only big industrialized country to notch up consistent surpluses in both its federal budgets and trade/current accounts (*Economist* 2005, 4).

However, many of the high-cost services such as health are provided by the provinces that have major differences in resource endowments and tax base strength. In response, the federal government provides major block and equalization transfer payments in an attempt to ensure equality of service provision among the provinces. For example, funds raised from wealthier Alberta and Ontario are sent to poorer Newfoundland. While this has reduced interprovincial differences in income levels, many argue that federal cash to the provinces encourages them to avoid needed efficiency reforms in service provision (*Economist* 2005, 14). The local response is that Canada works in practice even though it appears dysfunctional in theory (2005, 15)! Its fiscal space to respond to the current economic crisis in a measured way can be attributed to many of the prior reforms it has enacted successfully. In theory or practice, most agree with Petrei (1998, 60) that Canada is a "leader in the field."

Within the Commonwealth, the fiscal management and budgeting systems of Australia and New Zealand are most similar. They are especially similar in adoption of best practices. Their budgets were ranked first- and fourth-highest respectively in transparency. This means that their budget documents were the most available, widest in scope or coverage and clearest to understand in 2008 (*Economist* 2009b, 86). Reflecting similar budget structures and budget processes, their fiscal policies also seem to converge. For example, Australia and New Zealand responded similarly to roughly the same external circumstances in the same period of 1976–1984. Both were closed economies with substantial protection from external competition by tariffs, regulations, and subsidies (Petrei 1998, 148).

Both suffered foreign exchange crises, accumulated fiscal and trade deficits, high inflation and mounting debt about the same time and moved to deregulate their financial systems. More importantly, both introduced radical institutional reforms of their states to introduce competitive mechanisms. These reforms profoundly affected planning, public budgeting, state enterprises, civil service employment, and personnel management, and achieved major productivity gains, as will be described below.

The largest and most complex Commonwealth country is the UK. It may not be surprising then, that of the four countries, the UK endured the worst fiscal crises. The postwar era (both World War I and World War II) led to a substantial increase in the level of public expenditures that by most assessments was wasteful and disorderly. Spending was largely unrelated to revenue availability, which jeopardized macroeconomic stability (Petrei 1998, 82). The economy lunged unpredictably from periods of high growth to stagnation and high inflation. By the 1950s, it was evident that the overall UK fiscal policy process was dysfunctional. The size of the state in relation to GDP became unsustainably large, and because of weak expenditure planning and implementation control service delivery was inefficient and unstable. As will be evident, successive UK administrations responded with reforms of the state and budget processes at virtually all levels (i.e., strategic, management, and operations) and in all phases of the budget cycle (i.e., formulation, approval, execution and evaluation/audit). In short, reinforced by the common political culture noted in chapter 1, Commonwealth fiscal policies and programs have been similar. The composite response of Commonwealth countries to similar challenges has been to implement reforms to increase the consistency between policies and expenditures and to increase the efficiency of expenditures. These reforms have taken place in different forms and at different times in their history.

EXISTING BUDGET PROCESSES

Commonwealth budgeting is governed by the Westminster System, which facilitates institutional collaboration, managerial flexibility, and centralized control. In contrast with the more freewheeling presidential system based on institutional checks and balances (e.g., United States), the Westminster model achieves orderly and efficient public administration by drawing upon apparent opposites. This model applies to all four countries discussed here, even though two are unitary systems (UK and New Zealand) and two are federal systems (Australia and Canada). In all of them, budgeting is an ongoing exercise in which the necessary information flows well between the parties involved (Petrei 1998, 61). In the UK, the cabinet, and its leader the prime minister, and Parliament collaborate on building budgets and approving them. The difference with the presidential separation of powers model is underscored by the fact that the prime minister and cabinet members are also members of Parliament (i.e., the doctrine of collective responsibility). The U.S. president and his cabinet are definitely not members of Congress![1] In the Westminster model, the cabinet takes the lead in strategic policymaking and priority setting; Treasury takes the lead in economic forecasting, budget execution, and control. Parliament can approve or reject budgets after a lengthy period of discussion between the two branches governed by the annual calendar. The annual process moves forward within a system of informal rules and understandings made possible by a common law framework that permits wide managerial discretion. Given the high degree of collaboration and consultation during the budget calendar, the restriction that Parliament can only approve or reject budgets in their entirety is not that severe.

Cabinet groups prepare macroeconomic forecasts and set spending limits early on in the twelve-month calendar. Since the fiscal year begins in April (UK and Canada) and in July (New Zealand and Australia), the main institutional actors (i.e., MOFs, treasuries, cabinets, parliaments, central banks, and ministries) must begin work about twelve months earlier on draft spending and revenue estimates. Departments aggregate their spending preferences based on projected needs from the bottom up based on the budget department of the Treasury's annual instructions and guidelines. Skeptics such as Wildavsky (1989) argue that the relative weakness of the Treasury as a "guardian" gives force to spender arguments (i.e., departments). Despite all the talk about priorities, strategies, and rational allocations, the cabinet is unable to consider and decide on overall allocations because the calculation task is simply too large. He argues there are simply too many barriers to weighing expenditures against each other (1989, 107). However, since he wrote this, the accumulated force of expenditure forecasts, limits, and plans has largely overwhelmed spender arguments and Treasury has been able to play an effective guardian role in Commonwealth countries. The process continues as plans or spending packages (called "votes") are sent to the House of Commons where they are reviewed. During this period there is intense interaction and consultation between the cabinet and Treasury until agreement is reached on the financial law governing appropriations for the next fiscal year. The totals must agree with multiyear expenditure plans (Public Expenditure Survey Committee or PESC) and public sector borrowing requirements (PSBR)—not by law but through the force of common understandings hashed out in the process.

Budget approval is unique at the central government level. In contrast with the active role in budgeting of the U.S. Congress (some would say *disruptive* role!), the parliamentary role in budgeting is "essentially passive" (1989, 110). There is no professionally staffed CBO to advise Parliament. The dilemma is effectively that Parliament cannot exercise an independent critical voice on a budget that has been collectively developed by the government, without the possibility of bringing down that government itself through a loss of a vote on the House of Commons floor (1989,113). The Westminster model is parliamentary democracy exercised though cabinet government—a committee that tolerates no institutional rivals (1989, 112) in the budget process.

For budget implementation, the Treasury sets controls for each department that, consistent with the PESC, may include cash limits. Control totals can be set on a gross basis (irrespective of revenues) or net basis (meaning they can fluctuate in line with other revenue sources). In general, departments comply with them during execution of their approved spending plans. To help ensure this result, internal audit within each agency is coordinated and supervised by the Treasury. Each agency employs a chief accounting officer that reports first to the relevant minister and ultimately to the auditor general. External audit is the responsibility of the National Audit Office, which reports to Parliament. In case of internal ministry auditor disagreement with a minister over financial practice or value for money, that officer can report directly to the auditor-general (which then shares internal and external audit functions for some transactions).

With some variation in time left for legislative analysis and in the names of participant budgetary institutions, the budget calendars of Commonwealth countries reflect the same intended flow of fiscal information, reporting, and forecasting. If the rules can merge political forces and technical information to the satisfaction of major participants in the budget process, it should lead to an approved budget that is later implemented and audited. The real difference lies in the quality of the work that these institutions perform related to resource allocations and the vigor with which they ensure that spending matches purposes. In the Commonwealth countries, a penchant for brutally honest self-criticism and overt dissatisfaction with budgetary results led to reforms that improved overall fiscal performance.

RESPONSES TO FISCAL CRISES

What explains this apparently persistent need for fiscal reform? Reference back to our Comparative Budgeting Framework in chapter 1 provides some possible clues. We mentioned three distinctive factors that contribute to the reform objective: (1) context, (2) political culture, and (3) institutions. The context is important. The four Commonwealth countries are wealthy and economically strong. While their public sectors may be large, they are held accountable and deliver programs and services. Large Commonwealth bureaucracies and public sector do not simply feed off tax revenues and deliver nothing in return (though there were periods in each when this was the case). The political culture, as in many countries, is characterized by competing sets of values and attitudes that affect political behavior. On the one hand, the Protestant work ethic disciplines individual habits, producing a healthy disdain for rules that constrain individual effort and rewards. On the other, a strong sense of egalitarianism, community, and socialism underpin programs from education and housing to health. The result is a state that can focus on management of programs for social purposes.

Finally, institutions are relatively unique in Commonwealth countries. Beginning with the primacy of Common Law and contractual relations, documents such as property deeds, wills, employment contracts, procurement contracts, leases, and budget laws have unparalleled force. That is, anywhere except the United States, to which these institutions were transferred in the 1790s! In addition, the unitary state structure allows for exercise of reform power from the top down within a set of values that stress high trust, integrity, and professionalism. That the "bedrock of British political administration is the importance of trust" (Wildavsky 1989, 90) is no less true for the other Commonwealth countries. Many rules are unwritten and take the form of social understandings between and within social classes. If they are violated, responses come from interpersonal shame, the actions of an adversarial and freewheeling media, and the ultimately the criminal justice system.

The above three factors from our framework profoundly affect public budgeting and reform in Commonwealth countries. They also explain the aggressive and focused response of the UK public sector to the economic and financial sector crisis. While the UK has so far committed only 1.1 percent of GDP for economic support (as opposed to 5.8 percent of GDP in the United States), as in the United States, it is using all the tools available: tax cuts, infrastructure spending, non-bank bailouts, liquidity provisions, loan guarantees, capital injections, asset purchases, and nationalization (*Economist* 2009a, 79).

BUDGET POLICY INSTITUTIONS

The effectiveness of budgeting depends on how the function is organized in government. In some regions, historically there was no lead organization to coordinate the budget process, which of necessity included multiple institutional actors. Nor were the functions of planning and allocating resources very well defined. For example, in the FSU region, there was no budget function at all and allocations were handled by planning ministries with little cost-consciousness. The gap was particularly evident in public investment (i.e., infrastructure) budgeting. Modern capital budgeting systems require at least twelve separate steps that need to be coordinated by a lead organization with oversight responsibility (Guess and Todor 2005).

While there are several models available to determine the organizational structure, the one selected should ensure that the capital program and budget is based only on projects submitted by operating departments that meet economic (e.g., cost-benefit ratios) and broader social criteria (e.g., a water system project deemed essential to prevent risks to public health). Respective states will work out for themselves the respective roles and responsibilities between the prime minister/mayor's office and the parliament/city council. Within the adopted structure, responsibility should be assigned to a lead unit (e.g., public works or finance/budget office) for coordination of the entire process from planning and appraisal through implementation. The lead unit needs to control the flow of projects from the operating departments and to prevent systemic breaches of the capital system caused by inclusion of political projects supported by powerful clients. The lead unit should also work to prevent overruns during construction by decentralizing operational reporting and management responsibilities (Guess and Todor 2005).

The same requirement that a lead organization oversee the process with clearly defined roles and responsibilities exists for current services budgeting as well. Public financial management consists of multiple related functions and it is important to recognize this in organizing the functions of revenue systems, budgeting, accounting, treasury, cash management, procurement, internal audit, and capital planning and debt management. Lack of coordination and communications between units with these functional responsibilities, compounded by weak monitoring can destroy the best-made budgets on paper.

Organizational responsibilities for Commonwealth budget processes lie with parliaments (which allocate funds on a cash basis), which have been responsible for budget administration. Strong audit offices have also been historically important in controlling expenditures and preventing misappropriation. This was particularly true of Canada in the 1860s–1880s (Petrei 1998, 55). There, with growing programmatic and expenditure complexity, legislative budgeting evolved into executive institutional responsibility: Parliaments delegated authority to MOFs and technically equipped treasuries, which reviewed departmental estimates in line with macroeconomic constraints and sent agreed-upon totals to the cabinet and on to the House of Commons for final approval. After approval, parliament controls execution through the auditor-general office (external audit). Similar to the UK and Australia, Canada in the late 1980s began centralizing budget decision making (1998, 59). Canada's budget institutions have evolved and now have clearly defined functions, procedures, planning guidelines, and informational reporting requirements (1998, 60).

Beginning in the 1960s, executive budget agencies became interested in managing policy through the budget. This produced a major wave of reforms in the United States under the general label of "planning, programming, budgeting" or PPBS reforms that spread to executive budgeting agencies around the world— to Commonwealth countries such as the UK, Australia, and Canada, and to Latin America where PPBS ended up as constitutional requirements in some countries. The reform did not function as planned for reasons that have been exhaustively explored (Axelrod 1988, 281–94; Wildavsky 1989, 320–22), and which focus on how they unreasonably increased the calculation and transaction costs of elected officials. Despite such implementation problems, program budget reforms did stimulate interest in broader state modernization to ensure that budgets would be planned and spent more efficiently and effectively. Nowhere was this more evident than in the Commonwealth countries.

In the 1970s, it was recognized that to increase economy, efficiency, and effectiveness, more was needed than performance measures, multiyear planning estimates, and a new budget format. Institutional constraints would need to be removed and proper incentives provided to program managers to achieve results. Budget systems and formats had to be institutionalized to actually affect the allocation and control of expenditures. In this spirit, the British Financial Administration Initiative of 1982 attempted to decentralize operational responsibilities to departments and offices and elevate accountability to program managers. The vehicle was mainly a new information system for activity coordination (1998, 85). The problem with fiscal information systems that make data more transparent is that alone they do not provide managerial authority to take risks or achieve better program results. The fiscal information system failed to deal with the structural or disincentive problem that managers had no motivation to achieve cost savings or attain effectiveness. Since managers were not really autonomous (the central government continued to exert control), the departments could not keep any savings generated by any decisions made on the improved fiscal information. In 1992, the "Citizen's Charter" reforms were enacted to allow departments to keep their savings. That reform also introduced a market test to encourage competition in service delivery (1998, 86).

Australia and New Zealand went even farther down the path of "New Public Management" reforms. They focused on constraints created by the civil service personnel system to budget management and service results. Like the UK, they decentralized functions and gave greater management autonomy to chief program officers through various laws in the 1980s and '90s (e.g., New Zealand State Sector Act of 1988 and the Fiscal Responsibility Act of 1994). The State Sector Act separated policymaking from service delivery responsibilities (1998, 150) and increased incentives to perform by eliminating senior manager tenure and replacing it with medium-term contracts tied to preset objectives. The effect was to shift emphasis on quantity of inputs to fulfillment of policy objectives. By that Act, program managers were given the authority to hire and fire personnel and to set salaries and incentives (1998, 151). Canada and New Zealand have pioneered the use of fiscal incentive-institutional reform trade-offs (Wildavsky 1988, 258), for example, in intergovernmental performance transfers for health and education. As a quid pro quo for delegation of increased managerial autonomy over budget and personnel resources, managers have to stay within set expenditure limits. They are judged on their ability to attain preset service results and have the relative freedom to combine or eliminate resources to perform that task. Failure to achieve the program or service targets are a factor considered in renewal of their three-to-five-year employment contracts.

Thus, Commonwealth countries became laboratories for testing the ideas of "New Public Management." According to Barzelay (2001, cited in Moynihan 2006, 79), in the 1980s this bloc of countries engaged in several related institutional reforms that: (1) increased managerial authority by decentralizing financial management and human resource systems, (2) eliminated centralized civil service rules regarding tenure, promotion, and pay, (3) aggregated appropriations into performance contracts, and (4) initiated budget carryover authority to eliminate the incentive for year-end spending. In some cases, managers found achievement of preset program objectives cheaper and more efficient by using private contractors. Given their imminent accountability for service results, managers were given the autonomy and flexibility to look for service delivery alternatives as a logical adjunct of their "incentivized" positions.

BUDGET FORMULATION AND PLANNING

The process of issuing instructions and calls for budget requests begins the annual competition between staff finance offices (e.g., MOFs, prime ministers' offices), or macrobudgeting, and the line departments, or microbudgeting, as they build up their requests from last year's base. Instructions from finance departments impose top-down constraints: prior-year commitments, fixed costs (often entitlements and statutory grants), campaign promises, conformity with macroeconomic limits, and plans to concentrate on a few big issues (Axelrod 1988, 34). Budget offices also issue expenditure instructions that can require ceilings broken down by function, object of expenditure and program, multiyear projections of revenues and expenditures, capital construction plans and cost-benefits, and performance measures for core activities. In addition to guidelines on estimating staffing and nonpersonal service costs for the next fiscal year, a major focus of most instructions is the requirement that departments develop base budgets and changes to the base budget.

The baseline budget (often called "current services budget") is typically a calculation of real or constant currency requirements, assuming present trends without any policy changes. An important issue for base calculation is whether the department or the finance office should absorb expected inflationary increases (1988, 36). For discretionary programs, typically, the departments must absorb part or all of the increases. For mandatory programs, such as social assistance and social security payments, laws usually provide for CPI-indexed payments that do not have to be absorbed by the department or the individual. The 1961 UK reform known as the Public Expenditure Survey (PES) required development and reporting of budget service "volumes" to improve program performance. Departments calculated the inflation-adjusted funds required for delivery of a particular volume of services—which the Treasury was ultimately responsible for financing. In the name of performance, the system provided the wrong incentives and guaranteed loss of expenditure control when inflation increased (Petrei 1999, 84). In that the Treasury absorbed the inflation increase in order to achieve planned service volumes, departments had few incentives to spend efficiently or wisely. The treasuries of that period responded with some combination of cash limits, delays of MOF budget releases to departments, and payments deferrals. All of these were rather crude devices to try and stop the expenditure leakage at the source, and most of them are still used. The trouble is that these devices often end up creating expenditure arrears and pressure for even greater expenditure later. Moreover, cash limits and across-the-board cuts affect some service more than others (Premchand 1993, 77), which increases service instability. That put Commonwealth budget institutions back to square one, in that service stability was why *volume budgeting* was introduced in the first place.

Currently, and more logically, budgetary bases in Commonwealth countries are calculated in nominal terms to put the onus of cost control on the departments rather than the Treasury. Cash limits are still set, but on a gross or net basis depending on the type of expenditure. This means that departments, for example in New Zealand, must calculate both gross expenditures (excluding any revenue generated), and net expenditures for the next year in case cash limits need to be applied (Petrei 1998, 155). In the case of net calculations, departments or activities that have other revenue sources may include only the public budget funds requested (otherwise it would act as a disincentive to raise other revenues).

In an attempt to link revenues and expenditures to actual program results, Commonwealth countries developed several new approaches that have been followed elsewhere. In Canada, for example, "envelope budgeting" was developed in 1979 as a form of functional or program budgeting to integrate policy and expenditure decision making (Premchand 1993, 68). In fact, its main purpose was to control a "runaway budget" (Axelrod 1998, 265). All government programs were divided into ten functions or "spending envelopes" (1998, 265) with two elements—an operating reserve and a policy reserve. The operating premise was that the policy fund would encourage trade-offs between new initiatives by giving up old programs from the operating base. Instead of cost control, the system encouraged use of the policy reserve as an additional net claim on the new budget. Despite the ingenuity of this approach, it was given up for political and systemic reasons after ten years (1993, 69). In 1987–88, Australia developed a similar approach called "portfolio budgeting" (1993, 68). The idea was to bring many complementary programs under one "portfolio," set expenditure limits, and finance new policies through offsetting savings (1993, 69). This system is still in use there today.

Finally, perhaps the reform most identified with Commonwealth budget preparation is the Medium-Term Expenditure Framework (MTEF). Canadian envelope budgeting took place within a rolling five-year expenditure planning process that was updated each year. The purpose of an MTEF is to estimate budget requirements and revenues over a four-year period (budget year with an annual appropriation + three more). If applied, the framework will ensure macro-economic balance, permit allocation of funds to strategic priorities, and provide funding stability for line departments. Operating within typical MTEF rules, line departments estimate multiyear expenditures (mostly on a gross basis) based on guidelines provided by the finance department. In Australia, projections are based on assumptions for about thirty variables. The estimated budget is rolled forward each year and updated or reconciled with new estimates and a new hard budget constraint for the next year (Petrei 1998, 131).

The MTEF is designed to estimate downstream costs of major items such as personnel, benefits, O&M for capital investments, and debt service, and to forge a current budget constraint. Note that the framework relies on traditional object-of-expenditure budget data. To develop the "hard budget constraint," staff do not have to generate activity or program performance information. But staff must estimate multiyear expenditures and revenue requirements for each budget category. This ensures that expenditure decisions are made in the context of actual, multiyear program needs rather than annual budgets. Annual budgeting results in unpredictable funding within and between years and leads to poor operational and service results. MTEFs in practice often help allocation decisions if they are fully installed.

Figure 3.1 (Allen and Tommasi 2001, 184) illustrates a four-year budget planning framework (CY + 3 year plan). The framework requires linkage of current base estimates—the costs of current policies—with revenue and expenditure estimates over the planning period. Line agencies respond to calls issued by MOFs to estimate current program and running costs, then add in nominal costs for new policy changes for the same period. The MOFs reduce these estimates in real terms to compensate for inflation by providing a rate for budget calculation. This means that available funding for delivery of services and programs will be less in real terms. Line agencies must budget for this accordingly by reducing staff, changing how services are delivered (e.g., more technology and less personnel), or charging separate fees. The MTEF is a framework for expenditure planning and annual reconciliation of new revenue figures with expenditure needs. The aim is to plan for future program needs and revenue contingencies. Proper use of the MTEF framework allows managers to reprogram savings in response to expenditure ceilings and to plan for hidden expenditures (e.g., O&M for capital maintenance). To date in the UK, not all expenditures are included in this process. About 50 percent of total expenditures are for entitlements, such as social security and health care. Because of the volatile nature of these expenditures, they are planned

FIGURE 3.1. Preparing Multiyear Expenditure Estimates

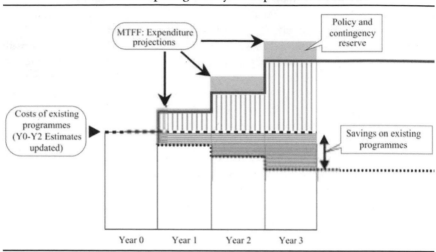

annually (Allen and Tommasi 2001, 179). Nevertheless, the reconciliation feature makes the framework a unique combination of regulation (the hard budget constraint) and flexibility (rolling plans and reconciliation exercises).

Often, MTEFs are developed separately from capital budgets because of institutional structures and jurisdictional rules that defeat the purpose of comprehensive fiscal planning. This institutional defect is as true in Commonwealth countries as in the other regions covered in our book. Limiting MTEF to current services budgeting calls into question the goal of programming all budget resources over a multiyear framework. International consultants and donors like exercises to develop MTEF frameworks. So, in many cases, MTEFs become trophy budgets (something like program budgets) that are not actually used except for display. Worse still, when implemented overseas either too narrowly focused as technical tools such as activity-based costing (Shah 2007, 128) or as part of broader budget reform projects that include performance budgeting, the frequent result is that the MTEF budgeting framework is not used for real planning, allocation, or implementation. So, the more traditional South African MTEF works well—expenditures are estimated in current prices and the rolling three-year process links the problem of growing personnel costs with expenditure management constraints (Schiavo-Campo and Tommasi 1999, 301). By contrast, the Mozambique MTEF does not work well. Budget staff there is unskilled and underpaid. Little confidence exists in the figures generated even for the annual budget in traditional object of expenditure format (1999, 300). In this context, it is difficult to imagine why the Mozambiquean MOF would push for a rolling five-year framework! Nevertheless, the MTEF concept is sound and it is a popular reform around the world.

APPROVAL

In Commonwealth countries, especially the UK, the budget is prepared almost collectively with regular consultations between the Parliament (House of Commons), cabinet, and the prime minister or executive offices (including the central bank and the Treasury). In the Commonwealth generally, as in most countries, legislative budgeting is relatively weak. The prime mover is the executive for major public financial management functions from macroeconomic forecasting to development of expenditure estimates (votes). The primary budget responsibilities of Parliament are to pass appropriations on time and get the fiscal year moving. During budget execution, parliaments also receive reports from their external or legislative audit units, called national audit offices. Performance of the legislative post-audit function in Commonwealth parliaments is typically stronger than in their counterparts elsewhere. Their role is clearly as authoritative as that of the U.S. Congress in relation to its external audit unit, the General Accountability Office (GAO).

In stronger legislative environments, such as the United States, the legislature performs the same functions as in Commonwealth countries—only much stronger. The U.S. Congress can in principle change the entire budget proposed by the executive branch and increase or decrease it. In the bicameral legislatures of Commonwealth countries, they can approve or reject but not modify the executive request. That is a fairly significant limit on parliamentary power. The structure of the approved budget consists of "votes" or line-item chapters/sections (250 in England). Otherwise, five legislative roles are universally important. First, after hearings and analysis, legislatures appropriate funds to proposed spending items (usually by line-item account or vote). This may be a one-stage or a two-stage process. In most countries, legislatures authorize and appropriate in the same stage. In the United States, to try and prevent funding from driving policymaking, standing committees adopt proposed legislation first, authorizing new programs and projects. After this stage, appropriations committees pass funding appropriations. In the United States, this is "budget authority," which permits agencies to incur obligations for expenditures (Axelrod 1988, 151). There are various types of budget authority depending on the purpose, for instance, multiyear (construction, housing subsidies), permanent (interest on national debt), or annual (most current programs—but actually the smallest part of available budget authority). Appropriations are broken down into apportionments and allotments for departmental and agency expenditure and legislative control purposes.

Second, where legislatures cannot agree on the annual budget, some form of continuing resolution is passed to keep the government from shutting down. In Commonwealth countries, such as Australia, parliaments attempt to pass the appropriations bill before the start of the July fiscal year. This replaces the normal process of authorizing "supply estimates" (Petrei 1988, 130) to cover expenditures during the first quarter when the legislature has failed to enact a budget. In the United States, when Congress cannot pass appropriations bills by the beginning of the fiscal year (not unusual), political battles can turn the interim device into a major game of brinkmanship—as in the mid-1990s when the Republican Congress could not even agree on continuing resolutions and brought the government to a halt to embarrass Democratic president Bill Clinton (Smith and Lynch 2004, 98).

Third, legislatures often develop forecasts, fiscal policies, and targets of their own. At the minimum, legislatures should have the capability to analyze expenditure requests and make changes. As indicated, many legislatures cannot change the executive request, which can act as a disincentive to development of analytic capability. The U.S. Congress has substantial technical staff support. This staff develops its own figures and data for budget forecasts and impact analyses—independently of the executive branch. Even at the state or intermediate level in the U.S. federal system, the quality of fiscal staff work is "exceptionally high (Axelrod 1988, 159). The U.S. Congressional Budget Office is the model for legislative fiscal work. This unit advises budget and other committees on request as well as by providing general analyses of fiscal trends. Its macroeconomic and fiscal forecasts are respected as objective and nonpolitical. Commonwealth countries do not include a strong legislative budget analysis resource as part of their institutional framework. In Commonwealth countries, the bulk of forecasting and analysis is performed by the treasury and prime minister's office. As noted by Petrei (1998, 88), the UK budget cycle takes place mostly within the executive branch. In contrast with the U.S. Congress, the UK Parliament receives macroeconomic reports two times per year from the executive when the budget bill is submitted for approval.

Fourth, legislatures participate to varying degrees in budget implementation. At a minimum, legislatures receive regular expenditure reports from MOFs on a cash basis (revenues and expenditures realized). Legislatures and audit units focus largely on variance analysis: comparison of planned versus actual expenditures and attempts at explanation. Commonwealth parliaments are no exception. In addition, the majority of legislatures have authority to decide on current-year adjustments by: transfers, reprogramming, and supplemental appropriation requests. These are standard budget management tools, useful as a safety valve in case of changing economic conditions, errors in revenue and expenditure estimates, poor fiscal management, unanticipated price increases affecting workload, or other unplanned developments (disasters, wars) (Smith and Lynch 2004, 249). Departments that make changes in approved expenditures must report them within the terms of their appropriations legislation to the appropriate legislative budget committee. Usually these are minor changes. For major changes that may amount to changes in policy, legislatures can grant supplemental funds to departments. In Commonwealth countries, the power to grant supplemental funds lies with the cabinet and treasury, not Parliament.

Fifth, legislatures effectively control budget execution through their external audit units. In the United States, the Government Accountability Office performs the function of a "supreme audit institution". In Commonwealth countries, auditor-general (AG) offices perform this function. In Canada, for example, the AG reports periodically to Parliament on economy, efficiency, and effectiveness of expenditures. Effectiveness is often termed "impact" evaluation or "value for money," which can include examination of policy objectives (Petrei 1998, 71). Reporting to the Parliamentary Public Accounts Committee is done though auditors in departments and ministries. It is said that about 50 percent of the AG's funds are now spent for value for money studies (1988, 70). In the UK the responsibilities are a bit more combined for external audit. The National Audit Office (NAO) was created in 1983 for this purpose. NAO is headed by the comptroller, who is appointed by the queen on the PM's recommendation and in consultation with the Public Accounts Committee of Parliament (1998, 99). Similarly, the Australian National Audit Office (ANAO) was created in 1901 and reports to Parliament. But the Parliamentary Public Accounts Committee was created only in the late 1990s. It spends about 33 percent of its funds on VFM studies (1998,138).

To summarize, parliamentary aspirations for increased analysis of budget approval decisions have not been achieved. To date, parliamentary budgeting has not been part of the Commonwealth reform model. How this has affected the quality, composition, and scope of expenditures should be examined in future comparative budget research.

IMPLEMENTATION CONTROL

In general, the budgetary literature likes to focus on budget formulation and tends to minimize the significance of budget implementation (Axelrod 1988, 169). A recent exception to this has been the treatment of Commonwealth countries and U.S. state and local budget implementation. Budget implementation focuses on the levers that control the budget in action, such as the allotment process, transfer of funds between budget items, and chapters and cash management (1988, 170). It requires a solid accounting foundation and requires regular reporting on spending, commitments, and outlays as well as anything measurable and attributable that can be developed for service results. OECD governments excel in the accounting and reporting of both fiscal and physical service information. As noted, after appropriations are approved and then broken into smaller parts for spending according to proposed agency spending plans. Post-approval quarterly apportionments of funds (called allotments elsewhere than the United States) to ministries for programs, projects, and objects of expense, are critically important to the stability and quality of program performance. In many countries, this apportionment-allotment process by ministries to their subunits is opaque, plagued by bureaucratic rigidity and rule-literalism. Post-approval processes often become tangled up in accounting rules that delay the release of funds. This profoundly affects expenditure planning for services and programs that expected their budgets to be released to them as approved by the legislature. Delayed release is less of a problem in common law countries such as the United States, and in Commonwealth systems.

In Commonwealth fiscal systems, successful major reforms have taken place at the implementation stage of the budget cycle. As indicated, program budgeting, MTEFs, and performance budgeting are largely reforms of budget presentation. For this reason, accounting offices responsible for implementation through existing charts of accounts are often opposed to reforms that require new categories of information for new budgeting systems, for example, programs, envelopes, and activities. The more important comparative budgeting questions are whether the reforms work and why, or why not? The answers lie in the implementation superstructure. Are there systems to allot funds properly and to flexibly change budget direction in response to new needs? Are there systems to measure the actual amounts of resources being consumed (i.e., costs or expenses) as opposed to only budget appropriations (i.e., expenditures)? This is important for service cost analysis and control. Are there backup systems to deal with short-term cash flow shortages, through either the treasury or commercial banking systems? At the U.S. state/local levels and in Commonwealth countries, the answer to these questions is largely yes. And these systems have worked quite well as aids to cash management.

A common theme to Commonwealth budgetary management is that all countries have followed the New Public Management (NPM) philosophy. This requires systems and methods of setting targets (for control and/or achievements), providing incentives for action, and developing program and service performance measurement systems for feedback in order to hold leaders accountable. Within this broad approach, there are differences. The Canadian system, for example, blends European stress on targets/norms and controls with the U.S. features of broad organic budget laws, market signals, and flexible budget management authority. The Canadian Expenditure Control Act of 1991 sets annual limits on expenditures but leaves deficit control to the market and regular Treasury Board spending reports that are shared with the public (Petrei 1998, 64). Similarly, provincial debt is not limited explicitly and controls are left to market institutions (i.e., transparently graded ratings by Moody's, Fitch, or S&P). Consistent with NPM tenets, fiscal managers are given incentives to actually manage services for results. Department managers can now carry over up to 5 percent of operational expenditures to the next fiscal year (instead of playing the usual games to avoid lapsed budget authority at the end of the year). They also have broad discretion to reallocate funds within their ministries. As public entrepreneurs, managers typically depend on budget savings to finance any new programs (1998, 65). To improve cost control, the accrual system of expenditure accounting is used to measure and to report the cost of resources consumed for each program (1998, 66). In accrual accounting/budgeting systems, resources are recorded in the period or year earned; expenses are recorded when consumed regardless of when payment is made (Finkler 2005, 49). This allows clear matching of resources to activities and prevents much of the manipulation that goes on in cash-based systems, for instance, delaying payments to reduce apparent expenditure levels in order to achieve virtual balance.

Within Commonwealth systems, the UK reforms have improved expenditure monitoring and evaluation by front-loading changes to the organization of government as well as the methodology of reporting budget figures and fiscal condition. Ministries now have CEOs that have significant authority to set salaries, hire staff, and rank positions. (Petrei 1998, 86). In the wake of structural reforms, many services were privatized and other agencies forced to reduce wage and salary staff expenditures. Despite these efforts, costs of services have not decreased—often because user demand increased to satisfy real needs. Similar to Canada, UK agency managers gained the authority to keep budget savings for their own departmental purposes. Departmental permanent secretaries can carry over 5.0 percent of capital expenditures and 0.5 percent of current expenditures to the next year (1998, 97). As a counterweight to the Treasury "guardian" tendency to control expenditures top-down through imposition of cash limits, this is an important managerial incentive (consistent with New Public Management operating premises) to achieve efficiency and effectiveness.

To align budget implementation more closely with the formulation phase, the methodology of budget preparation has also been improved. In many countries, because of a disconnect between budget planning and implementation, budgeting is actually done at the implementation phase—which generally produces poor service results. Beginning in 2000, the Public Expenditure Survey had to be submitted using the accrual method as a supplement to cash-based reporting. Reporting resources consumed, rather than inputs used to deliver services, allowed for cost measurement and easier assignment of prices for all resources, including fixed assets and basic services. Departments now submit regular statements or reports on resources consumed including capital, operating costs, cash flow, and financial balances. This has helped reconcile resource flows to cash flows and improved expenditure monitoring (Petrei 1998, 87). The executive branch

(NAO and Treasury) have also been behind the promotion of performance indicators to justify program existence. While there is some evidence that the obsession for service performance measurement was counterproductive and used to justify often minimal results (begun by the 1992 Citizen's Charter), emphasis on performance measurement has contributed positively to a change in the culture of UK government as well as those of other Commonwealth countries.

Beginning in 1983 with the Reid Report, for example, Australian budget implementation moved from emphasis on line-item and procedural controls to provision of incentives and authority for management to attain targeted service results. Policy and execution functions were separated across government. Managers became accountable for results and were given the authority to attain them. Fiscal controls were shifted to ex-post rather than ex-ante, which allowed for maximum discretion on the use of budgeted funds. The major ex-post control is the obligation for regular reporting (using the accrual accounting method and performance indicators provided by the central government and the states) to the cabinet and department of finance on fiscal transactions and service results. This "highly developed" program evaluation system is an important part of the overall budgeting and control system and was decentralized to the departmental level (Petrei 1998, 137).

New Zealand has achieved the greatest level of budget implementation reform of all the Commonwealth countries. This may not be surprising given its size and relatively simple governmental structure. Nevertheless, New Zealand closed the loop between formulation, implementation, and evaluation, which is the ultimate purpose of good budgeting systems. It combines the NPM incentive approach to service delivery, devolving authority and responsibility to managers while allowing them to "shop" for the cheapest and best service delivery alternatives, including privatization. It focuses on deregulation of the personnel system to make government more like the private sector, with higher salaries, clearer targets, less tenure security, and more authority to manage resources to attain results. In exchange for the authority, departments are responsible for regular reporting on expenditures and results. This quid pro quo exchange of increased managerial authority for program performance accountability is a central feature of NPM and works well in Commonwealth countries such as New Zealand. Managers must now submit annually and semiannually to the Department of Finance statements of: assets, liabilities, net worth, revenues-expenditures, cash flow, debt, contingent liabilities, extrabudgetary revenues and expenditures (i.e., gross and net expenditures), and management of trust funds (1998, 161). The minister of the treasury must certify that the reports are based on valid and reliable data. He/she must also certify that departmental internal control systems are operative. All reports are audited (externally) by the auditor-general and are ultimately submitted to New Zealand Parliament.

Transparent fiscal reporting is critical for political trust and the exercise of accountability measures. In September 2006, ten thousand people converged on the Hungarian Parliament demanding the resignation of Prime Minister Ferenc Gyurcsany. They burned cars and riot police fought with demonstrators, causing serious personal injuries and physical damage to the downtown area. What was the issue? The PM was caught on-mike saying that he lied to the Hungarian people about the state of public finances in order to get reelected in April 2006. For example, he told the public that the budget deficit was no larger than 4.7 percent of GDP when the GOH's own Central Bank had indicated that it was in fact at least 10 percent (Dempsey 2006). Many observers of the Hungarian public finances had been reporting the higher figures before and after the election, and many of them indicated that the fundamentals of public finance were far worse than presented by the PM. But few people (especially and ironically, the opposition Fidez Party) took notice. For example, *The Economist* (2006) reported in April that the budget deficit was between 8 and 10 perecent including off-balance sheet expenditure items as road building, and on-budget items such as preelection spending to drum up support for his own Socialist Party. Narrow budget coverage and cash-based accounting permitted the GOH to assert the lower deficit figure in public. These kinds of transparency and reporting gimmicks are less likely to occur in Commonwealth countries. In Commonwealth countries, independent institutions regularly check on each other, and the entire government financial picture is regularly reported and debated by think tanks, NGOs, and other quasi-public institutions. Many suggest that the Hungarian PM lied and tragically betrayed the people, and conversely that the opposition party (Fidez) capitalized on this error, but it is clear that if the PM had been honest and presented the actual figures (with broad coverage and accrued expenses) and gotten reelected anyway, the same people would have burned cars to protest the austerity program that would have had to include cutting down the size of the enormous state and its massive budget (total general government expenditure 50 percent of GDP versus 44.3 percent in the UK and only 37.3 percent in the United States in 2007 [OECD 2008]). As important as the size of the government budget and its transparency, then, is whether the public perceives that government goods and services are responsive to their needs. In Hungary, they apparently aren't!

AUDIT AND EVALUATION

There are, broadly, two kinds of audits: financial control and value for money or economy/efficiency studies. The latter evaluate budget policy and expenditure effectiveness. Modern controls try to prevent fraud, waste, or abuse and investigate it when it happens. The controls are viewed as a part of modern management. They are there to prevent or catch misappropriation of funds and also to help managers direct and regulate activities to achieve agency objectives (Petrei 1998, 44). There are two critical control points in any system: (1) the control institution, such as auditors-general and national audit offices, and (2) their functions, of which the most important is pre-audit. Axelrod (1988, 183) describes pre-audit as the "watchdog of budget implementation." This function consists of examination of all source documents for payments transactions, for example, vouchers, payrolls, purchase orders, and contracts. The purpose of preaudit is to ensure compliance with financial and appropriations laws as well as the availability of funds to pay for the proposed expenditure (Axelrod 1988, 184). The internal audit units are there to ensure that internal controls are working. Internal controls are the procedures for core government–wide transactions, for example, personnel recruitment and payment, procurement and acquisitions, treasury registry of payments, and registry of tax and customs receipts. While a central internal audit unit typically exists in any government, the bulk of pre-audit activity occurs within the agencies and departments. It has to be centralized to avoid overwhelming the departmental audit units. Modern Commonwealth audit systems have been designed as man-agement tools and excel in both financial control and value for money evalua-tions. Certification of the public accounts and expenditures in the UK began in the twelfth century. Reforms have progressed dramatically. In 1921, for example, the internal audit function abandoned the voucher system and moved to a more efficient sampling system (Petrei 1988, 98).

Currently, modern OECD systems operate from the premise that voucher verification (for pre-audit of payments as well as taxes and customs duties), is a time-consuming, corruption-generating system that does not really control expenditures. Rather, they often prevent effective performance of the program or system in question. For these reasons, most OECD countries have adopted source document sampling systems. Internal audit organizations receive their data from accounts officers in each ministry or department. They are technically audit employees and not subject to the will of the departmental minister or the finance department. Accounts officers are called "inspectors general" (IGs) in the United States. In the event of finding fraud, waste, or abuse of power, they can report directly to the head internal auditor, which is usually in the treasury, minister of finance, or other agency separate from external audit and parliament. External controls are exercised by parliamentary authorized units, often called a National Audit Office headed by an auditor-general and comptroller (which are also known as SAI's or supreme audit institutions). These focus on financial audits through reports to parliament and value for money studies of identified programs and projects. Even in Commonwealth countries, most external audit funds are spent on financial analyses and reporting rather than value for money analyses.

Fiscal information requirements vary by level of policy position. Policymakers at the strategic level are more interested in financial control, via real time reports comparing revenues and expenditures, and providing timely statements of financial position (i.e., balance sheets, operating statements, and cash flow statements). They need this information to ensure that deficit and debt targets are being met and that no unsustainable obligations are being accumulated that will lead to major crises later. At the "allocational" or sectoral level, policymakers need information on program and management performance. As indicated, internal audit units focus mainly on financial control through investigation of waste, fraud, and abuse of power issues. In the United States, internal auditors (IGs) in each department (i.e., ministry) report to the national budget office, or Office of Management and Budget. By having a separate line of reporting to the national OMB that circumvents both appointed department heads and the departmental finance office, IGs can function with relatively high independence. In Commonwealth countries, some internal audit units are moving to activity and program evaluations. For example, the UK Office of Comptroller and Auditor General was once limited to verification of individual vouchers—basically pre-audit for financial control. In 1921, as indicated, its responsibilities changed to sampling vouchers and later to value for money studies of particular programs.

Like the U.S. GAO, the UK NAO is responsible for external audit and reports to the elected parliament. Gradually, its responsibilities are shifting to value for money studies. Consistent with New Public Management tenets, the focus now is on using the budget process to pressure departments to improve management of their programs and projects. External audit units, such as NAO and ANAO are interested in productivity, impact, effectiveness, efficiency, and results, as well as in analysis of financial balances to maintain financial control. Finally, at the operational level of policy decision making, line managers are interested in specific information from auditors (as well as other sources) that can give them advance warning of program and service problems in both the physical (e.g., facilities condition and maintenance management) and financial areas (e.g., cash flow problems).

It is critically important for deregulation of the public sector and reforming management consistent with NPM principles (which are both major Commonwealth reform tenets) to develop strong ex ante controls over expenditure transactions that do not interfere with management interests in achieving program performance. Commonwealth internal audit systems have largely achieved this through its modern NAO offices with rules on pre-audit sampling enforced by highly trained accountants and financial professionals. In addition, internal audit is supplemented by strong external parliamentary audit units that focus on both financial and value for money or performance audits. Within this modern framework, budgets can be developed for more than one year, analyzed technically, and implemented on the basis of sound reporting and feedback to oversight authorities.

REMAINING ISSUES

There are two issues that remain for Commonwealth budget reformers: (1) performance management, and (2) local government finance. As indicated, a considerable effort has been made by Commonwealth systems to link expenditures and performance of services and programs. This is evident from the above discussion in all four countries. To a large extent, this effort is considered successful and has become a model for other regions and countries that seek to improve program performance via well-managed budgetary actions. More recently, the 1998 UK program of setting service targets and managing toward their achievement has been critically evaluated. The findings are relevant for not only Commonwealth systems but all performance budgeting and management systems worldwide. In the UK system, service targets are now agreed upon with Treasury by department managers (called production units) and budget allocations consistent with these agreements are provided to the extent possible. To enforce results, a Prime Minister's Delivery Unit (PMDU) was set up to provide targets, rewards (star ratings) and punishments (P45s or sacking notices).

On the other hand, Hood (2006) argues that many of the astonishingly positive results in performance that were reported as part of this program can be explained by gaming and strategic behavior. Three types of games were played that should have been known to the planners of this system, since they have also been documented in traditional public sector accounting systems, socialist planning systems (GOSPLAN and norms), and wartime production regimes (2006, 516). First, responding to target setter's incremental increases in output targets (the ratchet effect), production units restrict performance below their production possibility frontiers. Second, uniform targets provide no incentives to excel and good performers back off below the threshold (threshold effect). Third, managers rationally manipulate reported results to hit the target (output distortion). Hood suggests that these gaming responses (creative compliance) should have been anticipated and antidotes applied at the outset, such as refinement of targets, more audit investigations, and tightening the rules and data definitions (2006, 520). The findings of his study raise serious questions about the actual results achieved by "target and terror systems" that do not control for eagerness to report and to accept "good news" performance at face value (2006, 519). It is important that post-Blair regimes and other Commonwealth systems come to grips with these familiar problems before budget allocations are tied recklessly to "headline" performance targets.

The other important issue is the strengthening local government management and finance. According to Blond and Pabst (2006), one of the two most pressing needs now in Britain is "decentralization of political and economic power to localities, thereby enabling civic institutions to form and govern themselves." To a large extent, despite many reforms, local governments (LGUs) in the UK resemble, according to Wildavsky (1989, 114), "spending departments" of the central government. UK LGUs lack the financial clout of their U.S. counterparts and raise only 20 percent of their revenue from their main "own-source," which is the council tax. Even that source is controlled to some extent by Whitehall, according to Hambleton and Sweeting (2004, 482). Consistent with Wildavsky's earlier observation, they suggest that LGUs are little more than branch offices of Whitehall (2004, 483). In that about 80 percent of LGU funds flow from the central government, LGUs lack financial power and much incentive to be accountable to local electorates. This is a major difference in the intergovernmental structure and policy environments of the UK and the United States. Even though other Commonwealth countries permit election of LGU mayors and assemblies, in terms of financial dependence they are about as centralized in relation to local government autonomy and power as their counterparts in the UK. The UK, according to these observers, "is still one of the most centralized states in the Western world" (2004, 485).

But things are changing. As of 2004, the number of elected mayors in the UK had grown from zero to twelve out of 389 LGUs (2004, 479). Influenced by the U.S. model, the Local Government Act of 2000 introduced changes in management and political leadership, such as separation of powers between elected mayors and assemblies (councils) to replace the collective decision making of the cabinet model. It also included the possibility of popular referenda to install assembly-appointed city managers (2004, 476). These are positive reforms that should be extended to increase local fiscal autonomy and accountability for the financial substance of programs and services. Without that authority, few LGU officials (anywhere) have the incentives to take the risks required for improving service performance.

TRANSFER OF BUDGET METHODS AND SYSTEMS

As indicated, international donors, regimes, and policy reformers need to be cautious about transferring fiscal systems, methods and organizational models from one context to another. The target countries may not be comparable or even remotely compatible to begin with. Regime support for reforms varies widely. Verbal acceptance of the concept of modern reform is a crowd pleaser, even if followed by inaction. Cultural capacities to defer gratification also vary widely, allowing one to predict with reasonable certainty public tolerance for hard budget constraint–type reforms. More importantly, institutional development may differ. For example, models of fiscal corruption control are hard to transfer, because they require at minimum strong internal audit units, an aggressive and independent media, and an independent judiciary. Recognizing these constraints, Commonwealth countries nevertheless offer transferable models and practices in three areas: (1) the MTEF, (2) fiscal reporting and audit, and (3) New Public Management reforms.

First, the MTEF offers a good budget planning framework and an opportunity to develop a hard budget constraint for the current year based on downstream fiscal needs and estimated revenue availability. The multiyear framework allows fiscal planners and analysts to make cuts or additions based on future trends; it allows revenue estimates to lead to discussions of tax rates, bases, and the impact of user fees. These are some of the important analytic gains if the MTEF is used for planning and to develop a real constraint. If it is used simply as a massive data collection exercise, little of substance will be achieved in changing budget processes or allocation patterns. If the installation of an MTEF is combined with efforts to develop performance measures and turn the budget into a results-oriented system including parliamentary efforts, the entire project typically overloads and ends in failure. The absorptive capacity of most countries beyond the Commonwealth area is simply too limited for such complex reforms. Such design flaws that led to later implementation failures have occurred in a number of transitional and developing countries that eagerly accepted MTEF advocates from Commonwealth countries. The constraints of this framework need to be realized before attempted installation. More seriously, failure to install a workable MTEF can lead to a high-level public backlash against further fiscal reforms, and produce reform fatigue.

Second, the Commonwealth model is predicated on sound fiscal reporting and audit of both financial and program performance. The four countries' experiences reviewed here demonstrate strong systemic support for development of these institutions over many centuries. For sound budgeting, it is critical that: (1) fiscal data definition and classification rules are clear, (2) reported data can be verified, (3) reporting games, such as fictionalized data on nonreporting of embarrassing data, can be controlled. All this is required to ensure official and public confidence in the basic fiscal data of government. Revenue and expenditure definitions must be valid, reliable, and consistent according to recognized norms. As noted, GFS norms are clear, and the only question is whether they (or similar norms used by such units as Eurostat) are enforced. The IMF monitors fiscal and accounting reporting standards in member countries, through its Reports on the Observance of Standards and Codes (ROSC) series. Commonwealth audit units receive reports from departments and local governments to ensure that their internal control reporting systems are sound. The internal audit units also compile regular reports to the PMs and parliaments on the current and future projected states of the public finances. The reports are public and critiqued regularly by civil society budget watchdogs, think tanks, and fiscal policy analysis institutes. In Commonwealth countries, there is high confidence in these data and in the work of public sector audit institutions. Without sound fiscal data, neither the state of current finances nor projections of future trends can be properly and intelligently discussed.

Finally, Commonwealth countries have tested many of the tenets of the New Public Management (NPM) reform model. As indicated, the notion that the state can be deregulated internally, allowing managers the freedom to manage, depends to a large extent on the strength of internal and external audit and control units. Without sound fiscal data, reported and reviewed regularly, it is unwise to broaden line-item controls on personnel and purchasing, as well as to allow substantial carry-over or borrowing authority. With controls in place, these freedoms can be permitted, and managers can be held accountable to achieve measurable results. To the extent that gaming of the performance data can be controlled (Hood 2006), the NPM model offers rich possibilities for non-Commonwealth countries interested in linking fiscal reform to state modernization efforts.

4

BUDGETING IN EUROPE
AND THE EUROPEAN UNION

INTRODUCTION

Budgeting in Europe provides an important perspective on the global dimensions of taxing and spending. Each of the twenty-seven member states of the European Union (EU) goes through its own national budget process, making critical choices on social security, education, and other priorities. As European nations budget, they do so under a set of constraints on their fiscal balances agreed upon by EU treaty. At the same time, the EU itself as a supranational institution has its own budget and budget process. The interaction of budgeting at these different levels, including local and regional levels, makes Europe particularly fascinating for students of comparative budgeting. The twenty-seven member states are very different as well, including the original six members, which grew to fifteen by the 1990s, and the twelve new postcommunist member states that achieved accession into the EU in the twenty-first century. In this chapter, we will first examine budgeting in the EU, and then consider explanations for differences in levels of budget deficits and debt among the member states. Finally, we look at budgeting in France and Slovenia, an original member of "old Europe" and the first "new Europe" member state to join the Euro zone.

Today one of the wealthiest parts of the world, the twenty-seven nations of the European Union have become an economic powerhouse able to compete with the United States and Asia. For centuries, Europeans represented distinct, mutually suspicious cultures that often engaged in bloody wars among themselves. Determined to prevent future wars, since the end of World War II, European countries have integrated economically, and to a lesser extent, politically, as the European Union. The twenty-seven nations of the EU today have a population of 492 million, and a gross domestic product (GDP) of 10.9 trillion Euros

($15 trillion). The EU has strengthened Europe as a whole but has also resulted in some surrender of national sovereignty. Budgeting in the EU, then, is a story of parallel universes—taxing and spending decisions are hammered out annually in twenty-seven European capitals. In Brussels, the EU has a small budget of its own but also enforces a series of budget rules that constrain the actions of individual nations.

Several aspects of budgeting in the EU should be noted from the start. First, the size of the EU budget is relatively small compared to the budgets of individual member nations. The EU budget is limited by treaty to 1.24 percent of gross national income. By comparisons, the budgets of member states are proportionately forty times greater, often consuming one-half of a nation's GDP. Second, despite the relatively small amounts contained in the EU budget, those resources are fiercely contested between member states, between various interests throughout Europe (farmers, for example), and between EU institutions (the European parliament versus the Council of Ministers, for example). Third, the institutional configuration of the EU is extremely confusing, some would say convoluted, resulting in a budget process that is often hard to fathom. Additionally, those institutions have only indirect democratic links to citizens, meaning that EU budgeting appears more elite-driven than in many nations. Fourth, the bulk of the EU expenditure goes to a small number of programs, primarily agricultural subsidies, and what are called cohesion and regional funds, subsidies from the richest to the poorest member states. In the 1970s, agricultural subsidies from the Common Agricultural Policy (CAP) made up 70 percent of the EU budget. Today, after numerous attempts at reform, CAP spending is still nearly half of all EU spending. Fifth, contributions to the EU budget are partially based on the ability to pay (national income), leading to conflicts between nations that pay in more than they receive (UK and Germany, for example) and nations that reap much more from the EU than they contribute (Ireland and Portugal, for example). All these factors are important in understanding the context of European and EU budgeting.

European Integration

Europe had been devastated by World War II, leaving millions of Europeans without food or employment. Determined not to see the fourth major European war in a century, Germany and France looked for a way to tie themselves together economically in order to prevent a future conflict. Robert Schuman and Jean Monnet helped draft the 1953 Treaty of Paris, creating the European Coal and Steel Community (ECSC), including France, Germany, Italy, Netherlands, Belgium, and Luxembourg, the forerunner to today's EU. The ECSC created a common market in coal, steel, and scrap metals and led to further moves towards economic integration. Notably, the United Kingdom (UK) was not part of the

ECSC or an advocate of European integration at that time. In 1957, the Treaty of Rome set up the European Economic Community (EEC). By the late 1950s, British governments became more interested in joining, but after coming to power in 1958 under the new Fifth Republic, France's president, Charles DeGaulle, vetoed UK entry into the alliance.

As European integration proceeded to expand beyond economic cooperation, by the 1960s the alliance became known as the European Community (EC). With DeGaulle out of power in France by 1968, the EC expanded in 1973 to nine nations, bringing in Ireland, Denmark, and the United Kingdom. It expanded again in the 1980s twice, bringing Greece, Spain, and Portugal in as members. In 1995, the alliance grew again to fifteen with the addition of Austria, Finland, and Sweden.

In 1989, the collapse of the Berlin wall and the political changes that followed dramatically changed the situation in Europe. West Germany and East Germany reunited in 1990, and the members of the former Soviet-bloc in Central and Eastern Europe began to seek to become part of Europe. In 1992, the Treaty on European Union (commonly known as the Maastricht Treaty, named for the Belgian city where it was written) was adopted, and the EC became the EU. This treaty was tremendously important to European integration for several reasons. First, it expanded the basis of cooperation beyond economics and finance to foreign policy and justice (Neville 1999, 51) second, the Maastricht Treaty established criteria that had to be met by future members who would become part of a European Monetary Union (EMU) that would have a single currency. Member states were required to limit inflation, limit interest rates, restrict budget deficits to no more than 3 percent of GDP, and limit total national debt to 60 percent of GDP. The Euro was introduced in 1999 in eleven of the fifteen nations, notably excluding the UK. To ensure the stability of the common currency, a European Central Bank (ECB) was created. The ECB administers a common monetary policy for the member states, representing some loss of sovereignty for EMU members. (For example, prior to the creation of the ECB, the monetary policy of the Banque de France was often at odds with the inflation-wary German Bundesbank.) Conversely, the ECB has strengthened Europe's influence on world financial markets. The Treaty of Amsterdam was adopted by the fifteen member states in 1997 and continued the process of furthering European integration.

One of the most profound changes in Europe occurred fifteen years after the fall of the Berlin wall. Many of the states of Central and Eastern Europe such as Hungary, Poland, and the Czech Republic had made difficult but rapid transitions to democracy and market-based economies. In 2004, the EU added ten new member states from Central and Eastern Europe, and two more were added in 2006 (Bulgaria and Romania) for a grand total of twenty-seven by 2008. One of the new members, Slovenia, was the first to join the Euro zone in 2006. This rapid expansion created a large area both in terms of geography and population, but also introduced new sources of tension and conflict within the EU. The institutions from the era of a smaller EU—the Commission, Council of Ministers, European Council, and European Parliament—were increasingly inadequate to govern the enlarged union. But with expansion, the number of "Euro skeptics" increased. Reform efforts came to a screeching halt when a proposed new EU constitution was defeated in France and the Netherlands, two of the original six, in 2005. This outcome posed daunting challenges to the member states as they considered how to better govern themselves in areas such as national defense, law and justice, and agriculture. These challenges are particularly apparent in budgeting.

BUDGETING IN THE EUROPEAN UNION

The European Union Budget Process

Understanding the making of the EU budget requires some knowledge of European politics and the complexities of the EU. Many Europeans have a love-hate relationship with the EU. Politicians often find it convenient to use as political cover, blaming EU "eurocrats" for imposing unpopular rules or requirements, even if they know it is probably the right thing to do. The EU has an at least partially deserved reputation for unresponsiveness, a lack of transparency, convoluted rules, and excessive bureaucracy. Member states, even if they were part of making EU rules, still may resent those rules when applied to their country. There is a constant tension between protecting member-state sovereignty and those who want to gradually expand the scope of European cooperation and supranational institutions. That tension is visible in budgeting and explains in part the limitations imposed on the size of the EU budget.

Despite being proportionately small relative to the size of the twenty-seven European economies that make up the EU, the resources contained in the EU budget are fiercely contested by claimants. The cap on EU spending of 1.245 percent of gross national income is known as the "own resources ceiling." This represented spending of around 293 Euros per citizen of the EU in 2007 (EU, EU budget at a glance 2007). The EU budget is also not allowed to be in deficit. The EU is steeped in budgetary management techniques and "budgetese." Much of the language and approach to budgeting in the EU reflects earlier budget reforms tried in the 1960s and 1970s in the United States and around the world such as Planning, Programming Budgeting (PPB), Management by Objective (MBO), and Zero-base budgeting (ZBB). The EU budget procedures are laid out in Article 272 of the EEC Treaty, which sets out a timetable.

As with most sovereign nations, there are several distinct stages in budgeting. Executive bodies prepare the budget (EU departments, the Budget Directorate General, and the European Commission) and legislative or semilegislative authorities approve the budget (the European Council and the European Parliament). But unlike most countries, there is considerable overlap in EU budget institutions and much of the process proceeds through formal and informal negotiations between those institutions.

The European Commission

The Commission is a crucial institution in the EU system, both policy initiator and civil service at the same time. It is involved in policy formulation and drafting the EU budget and often fills a leadership void when other EU institutions stalemate (Nugent, 101). It is headed by twenty-seven commissioners, one for each member country, but many feel that number needs to be reduced (EU, The European Commission 2008). The Commission itself, however, is the bulk of EU employees—twenty thousand of the twenty-eight thousand total number of EU employees work for the Commission. They are organized in departments known as Directorates-General (DG). DG II is "Economic and Financial Affairs," and DG XIX is "Budgets." The DGs actually draft legislative and budget proposals but they must be adopted by a majority of the commissioners in order to move to the next stage of the process.

As with most nations, EU budgeting is continuous, a cycle taking several years between the drafting, approval, and execution of a budget. The European Commission begins the preliminary budget phase with an "Orientation Debate" and annual policy strategy discussion in the autumn, more than a year before the budget year starts on January 1 (EU, EU budget in detail 2007). The Annual Policy Strategy (APS) document that results from the debate attempts to:

- Clearly state policy priorities,
- Identify initiatives that contribute to achieving these priorities,
- Adopt the budget outline that allocates resources to those priorities.

Once the policy strategy is adopted in February, the Commission begins work on a Preliminary Draft Budget (PDB). At this point, departments of the EU in Brussels submit requests for appropriations, making sure that they conform to the policy priorities that have been set. Within the Directorate General on Budgets (DG XIX), hearings are held not dissimilar to agency meetings with OMB in the United States, or ministry meetings to plead their case with the central budget office in parliamentary systems. Like any central budget office, the DG on Budgets is subject to a variety of pressures by claimants for resources. Since 1993, in an effort to improve relationships between institutions of the EU, it has been agreed to have preliminary "trialogues" between the Commission, the Council, and the European Parliament (Nugent, 402) to reduce frictions later on. In April, the DG for Budgets submits its estimates to the Commission. Ultimately, the Commission establishes the numbers to be included in the draft budget, but relies heavily on the DG recommendations. Also included are activity statements and performance information from prior management plans that provide some justification for the requests. Because of treaty limitations and preexisting expenditure commitments, the Commission has limited degrees of freedom in drafting a budget. Once it has gone through these steps, the Commission finalizes a preliminary draft of the budget and submits it to the European Council in April or early May.

The European Council

The European Council is an institution that emerged in the 1970s because then-existing institutions did not appear capable of responding quickly or effectively to the changing environment (Nugent, 177). The Council is made up of the heads of state or government (prime ministers or presidents) of the member states, the president of the Commission, and occasionally other members. The Council has not been a formal institution (but would be made so if the Treaty of Lisbon is ratified by December 31, 2008), yet it is the most powerful institution in the EU as it consists of the top elected leaders of the member states. The Commission meets several times per year in Brussels. Given the makeup of the Council, its involvement with budgeting is at the highest level of macrobudgeting, although even prime ministers and presidents may fight with each other over seemingly small details of the budget.

When the Council receives the proposed budget from the Commission, it is referred to the Council's budgetary committee. This group reviews the budget chapter by chapter and tries to resolve as many conflicts as possible before the Council meets to approve it. After the budgetary committee, the proposed budget must be reviewed by the Committee of Permanent Representatives of the Member States (COREPER). The Permanent Representatives of the twenty-seven member states are appointed by their respective governments as ambassadors to the European Union. Like other ambassadors to nations, they all reside with their staff permanently in Brussels and are the key liaison between their home country and the EU. It too is an important body but its primary task is to prepare an agenda for the Council, including resolving budget disputes among member nations before they get to the level of the Council.

One of the key distinctions in EU budgeting is the distinction between compulsory and noncompulsory budgeting (comparable to mandatory and discretionary spending in the United States) The European Parliament's budgetary powers, up until the approach of the Treaty of Lisbon (2007), were limited to noncompulsory expenditures. There are often disagreements between the Council and the Parlia-

TABLE **4.1. Distribution of Votes to EU Member States**
to Determine a Qualified Majority

Distribution of votes for each Member State (from 01/01/2007)		
Germany, France, Italy, United Kingdom	X 29	= 116
Spain, Poland	X 27	= 54
Romania	X 14	= 14
Netherlands	X 13	= 13
Belgium, Czech Republic, Greece, Hungary, Portugal	X 12	= 60
Austria, Sweden, Bulgaria	X 10	= 30
Denmark, Finland, Ireland, Slovakia, Lithuania	X 7	= 35
Estonia, Latvia, Luxembourg, Slovenia Cyprus	X 4	= 20
Malta	X 3	= 3
TOTAL		345

Source: EU Budget in detail—Deciding the budget

ment over what exactly the distinctions are, so this is often a subject of negotiation during discussions with COREPER and the Council. Compulsory expenditures largely consist of agriculture subsidies as part of the Common Agricultural Policy. Noncompulsory expenditures constitute mostly non-agriculture spending.

As the Council members prepare to accept the proposed budget on their first reading, they are updated on financial perspectives, comparable to economic assumptions in national budgets, but also consisting of certain caps on spending. The Council normally meets in July for the purpose of approving the proposed budget. The meetings normally last several days made up of long sessions and informal negotiating and bargaining on the side. They finally come to agreement and approve the budget as a group and issue a statement from the summit on its outline. Neill Nugent (405) suggests that over recent decades, the Council tended to play the role of guardian in the budget process, by reducing amounts in the proposed budget and proposing transfers from noncompulsory to compulsory spending. However, the budget they approve is usually very close to the proposed budget they received.

The draft budget must be adopted by the Council using the EU's complicated weighted voting procedures to produce a "qualified majority." This is actually a supermajority (more than 50 percent needed) that allows a minority of member nations to block the budget. A qualified majority requires 252 votes out of 345 (74 percent) cast by at least two-thirds of the members that comprise at least 62 percent of the population of the EU (EU, EU budget in detail 2007). The qualified majority rules prevent the largest member states from imposing their will on the smaller states. The number of votes for each of the twenty-seven member states is shown in Table 4.1.

The European Parliament (EP)

Once the Council approves the budget, it is sent to the European Parliament. The Parliament began as a council of the original Coal and Steel Community and has evolved over the subsequent decades into the elected legislative body of the EU. Direct election of members of the European Parliament (MEPs) began in 1979. In budgeting, as in other areas of EU policymaking since that date, the European Parliament has not been as influential as either the Commission or the Council. But over the years, the EP has gradually increased its influence. If the Treaty of Lisbon is ratified by member states by the end of 2008 (see below), the Parliament will become co-equal with the European Council in budgeting.

The EP powers in budgeting include several key elements, but in many cases their decisions are subject to rejection or modification by the Council. In the budget's first reading, MEPs can propose modifications and amendments. First, the Parliament can propose "modifications" to compulsory expenditures in the proposed budget. These modifications must first be approved by an absolute majority of members of the EP (367 votes out of the 735 members of the EP) If Parliament wants to increase spending, those modifications have to also be approved by a qualified majority vote of the Council. If the modifications do not increase total expenditures (for example, if they are offset by revenues or other spending cuts) then they are approved unless they are rejected by a qualified majority vote of the Council. Second, members of the European Parliament (MEPs) may propose "amendments" to the noncompulsory expenditures, subject to ceilings set by the financial perspective. The Council can modify the Parliament's amendments by a qualified majority vote, but the EP can reassert them later. Third, the European Parliament, by a majority of its members and two-thirds of the vote, can reject the budget in its entirety (Nugent, 213).

Parliament concludes its first reading of the proposed budget in October and the budget goes back to the Council for their second reading during the third week in November after a reconciliation meeting with MEPs concerning differences. Generally, the Council's action during second reading to modify, accept, or reject modifications of compulsory expenditures passed by the EP are the final decision on those items (unless the Parliament rejects the entire budget). The budget then returns to Parliament for its second reading. With only two weeks to work on it, the EP concentrates on the noncompulsory expenditures that they have more influence over. The European Parliament then enacts the budget acting by a majority of its members and three-fifths of the votes cast (EU, EU budget in detail 2007).

In a number of years, Parliament has rejected the budget in its entirety and the EU faced having no legal budget when the fiscal year began on January 1. Budgets were defeated five out of nine years in the 1980s after the MEPs were first directly elected in 1979. If the budget is not enacted, the EU continues to function under a system such as "continuing resolutions" in the United States. The EU Directorates General, agencies, and transfer payment programs are funded at previous year's levels. The system is called "provisional twelfths" meaning that units can only spend the average per month of one-twelve of last year's total spending. In some cases, differences were reconciled in days or weeks. In others, a budget was not adopted until halfway through the year. Non-adoption of the budget has been less of a problem since the end of the 1980s.

Implementation of the budget shifts the cycle away from the Council and Parliament. Unlike most budgets, the EU budget is primarily implemented not by its own bureaucracy (Commission and DGs) but by ministries in the member states.

The Treaty of Lisbon (2007)

The budget process in the EU is cumbersome and confusing and relies on relationships and informal negotiations as much as established institutions and procedures. These problems were true in other areas of EU policymaking as well, leading to pressure for EU reform in recent years. In 2001, in anticipation of its largest expansion ever with the accession of ten new members anticipated in 2004, member states agreed to call a constitutional convention to create a new EU governance structure. Headed by former French president Valery Giscard D'Estaing, the fifteen members finally agreed on a draft in 2004. The proposed constitution, which needed to be ratified unanimously by all member states, faltered when voters in both France and the Netherlands rejected the new constitution in 2005. After a year of "reflection," EU reformers abandoned the constitution and decided to try to implement many of the changes through a new treaty that would be ratified by parliament rather than be ratified by voters (except in Ireland as required by its constitution).

By December 2007, agreement was reached on the Treaty of Lisbon. The twenty-seven member states would have until the end of 2008 to ratify the treaty, in which case it would go into effect in 2009. If ratified, the treaty will make significant changes in EU institutions and in budgeting. First, key political institutions will be changed. For the first time there will be a real president of the European Council with a two-and-a-half-year term to provide greater leadership, and the size of the Council will be reduced to make it more workable. Second, the powers of the European Parliament are expanded to more nearly match those of the Council. If ratified, the EP and Council will function like a bicameral legislature with approximately equal powers as co-decision makers. Third, the Parliament gains significant power in budgeting, and would be able to make changes to compulsory spending as well as noncompulsory spending. Changes are also proposed for defining qualified voting majorities that would go into effect in 2014 if ratified. The treaty has a number of other provisions dealing with human rights, parliaments, foreign policy, transparency, and other issues.

The EU Budget

Traditionally, the largest single expenditure for the EU has been for agricultural subsidies under the Common Agricultural Policy. CAP has been one of the most criticized of EU policies over the years both inside and outside of Europe. But support of small, often inefficient farmers has strong political appeal among European nations, particularly France. CAP resulted in excessive surpluses of food in the 1980s and 1990s, lambasted as "butter mountains and wine lakes" (Reinhorn 2007). The percentage going to agriculture support payments has gradually been reduced. Figure 4.1 examines EU spending in 2007. Natural resources, primarily agriculture, composes 43 percent of the EU's EUR 126.5 billion (US$175 billion) budget (EU, EU budget in 2007). Agriculture alone accounts for 34 percent of all spending in 2007. What the EU calls competitiveness and cohesion constitutes 44 percent of the budget. Under these programs, less-developed member nations will receive structural funds and cohesion funds in the amount of EUR 35 billion in 2007.

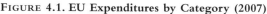

FIGURE 4.1. EU Expenditures by Category (2007)

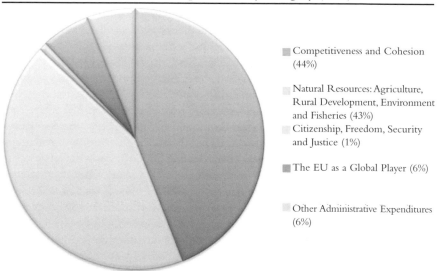

- Competitiveness and Cohesion (44%)
- Natural Resources: Agriculture, Rural Development, Environment and Fisheries (43%)
- Citizenship, Freedom, Security and Justice (1%)
- The EU as a Global Player (6%)
- Other Administrative Expenditures (6%)

Source: European Commission, "Financial Programming and Budgeting," 2007.

FIGURE 4.2. EU Sources of Revenue (11996, 2007)

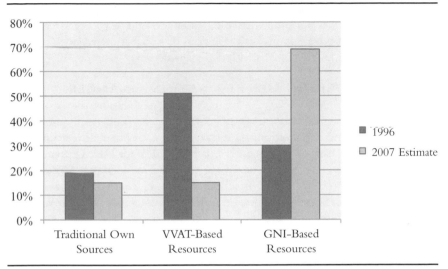

Source: European Commission, "Financial Programming and Budgeting," 2007.

As noted earlier, EU revenues are limited by treaty to 1.24 percent of EU national income and the EU itself may not run a deficit. Where do EU revenues come from? The sources have changed significantly in the last decade. In the mid-1990s, as Figure 4.2 shows, more than half of the EU revenues came from a fraction of the Value Added Taxes (VAT), a consumption tax, levied in all of the member states. By 2007, the main source of income had shifted to payments from member states based on a uniform rate applied across the Gross National Income (GNI) of each state. The remaining 15 percent in 2007 came from traditional sources based on custom duties and agricultural duties imposed on imports into the EU.

The EU likes to point out to its citizens that its total budget only comes to EUR 0.70 per day per person. However, the allocation of 126.5 billion Euros is of critical importance to farmers, fishers, poorer nations, and others across the union. EU sectoral funds have transformed nations such as Ireland in a generation from an economic backwater with massive out-migration to a booming economy attracting workers from around the world. EU budgeting is unique in the world of comparative budgeting and in some ways is not like any other countries. But for comparative purposes, its contrasts and similarities provide some important insights. Budgeting by a supranational entity is fundamentally different because of the inherent tension between the governments of the member states and the EU bureaucracy, and the competition between members. Yet we still see basic stages of budgeting, claimants and conservers, and legislative-executive conflicts, although in a somewhat unique fashion because of EU institutions. The EU is significantly different in that it does not implement its own budget and that has consequences on its ability to enforce sanctions against nations that do not meet budget rules.

COMPARING MEMBER NATION FINANCES

As we saw in chapter 1, many European countries spend substantially more than the United States and Asian nations on social programs. In Figure 1.1, we saw that the median level of tax revenue as a percentage of GDP for OECD countries (a broader group of industrialized countries) was about 37 percent. Most of the European countries were above that level with only the UK and Germany slightly below that among the original fifteen member nations. Sweden was over 50 percent of GDP (see chapter 1).

The Maastricht Treaty not only set new boundaries for admission to the monetary union but set macrobudgetary guidelines for existing members. Most notably, annual budget deficits of member states are required by the Stability and Growth Pact (SGP) to be less than 3 percent of GDP and the total national debt must be under 60 percent of GDP. As part of the Maastricht Treaty's fiscal framework, the terms of the SGP combine discipline and flexibility. They require countries to reach fiscal positions "close to balance or surplus" over the medium term and keep their actual deficits below 3 percent of GDP except in the case of unusually large shocks (Annett and Jaeger 2004, 22). Otherwise, the "excessive-deficit procedure" is initiated when a country's deficit exceeds this 3 percent level. If a member state is out of compliance, a process called "excessive deficit procedure" can be initiated. The EU has a system of multilateral surveillance. The EC agency known as ECOFIN (the Council of Economic and Financial Affairs) is charged with fiscal surveillance and monitoring of member state budgetary policies. This relatively minor EC agency is the decision-making forum for the EU's ministers of finance and economics. It also is responsible for ensuring that Eurostat budgetary data and reporting standards are harmonized (Savage 2005). Decisions by ECOFIN can lead to a series of warnings of increasing severity, up to imposing financial penalties. However, a number of countries, including founding members France and Germany, have had excessive deficits on several occasions and not been penalized. This is emblematic of the tensions in budgeting in the EU—member states' autonomy versus the constraints they agreed to in forming the European Union. The EU is limited in its ability to sanction member states who do not abide by these budget guidelines.

Figure 4.3 provides a comparison of member state performance on two of the key Maastricht budget criteria: deficit and debt as a percent of GDP. The two

FIGURE 4.3. The EU Member States and the Maastricht Criteria in 2005

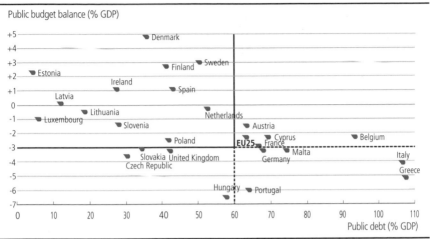

Source: Sub-national public finance in the European Union, Dexia, November 2006, 5.

axes of the grid are the 3 percent requirement for the deficit and the 60 percent for debt. All of the nations falling below the horizontal axis have a deficit above the 3 percent limit. All the countries to the right of the vertical axis have a debt greater than the allowable 60 percent. The countries in the lower right quadrant are violating both criteria; in 2005 they were Greece, Italy, Malta, France, Germany, and Portugal.

Despite these instances of excess deficits, perhaps what is more remarkable is that it appears as if the EU budget rules actually do serve as constraints on member states' budget actions. When states are out of compliance, there are strong political pressures both inside and outside the country to devise budget policies that will lead back to compliance. At the same time, those pressures are tempered by domestic pressures to not allow EU rules to threaten employment or economic growth.

Another important difference among EU countries is the degree to which they are federal or unitary states. Historically, France has been considered a unitary state with relatively little authority exercised by subnational governments. Conversely, Germany had a strong tradition of federalism with the German states (*Lander*) exercising significant power. One way to compare EU nations on this score is to compare the level of state and local (subnational) taxation to revenues raised by the national government. All nations, whether unitary or federal, have some form of subnational governments that perform important functions such as police, fire, public safety, schools, sanitation, etc. How much budgetary discretion these local governments have differs considerably. Figure 4.4 compares subnational

FIGURE 4.4. General Government Tax Revenues as a
Percentage of GDP (2000, 2005)

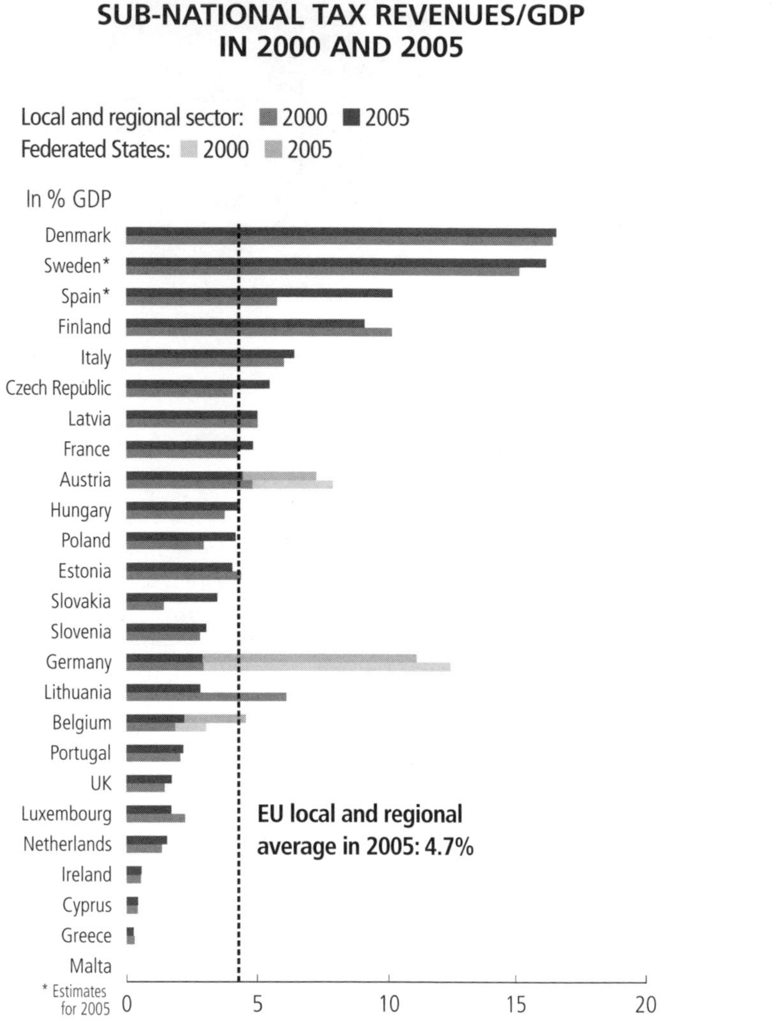

SUB-NATIONAL TAX REVENUES/GDP
IN 2000 AND 2005

Local and regional sector: ■ 2000 ■ 2005
Federated States: 2000 2005

In % GDP

Denmark
Sweden*
Spain*
Finland
Italy
Czech Republic
Latvia
France
Austria
Hungary
Poland
Estonia
Slovakia
Slovenia
Germany
Lithuania
Belgium
Portugal
UK
Luxembourg
Netherlands
Ireland
Cyprus
Greece
Malta

EU local and regional
average in 2005: 4.7%

* Estimates
for 2005   0   5   10   15   20

Source: Sub-national public finance in the European Union, Dexia, November 2006, 15.

tax revenues as a proportion of GDP across the twenty-five EU members in 2005
in comparison to 2000. The EU local and regional average is 4.7 percent but the
range is considerable. In Denmark, local and regional governments collect and
spend around 17 percent of GDP. Subnational government in Germany is at

about 13 percent. At the other extreme Ireland, Cyprus, and Greece are less than 1 percent of GDP, meaning that the national government collects virtually all the taxes and then transfers them to local and regional governments for any services that are provided at that level.

Explaining Macrobudgetary Differences in Europe

In chapter 1, we suggested that constitutional systems and political institutions were important factors in influencing both budget processes and budget outcomes. We suggested that countries differ in their ability to make decisions in a timely fashion, to keep revenues and spending in balance, or to make difficult decisions that impose losses on powerful interests. Looking back to Table 1.2 in chapter 1, recall that most European nations have a parliamentary and representational legislature. The French system is a hybrid of this with an independent president. After the collapse of the Soviet Union, the nations of Central and Eastern Europe all adopted some form of European parliamentary system. The other exceptions in the EU are the UK and Ireland, which as noted in chapter 3, are based on the British Westminster parliamentary and majoritarian legislative model. Where more differences are apparent is in the party systems and the nature of governing coalitions.

A number of empirical studies have been undertaken to explain how some European nations were able to conform to EMU guidelines after decades of large deficits and debt. They have also tested several theories of why certain countries, such as Italy and Greece, seem to have trouble keeping their fiscal balances within limits compared to other countries, such as Estonia and Latvia. Scholars have focused on both external variables and domestic variables. Because a number of nations did significantly improve their budget balances after committing to the EMU, there appears to be prima facie evidence of a "Maastricht effect," that is, external influences were critical in policy change. Others, however, found that internal variables based on party system, institutions, and budget rules are more powerful explanations of budget choices.

At least one study (Dafflon and Rossi) argued that conformance to macrobudgetary targets was accomplished simply through accounting maneuvers and "tricks" to make the balances look better. However, most studies generally agree that member states did change budgetary behavior. Partisan control of parliament and its ideological composition have been examined by several studies. The hypothesis is based on the fact that traditionally left-oriented parties tend to prefer higher levels of government spending and have a higher tolerance for deficits (Hibbs 1977). Oatley found that from the 1960s to the 1990s, left-leaning governments generally had lower interest rates and higher deficits than more right-leaning governments (1999, 1005).

In addition to the partisan composition of majorities, studies of macrobud-getary decision making in the EU have focused on government structure, institutions, majority versus minority status of a government, and budget rules. Roubini and Sachs (1989) suggested that minority governments tend to be more prone to deficits than majority governments. Von Hagen (1998) developed a typology of budgetary institutions based on their degree of centralization. Two main types of centralization are "delegation" and "fiscal contracts." Delegation involves the granting of special powers to individual participants in the budget process (such as a powerful finance minister or prime minister), which have more of a macrolevel perspective than other participants. Fiscal contracts are budget rules—binding agreements negotiated among participants without lending special authority to any particular one. Hallerberg and Van Hagen's 1999 study examined the effect of these two types of budget institutions on fiscal deficits in the fifteen EU member states between 1981 and 1994. They suggested that the choice of delegation or fiscal contract as a way to achieve fiscal balance was a function of the number of parties within a government, arguing that single-party majority governments are more likely to delegate authority to a powerful finance minister while multiparty coalition governments are more likely to choose a fiscal contract that is agreed upon by the different parties.

Hallerberg (2004) builds upon this earlier work by suggesting that there are two crucial institutional variables that determine the type of fiscal framework a government puts in place: the nature of the party system and whether it is a majority or minority government. Hallerberg claims that the most significant aspect of the party system is whether governments are more unified ideologically or whether there are significant ideological differences between coalition partners. In the first case, it would be easier to delegate to a strong finance minister, maintaining tighter fiscal discipline. The best example of this is the UK, which consistently has a single-party majority and has a relatively powerful chancellor of the exchequer. In France, although governments are rarely single-party majorities, the ideological differences between coalition partners, whether on the right or left, are relatively small. Hence, in France as well, delegation to a powerful finance minister takes place. In contrast, ideological divisions between coalition partners tend to be greater in the Netherlands and Finland, hence participants are more reluctant to delegate to the finance minister. In these countries, budgetary restraint is more frequently imposed by negotiated budget agreements.

Hallerberg (2004) also examined the consequences of minority versus majority governments for macrobudgetary outcomes. He argues that a majority government, whether single- or multiparty, will be more likely to either delegate power to a fiscal guardian or come up with a negotiated set of budget rules. Minority governments, in turn, must rely on the support of at least one opposition party, making it more difficult to impose fiscal discipline. He concludes that based on his research, the link between the ideological composition of a government is a less important determinant of budget outcomes than the number of parties in the government and whether it constitutes a majority or a minority government. In general, one can conclude that the adoption of the Maastricht treaty and EMU did provide impetus for EU member states to conform their fiscal totals, but how they did so depended primarily on the nature of political institutions and the party system. Next, we turn to two cases of budgeting in Europe, making comparisons between the one of the original fifteen EU members and one of the twelve new member states.

BUDGETING IN FRANCE

French Political System and Budget Process

The French political system differs from the systems in other EU members because of the independence and strength of the French presidency. The legacy of weak and unstable governments under the Fourth Republic (1946–1957) led General Charles DeGaulle to spur the creation of the Fifth Republic, a parliamentary system but one dominated by a strong, independent president. Today, France remains a hybrid system. As we have seen, France along with Germany provided the impetus for European integration, and France had been a consistent supporter of the EU up until the rejection of the European constitution in 2005. As in other EU nations, however, public sentiment toward the EU has always been somewhat ambivalent, appreciating the benefits of integration but resenting the strictures of the EU. That latter sentiment came to the fore in 2005 when voters decided that the EU constitution was too much a threat to French sovereignty. France has long been seen as a centralized state, and one dominated by Paris. While this remains true today, there is evidence that political and budgetary power has fragmented somewhat since the 1950s.

France has a multiparty system, with the parties evolving and morphing from election to election, making it difficult at times to keep track of the evolution of parties. At election time, as many as a dozen parties may contest national elections and because of French election rules, as many as five or six parties may hold seats in parliament. Parliament is less fragmented than that may suggest, however, since the parties tend to form fairly unified coalitions of the Left or Right. French parliamentary elections are conducted on the basic of electoral districts in two stages. If a candidate gains at least 50 percent of the vote on the first round, he or she is elected. If not, there is a runoff where the candidate amassing a plurality is the winner. The result is extensive bargaining between the parties between the first and second rounds of elections that produces relatively stable coalitions. France has a bicameral legislature with the National Assembly, the lower house, and the Senate, the less powerful upper house.

The budget process in France follows the familiar stages of most parliamentary systems. The budget is drawn up by the Ministry of Finance, where the key actor is traditionally the finance minister. After winning the presidential election of 2007, Nickolas Sarkozy split the Ministry of Finance into two entities, the Ministry of Budget and Public Accounts and second, the Ministry of Economy, Finance, and Employment. These changes were meant to emphasize both public sector reform and reducing government spending, as well as a return to full employment in France. In April of the year before the fiscal year (calendar year), the prime minister sends each ministry a "framework letter" that specifies spending caps and provides an overall macroeconomic context for ministry requests. Conferences between ministries and the budget ministry are used to negotiate what totals will be included in the government's budget to be submitted to parliament. If negotiations cannot resolve differences, the prime minister is brought in to resolve them. Budget issues are rarely resolved in cabinet sessions (Hallerberg 2004, 165).

The President of the Republic has little direct impact on France's annual budget—it is under the purview of the prime minister and cabinet. However, presidents can insist on certain budget items being included. For example, in 1991, President Francois Mitterand demanded that a major increase in education be included in Prime Minister Michel Rocard's budget (Knapp and Wright 2001, 108). President Sarkozy certainly set the tone in the preparation of the 2008 budget in terms of proposing reforms of social programs with major budgetary consequences. Because presidents were elected for seven-year terms until 2002, and now five-year terms, parliamentary elections may be called in the middle of a presidential term. This has occasionally led to divided control of parliament and the French presidency, a situation referred to as "cohabitation." Under these conditions, with a prime minister of the opposite political side, the president has virtually no impact on the content of the budget.

When the budget is finalized, it is submitted to the National Assembly. Parliament has little direct impact on the budget but majority support is ultimately required for the government's proposals to succeed. MPs have indirect influences through parliamentary debates and public comments on proposals. The *"loi de finances"* must be submitted to parliament no later than October 1, and parliament then has sixty days to debate and approve. The amendment powers of parliament are greatly restricted. For example, Article 40 of the French constitution states that the National Assembly may offer amendments that reduce the deficit, but no amendments that would increase it. If necessary, the government has a powerful tool to compel parliamentary approval of the budget. If the government invokes the power, it may deem that after debate is ended, the budget is considered to have passed (Article 49.3). The only recourse for parliament is to censure the government within twenty-four hours (Hallerberg 2004, 105). The censure measure is the equivalent of a vote of no confidence—a very extreme measure. Even when the Communist Party members refused to support the Socialist government's budget in 1990, they refused to approve a censure motion that would have toppled the government (Hallerberg 2004, 107).

The parliament traditionally had little oversight responsibility over the budget, but since 2001, the government must provide the National Assembly with more detailed information, and MPs may reallocate spending among categories as long as the aggregate totals do not change.

On several occasions, changes in the governing coalitions after national elections have had major effects on budget policy. In 1981, the election of Francois Mitterand as president represented the first time in the Fifth Republic that a left-leaning coalition would control the presidency and parliament. Mitterand immediately initiated a series of leftist budget policy changes and social policy changes that had budgetary consequences, such as lowering the retirement age to sixty and giving state workers an extra week of vacation. After the resulting increase in France's budget deficit, the Mitterand government was forced to pursue a number of austerity measures to keep fiscal balances under control.

Major Trends in French Budgeting

France has traditionally been one of Europe's most centralized states, with the bulk of taxing and spending taking place at the national level by the national government. In recent years, however, France has changed politically and budgetarily, becoming somewhat more decentralized. More political autonomy and spending authority has shifted to the local and regional level in France since the 1950s. Other shifts have occurred over time, many of them paralleling budget developments in countries around the world. Baumgartner, Foucault, and Francois have done a comprehensive study of macrobudgetary trends in France between 1959 and 2006 (2007). They conclude that since the 1970s, "deficit spending has increased, transfer payments to individuals have become the single largest type of public expenditure, capital and infrastructure projects have declined dramatically, and power has been systematically fragmented" (2007, 3).

As with other European nations, the scope of the public sector in France has grown dramatically since the 1950s when Europe was still recovering from the war. Figure 4.5 shows overall taxing and spending rates over the period 1959–2006. In 1959, France had a surplus budget with revenues of the equivalent of EUR 142 billion in constant 2000 Euros, and outlays of EUR 123 billion (INSEE 2007). At the beginning of the Fifth Republic, government made up around one-third of GDP in France. As Figure 4.5 shows, that has increased to over 50 percent of GDP since the end of the 1980s. In 2006, government spending represented 58 percent of GDP, about 10 percent higher than the mean level for Europe and generally higher than the rest of the world. Much of that spend-

FIGURE 4.5. **French Government Spending and Receipts, 1959-2006**

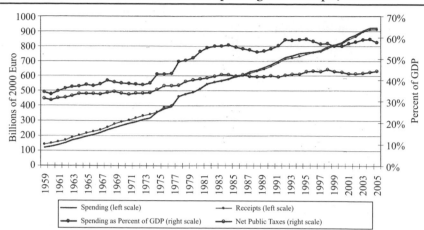

Source: Baumgartner, Foucault, and Francois, 2007.

ing funds the French "social contract" with its citizens, a belief that France could be a competitive capitalist economy but one that was particularly caring of its citizens in terms of providing generous social services.

Growth in government spending in Europe, as in the rest of the world, is tied to economic growth. Linking economic growth to levels of budget outlays, Baumgartner et al. (2007, 6) found that earlier French governments, whether left- or right-leaning coalitions, tended to act countercyclically, raising spending during economic downturns. Later conservative governments under prime ministers Chirac (1986–88), Balladur (1993–95), and Juppe (1995–97) all attempted to make significant cuts in public spending during periods of low economic growth. Since the mid-1990s, spending has largely tracked economic growth. The election of President Sarkozy in 2007 was followed by an attempt by the government to once again slow the growth of public spending to make the French economy more vibrant and competitive.

Between the 1950s and the 1970s, France generally ran a surplus budget. Both left- and right-leaning governments since 1974 have run budget deficits, reaching a high in 1994 with a deficit just under 6 percent of GDP (Baumgartner et al., 7) Figure 4.6 looks at the public debt and annual budget deficits in France during this time period. In 2008, total public debt in France was equal to 64.5 percent of GDP, comparable to the United States. As monetary union approached, the limitations on deficits and debt became very challenging for France to meet, and governments made concerted efforts to conform to the requirements.

FIGURE 4.6. **Public Debt and Annual Deficit, 1959–2006**

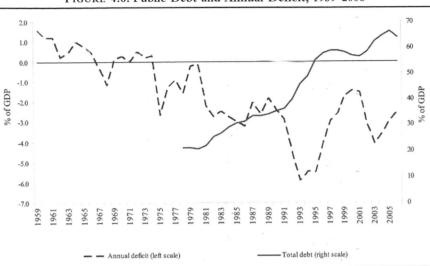

— — Annual deficit (left scale)   ———— Total debt (right scale)

Source: Baumgartner, Foucault, and Francois, 2007.

The composition of public spending in France has also shown significant changes during the Fifth Republic. At the beginning, the central state was the source of most of the spending. Local governments, including regions, departments, and municipalities, were a relatively small portion of the total. Social security spending was also relatively small in the late 1950s as a proportion of government spending. Figure 4.7 shows government spending by source from 1959–2006. In 1959, some 60 percent of all outlays were central state spending, which includes what the government ministries in Paris spend as well as the large amount of infrastructure spending on monuments, museums, and rail transportation, which France is so well known for. By 2006, central state spending was down to just over 40 percent of all outlays.

Local governments, in contrast, have increased their relative share of outlays from about 15 percent to 20 percent. The most dramatic growth has come in social welfare transfer payments, rising from 25 percent to around 40 percent of GDP. Baumgartner et al. put a heavy emphasis on the decline of the central state in France (2007). The causes of those changes are the growth in the powers and budgetary resources of subnational governments in France, the growth of social security (entitlement) spending, and the influence of the EU. Europeanization has had the same effect on all member states, but more so for those who have tended to run deficit budgets. Another common budget trend in Europe and across the

FIGURE 4.7. Government Spending by Source, 1959–2006

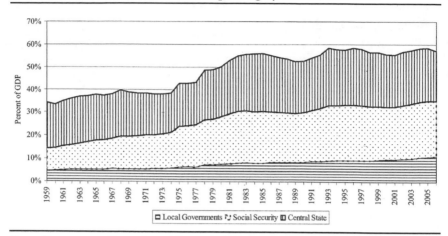

Source: Baumgartner, Foucault, and Francois, 2007.

developed world is the rapid growth of social transfer payments. In the United States, entitlements doubled their budget share in the 1970s and have continued to grow ever since. Today in the United States, discretionary spending by the federal government (comparable to central state spending in France) is less than 15 percent of all outlays, much smaller than in France. The growth of social entitlements, much more than decentralization and the growth of local government spending, is responsible for the overall spending trends in France. While local and regional governments are much more important than they were two generations ago in France, one must be careful not to exaggerate the shifts. France does not spend on infrastructure as it used to and there are sharp constraints on central state spending, but it remains one of the more centralized countries in Europe and the world in terms of national budgeting.

BUDGETING IN SLOVENIA
AND THE NEW MEMBER STATES

Compared with her neighbors, Slovenia has been one of the most successful of the former Eastern-bloc nations. It has developed a stable, multiparty democracy with regular elections, a free press, and good human rights record. It is the first of the new member states to enter the European Monetary Union and change to the Euro. It is prosperous, with per capita income that is about 80 percent of the level of the original fifteen members of the EU (EU-15). Many factors could explain Slovenia's success—its consensus-building political culture carrying over from the days of self-management, its more open economy when it was part of Yugoslavia, its size and relative homogeneity, its proximity to the West, or its very early experiences with democracy.

The nations in Central and Eastern Europe (CEE) had to adapt from a command economy with centralized resource allocation to a budget system driven by democratically elected political institutions. The fact that Slovenia did not have as rigid a command structure as her neighbors should not obscure how profound a change it was. Slovenia had to adopt dramatically new budget policies while protecting domestic constituencies from economic upheaval and to reinvent budgetary institutions to facilitate both economic restructuring and democratization.

Budget Transformation in the 1990s

When independence was declared in 1991, a limited armed conflict took place between Slovenian troops and the forces of Yugoslavia that lasted some ten days. The European Union intervened five days into the conflict and a cease-fire and peace agreement was signed. During the fall of 1991 and the winter of 1992, the transition government established the Bank of Slovenia, with the Tolar (SIT) as the nation's currency, and adopted a new constitution. Slovenia was one of the first transition countries where growth resumed and by 1996 GDP had recovered to the pre-independence level (OECD 1997, 2). The loss of internal (Yugoslav) and Eastern-bloc markets initially hurt, but was soon compensated through trade with Europe. By the end of the 1990s, one could make the following conclusions about the transformation of Slovenian national budgeting after independence (LeLoup et al. 2000).

- *Deficits and Debt:* One of the most significant features of budget policy in Slovenia during the 1990s was its ability to maintain low budget deficits, in the range of 1 percent of GDP, and a relatively low external debt.
- *Stability:* Slovenia demonstrated more certainty in its budget process than many of its neighbors, making it unnecessary to revisit and revise earlier budget decisions made in that year. It reflected the more advanced development of Slovenian budgeting and the relative stability provided by its lack of large deficits or external debt.
- *Fragmentation/Centralization:* Slovenia was able to centralize what had been a very fragmented budget process under the Yugoslavian self-management system, with more than six hundred separate budgets before 1992. During the 1990s, Slovenia developed a budget system that despite its initial fragmentation was characterized by a strong finance minister, strengthening the hand of central guardians/conservers over the demands of claimants.

- *Political Culture:* Political culture was important to budgeting transformation. Slovenia's relative success was facilitated by experience with market capitalism as early as the late 1940s and 1950s. Although Slovenes escaped the brutal violence that plagued the Balkans in the 1990s, surveys during those years found a persistence of ethnocentric and xenophobic attitudes and attitudes of dependency strongly affected by a half-century of communism. These attitudes were tempered by growing underlying support of democracy. Slovenia also had a cultural acceptance of trade with the West.

- *Delegation to Powerful Finance Minister:* Slovenia showed strong evidence of a system that relied in the 1990s on delegation of power to the finance minister. Finance Ministry officials have extraordinary flexibility in the budget implementation stage to achieve macrobudgetary and fiscal objectives. Examples exist of adjusting outlays during the fiscal year of as much as 10 percent to maintain desired fiscal balances. This is largely unprecedented in either the United States or Europe.

- *Governing Ability:* Institutional capacity and the kind of governing coalition affected the budget process. Greater fragmentation among parties in the governing coalition sometimes limited the ability of the government to make hard choices or impose losses on certain constituencies. When the governing coalition was stronger and more unified, it was easier to maintain fiscal balances. When the Pensioners Party was part of the governing coalition, it was more difficult to hold the line on social security spending.

- *The Budget Agenda:* Slovenia was more advanced than other Central and Eastern European nations in terms of its "budget agenda." While other nations were constructing basic budget institutions such as a Treasury system, Slovenia was already planning for EU accession and looking at advanced reforms such as performance budgeting.

- *External Influences:* Because of favorable fiscal balances, external organizations such as the World Bank and IMF were less influential than in neighboring countries in terms of prescribed "shock therapy" approaches. On the other hand, IMF held sway in terms of modernizing the budget system, but its influence was sought rather than imposed. Determination to win EU membership made EU accession criteria a dominant external force that shaped budget priorities and processes.

- *Privatization:* Economic restructuring and privatization proceeded with caution and was incomplete. Many citizens, as in other CEE countries, felt that privatization benefited the "haves" at the expense of the "have nots."

BUDGET DEVELOPMENTS SINCE 2000 AND COMPARISONS WITH NEW MEMBER STATES (NMS)

In late 2002, Slovenia successfully completed negotiations for their accession to the European Union. From Slovenia's perspective, the terms were judged favorable in both the short and long term (Republic of Slovenia 2002). Regarding agriculture, Slovene farmers were granted access to the same level of direct payments as other member states. In terms of regional policy, Slovenia would receive 404 million Euros from structural and cohesion funds. Slovenia would be a net recipient at least through 2013.

Debt and Deficits

Slovenia's fiscal balances deteriorated after the turn of the century, with budget deficits increasing to around 4 percent of GDP in 2000 and 2001. This was both a function of recession and discretionary increases in spending and reductions in revenues. A large part of the deficit in 2002 was the result of discretionary policy. As the economy recovered, cyclical dimensions of the deficits went to zero by 2004 while discretionary changes fell after 2002 as well, reducing the deficit to 2 percent of GDP by 2004 and close to 1 percent by 2006 (IMF 2007).

Figure 4.8 compares Slovenia's budget deficits and gross debt to seven other new member states. Slovenia's fiscal balances were superior to those of Hungary,

FIGURE 4.8. A Comparison of Budget Deficits and Debt, 2005 (% GDP)

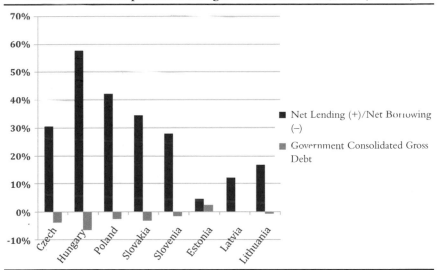

Source: Eurostat, IMF 2007.

the Czech Republic, Poland, and Slovakia both in terms of the relative size of the debt and the amount of borrowing needed to finance deficits (blue bar). Only the Baltic Republics had superior positions. In the coming years, Slovenia wants to consolidate revenue sources while lowering the structural deficit—a daunting challenge. Officials hope to reduce spending to 41.7 percent by 2009 while balancing the budget.

Trends in Taxing and Spending

Among these eight new member states, Slovenia remains relatively high in the amount of revenues raised and spent. Figure 4.9 compares government revenue and expenditures. Slovenia has the highest level of taxation (25 percent GDP) and

FIGURE 4.9. A Comparison of Revenue and Expenditure Levels in Eight New Member States (Percent of GDP)

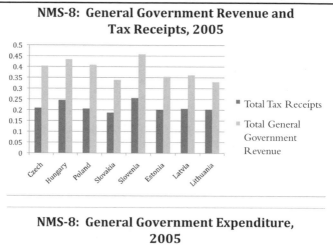

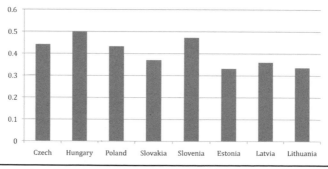

Source: Eurostat, Slovenia Ministry of Finance, IMF, 2007.

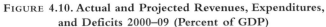

FIGURE 4.10. Actual and Projected Revenues, Expenditures, and Deficits 2000–09 (Percent of GDP)

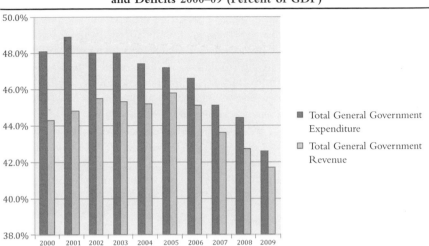

■ Total General Government Expenditure

☐ Total General Government Revenue

Source: Slovenian Ministry of Finance, IMF 2007.

total revenue (45.8 percent GDP). It is second to Hungary in expenditures at 47.2 percent of GDP. This has changed little since the mid-1990s and may actually be slightly higher, raising concerns about budgetary inflexibility and the size of the public sector. High taxation levels may be dampening economic growth and inflexible spending patterns may hinder the effectiveness of countercyclical fiscal policy (IMF 2007).

Given those concerns, the government planned to lower taxes, which required spending restraint. Successfully lowering the amount of spending with the intent to increase flexibility could provide more discretion in fiscal policy and allow decision makers more leverage to respond to age-related spending pressures. Figure 4.10 shows the projected reductions in revenues and expenditures through 2009. The black line shows the projected budget deficits.

BUDGETARY CHALLENGES TO NEW MEMBER STATES

Age-Related Spending

Perhaps the greatest budgetary policy challenge over the coming decade is age-related spending, including health and social security. The demographics in Slovenia are less favorable than those in other EU nations in terms of the ratio of pensioners to workers, and it is only projected to worsen. It is forecast that pensions and health care will increase by 7 percent of GDP from current levels by 2050 at which time the system would be insolvent under current policy. Beginning in the late 1990s, long and difficult negotiations on restructuring the pension system resulted in a new Law on Pension and Disability Insurance that was adopted in December 1999. The average retirement age rose from fifty-two in 1992 to fifty-seven in 2007, but this is still left the system one of the most generous in Europe. The system is not utilizing the productive capacity of older workers, whose numbers will double over the next two generations. Reform proposals include raising the retirement age, lowering the growth of benefits, and relying more on supplementary private pensions. These additional reforms are opposed by labor organizations. The Union of Free Trade Unions (ZSSS) contends that the 1999 pension system works well and should not be changed. Working out further reforms of the pension system without creating intergenerational conflicts will be a difficult challenge.

Expenditure Inefficiency

Because of its generous social spending, poverty levels in Slovenia were lower than in many other European countries. Only Czech Republic, Netherlands, and Sweden had lower poverty rates. Income inequality is also relatively low in Slovenia compared to Europe. Only Sweden and Denmark had a more even distribution of income than Slovenia among EU countries.

However, a recent study suggests that overall spending, and particularly social spending, is relatively high for what it actually buys for society. Matina and Gunnarson conclude that expenditures are inefficient because of funding mechanisms, institutional arrangements, that coverage is broad rather than targeted to where needs are greatest, and inadequate cost recovery. For example, Slovenia has some of the most generous social benefits in Europe including both old and new member states. Table 4.2 compares the benefit levels in three key social policies—maternity benefits, child allowance, and unemployment benefits. Slovenia generally provides higher benefits for longer duration than other EU members.

Despite relatively high levels of spending, policy results in areas of education and health are less effective than nations that spend less. In terms of the health sector, for example, Slovenia ranked eighteenth out of twenty-two nations on health sector efficiency. While spending 6.4 percent of GDP on health, they ranked lower in measures of infant mortality, life expectancy, or maternal mortality than countries spending far less on health care. Table 4.3 examines a similar comparison for education efficiency. Here, Slovenia ranks twenty-second of twenty-three countries, spending 6.68 percent of GDP on education but ranking lower on student-teacher ratio, and the percent attending and graduating from high school.

TABLE 4.2. Benefit Levels and Duration of Social Programs in Selected EU Nations

	Maternity Leave Benefit		Child Allowance		Unemployment Benefit	
	Benefit (% of earnings)	Duration of Benefit (weeks)	Duration of Benefit (age limit)	Duration if Student (age limit)	Benefit (% of earnings)	Duration Benefit (months)
Slovenia	100	52	18	26	60–70	3–24
			NMS-8			
Czech Republic	... 1/	28–37	26	26	40–50	...
Estonia	100	20–22	16	18	...	6
Hungary	70	24	16	20	65	9
Latvia	100	16	14	20	50	9
Lithuania	100	18	...	...	...	6
Slovak Republic	...	28	...	...	...	6
Poland	100	16	18	21	...	6–18
			EU-15			
Austria	100	16	18	26	55	20–52
Denmark	...	52	18	18	...	52
France	100	16–34	20	...	...	4–60
Germany	100	14	18	27	60–67	3–32
UK	90 for 6 weeks	26	16	19	...	6

Source: U.S. Social Security Administration, 2007, www.ssa.gov/policy/docs/progdesc/ssptw/.

TABLE 4.3. Expenditure Efficiency: Comparing Education Spending to Outcome Measures

	Primary Student-Teacher Ratio	Secondary Enrollment (%)	Tertiary Total Graduates (%)	Public Education Spending (% of GDP)	Efficiency Score	Rank
Hungary	10.4	94.9	7.3	5.89	1.00	1
Italy	10.9	76.7	5.8	5.02	1.00	1
Sweden	11.6	104.1	8.5	6.86	1.00	1
Spain	14.4	98.3	8.8	4.24	1.00	1
Poland	11.2	63.7	12.5	5.58	1.00	1
Ireland	20.3	105.2	13.0	4.20	1.00	1
Bulgaria	17.3	68.1	7.8	3.87	1.00	1
United Kingdom	18.0	81.4	15.3	5.19	1.00	1
Denmark	10.0	93.2	11.5	8.05	1.00	1
Germany	15.1	78.5	6.7	4.30	0.96	10
Slovakia	18.7	59.6	5.5	4.04	0.96	11
Norway	10.3	75.8	11.0	7.68	0.95	12
Czech Republic	17.4	57.2	4.9	4.11	0.94	13
Romania	17.9	59.3	4.6	4.15	0.93	14
Croatia	18.4	56.4	4.8	4.48	0.86	15
Portugal	12.1	97.6	8.5	6.97	0.81	16
Austria	13.3	63.7	5.8	5.69	0.79	17
France	18.7	81.4	13.4	6.12	0.75	18
Latvia	14.7	79.0	10.9	6.30	0.74	19
Finland	16.2	82.8	11.6	6.44	0.71	20
Belgium	12.0	66.1	10.0	7.24	0.70	21
Slovenia	13.0	63.1	8.5	6.68	0.69	22
Estonia	14.5	79.8	8.1	7.20	0.59	23

Source: UNESCO and Eurostat data; reported in Mattina and Gunnarson 2007, 17.

Several recommendations have been made for making expenditures more efficient: institutional reforms to consolidate and contain costs; reform social service funding such as shifting education financing to capita-based formulas to penalize high cost providers; target social benefits to add resources to the most impoverished households while reducing benefits to the middle class; and make work rules more flexible in the civil service and education sectors to enhance flexibility.

The nature of governing coalitions since 2000 has made delegation more difficult, suggesting Slovenia may have to turn to negotiated budget agreements. To deal with the deficits and debt, IMF has suggested that Slovenia needs a set of rules that guide taxing and spending decisions (IMF 2007). This would take the form of fixed deficit targets and expenditure ceilings. In the case of revenue shortfalls, expenditures would have to be cut accordingly. Over the past two decades national fiscal rules have increased in the EU. For example, Denmark, Germany, Netherlands, Spain, Sweden, and the UK all have enacted some sort of deficit rules.

Although fiscal discipline declined and deficits increased after 1999, policymakers were able to use the existing budget process to shift back toward fiscal balance. The goal of reducing taxing and spending levels while maintaining a balanced budget will be a severe test of both the budget system and the political will of the government. Political culture has continued to evolve as the Yugoslav era grows distant and more and more young people grow up in a democratic, capitalist society. However, as the previous discussion of reforming age-related spending suggests, adhesion to extensive and broadly distributed social spending remains strong. This aspect of political culture will continue to present obstacles to the government in their reform efforts.

CONCLUSION

Budgeting in the EU encompasses budget processes and budget choices in each of the twenty-seven member states as well budgeting for the European Union itself. In this chapter, we have focused on budgeting in the EU and chosen two specific countries, France and Slovenia, to examine more closely. There are innumerable differences between the twenty-seven member states in terms of size, wealth, political culture, and government structure. These differences are instructive as we attempt to understand what explains differences in fiscal balances, levels of government spending, and ability to effectively restrain spending pressures. In terms of macrobudgetary policy, we have seen that control of fiscal balances is achieved either by delegation to a powerful finance minister, or by negotiating a set of budget rules or fiscal contracts among participants. The kind of budget policy that is adopted depends in part on whether the government is based on a majority party or coalition.

Europe faces many budget challenges in the coming years, similar to the developed countries around the world. Perhaps the greatest challenge in Europe is to protect their social safety net while keeping their economies vibrant by lowering taxes and holding down spending. Different countries have taken different paths, but all will continue to be challenged in the coming decades. Much of this will be driven by demographics of an aging population and stagnant birthrates in many countries, foreshadowing a growing burden on workers to support the expanding ranks of retirees. Health care costs are a serious problem as well. The UK has taken a different path than much of the rest of Europe since 1980, cutting government programs and benefits and privatizing government assets such as British Rail. How budget in the UK and other Commonwealth countries compares to the rest of Europe is the subject of another chapter.

5

CENTRAL AND EASTERN EUROPE
AND THE FORMER SOVIET UNION

INTRODUCTION

When the CEE/FSU region is examined, the value of comparing budgeting and fiscal management systems and transferring successful examples becomes clearer. In the world of public budgeting, the Soviet system was a hermetic and quite unique means of allocating state resources to programs and projects. Since the "collapse" or "transition," it has been a veritable fiscal laboratory in which to install reforms from other regions and countries. So, what applicable lessons are available to this region from others? Conversely, are there systemic lessons which the post-transition reform process in CEE/FSU can teach other regions? With the economic meltdown of market-driven financial systems in 2007–08, are there methods and models from the pre-reform Soviet era that might be transferred back to the West? Some argued that this is a relatively unique region; systems, methods, and practices from market and quasi-market economies would not be transferable. Authoritarian and state socialist political cultures might resist introduction of Western budgetary management systems. Others disagreed with this conclusion. The more practical question has been how the experiences, conditions, and systems of the CEE/FSU region could be compared with similar regions in order to generate relevant lessons? If other regions, such as Latin America, experienced a similar range of economic conditions and cases of political transformation, then the similarities and differences in their budgetary systems and institutional practices should be of practical importance. How might the experiences of the North American region be relevant to the CEE/FSU? Can we compare the sub-regions, such as Central Asia and poorer Latin American country fiscal systems at the central and local levels? An important distinguishing feature of the CEE/FSU region is that fiscal and governmental systems in place were found wanting after the Soviet economy underpinning them collapsed. The systems that functioned rather well under the economic autarky of the fifty-to-seventy-year period would no longer suffice for socioeconomic development in the context of a market-driven world. The fiscal management systems had to be replaced and to a large extent, in the short time of only about twenty years, they have been. As will be indicated, the political systems and regimes of these "transitional" countries have had problems in democratic consolidation. Now, with the addition of global recession and economic meltdown problems (spawned by collapse of the commercial property and housing debt bubbles), there are major threats to the gains made in economic and fiscal reform.

By contrast, fiscal systems in the developing countries of Asia, Latin America, and Africa were weak and needed to become functional. One might say that it is often easier to adapt systems or demolish them and start over, than to build from scratch. Success in "developing" countries has been almost on a country by country basis. Systemic reforms have taken much longer, beginning in the 1950s and continuing until today. Corruption, poverty, and political instability inhibit fiscal reforms from deepening in many developing countries, especially in Latin America. Similar to the conditions found in Central Asia (especially in rural areas), governments of poorer developing countries lack technical skills and functioning accounting, budgeting, and financing systems at both central and local levels. As will be evident in this chapter, reforms of CEE/FSU economic systems moved forward quickly. The fiscal systems at the central and local levels are now largely in place for most of the developed parts of the CEE/FSU region and the question is how to make them work better (Davey, cited in Guess 2007a, 1). Still, the legacies of many uncompetitive state firms, huge public bureaucracies, and ingrained welfare mentalities among voters survive to some extent in all CEE/FSU countries. These have impeded the deepening of both economic and political reforms. Most of the post-Soviet regimes remain quite distant and out of touch with their voters and distrust is growing.

To focus on budgeting and financial management, it is useful to note that within the FSU/CEE region, there are at least five sub-regions that have reformed at different speeds and levels of achievement: (1) the Baltic Republics, (2) Central and Eastern Europe, (3) Former Soviet Republics, (4) Central Asia, and (5) Southeast Eastern Europe. For example, the Baltic "tigers" (e.g., Estonia and Latvia) until recently were speeding ahead with reforms of budgeting and financing to deepen their institutional foundations. In 2006, Latvia was growing at an astonishing 12 percent per year (*Economist* 2009a, 56). They maintained aggregate fiscal discipline and encouraged growth as recommended by Western advisors. At the same time, reforms widened the base of public participation in budgeting and policymaking via diffusion of information technology such as e-governance. The Baltics looked to Finland as a developmental role model—and this worked well for more than a decade. With the collapse of the largest local bank in Riga (Parex) and subsequent nationalization, taxpayer funds and IMF credits are now being applied to restore economic competitiveness. In the search for revenue sources to finance growing fiscal deficits, even such reforms as the flat tax may be replaced by progressive income taxes (*Economist* 2009, 56). By contrast, reform fatigue seems to have taken hold of countries in the EU-8 (e.g., Hungary and Poland) where growth is leveling off and fiscal deficits are climbing steadily past the Stability Pact limit of 3 percent GDP. Since Fall 2008, the IMF has loaned more than $30 billion to countries of the FSU/CEE region, in particular to Latvia and Hungary (Shin 2009). Other countries such as Estonia were more prudent and increased net public assets to 7 percent of GDP, which allows them more room to run expansionary fiscal policies to offset the recession (*Economist* 2009a, 57). The rest of the CEE region has followed the Austrian model, which has been appropriate for economic reform but questionable for political reform given their politicized civil service and private special interest–driven budget process.

This chapter argues that despite recent reversals, the successful evolution of budgeting and financial management systems in post-transition CEE/FSU for more than fifteen years offers many lessons for other countries. A major remaining problem is how to integrate the popular concerns of civil society with the need for hard choices to maintain sustainable public finances. Underlying these concerns are improved budgeting and financial management systems that generate viable fiscal options and point to the right policy choices. While the budgetary systems produce appropriate options, the choices are often not selected by political leaders. What is evident is that the administrative and policy systems are sound—but those that use them may not be. In many countries of this region, unworkable partisan coalitions have formed that paralyze reform efforts. Many of the parties offer retrograde, state socialist, and crypto-fascist platforms with public financing—just like the old days. Partisan maneuvering tends to distract rational debate on fiscal issues by shifting from practical operational matters to questionable historical analogies, high abstractions, and ideological considerations. Relatively simple problems of budgetary accounting in countries of this region often become excuses to rave about communist terror after World War II, to which rational responses or sound policy formulation is difficult. The explanation is often that issues are complex and need to be addressed at different levels of meaning. The practical response is that efforts need to be made to establish problem boundaries and to utilize the many problem-definition methodologies that are readily available. The policy and budgetary process should be strong enough to ensure that problems are defined and reviewed at the same analytical level so that problem definitions lead to solutions—not more debate. In this chapter, we examine first what is meant by fiscal and budgetary reform. Second, we employ the five-variable comparative framework in an attempt to explain the important changes in this region. Third, we examine how context, institutions, and culture have been used to set an appropriate post-transition policy agenda in many if not most of the countries in the CEE/FSU region.

BUDGETING SYSTEMS REFORM

Countries reform their budget systems for various reasons. They may need to increase fiscal discipline to control deficits; to improve the allocation and targeting of resources to different sectors or functions; and/or to improve funding for operations of existing services and facilities. Budget reforms may seek to increase "transparency" or the coverage and clarity of budget documents. Budget reforms may also focus on "sustainability" or developing hard budget constraints for the current year from medium-term forecasts of revenues and expenses. For these different types of reform, there are major and minor projects and activities. A problem is that the term *reform* is typically used for modification of the fiscal management system, which often leads to exaggerated expectations, disappointments, and even political backlash. It is important to present the changes consistent with their narrowest intent. Larger structural reforms require more complex databases and modification of system requirements, for example, IFMS, Zero-Based Budgeting, and Performance Budgeting Systems. They are more costly, time-consuming, and more prone to failure. Marginal reforms require focus on presentations and formats—the forms and formalities of budgeting, for instance, calendars, capital project presentation, and accounting and reporting forms (as will be explained further in chapter 7) Clarification of a definition of "minor maintenance" would appear marginal despite the potential for improved budget control and potential reprogramming of savings to underfunded activities. While the intent of these types of reforms may be marginal or minor, their institutionalization may lead to broader structural reforms. For instance, changes in budgetary accounting systems and charts of accounts might appear minor but often result in comprehensive changes that affect the entire financial management system. This has frequently been the case with apparently minor and innocuous local government budget reforms in the CEE/FSU region. Ideally then, the budget reform path should lead from forms and formats to new and improved systems.

Budgetary reform is often implied in larger state modernization programs that seek to re-engineer public sector processes and programs such as health and education to increase their efficiency and effectiveness. Budgetary reforms can facilitate the achievement of all these objectives, but are unlikely to result in major improvements by themselves. Budgetary reform may also be part of broader public financial management reform. This consists of the interrelated fiscal framework of which budgeting is perhaps the most important function: treasury payment, accounting and reporting, cash management, debt management, revenue policy and administration, procurement and contracting, internal audit, and budget formulation and planning. Budgeting in this context is the central incentive system of the state, the nerve center or heart of the body politic—what is needed to plan, fund, and implement services and programs in the public interest. Some countries overpromise and overextend themselves (perhaps from consultants' exaggerated claims of probable successes) by engaging in multiple reforms at once (e.g., program–performance budgeting, state modernization, and political and fiscal decentralization). This tendency was noted in chapter 3 where MTEF fiscal planning reforms exported from Commonwealth countries often included program/performance reforms as well. The current budgetary reform portfolio of the Peruvian government includes civil service and local government fiscal decentralization—a recipe for overcommitment and probable failure. Even wealthier OECD countries are rarely successful with the fiscal reform saturation approach. Transitional and developing countries often forget this and forge ahead blindly. In short, reform efforts should be focused and sequenced to avoid overloading existing institutional capacity. Focusing on comprehensive fiscal reform requires change in one or more functions or components of the financial management system. The component changes may be preconditions or required simultaneously. Either way, the system requirements may add up to delay of the fiscal reforms for political leaders that had been banking on them to enhance regime credentials. But, the fact remains that changing budget formats without making corresponding changes to the budgetary accounting system, reporting requirements, internal audit routines, or staff incentives is unlikely to be much of a reform.

When is a reform not a reform? In terms of cost, complexity, and potential systemic implications one should distinguish incremental or marginal from structural and comprehensive reforms. A $50 million project to computerize an entire local government financial management system, allow real-time reporting, and integrate the general ledger with the treasury single account (often called IFMS) would be a major undertaking that could take years. It could lead to major public administration changes, such as elimination of redundant reporting and clearance requirements that plague all bureaucracies in the form of red tape. At the same time, a program to upgrade internal audit to value for money auditing from financial compliance audits would be smaller—but could also produce major service gains that would be more saleable to the public and politically more important than the expensive IFMS. So which is the major and which is the minor reform? Much depends on project definition, cost/time, and medium-term purposes or expectations.

In the medium term, financial management reforms focus on one or more of the following purposes: (1) maintenance of fiscal discipline and control at the aggregate macroeconomic level; (2) allocation of resources to meet planned needs; and (3) efficient management of expenditures to maintain services and operations (Guess 2007a, 3). The purposes are related in that, for example, controlling weaknesses at the aggregate level affects available funding for sectoral allocation, which affects the efficiency and stability of service delivery expenditures. While fiscal management problems rarely affect all three levels at the same time, problems at one level can cause problems at other levels (e.g., operational-level undermaintenance of facilities, requiring more capital investment at the strategic level). FSU/CEE governments in the post-transition period have had problems maintaining fiscal discipline and control at the aggregate macroeconomic level. For deficit and debt management and to avoid legal sanctions from the EU (or downgrades from credit agencies), there have had to be systemic improvements. This took the form of improved budget coverage and classification consistent with the charts of accounts, improved internal audits, and regular reporting of outlays, commitments, and arrears. Most of these requirements were mandated by central governments, which had to certify to the IMF and/or Eurostat that all units of "general government" now conformed to those standards and that the MOF would enforce them. Reform at the strategic or aggregate level means that a capable budget/finance organization can and will act promptly on reported fiscal information. Many fiscal reforms in this region have focused on enforcing expenditure control to reduce operating deficits, reduction of within-year cash flow problems, and making sense of poorly reconciled accounts after the fiscal year has ended. At the intermediate level, local governments have also had problems in allocating resources to meet planned needs. Their revenue forecasting problems, for instance, often have less do to local technical incapacities (e.g., unreliable methodologies) than from delayed fiscal transfers from the central government or lack of an assigned tax base that can cover local financing needs for education, health, and other programs. As a legacy of the fiscal and political centralization of the Soviet period, many local governments throughout the region still lack sufficient own-source revenues to finance their needs.

COMPARISON OF CEE/FSU BUDGET SYSTEMS

Using our comparative model, it will be seen that the variables of: (1) context, (2) political culture, and (3) budgetary institutions explain much of the difference in fiscal systems modernization, advancement, and reform in this region.

Context

The period of whole-systems collapse and "transition" (a euphemism that for many countries in this region meant civil war, destruction of property and loss of legitimate governing institutions) ended about 1992. This exposed the weaknesses of both the overall Soviet financial management system as well as those at the country level. Most countries had governance systems unable to cope with or respond to the needs of their respective populations. As is known, state socialist systems were centralized and lacked independent lower-tier governmental units. Services were dispensed by local officials integrated into the central ministry system—or "deconcentrated" from the center. Their roles and responsibilities as well as financing emanated from the central government. State-financed enterprises functioned in parallel to provide services to employees of functional state services, such as education and health, and producers of material products. The sudden, forced independence of particular countries from the Russian orbit produced shocks that required radical and rapid actions by one or more legitimate actors to avoid chaos and civil war. In some cases, state actions were insufficient— because the new states were weak and lacked professional capacity to target programs and policies for their beneficiaries. In others, they bought time before international donors could offer relief to support their transition efforts.

For example, effective Albanian efforts, supported by the World Bank, to distribute social safety net payments rapidly throughout the country prevented starvation and civil war, and held that country together from the late 1980s to the early 1990s. Initial efforts of other countries to raise and spend public funds for local needs were insufficient. This could be seen in the institutional context of: (1) contradictory legal and regulatory frameworks for budgeting and fiscal management, (2) distorted intergovernmental fiscal roles and responsibilities, (3) lack of civic participation traditions in public finance decision making—national or local.

Budgeting in CEE/FSU countries was not a real function of government. There was no formal process of analyzing the costs and consequences of how funds should be spent before approval. This function was handled by the communist party apparatus advised by technocrats that allocated funds for infrastructure projects according to "scientific" plans. The plans were politically scientific, and produced allocations based on simple political criteria, such as party planning directives on where people should live and work. There were many in the line ministries responsible for functions, such as health or education, that actually wanted to allocate funds on the rational analytic basis of need and efficiency. But they were stymied at the center from advocating this peculiar mix of partisan politics and technocratic criteria to improve program results. The line officials often wanted to budget; their staff superiors wanted to allocate by plan. The budget function was weak and designed only to account for expenditures after they were made, and to receive regular reports on their use for narrow, legalistic control purposes. Intergovernmental fiscal roles and responsibilities were relatively simple—funds and responsibilities flowed from the center through a network of deconcentrated administrative structures around the country and the region. Role definitions and responsibilities were "broadened" only if expenditure efficiency and service responsiveness were the goals, which they were not. Otherwise, the funds flowed and the reports returned with brisk efficiency.

Finally, there was no civil society to speak of—some countries had major singular influences, such as the Catholic Church in Poland and Hungary. In most of the region, there were no intermediary organizations such as the media or independent labor unions, between citizens and the state. The state was the society into which citizens integrated through the party. This left quite sensibly, a legacy of passive compliance and fear of the state bureaucracy and its security apparatus. To paraphrase a pilot's heated conversation with the control tower, they (bureaucrats) were not here to serve citizens—the citizens were there to serve the bureaucrats! In the West, the media and NGOs play an important critical role in forcing the state to take proper actions—to deliver services, provide due process, give restitution, etc. In this region, for fifty to seventy years, there were no indigenous institutions (including even parliaments or legislatures, which were not checks on the executive but rather part of the entire apparatus) to force accountability from the state.

Fiscal reform efforts in this region might be likened to peeling away layers of skin from a ripe fruit. At the core is or will be a good system that will govern and allocate funds consistently with plans. Fiscal database improvements have moved forward in tandem with changes to legal frameworks, forms, calendars, budget formats, analytic methods, and on into new systems. But in many countries progress has been disjointed. For example, the legal and policy framework in several CEE/FSU countries has still not changed. Rigid and literalistic operating premises stifle budget policymaking and management. Decisions are taken at the center and few are delegated; each action must be authorized individually, which discourages initiative and induces a climate of fear. This behavior is due in part to the different "structural premises" of European and Anglo-American public administration. In the former, as adopted now by FSU/CEE countries, there is effectively no implied authority. Discretionary space to shift funds or reprogram them is limited by the letter of the law. Budgets become almost fixed, legal records made at the beginning of the year. The budgetary script approach contrasts with common law countries in which actions are permitted unless prohibited (i.e., one need only seek subsequent "forgiveness"—not prior permission). The civil-law framework of Europe as adopted in other regions such as CEE/FSU and Latin America (see Table 5.1), leaves little room for management discretion or risk taking. According to the "state-centered dominance of public law" approach in Europe (Wright 2002, 21), which now governs Eastern European thinking, all public administration decision making is derived from rule of law. In contrast with the U.S. approach, this imposes limits on "managerialism" and the power of managers (2002, 22) to shift resources in order to attain service objectives efficiently and effectively. The continental European legal framework tends to encourage passive behavior and a compliance mentality. It inhibits incentives for active government action to solve policy problems and to undertake reforms of public budgeting systems.

TABLE 5.1. Common vs. Civil Law Countries

Country	Legal Framework
United States	Common Law
United Kingdom	Common Law
Australia	Common Law
Canada	Common Law
France	Civil Law
Germany	Civil Law
Russia	Civil Law
Hungary	Civil Law
Latin America with exception of Belize	Civil Law

Note: The vast majority of countries develop and execute government budgets within a civil law framework.

Political Culture

The values and attitudes of a society that affect institutional and policy decisions refers to its "political culture" (Inglehart 1988). Among other variables, Wildavsky (1986) used the concept of political culture as a determinant of budgetary change. In his terms, the cultural problem for modernizing FSU/CEE budgeting systems was how to change "collectivist" cultures with "hierarchical" regimes into "individualist" cultures with "market" regimes. While this was a pioneering typological effort, it is still generally accepted that a major weakness with the political culture approach is the inability to specify mechanisms linking culture to structure, and the tendency to include ever more lines of causal influence rather than specifying more precisely the parameters of a cultural model of politics (Laitin 1989).

To craft a better future, FSU/CEE policymakers (and external advisors) need to work on those institutional elements of the culture that can be changed. Focusing on the resource allocation process is important in that budgeting, as noted, is the central incentive system of the state. Emphasis on changing the larger culture through incremental modification of microfinancial management routines has been successful in similar contexts, such as Latin America (Guess 1992). Budgeting and financial management offers small decision levers that can be moved to change the culture and institutionalize new budget practices. In the FSU/CEE region, the municipal finances were the product of a common institutional history. Utilizing the comparative method allows us to examine the common features of FSU/CEE public finances and within this framework to isolate those differences that may allow decision makers ways to achieve modernization and improvements (Guess 2001b).

FSU/CEE public finances developed subject to at least five common cultural forces. First, the FSU/CEE countries developed within the less-enlightened and poorer Byzantine and Ottoman realms. This inhibited economic performance and gave them a lower base from which to start. Second, the Orthodox Church facilitated tolerance of brutal and corrupt governance. In contrast to the active community involvement preached by Catholicism and Protestantism, the Orthodox Church was passive and contemplative, accepting the physical world and whatever regime was in power (Kaplan 1998, 33).

Third, FSU/CEE, and especially Balkan, practices were strongly influenced by the Soviet political culture. It is debatable whether the influence of the Soviet system made the change of Balkan budgetary systems more or less difficult than it would have been without that influence. The effect of the Soviet system was to reinforce Ottoman top-down, secretive, rigidly legalistic policy-making tendencies but also to upgrade statistical and record-keeping abilities of government officials. Structurally, this meant that public expenditures were fully centralized, though considerable shares were allocated to local government departments (Martinez-Vazquez 1995, 183). While Balkan administrative and governing systems were formed only after the late 1940s, at which point they joined the "communist Second World," the Soviet political culture had been reinforcing itself since the 1920s. But some countries in the Balkans, especially Albania, were very similar to the earlier, purer "Stalinist" form of Soviet state central control. Central governments in the Soviet-Balkan orbit still viewed local governments as their administrative arms. By contrast, Tito created and operated a Yugoslav form of decentralization that was unique in the Eastern bloc until his death in May 1980.

One could argue that the Soviet political culture reinforced not just Ottoman influences but long-standing European corporatist practices. Corporatism as practiced in Europe for centuries meant two things: lack of transparency and consensus decision making. Governance in most European countries occurs through social partnerships between the dominant coalition and key organizations such as unions and financial institutions. This means that resources in most EU states are allocated often behind closed doors (e.g., *proporz* or posts and contracts "for the boys," divvied up by Austria's two big political parties) to ensure broad consensus (*Economist* 2007). The populace must work through entrenched institutions to forge consensus. While this is slow, the method accounts for interpersonal distrust and a tradition of official secrecy.

The effects of the Soviet/Ottoman/European cultural practices on public administration and governance in the FSU/CEE region have been substantial. The quantitative norm-driven Soviet system created a subculture of calculations and emphasis on quantitative and numerical expressions. The security considerations of police state operations produced a fondness for tight administrative systems—effective if not efficient administrative systems that produced services, such as housing and transport, that met basic needs. Consistent with focus on narrow rules rather than broad allocations of management discretion, the emphasis of administrative systems was on rule-obedience and severe punishment for failure to comply. Within governmental structures the communist party apparatus dominated. Fear or retribution produced a general avoidance of risk taking derived from the everyday experiences of colleagues being punished for putting their heads up. As noted, the basic decision framework and structural premise was legal authorization. There was no implied authority.

Fourth, private property ownership and autonomous institutions apart from the state were virtually unknown in Tito's Yugoslavia or in the Soviet system. Allowing the state to be the agent of societal change created an anti-entrepreneurial ethos that worked against economic development and autonomous decision making by lower tier (municipal) governments. In contrast with Western civil societies, where contending power centers largely created the state, in Eastern Europe the bureaucratic state (later controlled by the Communist Party) discouraged contending power centers—the media, church, private property, unions, or a commercial class. For this reason, countries with functioning civic and economic institutions such as Poland, Hungary, Estonia, Czech Republic, and Slovenia achieved growth and modernization after 1990 more quickly than countries that lacked this civic tradition, such as Russia, Ukraine, and the Balkans. Fifth and finally, in contrast with Western European and U.S. cities that developed as contending and autonomous power centers from the rulers and the Church, Eastern European and Balkan cities were simply part of the central apparatus of the state. They were either bureaucratic agglomerations—the seats of administration—garrison towns, or static introverted settlements (Schopflin 1991, 72). Their budgeting and financial functions were controlled and dominated by those of the central government.

While these are the features of a common history that cannot be changed, some of them can be modified. It needs to be emphasized that political culture is a variable and not a constant (Harrison 1985). Evident to those who work in and live in this region, what is needed is a type of psychological regulatory deprogramming to rid public officials of their rigid, number-crunching small print mindsets. That cultural perspective will not change from within but needs force from outside—from competition with the successful political economies of the CEE/FSU region and from the exercise of real public management—cadres of managers that are both responsible and accountable for better public service delivery in behalf of citizens. Despite cultural similarities in this region, examined at the micro level there are some important differences in Balkan as well as CEE/FSU development. Though similarities exist in Balkan municipal budgetary practices, there are country variations in the achievement of financial management reform at the three levels noted above (aggregate fiscal discipline, sectoral allocation to meet need, and efficient management of service expenditures). The explanation for performance differences among the five subregions of FSU/CEE region are largely institutional and political culture.

Budgetary and Political Institutions

Beneath surface uniformity, there were an impressive range of regimes under Soviet communism (despite the capacity of the latter to enforce order and to alter the course of domestic politics). Observers frequently miss both the degree of heterogeneity and range of sovereignty under Soviet communism. There was limited pluralism in the CEE states (civil society institutions such as the Catholic Church still functioned and farmer's groups still organized). Civic institutions still functioned, and if Hungary, for example, had been in the "political space" of Spain or Brazil in 1956, communism would have been stayed or reversed and a democratic tradition might then have been started (Linz and Stepan 1996, 237). Likewise, observers often underestimate the power of the Soviet military presence in beating back the impressive range of heterogeneous resistance these "satellites" managed to generate (1996, 237). In the "inner empire" of Albania and Central Asia, any resistance was much easier to control and civil society had been mostly eliminated by force. In budgetary and fiscal terms, all authority emanated from Moscow, including budget forms and local policies from fees to debt. The centralized fiscal system reflected this almost total centralization of political power.

Pre-transition budgetary institutions in this region were relatively unique. The need now is to de-claw, unwind, and perhaps unlearn the old lessons and methods of the past. The need is to adjust, adapt, and retool those practices that can serve the ends of an active budget process that analyzes needs in relation to resources and ensures that allocations have the intended effects. The cultural roots of preexisting systems and practices are deep. Grafting new practices, developing new regulations, uprooting old rule-making processes completely, and training already skilled people to think about citizens and consumers are challenging but in many ways enviable tasks. They are entirely different from the contexts of those developing countries in which budgetary institutions remain underdeveloped, and never institutionalized the wrong lessons or developed sophisticated systems that became obsolete. The Soviet system generated a high-capacity, misdirected fiscal system, one that provided generations of officials with the needed skills to make adjustments quickly. This is a solid base from which to build budgetary institutions.

Newly functioning public budget systems do not simply emerge like markets but must be planned and installed carefully—balancing needs with existing constraints. Legions of consultants and budget/finance experts descended on this region in the early 1990s from most Western countries, bringing enthusiastically the latest tools from their own countries. As noted by Mikesell and Mullins (2001,

549), they did achieve a semblance of superficial success. Then, the crises of debt defaults and accumulated deficits in Russia in 1998 revealed, among other things, the paucity of underlying structural reforms of the state and its core taxation and budget systems. Tax systems simply punished firms and citizens and raised little revenue for the treasury; budget systems could not measure progress or control deficits. The systems were set up for stable fiscal conditions and were managed rigidly within their narrow rule frameworks. If there were fiscal deficits, for example, these were treated as accounting problems to be covered by printing money and state bank transfers. After the transition, political systems in the FSU/CEE region had to cope with massive revenue and expenditure reductions, termination of artificially low administered prices, and increasing social needs as inflation soared and services collapsed. They were too inflexible to do this.

As is now evident, the pre-transitional institutional context was illusory stability only. Market forces had been artificially suspended for fifty to seventy years and both governmental institutions and citizens relied on this stability (they adapted to its defects with queues and black markets—but these were normal headaches). Citizens of this region came to expect little from life or from their governments. They are perhaps the toughest people on earth! For them, the state was the economy and its sole employer. It produced and distributed everything. Prices of goods and services were administered to prevent inflation. Distribution of goods and services were part of the plan which required controlled demographic patterns (i.e., internal passports). Schools, hospitals, and factories provided for every employee and client need. In practice, this was extended to non-core activities, such as ministries of defense operating hotels and restaurants and schools running farms (Mikesell and Mullins 2001, 554). As noted, local governments were part of the central government apparatus. The banking system financed current losses and all the investment needs of the public sector. There was no real separation of fiscal and monetary accounts. For personal accounts, loans were treated perversely as liabilities by state banks and deposits were assets—meaning that credit were either scarce or politically allocated. Putting personal savings into state banks was like throwing money into a black hole—hence the notion that banks treated deposits as their assets. The banking system served effectively as a financial printing press for government that also kept tabs on personal savings. As indicated, people grumbled. But they were used to these systems and they functioned.

The budget structures of the Soviet era were designed for the central physical plan—to cover planned needs of spheres or functions (e.g., agriculture) with resources allocated by the plan. The resources were not allocated by a resource-conscious budget process, because financing was not limited and prices were controlled. The MOF and its financial budget were irrelevant. Most of the allocations were for capital or "net material products" by sphere rather than for non-material services. The plan "scientifically" allocated material product funds and budget officials kept track of them. They were simply "bookkeepers" (2001, 551) that verified the calculation coefficients for physical norms (2001, 557)—the rigid number-crunching small print mindset in action. Despite the substantial technical and statistical capacities of finance officials in this region, there was little budget analysis.[1] The narrow role of these weak MOF institutions was to track allocations for state orders and to cover physical norm financing requirements—consistent with the latest plan.

Since physical norm-driven budgeting is a relatively unique phenomenon of this region it will be described briefly. Norms were not just physical or industrial standards. They were also allocation mechanisms. Norms were usually designed to fund and support public physical infrastructure (e.g., staff/hospital bed) and not to deliver services to the citizenry (2001, 556). In Ukraine, for example, the health care system (which consists of both infrastructure and current services) was norm-based and is now in the process of shifting toward cost-based transfers that provide positive incentives to both health managers and patients. The former health system was driven by service norms such as beds per thousand residents, medical doctors per thousand citizens, or numbers of hospitals and polyclinics (Guess and Sitko 2004). These formed the basis on which performance was judged for the purposes of both planning and budgeting. The result was an excessively high hospital capacity and low quality services. Limited resources were dispersed over an unnecessarily large number of facilities. Smaller institutions had lower occupancy rates. For example, the Ukrainian bed/10,000 population ratio was almost 40 percent higher than in Europe and 66.8 percent higher than in the EU (Vitrenko and Nagorna 1999). The number of doctors/10,000 population also was about 35.8 percent higher in Ukraine than Europe and 48.1 percent higher than the EU (1999). The availability of doctors and assistants should be a positive feature from the perspective of the patient. But the excessive supply simply led to greater demand pressures for wage payments that did not translate into the non-wage expenditures required for quality patient care. Moreover, the distribution of doctors/assistants was skewed in favor of urban areas: there are still an insufficient number of trained personnel, doctors, or nurses in rural areas. Hospitals such as Kyiv # 1 compare favorably with any in Europe. But rural Ukraine where nearly 16.3 million (33 percent) out of a total 49.5 million population live was another story (World Bank 2001, 114).[2]

Health care budgeting in Ukraine is almost continuously performed during the year and obligations are financed on a cash availability basis. In the context of artificial norms that could not be met and chronically unstable/reduced resources (essentially revenue collapse), actual health care expenditures in 1999 were only 61.9 percent of planned outlays as opposed to 98.0 percent in 1991 (World Bank 2001, Appendix 2). Following approval of the proposed budget by December 31, the budget is implemented over twelve months. MINFIN prepares a financial plan with Ministry of Health (MOE) inputs covering all expenses and revenues by item for each quarter. This is the object of the expenditure financial plan on which ministry releases or apportionments (*rozpys*) are based. Because of revenue uncertainty, as noted, actual releases are based less on agreed budgets than cash flow and daily cash position.

In the context of rigid norms that could not be met, during budget execution officials deal with revenue shortfalls by cutting back functional priorities according to the economic categories, that is, traditional line-item inputs. To deal with the cash management problem, the budget law required a priority list of "safe expenditures" that protected salaries and utilities/heat/food first. Oblast officials often prepared their budgets knowing in advance that they would not meet per capital norms or priority levels and that the real budget would be far different from that approved by MINFIN and the *Rada*. They tried and still try to bridge the funding gap with wealthy "sponsors" interested in health care and by creative transfers that avoid rather than evade the budget law. For example, Lviv hospital officials had to return funds unspent for heating unoccupied hospital beds (calculated by the bed-day norm). Acting as any rational manager would do under the circumstances they "redefined" the facility to be a warehouse, reprogrammed the funds to roof repairs, and then obligated them. Since the Ukraine model of health care still relies mostly on tax financing, managers cannot legally charge fees, though they do so informally for wealthier patients. This makes an already inefficient and inequitable system even more so.

In addition to the peculiar physical norm system, budget structures were also fragmented across institutions according to broad Soviet-style classification codes, such as "national economy," that in some cases included up to 40 percent of total expenditures. Control was exercised through this broad legal and financially irrelevant category. While use of this line item would make planning and control of funds difficult, such expenditure control activities were not really needed under the legal framework of state socialism. Now they are! Overbroad categories effectively remove the expenditure item from budgetary coverage and control. The coverage and classification problem, of course, is well known in other regions, particularly Latin America. At one point, the Ecuadorian state budget featured 1,300 extrabudgetary or off-budget funds that were outside the scope of the general government budget! Extrabudgetary accounts offer ripe opportunities for corrupt funneling of funds through bank accounts outside governmental controls and they can conceal, for instance, large amounts for earmarked subsidies and subsidies to state enterprises. In a narrow accounting sense, extrabudgetary funds are acceptable, so long as balances and flows are transparent and can be reconciled by the financial management system. Recall that U.S. local governments are effectively legalized collections of general and special funds—but the stock and flow of such amounts are transparent to officials and to the media.

In the FSU/CEE region, the fragmentation of special funds and use of overbroad line items preventing use of the budget for mobilization, control, or monitoring (Mikesell and Mullins 2001, 552) have been corrected. In Kyrgyzstan, there were 1,100 special funds in 1995–96, most of which have now been closed (2001, 552). In Georgia, all special accounts of central government spending units were closed by 2001 (2001, 552) and budget funds have been consolidated. It is also critically important that formal and informal fees paid to contribute to service delivery (to doctors, for textbooks, for school trips) be made transparent and flow through systems of public fiscal controls. In practice, payments are often kept informal to avoid subjecting them to even more corrupt governmental controls. In short, managers often illegally hide payments for legitimate public purposes to avoid confiscation by corrupt governmental officials using their own informal control systems! Paradoxically, keeping them informal can raise the level of actual services to students, patients, etc., while generating even more transparency and equity problems. Estimates of "non-cash revenues" such as in-kind payments and "offsets"—receivables and products used to cover taxes or other invoices owed to the government (e.g., cars from auto factories instead of taxes owed to local government in Russia) amounted to 15 percent of total revenues at the federal level and 50 percent of total local revenues in 1999 (2001, 560). Non-cash revenues have been a device or gimmick to clear debts to suppliers. If they could not use this, the other option was arrears or forced non–interest bearing loans to the government (2001, 561) which in Russia reached 3.2 percent of GDP in 1998.

The problem with off-budget revenue and expenditure accounts is that they violate the norm of "comprehensiveness" that applies to all budgets. A related problem, as noted, was overbroad classification, which inhibits expenditure accountability. If auditors cannot distinguish whether outlays are made for rehabilitation or maintenance, this affects the calculation of current budgetary balance. "Capitalization of operating expenses" (i.e., entering a current expenditure commitment as a capital item to be debt-financed), based on vague legal and accounting definitions of basic terms and/or weak control of actual journal entries, is a familiar dodge or gimmick to reduce fiscal deficits in most Western countries. In the FSU/CEE region, budget categories were much more porous than vague types of maintenance. Objects of expenditure were not really needed for accountability. So, the catch-all "National Economy" category was an opaque mixture of capital and current, wage and non-wage expenditures. Those who worked in the FSU region during the early 1990s on classification and coverage issues (especially IMF fiscal economists) spent months of frustration trying to sort these items out and classify them properly to get control of public expenditures.

As budgeting was largely an accounting function in the FSU/CEE region, the document was an accounting document. Effectively, operating budgets were reports on income or operations (i.e., operating statements). They were not real fiscal plans. Budgets provided only broad totals by functional classification and economic article. They looked like airline timetables with legal citations to add confidence in the veracity of the schedule. There was no comparison of past, current, and budget planning years from which to analyze variance trends. The budget document (i.e., format or presentation) was designed to meet two criteria: (1) regulatory compliance, and (2) correct arithmetic (Mikesell and Mullins 2001, 557). As a framework for analysis and accountability of actual expenditure results in financial or physical terms, it was less useful. The spherical classification of FSU budgeting did allow control across economic line items and facilitated translation into GFS functional budgets. But from there it was often difficult to track functional expenditures down to the organizational units, namely, cost and responsibility centers. This impeded identification of organizational and managerial accountability for expenditures (2001,558).

Budgetary control during execution was rigid and rule-driven. Consistent with the "public law" approach to finance noted above, emphasis was on control and execution of the budget as approved rather than management discretion to shift funds to deliver efficient and effective programs. In a plan-driven world, where legal compliance and correct math were all that mattered, this made some sense. In the real world of revenue forecasting errors and changes in expenditure needs, more flexibility is needed. In poor and uncertain budgetary contexts, where officials make and remake their financial plans during execution (as in the Ukrainian health care ministry noted above), managerial flexibility is needed. This did not exist in the FSU/CEE fiscal system. The use of extrabudgetary accounts, to some extent, was a real-world response to the managerial rigidity problem. Control was exercised at the appropriations point of a largely cash-based system to prevent overcommitment of funds. This ignored the need for commitments recording and control and for the need to verify the commitment before payment. In a modern budgeting system, the internal control function of the financial management system withholds payment approval until a pay or transfer order is approved. The internal control system indicates that sufficient funds exist and that the proposed outlay is for approved purposes—allowing approval. Modern computerized treasury systems do this in real time, preventing arrears and overcommitment, and ensuring that variances caused by within-year transfers and reprogramming decisions are accounted for and reconciled properly. Systems in the FSU/CEE did not, resulting in massive arrears (pensions, salaries, transfers) and overcommitments that translated into major fiscal deficits. To control expenditures in the early years after transition, ministries of finance (MOFs) resorted to weekly and monthly cash limit controls based on a priority list approved daily. Faced with chaos and total loss of financial control, they used these crude systems to cut funds off at the source.

Post-Transition Comparison (Reforming and Reformed Systems)

At the outset of the "transition" in the early 1990s, it was thought by specialists in the International Financial Institutions (IFIs) such as World Bank and International Monetary Fund, that the way ahead in FSU/CEE was to apply solutions learned from other regions. These included: orthodox macroeconomic policies (e.g., tight budgets and controls on inflation), cautious liberalization of the financial sector (e.g., tariff reduction, floating exchange rates), mass privatization, support for social institutions and for state reform—fewer but more capable civil servants operating within deregulated and smaller-sized state bureaucracies. These reforms were known as the "Washington Consensus" since they were also endorsed by the U.S. Treasury, which indirectly provided much of the funding (Burki and Perry 1998).

It was expected that these kinds of reforms would facilitate private sector–led growth in developing and transitional societies. Since then, it has been learned that sound economic policies, reduction of the size of the state, and administrative improvements are necessary but not sufficient conditions for sustained development. In many cases, recurring problems in public policymaking and financial management have been a more direct consequence of the absence of competitive and responsive institutions, or the absence of political democracy. For example, "shock therapy" worked in Poland. In Albania it worked at the macroeconomic level until the country flew apart into warring tribal factions in 1996–97. And radical "mass privatization" programs were quickly overwhelmed by thousands of busted state firms and hundreds of thousands of unemployed people all at once. Policymakers had to consider institutions and the reforms had to be sequenced properly. IFIs had few tools and lessons to apply to a region that had collapsed (imploded) and that did not employ concepts such as "supply," "demand," "market," or "profit." In Latin America and Africa, there were market economies, albeit imperfect ones, that could be used as the basis for devising reform strategies (Bokros 2006). Many "experts" in the IFIs were slow to realize the substantively different challenge. Those experts that did understand had few tools to apply except common sense and past experience elsewhere.

Fiscal management specialists discovered that there were major development differences in the FSU/CEE region, and that one strategy would not fit all of them. As noted, one can distinguish at least five subregions within the FSU/CEE region: (1) the Balkans, such as Romania and Bulgaria, (2) Central and Eastern Europe, such as Hungary and Poland, (3) Former Soviet Republics, such as the Baltic Republics (Latvia, Estonia, and Lithuania) and Ukraine and Moldova, (4) Central Asia, such as Kyrgyzstan and Kazakhstan, and (5) Southeast Eastern Europe (SEE), such as Albania and Macedonia. The tasks of former IMF/World Bank budget and public expenditure management reform efforts in CEE and Balkan countries have now largely been taken over by EU. IMF/World Bank continues to work in SEE and Central Asia, along with other donors such as the Asian Development Bank, British DFID, and USAID. In all five subregions, the "transition" is probably over in the sense of setting policies and establishing basic institutions. To deepen reforms in SEE, FSU, and Central Asia, however, assistance will be needed for many years in the financial sector (i.e., banking), poverty reduction, and functional areas such as agriculture, infrastructure, and municipal services.

Despite these acute needs, in the CEE, Balkans (especially in the new EU entrants Bulgaria and Romania), and FSU countries there are increasing problems of "reform fatigue." This is largely because macro fiscal reform issues are not part of the democratic debate. Civil society, media, and other nongovernmental stakeholders have not progressed to the stage where technical public finance issues are well understood and included in the political agenda. Thus, in Hungary, populists and the opposition Fidesz party wanted Prime Minister Gyurcsany to resign from office over the "lies" he made about the public finances and his support for an austerity package back in 2006 (Logan 2006). Much of the Hungarian populace still believes the state can provide for most needs without fees or taxes. Fueled by opposition parties that care little for EU Stability Pact requirements or fiscal austerity packages, they demand more benefits, jobs, and perks from the state. Opponents of austerity and reform (i.e., cutting state jobs and raising taxes and fees) in the CEE (e.g., Hungary) and FSU (e.g., Ukraine) are a toxic mixture of ultranationalists (claiming patriotism in keeping foreign influences out—such as austerity packages) and crypto-communists (who want to continue the stable benefits of the socialist welfare state). In the context of growing media influence and demands for democratic responsiveness, austerity programs are increasingly unpopular and illegitimate (because they are not popularly approved) (Guess 2006).

This restrictive political context puts FSU/CEE candidates campaigning for office in the bind of pretending that all is well until elected and then springing austerity on a population that has not been prepared for it. Witnessing the massive protests and the near fall of his colleague in Hungary over the poor state of public finances, the Ukrainian PM went on record immediately for social stability over reform (as if putting off the latter will increase the former) (Dempsey 2006). Control of the public finances is a necessary part of good governance. Designing proper fiscal reform strategies is critical for the growing mass democracies of this region. While elected leaders are needed that can build support and consensus for fiscal reform, there are few in power now and most oppose even the thought of it. Even in Latin America, noted for decades of social instability, hyperinflation, mass protest, rapid political regime changes, and cultural inability to defer gratification, the deteriorating state of public finances and the need for reform appear on campaign agendas and are debated openly. For example, the public debate in the last presidential campaign in Brazil was mainly about: financing pension reform, the scope and type of cuts in state spending programs, the effectiveness of regulatory agencies, and the use of private services management for assets such as roads (*Economist* 2006a, 59). In this context, the Brazilian budget was recently classified behind that of the United States as one of the top five most transparent budgets in the world (*Economist* 2009b, 86). While Brazilian budgetary debates are

TABLE 5.2. 2009 Projections of Fiscal Deficits as a Percentage of GDP

Country	Deficit	2008 OBI Rating	Region
Bulgaria	-0.30%	57	Balkans
Romania	-2.40%	No Data	
Kazakhstan	-3.60%	34	Central Asia
Uzbekistan	3.40%	No Data	
Hungary	-2.70%	No Data	Central and Eastern
Poland	-2.80%	67	Europe
Russia	-6.10%	58	Former Soviet
Moldova	-1.40%	No Data	Republics
Ukraine	-3.80%	55	
Albania		37	South Eastern Europe
Macedonia	-2.40%	54	

Source: The Economist (2009), World Bank (2008), OBI (2009). OBI index scores range from 0-100 with 88 as the currently highest rated country (UK) and Ecuatorial Guinea as the lowest (0) www.openbudgetindex.org.

not about major structural reforms proposals, the fact that technical sub-issues can be debated openly suggests that the public trusts officials to deal with larger design matters. In CEE/FSU, public finance issues are still not debated openly and there is growing distrust of the crop of officials that continues in 2010. This is the case despite high public tolerance (and desperation) for early 1990s "transition" efforts at the strategic or macroeconomic level. It may be that the FSU/CEE region can learn from Latin American experience (countries such as Chile and Brazil) that public expenditure reforms can stimulate larger structural reforms by providing a transparent process for the analysis of means-ends and a transparent allocation of public resources.

The larger economic challenge for governments in the FSU/CEE region in 2010 is that they are faced with global recession, collapse of the financial, banking, and mortgage industries, and potential social explosion at home. Many countries did not exercise prudent fiscal policies, raising taxes, cutting expenditures, limiting debt to sustainable levels. Instead, many spent and borrowed and are now faced with the deficit situations described in Table 5.2. In that the figures reflect the GDP contraction in many countries of this region, public deficits and debt ratios increase and are, in fact, much more of a fiscal policy burden. Those with prudent fiscal policies now have more space to stimulate their economies with infrastructure spending and to contract debt (gross or net) in support of financial sector recovery. Countries with less than prudent policies over the past ten years (1999–2009, such as Hungary with gross public debt at 100 percent of GDP, have been shunned by the EU (Whitlock 2009) because lenders recognize the kinds of major fiscal policy results expressed in Table 5.2.

LEVELS OF REFORM

As indicated, the collapse of the Soviet Union (and Russia, which drove most of these economies and controlled their political systems) affected the abilities of their public sector financial institutions to: (1) maintain fiscal discipline and control at the aggregate macroeconomic level; (2) allocate resources to meet planned needs; and (3) manage expenditures efficiently to maintain services and operations. Prior to collapse of the Soviet administrative system and its capacity to finance the budgets of its empire, the region was ruled by a variety of totalitarian-type regimes. Albania under Enver Hoxja, for example, represented perhaps the most brutal and pure type of totalitarian regime, a mixture of highly personalistic and arbitrary rule tempered only by his peculiar interpretation of Marxist-Leninist doctrine. After the "transition," depending on the extent of their economic sophistication and institutional complexity, regimes shifted toward authoritarianism. This left some space for a semi-opposition. But they were basically elitist systems with weak oppositions, for example, Poland in the 1980s and Brazil in the 1970s (Linz and Stepan 1996, 45). Others shifted toward post-totalitarianism. This meant a limited but weakly responsible social, economic, and institutional pluralism in which there was a second culture and parallel society, for example, Hungary 1982–88 (1996, 45).

As with any external shock, the loss of financing and ideological legitimacy affected countries differently. Those that had some prior functioning market sectors (e.g., Poland) responded better at one or more levels of fiscal management than those that did not (e.g., Belarus). The major distinguishing feature (other than the emergence of local reformist leaders) was the grip on local practices and institutions by the past Soviet system. "Other things being equal" (a quite meaningless phrase here!), the tighter and longer that grip, the more difficult it has been to reform public budgeting and financial management systems, for example, Poland and Estonia (less grip, more reform), Belarus and Moldova (strong grip, less reform). By contrast, Albania (tight grip but strong locally reformist leaders) has made several radical attempts at reform and is succeeding in breaking out of the cultural grip of a radically communist, autarkic country governed by a regime of state terror

Aggregate Fiscal Discipline

In order to develop a hard budget constraint that would produce sustainable growth and stability, estimates must flow from a realistic model of the macroeconomy. Macroeconomic projections leading to a hard budget constraint are needed to ensure fiscal sustainability (solid fiscal position, often indicated by a lower fiscal deficit/GDP ratio) and limited vulnerability to shocks (from short-term capital outflows flows, debt payment maturity structure, and the degree of dependence on Russia for oil—which in this region constitute major risks!). Economists must estimate rates of growth, employment, and inflation that are likely to result from internal and external factors, together with existing fiscal policies. To do this, they need valid and reliable data and a sound projection methodology. Both were missing in the early 1990s as economists (mainly from IMF) tried to get control of macroeconomic policy. Data and projection methods were needed for the: (1) real sector (production), (2) external sector (balance of payments), (3) fiscal account (balances and financing—this was the area of least data confidence), and (4) monetary sector (bank and monetary authority assets and liabilities—a big problem since whole countries were effectively large noncommercial sectors. If the actual values and rates of change for each variable were hard to estimate because of local peculiarities and lack of time-series data (there was really no macroeconomic history here yet!), rational economic and institutional policy responses to them were even harder to devise. Predictably, in the early 1990s "transition" period, economists made wildly unrealistic estimates (e.g., number of unemployed, amount of revenue collapse) that led to unrealistic policy recommendations (e.g., mass privatization, unrealistic exchange rates imposed on Russia, and inconsistent implementation sequences).

Following a difficult learning period by both country-level and IFI specialists, by the late 1990s, FSU/CEE countries began to get control of their macroeconomic policies. Employment increased as private investment increased. Country fiscal performance improved and inflation was reduced. Stability was increased and most of the indicators moved in the right direction. Social safety nets were in place to provide benefits to most of the displaced and unemployed populations affected by the transition. It was deemed that further structural reforms of strategic industrial sectors and deregulation of economies were needed to stimulate more growth. With a semblance of macroeconomic stability achieved, sustainable hard budget constraints could then be properly imposed.

After macroeconomic variables are under control, in order to maintain aggregate fiscal control, governments should be able to control planned expenditures consistent with the hard budget constraints. For example, Moldova achieved macroeconomic stabilization relatively quickly by the mid-1990s. This allowed them to move to the "first generation" reforms of trade, price, and exchange rate liberalization (World Bank 2004, 2). Their reform efforts since have been stop go with weak support for further deepening of reform and much state corruption. Moldova remains the poorest country in Europe and pays 45 percent of its revenues in debt service (2004, 5). In this context, it is not surprising that reformist leaders have little support among the citizenry. In Moldova, as elsewhere in this region, with weakening expenditure controls the benefits of a precise hard budget constraint are lost and macroeconomic gains diminished. By the late 1990s, many countries of this region had improved their fiscal data and projection methodologies, expenditure control institutions (e.g., accounting and reporting systems, computerized IFMS/ treasury single-account systems, internal control and audit systems, budget classification and coverage systems). These systemic reforms combined with better policies and control systems over such vital functions as purchasing, led to lowered levels of general government fiscal deficit (as a percentage of GDP). Vickland and Nieuwenhuijs, (2005, 95–103), for example, document the factors contributing to the success of installing an IFMS system in Bosnia and Herzegovina. With the major fiscal policy responses (such as installation of IFMS systems) to the external shock of transition over by the late 1990s, the subregions began to move in their own quite different directions.

In general, upper-middle-income countries (OECD) have registered better fiscal balances than low- and lower-middle-income groups between 1980 and 2005. FSU/CEE countries can also be separated into low- (e.g., Moldova), lower-middle-income (e.g., Bulgaria) and upper-middle-income groups (e.g., Hungary). Using this classification, a similar fiscal balance pattern holds over the same period (World Bank 2006a, 29). However, the fiscal data can be somewhat misleading because they may mask "reform fatigue." In some settings, earlier reforms either took place or were not needed because of higher incomes and growth in the first place. Moldova, for example, was a slow "first-generation" reformer due to the iron grip of its FSU institutional heritage. But, stimulated by hopes of EU accession and the opportunity to join Europe, reformers quickly gained momentum and its fiscal deficit dropped from -9.0 percent of GDP in 1993 to a primary surplus of 0.4 percent of GDP in 2003 (World Bank 2004, Annex A2).

By contrast, in the EU-8 (those acceding after the original seventeen EU members but before the most recent two) there have been problems of: upward deficit bias, overoptimistic revenue projections, creative accounting and one-off measures that may all be linked to institutional weaknesses (World Bank 2005, 27). Lack of reformed budgeting and financial management systems constitute one of the major institutional weaknesses—in particular the lack of obligation by MOFs and audit institutions to report regular macroeconomic information to the public in understandable terms. Even within the EU-8, some Baltic countries have pursued (along with Czech Republic and Slovakia) "ambitious fiscal consolidation" (meaning control of deficits to sustainable levels consistent with EU criteria), while countries such as Hungary and Poland "allowed deficits and debt to widen to worrisome levels in recent years" (World Bank 2005, 27). They have pursued "erratic fiscal policies and postponed politically difficult reform measures" (2005, 27). By 2006, the expansionary fiscal policies of even Baltic countries were eroding revenue overperformance and complicating inflation control (2006b, 15). As noted, countries that were more prudent in the late 1990s and early 2000s, such as Estonia, are now better positioned than others that were not (such as Latvia) to finance stimulus programs in order to deal with the 2007–08 recession and meltdown of the financial sector without generating excessive deficits or debt (at least for the next few years) (*Economist* 2009a, 57).

Hungary may be a negative bellwether of things to come along the aggregate fiscal discipline front (the Latin Americanization of Eastern Europe?). Its recent behavior has provided a warning to leaders of other EU–8 countries as well as those in the pre-accession and no-accession categories of the FSU/CEE region. By 2006, the underlying Hungarian fiscal position by most accounts was unsustainable. By 2009, it was the most indebted country in the region at nearly 100 percent of GDP (*Economist* 2009a, 57). With the largest state expenditures per capita in the region (if all off-budget state institutions were included, such as the railroad MAV), Hungary racked up the worst fiscal deficits in the region after 2004. In the context of deficit projections beyond 2008, it was clear that Hungary needed a fiscal austerity program. Including costs of pension reform and motor-way construction, the projected deficit for 2005 came to 7.4 percent of GDP. This figure excluded costs of leasing military aircraft (0.3 percent of GDP), planned postelection transfers from the state budget to the state railroad (MAV), and other pre-election expenditures. Including these, the estimated deficit for 2006 reached 10.1 percent of GDP (Higginson 2006, 7). By early 2007, it was evident that using the peculiar European System of Accounts (ESA-95)—consistent definition of the deficit, which still excluded all local government expenditures—the 2006 fiscal deficit was still 9.4 percent of GDP.

The ruling Socialists in Hungary recognized this emerging problem early on and began tax reform efforts in 2005 by lowering the top VAT and corporate income tax rates. When this effort led to increased deficit projections, the government reversed course and then increased taxes. In the run-up to the April 2006 elections, the opposition Fidesz Party campaigned on a no-reform platform, urging more state expenditures and lower taxes. This platform was, of course, wildly popular with the electorate. 2006 polls predicted that Fidesz would very likely win with this strategy, causing the Socialists to adopt a low-visibility strategy of silence until after the results. Reelected, the Socialists then admitted, off the record, that they withheld information on deterioration of the public finances. They then castigated themselves at a party meeting for not implementing a severe austerity program faster. Since the poor fiscal position of Hungary had been known and discussed in the media for several years before the election, an outsider would have to wonder if PM Gyurcsany's discourse was less an admission of lying than an attack of guilt mixed with political stupidity (Guess 2007). In any case, the do-nothing strategy proposed by the opposition (opposition movements here in the Ukraine, Moldova, and elsewhere) was also in fact a form of "lying" since it implied a sustainable future based on state benefits expenditures—jobs and payments. Clearly, more nationalist and populist opponents in the region seem to be lining up against fiscal reform and austerity packages. As the current (2008–09) economic crisis spreads rapidly to this region, more populist right-wing parties in CEE/FSU countries with unsustainable fiscal positions can be expected to push for more state expenditures and lower taxes, and to succeed at the ballot boxes.

It should not be imagined that only transitional countries in the FSU/CEE face these kinds of populist fiscal dilemmas. Regardless of the quality of fiscal information and the objective need to reform recommended by fiscal experts, local political leaders must act on the advice and information. And therein lies the problem. For example, EU member Italy now registers the third-largest public sector debt in the world (!) at 108 percent of GDP. Despite this level, it has been able to run near-balanced budgets or primary surpluses. In order to reduce the debt to EU criteria (60 percent of GDP), it would have to run primary surpluses (again, before interest payments) of 2–3 percent of GDP every year to prevent the debt/GDP ratio from rising. Opposition by ruling coalition Communist Party members to such an austerity program (i.e., cuts in government employment and pension and health spending) jeopardized Italy's investment grade sovereign rating (*Economist* 2006b, 33). Standard and Poor's rating agency nevertheless downgraded Italy to A+ from AA- because it concluded the prime minister would not be able to get a reform package through parliament with meaningful debt-reduction measures (Sylvers 2006). The downgrade raised borrowing costs—increasing recurrent debt servicing costs on government debt that will lead to more spending and fiscal deficits in the future. It also suggests that political support for fiscal reform is even lower in some of the older EU countries than the new EU-8.

To summarize, the macroeconomic policy trajectory of the three kinds of FSU/CEE countries (upper-middle, lower-middle, and low income) is affected powerfully by the growing contest between reformist regimes and populist regimes (i.e., parties and party coalitions). It can be said that the three types of FSU/CEE countries are moving at different speeds toward mass democratic systems. Those at the top of the league, such as Hungary, now face the most intense competition to sustain the fiscal reforms from those who want more distributive benefits and greater responsiveness from governmental institutions. The historical period may be similar to Latin America in the 1980s, when Bureaucratic-Authoritarian (BA) regimes (or complex, highly institutionalized corporatist, higher-income countries with nondemocratic, military regimes such as Brazil, Uruguay, and Argentina) were in transition to democratic regimes (Linz and Stepan 1996, 151). The rationale and benefits of further austerity programs will have to be demonstrated more clearly and persuasively by FSU/CEE regimes to their citizenry. Leaders in the poorest countries with high levels of external indebtedness, such as Moldova, will have the hardest time doing this. The era of trust out of desperation (the "transition" period) is over and officials will have to make their economic case more practically and with fewer textbook abstractions. If the MOF wants more "fiscal space" to cut inefficient state jobs and increase fees/taxes to reduce deficits, it will need to demonstrate that in neighboring Slovakia or Czech

Republic, for instance, expenditures for social safety net increased, private sector investment increased and absorbed 60 percent of those made redundant, and most were better off than before. Use of slogans like "more fiscal consolidation!" in front of an increasingly skeptical media and public is unlikely to persuade anyone! As in many cases with the communication of figures indicating fiscal problems, available options, and required responses, political courage and a glib tongue are probably more important than managerial expertise!

There are at least two data use models of relevance to fiscal reform in this region. The "rational choice" model seeks to increase the access of policy consumers to summary statistics and research. Policymakers, consistent with this perspective, receive, use, and understand this research and create better policy and outcomes. Conversely, the "deliberative democracy" model is also based on public access to microdata, summary statistics, and fiscal research. But the onus shifts to the public to comprehend the meaning of the data. That means that the media, think tanks, and civil society interpret the data and provide recommendations to the public indirectly. Officials take cues from this interactive learning process and implement policy (Weitzman et al. 2006, 387–88). In the FSU/CEE countries where democracy is consolidating fast, the public believes it should be the final arbiter of policymaking (i.e., the second model). The belief is growing that civil society should decide on the scope and severity of such programs as fiscal stabilization. Populist leaders call their deliberative approach "democratic fiscal reform" as juxtaposed to what they have termed "fascist fiscal reform" or the top-down austerity programs imposed on them by IFI economists and their local MOF colleagues. This is a direct consequence of a shift from "trustee" to "delegate" role for public officials in OECD countries. In FSU/CEE, it appears now that public officials may have been trustees for only a short period in the early 1990s.

Austerity packages are frequently necessary for stabilization and improvement of the public finances. Comparative research on implementation of fiscal austerity packages in the EU suggests that expenditure-based fiscal adjustments can be made "successfully" (meaning not just for economic growth but also reelection of the reformist government) if labor market reforms to increase labor supply can be implemented simultaneously. This worked, for example, in Ireland, Denmark, and the UK. Designing austerity packages to control public finance, increase labor supply, and allow space for tax reductions, has also worked in some EU countries (Annett 2006, 35) and those lessons can be transferred to FSU/CEE countries.

As is well known, not all austerity packages are designed or implemented properly. Bad ones can do more harm than good. In addition to the macroeconomic program "marketing" concerns noted previously, poorly implemented austerity packages to trim fiscal deficits may not be a good macroeconomic solution in that they can actually lower economic growth. World Bank research suggests that reduction in fiscal deficits (1980–2005) in low-, lower-middle-, and upper-middle-income countries has often been achieved by expenditure reductions rather than revenue enhancements. The expenditure reductions to achieve fiscal stabilization consisted mainly of cuts in public capital formation, that is, infrastructure investments in mostly non-health and educational areas (which had been protected) (2006a, 2). This was particularly true in Latin America where public investment dropped from 3 percent of GDP in 1980 to 1 percent of GDP in 2001. If depreciation is included, this means that the stock of public capital actually declined in Latin America as a response to fiscal stabilization efforts (2006a, 3). Though public financing of capital investment is not the only way to fund productive investment, it is the major means in most countries with limited capital markets and low capacities to manage public-private partnerships, concessions, or even to lease or purchase capital without major corruption. Nor does it mean that public investments, contracted properly and constructed without corruption, were actually needed in the first place (capital planning is often an insider process that excludes most of the public). Despite these reservations, stabilization efforts often translate into adjustments that reduce capital expenditures. The stabilization programs may impede economic growth, while perpetuating current services delivery problems (because salaries and public administration structures remain about the same).

Allocation to Meet Planned Needs

Countries within the FSU/CEE region vary widely in their capacities to achieve "allocative efficiency." This kind of efficiency means that they can establish priorities within their budgets. Planned budgets reflect resources to be distributed according to the government's priorities and potential program effectiveness. Budgets will also reveal any shifts in resources from old to new priorities (Kasso 2006). The capacity of governments in this region to do this depends on: (1) the proper assignment of intergovernmental roles and responsibilities (i.e., authority and responsibility are matched), and (2) substantive budgeting systems that allocate resources based on need and effectiveness criteria (usually through some form of "targeting" system that monitors performance via benchmarks) (see Morse and Struyk 2006, 85–120). In addition, capacity depends on macroeconomic stability since without it revenues will fluctuate wildly. Macroeconomic instability prevents accurate revenue and expenditure forecasting. For instance, MOF releases to ministries and local governments are typically disrupted in order to try and maintain a semblance of fiscal balance and control. Under these conditions, core services such as health, education, and transport suffer badly. Program and service managers need fiscal stability—meaning budget receipts received as planned and expenditure variation kept within the range expected for the fiscal year.

Substantial fiscal management achievements have been made in all five regional sub-areas. Allocative efficiency has increased largely through installation and use of performance-based budgeting systems mainly at the subnational level. With the exception of Central Asia, which remains very poor in most parts and underserved by services and programs, allocative efficiencies are increasingly evident. In large part, they have been attained because of the institutional and cultural features noted above—high quantitative and statistical skill levels, and general tendencies to work hard where financial and nonfinancial incentives are made clear. In most cases, finance ministries, and regional/local government finance offices have made good use of the technical assistance and training received from overseas assistance programs funded by such donors as IMF, World Bank, USAID, Asian Development Bank, and British DFID.

Nonetheless, three constraints to achieving successful allocative efficiency in this region should be noted:

CULTURE OF PHYSICAL NORMS STILL ACTIVE FOR EXPENDITURE PLANNING

Prior to the transition in the early 1990s, priorities for current services and capital investment were established nationally by the central government. After the transition, resources for operations and refurbishment of hospitals in Lviv, Ukraine, for example, were planned by the MOH, Ministry of Economy, and MOF with some inputs by local officials. As noted, resource plans for health and education services were largely determined by physical norms. Capital investment followed a five-year plan with major inputs from engineers in the Ministry of Construction.. Following the transition, much of the construction became the responsibility of "private" state firms. Former ministry employees then worked for "outsourced" firms on state contracts, and had substantial political influence on the determination of capital investment priorities. This was true to a greater or lesser extent throughout the region.

Efforts have been made to replace norm-based allocations with needs-based allocations for both current programs and capital investments. For example, from 2002 to 2004, technical assistance efforts financed by USAID for Romanian cities produced important successes in the modernization of their capital planning and budgeting processes (Guess and Todor 2005). The new systems allowed them to establish capital priorities (linked to future current service expenditure requirements in a multiyear planning framework). In many medium-sized Romanian cities, the twelve-step process noted below in Table 5.3 continues to produce a full list of approved projects in rank-order, to be matched against funds available from current financing as well as borrowing. The process of CIP development thus began by producing a ranked list of cost-beneficial projects. This was not the final capital program. Nor was is it actually a capital budget. As in the case of many capital budgeting systems (e.g., in the U.S. government), the lists developed were sector-specific and did not compare projects in different sectors with each other or indicate objectively which ones should be approved. Local sectoral priorities still had to be inserted into the project approval process.

Moreover, using benefit-cost ratios alone, neither officials nor citizens could compare the benefits, for example, of educated students and productive farmers with those of hospital patients receiving quality health care. Efforts to allocate funds by function or sector ran up against the methodological problem of inability to compare the values of different individual utility preferences for different services. Thus, for Romania a method had to be used to approximate the comparative benefits of different projects for dissimilar groups. The ranking system used by many OECD cities tries to adapt economic interpersonal utility benefit models and marginal productivity curves to suit administrative needs. Consistent with decision requirements and methodological limitations, to develop a capital program, cities (as well as central governments) in the FSU/CEE region needed to develop a rational system of transparent project ranking. Before projects were prepared and reviewed, the ranking system had to be agreed upon by multiple stakeholders, including citizens groups, community watchdog organizations, producers, and consumers (Vogt 2004; Calia 2001).

Romanian cities with effective capital planning and budgeting systems now ensure that local stakeholders agree on a weighted ranking system that incorporates multiple values and criteria. This is the most difficult part of the entire capital planning and budgeting process—here and elsewhere in the world! But, in developing and transitional countries, personal, partisan, and institutional problems often combine more viciously to work against modernization of local capital budgeting and planning processes. Some OECD cities use single-standard systems, and employ benefit-cost ratios. The obvious problem with this approach is how to use such ratios to compare the worth of projects in different sectors such as health and transportation? For this reason, more OECD cities use "value" categories, such as *urgent* (danger to health), *desirable* (to replace obsolete facilities), or *deferrable* (duplicates other projects) to classify and select projects for capital financing. But the problem with this approach is how to find a rational basis to achieve consensus on these categories among the many community groups. Defining agreeable criteria for such categories as "desirable" projects often wastes substantial amounts of time and political capital.

Thus, technical assistance to Romania focused on institutionalization of the multiple criteria approach used by most cities in OECD countries. This allowed balancing of competing needs and efficiency-welfare values, such as economic worth, existing occupancy or user rates (as measures of need), fiscal and economic impact, health, safety effects, and environmental costs/benefits. As a successful example of technical assistance in fiscal reform, program values and priorities are

TABLE 5.3. Elements of a Successful Capital Programming,
Financing, and Implementation System

1. Determine organizational responsibility structure
2. Establish capital policies
3. Develop realistic calendar and useful forms
4. Assess capital needs: inventory
5. Analyze city financial capacity
6. Prepare project requests
7. Review project requests
8. Rank project requests
9. Evaluate financing options
10. Draft capital program (CIP) and budget documents
11. Adopt the capital program and budget
12. Implement and monitor the capital budget

now made explicit and quantified. Romanian city officials, working with community stakeholders, now propose their own criteria (e.g., level of public supporting services required; availability of cost sharing; and forecasted demand), weights for each criteria (i.e., facilities with poor existing conditions should receive higher weights than those in better condition), and scores from which to determine project rankings (Calia 2001). The multiyear integrated capital–current services framework has the strategic value in allowing more transparent cutbacks of projects in times of revenue shortfalls—or budget add-ons in time of buoyant revenues. While agreement on criteria and weights can be a lengthy and contentious process even before projects are inserted for overall scoring, as noted many OECD country cities use this approach. More importantly, it has proved successful in Romania since 2004 and we believe can be transferred to other countries of the region.

The advantage of formal capital planning/budgeting systems for priority setting is their transparency. If developed properly, they combine strategic plans and budgets in one document and one process. Ranked projects can be justified to voters as having been financed with sustainable city finances and tax/fee levels in mind—up to a clear cutoff point based on available resources. Should funding shortfalls occur (as is common), with clear policy priorities established during the process, elected officials need only move up the list and shorten the capital budget. This is a major advantage over simple, across-the-board cutting methods used in many places in the FSU/CEE region in capital investment in response to austerity/stabilization programs. Traditionally, opaque capital investment planning systems permitted substantial political maneuvering to get favored projects on the list of financed projects. This is now harder to do under reformed systems used by Romanian cities. Modern multiyear capital budgeting systems also permit rational shifts of policy priorities. Should a city want to shift its main project portfolio in the coming budget year from environment to transport (i.e., to roads, bridges, and trams), it could either reopen the ranking process in order to publicly determine the best mix of transport and environmental projects with less funding, or, it could leave the rankings as they were and replace educational projects, for instance, with a slate of environmental projects. Either way, the system allows for transparent ranking and financing. Civil society "budget watchdog" groups can assess results through establishment of performance benchmarks. Internal and external audit units can assess whether projects selected are consistent with city priorities and the media can tell immediately if some projects appear at the top of the list when they were obviously missing before (see Ott 2006).

At the national level, service and investment priority systems have been designed, installed and driven mostly by donor-funded fiscal reform projects. For example, in this region, British DFID has been installing medium-term expenditure frameworks (MTEFs) in a number of countries, such as Armenia and Ukraine. As indicated in chapter 3, this is a multiyear budget priority-setting tool that allows calculation of downstream effects of current revenue and expenditure trends. The ability to track the progress of capital projects from planning (as a new start or rehabilitation effort), completion of construction, to their final transfer onto the current budget for O&M financing and debt service, is a critical necessity for any kind of budgeting system. The MTEF allows a comprehensive picture of fiscal obligations and available resources for at least current items over a three-to-five-year planning period There is no technical reason not to include capital items in the MTEF framework and integrate them with current expenditures. Each year, the fiscal plan for a typical MTEF is rolled forward to account for changes in priority, revenue/expenditure estimates, and changes in the macroeconomic environment. World Bank has financed public investment planning (PIP) systems in such countries as Kyrgyzstan. PIPs are similar to MTEFs but focus only on capital plans for the national government as well as those local projects financed by central ministry transfers, for example, hospitals and airports. MTEFs can also be used to target expenditures to functional sectors or income-based beneficiaries. Asian Development Bank (ADB), for instance, has financed installation of poverty-budgeting systems in several countries, including Kazakhstan (Guess 2001). These were designed to develop priorities and target resources for pro-poor projects consistent with country *poverty reduction strategy papers* (PRSPs) in order to deal with the important problem of rural poverty.

In addition, international donors have initiated and funded several forms of results-based budgeting systems at the national and/or local levels in most countries of this region. These may take the form of program budgeting (U.S. Treasury Romania Program), program-performance budgets (World Bank, USAID), and integrated financial management systems that include flexible charts of accounts. The latter can be used to measure the activity and service costs of budget allocations. None of these systems address comprehensively the need to match policy priorities with optimal means of attaining them, that is, the institutional issue of how to organize efficient expenditures and subsidies that reach their intended targets. Program budgeting reforms should do this but most systems implemented consist only of the addition of new program structures. In Hungary, according to Tonko (2007, 107), three cities implemented program budgeting systems via new documents and databases. The documents served the standard fiscal objectives of operations guide, planning tool, communications device and policy statement. The major implementation improvements consisted of better workplans, improved systemic thinking, better decision making, and ease of fiscal monitoring (2007, 125). But there is, so far, little evidence that budget allocations have dramatically changed in response to or based on program budgeting analyses. To improve matters further, the system might be deepened with a zero-based (ZBB) type system that would allows line managers to analyze the costs and performance consequences of different expenditure options in order to attain their program objectives. Since more than one organizational unit is normally involved in program delivery, ZBB allowed for multiorganizational "decision units," mostly at the U.S. state and local level. This system allows managers to indicate to their staff superiors and to legislators whether program objectives can be attained under conditions of existing, reduced, or expansion budgets. ZBB instructions typically use realistic bases of -50 percent, -85 percent, no changes from past year, and +25 percent instead of the magic "zero" base calculation. ZBB has not been installed anywhere in this region and, because of calculation complexity and legislative resistance, remains largely an unimplemented reform in most OECD countries as well. In the United States, the organic practices of ZBB still exist under other names, for instance, "results-oriented budgeting" (Guess 1988). But ZBB has largely been superseded by other fiscal reforms.

MISMATCHED FISCAL AUTHORITY–MANAGEMENT RESPONSIBILITY ROLES

Devolution of functional responsibilities requires both fiscal resources and the appropriate level of management discretion to use them. In the Soviet era, both were centralized and the system was relatively simple. With scarce resources and the need to finance diverse services for an increasingly mobile population, roles have to be defined more consistently with need. So far, this has happened in only a few of the EU-8 countries. Other regions of the FSU/CEE region still maintain a rigid bureaucratic centralization that impedes service delivery and program performance. Nevertheless, with international donors pushing for reformed systems to target funds more precisely to needs, important achievements have been made in the social services area.

For example, the role of educational financing has been assigned to local governments in the EU-8. This is the largest item of expenditure in most local budgets in EU-8 countries and in many other countries of the FSU/CEE region. The establishment of educational management norms, such as teaching loads, salary schedules, and rules for recruitment/ promotion remain national functions—even though school directors are appointed locally (World Bank 2005, 63). By contrast, responsibility for health care management was assigned to local governments, without the authority to raise financial resources (which remained centrally funded or through compulsory health care insurance programs). In both education and health program areas, capital investment has been centrally funded with local input. This mismatched set of role assignments still impedes local capacity to allocate resources in order to achieve planned priorities. To the extent that they are allocated properly, performance norms and other quasi-effectiveness indicators serve to provide funds to schools and clinics for construction, rehabilitation, and repair. Where countries have installed local capital planning and budgeting systems and allowed local governments to finance capital partially by debt (i.e., Romania), results have been better. The third area of social services, social assistance, remains a centrally funded program with some local discretion to determine eligibility criteria and to allocate funds accordingly (2005, 64).

BUREAUCRATIC CONSTRAINTS TO SHIFT OF FUNDS FROM LOW TO HIGH PRIORITY

Given the public law/civil law constraint on public administration noted above, managerial discretion to shift resources is limited. Discretion to shift funds through transfer or reprogramming of current service budget items is governed by restrictive laws and subsidiary regulations. So far, this is not New Public Management territory! Discretion of officials to eliminate, modify, or add capital investment projects is also quite restricted—often by signed construction contracts that impose penalties if any of this is done. Thus, local government and ministry line managers are restricted by poor assignment of intergovernmental roles and by narrow limits on their discretion to transfer funds during budget implementation.

Institutional and legal constraints on shifting funds during budget execution (within the norms of normal expenditure variance reporting) affect the capacity to manage services effectively (the operational level to be discussed below). At the strategic or policy level, funds are allocated to health, education, transport, and social assistance from overhead, defense, and other categories. Governments in the FSU/CEE region have made these policy choices consistent with some notion of local or national preferences. However, providing sustainable fiscal space to finance these policy priorities through such means as cutting the size of the state, downsizing ministries, or requiring internal operating efficiencies have been made in only a few countries of this region. Most countries have not reformed their state organizational structure or the functioning of their public administrations. Problems of bloated size, weak and corrupt contracting systems, ineffectual control systems, and inflexible and unresponsive program and service delivery institutions remain throughout the region. The major response has been

to shift functional responsibilities to the local governments often without sufficient funding.

Nevertheless, systemic changes have been made in the broad and financially
important area of social services to increase efficiency and effectiveness. Similar in
scope and fiscal importance to those of Latin America, these services absorb on
average of 60 to 70 percent of FSU/CEE national budgets. Many analysts view
Latin America as the major comparative example for CEE/FSU budget systems
reform precisely for this structural reason. The *horizontal* shift in social services
spending has been intersectoral, from one function such as health to another, such
as environment, based on explicit changes in priorities. This policy shift has been
relatively smooth across the region. The major country differences have been in
the technical capacity to assess social welfare needs, measure performance, and
reallocate funds based on them, rather than to allocate based on donor priority or
local partisan political preferences. Not surprisingly, countries in the EU-8 seem
more adept at these tasks than Central Asian or Southeastern Eastern Europe
(SEE). The *vertical* shift of priority has been decentralization of functional responsibilities (along with substantial revenues to finance them) down to lower tier
governments from the center. This shift has been motivated by democratic pressure to consolidate post-transition political reforms, and by those who recognize
that local needs can best be met by locally accountable officials for most services.

As noted, pre-transition local governments derived revenues from the enterprise profits of firms located within their boundaries or from revenues designated
to local units from the center. This was based entirely on the socialist administrative system, with no real competition or profits in the Western sense. In the post-
transition period, the fiscal federalism model accepted in the West was used to
assign expenditure responsibility for stabilization and distribution functions to the
center, and to assign responsibility for allocation and regulation to the lower tiers
(World Bank 2005, 59). This functional definition still holds with social assistance
largely a centrally financed and managed function and social services as local programs. Within this general model, modifications have been made on the basis of
local practice. As noted, some EU-8 countries assigned educational financing to
local units and restricted their management. For example, in Poland, the local
share of educational financing is 72 percent. Conversely, health sector financing
remained largely at the center (along with insurance schemes) and operational
management was decentralized (2005,63). In Czech Republic, the local financing
share for health is only 2 percent (2005, 64).

Does more funding mean greater performance results? Often not. While
minimum funding is needed for social services, it is often discovered that better
personnel and incentives for their advancement matter more than financing for
salaries or technology aids. Again, Latin American policy examples are useful for
this region. In Chile, secondary school teachers already make salaries comparable
to industrial countries, for example, but student performance remains low (below

Argentina and Mexico, which have low teacher pay). Total spending on education is 7.3 percent of GDP (also similar to industrial country levels). The need is to improve teacher recruitment and allow for at least some of the salary to be based on performance (*Economist* 2000c, 60). As discovered in other Latin American (and U.S.) contexts, this policy reform often meets resistance from teaching unions—which they often claim converts a legal obligation to pay salaries to a conditional obligation based on an extraneous condition: performance (!).

An important area of post-transition institutional and budgetary confusion is capital budgeting and financing. This is important because any service, for example, education, health, or transport, ultimately depends on a mix of recurrent (e.g., salaries, routine maintenance) and capital (e.g., equipment, infrastructure, and rehabilitation) to achieve results. In the fiscal accounts, current and capital expenses are separated and this leads to institutional separation that affects budget planning and implementation. Capital investments were traditionally provided by the central government because most local units lacked revenues or capacities to manage construction projects and place them afterward on their current budgets. Investments were all part of the "material product" system that remained the responsibility of the Communist Party and the central government apparatus. As indicated, moving away from this system has been slow in the transition period. Whenever the word *planning* is mentioned by consultants, host country officials perk up, thinking it is the good old days again. But Western "planning" has to do (or should have!) with forecasted program or project options constrained by scarce resources that, unless economically justifiable, should be used elsewhere (i.e., planning constrained by opportunity cost). Responsibilities for service and program provision remain institutionally fragmented across MOFs and ministries of construction/public works. They have separate pots of money in budgeting and typically engage in separate planning processes. At the local level, with greater fiscal and management responsibilities, the two types of expenditure processes have been integrated in parts of the FSU/CEE. In the capital investment area, installation of new CIP processes in Romanian cities, as noted above and in Table 5.3, has allowed the transparency and flexibility to rid the system of some of its worst projects and to save funds.

One of the advantages of decentralized, autonomous local governments is that they can plan and finance their own infrastructure and capital needs. Many local governments in the FSU/CEE region still cannot do this—because of legal restrictions on borrowing (see Swianiewicz 2004) or lack of technical capacity. To plan and manage capital programs, they need capital budgeting processes that rigorously evaluate projects that will create assets (those which meet useful life standards of one to two years and cost threshold minimums), such as roads, public transport, water and sewer systems, solid waste, sanitation facilities, and projects for local economic development. Capital planning and budgeting "institutions" provide the rules of the game and they are critical to the success of local government programs. For best results, there needs to be a lead organization with responsibilities for financing, construction, and project management (even if some of these are performed by private contractors). Program results in any budgetary function, whether education, health, transport, or agriculture, depend upon the judicious allocation of resources to salaries (current) and to the construction and maintenance of the infrastructure (capital). Institutional requirements include the efficiency of organizational processes; the efficacy of regulatory rules and systems; clear definition of management roles; and linkage of financial management processes and rules to service and program results. Such institutions are all critical to planning, financing, and implementing local capital programs (Burki and Perry 1998). Based on training and technical assistance experiences overseas, particularly in Central and Eastern Europe, there are twelve essential steps for the development of capital planning and budgeting systems (Guess and Todor 2005 and Table 5.3). Where any of them are missing, especially the right institutions and project ranking process, problems can occur.

For example, the sixth step is to have a system for evaluating projects—to weed out the bad ones and rank up the good ones. Having the right capital budgeting and planning process may not be sufficient to shift funds from low to high priority, but they are certainly necessary. A good capital improvements process may not singularly be able to get rid of large "white elephant" projects, such as highways to be constructed with the commonly used panacea: public-private partnerships or "PPP"s. But, they can often eliminate small white elephants from the queue. The problem for capital budget planning and financing is that many capital projects are served up as essentially free goods, to be paid for by donor grants or via magic financing techniques that will cost city or national governments nothing.

For, once a term like "PPP" is used, many forget that while public investments involve large upfront costs that are reported in the fiscal accounts as deficit and debt obligations, many of the long-term fiscal effects of PPPs can be hidden. The effect on future fiscal position is often hidden from public view. In Hungary, as noted, this might be called "lying." As mature budget analysts, we might say that proponents are simply "expanding the truth," and that it is our obligation to recognize their little practices, habits and innocent accounting oversights. It is well known that PPPs can create unreported contingent liabilities in the form of guarantees to cover future losses of concessionaires, or "availability payments" that must be made if the government is the sole purchaser of the output. These obligations may mean the "private" debt is the same size as that incurred had public finance been used (World Bank 2005,138). Use of dodgy financing techniques can thus vitiate the best capital planning and financing systems, if no one is there to catch their misuse.

Good capital project evaluation systems can eliminate small white elephants from the queue—and the net result is a lot of savings that can be used for other community projects. For example, in 2002, the Iasi (Romania) County Council decided that a new airport cargo terminal would be useful for local economic development. They drafted a proposal to EC Phare (aka Euro AID) which was correctly rejected on economic benefit grounds. They then turned to local public funding and had it placed in the queue for local capital financing. Since there was no real CIP process in Iasi, this was easy for them to do. The airport was managed by a separate county department staffed by aviation professionals (a pilot and a former aviation mechanic). Both opposed the project as a waste of money. They had noted to county council officials without success for several years, that without strengthening the depth of the concrete runway (PCN factor), the new and larger cargo planes would sink in the mud. The airport lacked current funds to deal with major flying hazards, such as the elimination of the packs of stray dogs that roamed around scavenging for food. Many dogs had been hit by landing planes (especially at night), but to date there had still been no aircraft accidents. There was also a danger that unless the runway was strengthened (not necessarily lengthened), the investment in the existing relatively new airport terminal would be wasted—as it would have to close down. These systemic factors had been ignored repeatedly by the council in its quest for a new symbol of modern urban development. It was said repeatedly their model was Arad (in western Romania), where a new cargo terminal had been constructed the previous year. They ignored the fact that neither the expected traffic nor development had been yet generated by that terminal.

In 2003, a team of local government technical assistants worked with Iasi officials to design and install a new capital improvements process (CIP) that required economic evaluation and ranking by formal criteria before financing would become available. Even after ranking, financing would become available only to the level of the project ranking. Using this system, and comparing this project with others proposed in other functional areas based on local economic development priorities, the cargo terminal ranked somewhere near the bottom of the list. It should be added that the project did not finally receive public funding from the Iasi budget. Iasi officials then claimed to the media that the cargo project had been hijacked by outside consultants and indicated that they remained committed to obtaining a grant from EU for the project. This was unlikely and it didn't happen. As luck would have it, since Romania joined the EU in 2007, it was no longer eligible for pre-accession funding!

Everyone is in favor of better analysis and decision processes with which to allocate funds more professionally. In this regard, FSU/CEE professionals are no different than their counterparts in such regions as Latin America. For capital budgeting and financing, the more difficult question is, How to design the process and to sequence their installation? Which of the twelve steps or institutional systems indicated in Table 5.3 should be installed first? They all cannot be installed at once. Which are most important for transitional countries? Obviously, because of resource and absorptive capacity constraints in most countries (in this region or elsewhere), it is impossible to do everything at once. Based on relevant overseas experience, implementation of a capital programming and budgeting system should likely follow this four-step sequence (Guess and Todor 2005):

1. Cities should first fix the organizational and policy framework. Cities need to clarify planning and implementation responsibilities and eliminate negative institutional redundancies, such as excessive approval steps that produce corruption opportunities and drive up project costs. There has to be a lead organization. Cities should perform reviews of core transactions in capital planning, such as project approvals and contracting, to ensure that these processes are performed as efficiently and with as few redundant steps as possible.

2. Professional management skills need to be improved. Managers should have the skills (as well as the authority) to analyze project proposals and develop weighting and scoring matrices from which to develop overall capital programs.

3. Capital plans and budgets should be integrated with the current budget process in a multiyear framework. This allows the finance department to oversee planning of the capital program and to ensure that financing is available for future years to cover maintenance and debt service requirements (Schiavo-Campo and Tommasi 1999).

4. Cities need to improve their overall practices of municipal budgeting and financing. This means more than just installation of computerized accrual accounting and integrated procurement and budgeting systems. Officials need to know how to operate and modify such systems to meet their future needs. They also need to know how to apply innovative options for project financing, such as leasing, tax increment districts, and note/ bond relationships with commercial banks. To do this requires more flexible administrative operating and budget management rules. More flexible rules without strong internal controls and audit can lead to waste and corruption. Thus, stronger municipal budgeting should focus on internal control systems and audit units and then argue for the kind of New Public Management (NPM) type incentives that work well in Commonwealth countries.

After expenditure responsibilities are properly assigned and controls put in place, it is probably safe to assign the funds needed to achieve functional objectives. Much of the funding flows directly from the state budget; other funds flow through ministries and their local units. A difficult problem for governments in the FSU/CEE region has been the degree of regional differences and the high poverty levels exposed by the collapse of the Moscow-driven financing system.

This is especially true in rural Central Asia and is comparable to rural Andean and Central American countries. Thus, on the revenue side, post-transition governments have attempted to provide subsidies to make up for the large regional economic differences. The objective has been to provide an equal level of relevant service spending (to comply with assigned and legislated local tasks) in all jurisdictions. The major equalization vehicle is to develop mechanisms to share some or all of personal income tax revenues with local governments. For example, Latvia shares 94 percent of its PIT with local units. There are various equalization formulae (World Bank 2005, 67), but the general idea is to distribute some or all of PIT collections on an origin basis and provide an additional subsidy using adjustment factors (e.g., population plus people over 65, number of children, etc.). In this fashion, the revenues of poorer jurisdictions are supplemented by those derived from the formula. The formulae work well in more advanced EU-8 countries and less well in Southeastern Eastern Europe and Central Asia where differences are much greater between poor and rich regions. The point is that CEE/FSU countries are making major efforts to adjust for revenue differences by transparently and flexibly shifting resources. They have also been creative in developing revenue generation techniques for "informal sectors" where most of the population is too poor to pay PIT or even fees and service needs are high.

EFFICIENT AND EFFECTIVE MANAGEMENT OF SERVICE OPERATIONS

At the ground level, the citizenry of the FSU/CEE region care mostly about their services—transit, health, roads, water/sewer, and education. If these are not delivered effectively, they get mad. For policymakers, the current tendency is to offload these responsibilities from central to local governments, provide them minimum funds, and tackle larger matters. This sounds good, as it can be called decentralization; but in practice responsibilities and mandates without money result in poor services, which encourages backlash against both local officials and the important concept of democratic decentralization. But for national-level officials larger matters of maintaining fiscal discipline and allocating resources to sectors properly also require hard choices. As noted, many of these are now stalled in dysfunctional partisan politics. For example, the operations and maintenance costs of capital investment are rarely provided for in national PIPs or capital budgets—other than on paper. There is no hard budget constraint imposed by the maintenance requirement through multiyear expenditure planning frameworks—they are advisory only. Where the maintenance requirements have been devolved to local governments, local governments (logically) spend for higher priority needs such as salaries, and officials rarely consider O&M important—unless a bridge collapses or a school roof caves in, generating a public outcry and a single maintenance repair response. Either local governments lack the funds, do not want to pay for repairs over salaries, or calculate that undermaintenance will lead to replacement by national governments anyway. Viewing these motives, it is clear that FSU/CEE local government officials differ little from their U.S. or European counterparts.

In 2006, the FSU/CEE region was described as an economic success but a "remarkable political failure" (*Economist* 2006f, 13). Throughout the region, there is not one united, modernizing government. For example, it is said that Slovakia may have the sleaziest and nastiest coalition of political parties running the country—they seem to be united only by their common hatred of Hungarians. Politicized civil services and tight links between government and business have encouraged rot to set in. The regimes are described as "thuggish," "corrupt," and "squabbling." The gulf between political elites and the people seems to be growing. The popular perception is of "bossy bureaucrats" and "snooty politicians" (*Economist* 2006g, 34) driving black Mercedes and overeating at posh restaurants. The net result is official resistance to fiscal and macroeconomic stabilization reforms because imposition of higher taxes, cutting state jobs, and selling state firms puts them in jeopardy with the voters. Fiscal policy non-decision making where structural reforms are still needed leads to lower economic growth and will worsen the state of public finances. Increased discontent and populism are forming a vicious circle that is both causing economic failure and worsening it (2006g, 34).

Needed are bold reformist governments in the FSU/CEE region. The drive for democratic consolidation and fiscal reform has apparently halted at parliament. EU countries have not provided solid examples of fiscal prudence for their CEE/FSU counterparts. Countries such as Italy have been downgraded by rating agencies for their level of debt (at 108 percent of GDP, the third highest in the world) and failure to execute reforms of the deteriorating public finances. In Italy, the debt ratio came in this high, even with gimmicks that classified large amount of debt (pension payments) as cash revenues. Roughly $6.7 billion in such payments were used to claim an increase in revenues (*Economist* 2006d, 36) and therefore a reduction in the annual fiscal deficits that accumulate into long-term debt. All this really means higher borrowing costs, more debt service and more current expenditures (with probably higher fiscal deficits in the future) (Sylvers 2006). The need is for reformist elected leaders that have the courage to take the risks of linking strategic policy priorities with service and operational needs within a market economy. Good governance requires regimes that take resource planning and allocation seriously and support budget and financial management reforms.

Technical accounting and budgeting issues require a response at the same level. Too often in this region, the debate shifts to quite different levels of abstraction and problem definition—definition and resolution of practical service problems quickly degenerate into ideological battles. Public complaints tend not to be translated by the policy processes into actionable problem definitions and practical policy responses. Owing perhaps to the civil/public law tradition, it has been difficult to translate ideological concerns through coalition governments (that almost reward lack of courage or indecisiveness) into practicalities. When problems are defined, they are often misinterpreted or mistranslated. For example, program budgeting was recently proposed as a policy response to the need for fiscal austerity in Georgia; and a thirty-five-hour work week was proposed as a policy solution to high French youth unemployment.

As noted, reforms have been made and funds shifted to social services based on real needs. Successful decentralization programs (e.g., Romania) and provision of fiscal autonomy in many countries of this region means that officials must be more responsive, and produce real results in education and health spending, since voters know that (unlike before) these officials are now actually accountable. For services such as urban transport, FSU/CEE city officials have often been at a relative loss on what to do or how to do it. Central government funding for these massive metropolitan systems has dried up. The well-functioning and multi-modal systems of the Soviet era are now falling apart and unable to keep up demand in face of competition from private cars and minibuses. There was no transparent and rational subsidy system in the Soviet era, such as the multiprogram U.S. system that covers public transit operating costs from the federal level and allows local units to impose fiscal constraints on operating systems. This keeps fares, service performance, transit operations, and transit system employment in line in most U.S. cities. Raising fares for a largely poor population reduces transit demand, encourages auto ownership, and generates revenues that rarely cover even 50 percent of operating costs—let alone capital replacement costs. Officials in many CEE/FSU cities remain wedded to the idea of public monopoly provision of transit and they tend to view the problem and the solution as public transit. In this mindset, private alternatives whether minibuses, contracted routes, or private cars become threats to their livelihood. Trams, trolley-buses, and subways are still run by city enterprises. This is true in cities as diverse as Chisinau, Moldova (Dumitru and Mihai 2005, 14), and Yerevan, Armenia (Arakelyan 2005, 18). Needed is a new framework for effective service delivery of most services. For urban transport, it has to include multi-stakeholder public and private transport planning and various financing schemes (e.g., value capture through improvement districts or tax increment financing assessment districts or catchment areas). The new policy framework for transit should include: capital planning, route scheduling, transit system maintenance, monitoring of system condition for safety and comfort, capital financing, and fare policies.

FSU/CEE cities have already started to develop new planning and service delivery frameworks and financing systems. Some cities in the region have broken the historic public monopoly enjoyed by city enterprises and moved toward integration of alternative providers. For example, Warsaw, Belgrade, and Budapest began three-stage transformations of their systems in the mid-1990s. With some variation in practice by each city transit system, first, they transformed city/state enterprises into one or more joint stock companies subject to commercial law. This allowed the city to produce a contract with a new company that included remuneration, responsibilities, performance benchmarks, positive and negative incentives, and cancellation. Second, the cities tendered contracts to private and joint stock operators for particular parts of their network—specific routes. Depending on the outcome of the tender, the public-owned part often began to disappear. Third, they passed revenue risks to the operators—although state guarantees were still possible for purchase of equipment in some cases. The three-stage approach worked well for buses but had to be more complicated to deal with trams and trolley-buses. For those modes, management contracts are now used and evolved into long-term concessions with pubic retention of infrastructure ownership (Mitric 2003, 18).

The three-stage approach seems to work best where the transit system did not deteriorate too badly after the transition (e.g., Budapest but not Yerevan). In the case of cities such as Yerevan, the governance capacity of the city and city enterprises to manage contracts may need to be reconstructed (or perhaps constructed!) first before moving toward management contracts and concessions. Service models also exist from Europe and North America that are catching the attention of FSU/CEE policymakers. For example, Vancouver includes private stakeholders in land use and transportation planning for the metropolitan region. Delivery is the responsibility of one authority (Translink), which is at the forefront of experimentation with models to infuse competition and market forces into planning, financing, and delivery of services. Vancouver has partly shifted from the traditional model of public financing of operating deficits and infrastructure debt to procurement of transit services through contracting (similar to Belgrade and Warsaw) and use of PPPs and private concessions for capital financing (Siemiatycki, cited in Guess 2008). Based on high customer satisfaction with services, this approach seems to be working.

For all services, not just transit, financial management methods and systems have improved. Operations have improved for many services based on introduction of modern management systems that allow funds to be shifted according to targets and results. After the transition, management experts from the West descended on this region. Some had language skills from their family heritage; most did not. Few had in-country experience, and most wanted simply to transfer what they thought had worked in their own countries. Examples of this phenomenon include the proffering of program budgeting as a miracle of budget reform and the introduction of performance indicators and targets. The defects of the former have been much noted. The latter problem centered on introduction of top-down target regimes from countries such as the UK. They were also introduced from the United States, but mostly from the local level, that is, set by local authorities whose officials had discretion to change both targets and resource patterns. From the UK, the targets often tied managers' hands, especially in the health area (*Economist* 2006c, 39). The performance measurement problem was threefold. First, local health officials lacked discretion to actually manage services to achieve the targets. Second, they were held responsible for targets in a narrow evaluative framework that stressed efficiency and cost. In health as in most services, there is often a tradeoff (with unintended consequences in between) between quality and cost. Reduction of hospital waiting times might increase bed occupancy rates, which make MRSA infections more likely to spread (2006c, 39). This tradeoff is often based on experience with particular services and often does not fit neatly into logical frameworks developed by generalist efficiency experts.

Third, international consultants often assumed the intergovernmental assignment of responsibilities in FSU/CEE countries was about the same as in the UK or other European countries—and if they weren't they could be easily changed by passing a law. They often failed to note that the UK was a rather centralized, unitary government and still is. FSU/CEE countries want to move to multi-tier federal systems, such as Poland. The mismatch of managerial and financial authority in service delivery continues to plague performance and it is clear that operational authority needs to be decentralized in most cases and better norms developed and enforced from the center. That is easier said than done.

One solution (in Europe as well as this region) is more intelligent monitoring and evaluation systems. Rating systems need to be based on a few, sound indicators of quality that encompass financial as well as service performance. This allows a more comprehensive response by technical professionals who deliver services and often have to explain their actions to generalists that may not understand the complexities of multi-objective service delivery. The false analogy is monetary policy—there is no doubt that interest rates can be used to bring down inflation. Despite the ease of measuring inputs and outputs in health, education, and social assistance, there is substantial doubt about the best means to balance quality and cost to achieve, for instance, the best medical services for different clients. Evaluation systems tied to budget allocations are the way forward and designers must ensure that the right things are being measured—to ensure quality and effectiveness of service delivery.

CONCLUSIONS

Reformers have often noted that progress is needed in one or more of the three levels of fiscal decision making: strategic, allocations, and operations. They have also tried to install policy analysis capacity and multiyear integrated current-capital budgeting systems that allow decision makers to have information on problems and progress at more than one level. Many have noted that the interrelation of fiscal management problems across levels is ignored. Whether this requires more information or less data and better and more useful information, it is clear that incentives are also needed for policymakers to take risks and search for problems across organizational lines and the legal/regulatory limits of their job descriptions. In many cases, narrow job descriptions encourage insulation and isolation, which rewards failure to find and define actionable problems.

National governments and subnational tiers in the FSU/CEE region have made remarkable economic progress. They have established and maintained aggregate fiscal discipline, and inflation remains under control. While some countries of this region have relatively high debt/GDP ratios, they are not close to Italy or other older EU members. There is a cultural predisposition in this region away from debt and borrowing that is hard for outsiders, particularly counterparts from Latin America, where overborrowing has been a big problem, to comprehend. They have also assigned intergovernmental fiscal roles reasonably well. Where role definitions have not worked, they have been redefined as part of ongoing fiscal decentralization programs. Countries of the FSU/CEE have decentralized their political and economic resources, and this has been an important factor in consolidation of democracy and producing better municipal services. FSU/CEE countries have also allocated resources by function to real needs. More discretion is needed by line managers and better performance management systems are necessary to consolidate these gains. Programs such as social assistance, based on substantial analytic inputs and targeting efforts, have performed well overall. Since they have been established and managed for only fifteen or sixteen years, this is a remarkable accomplishment. At the municipal level, more efforts are needed to strengthen internal control and audit systems and to modernize local public administrations based on NPM principles used successfully elsewhere. This will consolidate existing reforms and improve municipal service even more. Finally, the danger for all countries of this region is that populist parties will manipulate public opinion further, generating mass opposition to further fiscal reforms. Regimes elected on false populist claims can only damage economic growth and ultimately weaken the political stability that so far has been a hallmark of reform in this region.

6

INTERNATIONAL BUDGET PROBLEMS AND PRACTICES

Latin America

INTRODUCTION

This chapter considers selected fiscal and budget issues in Latin America. The region is critically important to the rest of the globe in providing comparative lessons on what to do and not do in fiscal management and budgeting. Its current budgetary practices are the product of historical influences from Spain, the United States, advice from multilateral (World Bank, UNDP) and regional institutions (IADB), and home-grown ideas. There are at least four features of the Latin American region that make it important for budgetary analysis and comparison. The features are only *important,* not unique, as this would make comparison and lesson-generation to other regions difficult.

First, within each country there is a wide gap between rich and poor. This is a well known socio-fiscal distortion that makes expenditure financing and revenue raising a difficult task for governments of this region. What is less recognized is the wide range in income and GDP levels between Latin American countries themselves—they range from the bottom (e.g., Haiti) to almost-European living and income standards (e.g., Chile). Within our comparative framework, this has important implications for the context of budgeting, especially social spending. EU countries such as Hungary spend 20 percent of their GDP on social services while mid- to upper-range Latin countries spend only about 5 percent (e.g., Mexico) (World Bank 2003, 93). Because of institutional weaknesses, even the small amounts/GDP spent for social welfare programs are often poorly targeted and "leak" out.

Second, perhaps presaging what may come to pass in other regions such as Eastern Europe, Latin America has experienced wide variations in political regime types. It is not simply that administrations change often (e.g., Ecuador has had three presidents in the past ten years, none of whom have finished their terms). It is that the underlying regime structures vary qualitatively. Populist, democratic, socialist, and bureaucratic authoritarian or crypto-fascist regimes can all be found in different historical periods, over which several radically different types of regimes try to govern the same country. This pattern has important implications for macro-micro budgetary behavior and institutionalization of budgetary roles. For budgetary stability, predictability, and effectiveness, it makes things very difficult. For example, the Venezuelan state oil company (PDVSA) operates as a parallel state within the populist-authoritarian regime of President Hugo Chavez to provide billions of dollars in financing for a wide range of social projects that are normally the budgetary and program responsibility of the education, housing and health ministries (*Economist* 2008b, 43).

Third, in this region fiscal and budget policies have varied widely, with almost predictable results, from austerity and fiscal discipline to spending sprees in the wake of populist state socialist policies (as with Venezuelan PDVSA noted above). The linkage within regime types is not very predictable. But historically, programs have ranged from centralization of spending/taxation decisions as well as political decisions to engage in varying types of fiscal decentralization. For example, Brazil and Argentina were decentralizing their systems to local governments as early as the nineteenth century (Daughters and Harper 2006, 1). Despite the usual caveat about centralist political culture derived from the heritage of Spanish-Portuguese rule, Latin America has been an important international generator of successful lessons on political and fiscal decentralization. Finally, the Latin American region offers a wide range of design/implementation lessons from successful and unsuccessful cases of budgetary practices. For example, Latin American countries were early leaders in installing integrated financial management systems (IFMSs) and in modernizing their internal audit systems to replace the classical tradition of strong ex-ante external audit of all expenditure transactions. Some of these larger reforms are described in more detail in chapter 7. The region also has some special problems of its own, such as inordinate budget inflexibility (arising from legal rigidity and fragmentation of budget accounts).

It is difficult to generalize about fiscal and political patterns in this region (or in others such as Eastern Europe). But by identifying several blocks of country-types (poorer, middle range, advanced) it can be argued that the trends at least in the middle and advanced range countries have been positive—institutional modernization, wider development, better service delivery, better fiscal planning and control, improved program implementation, and more electoral accountability. Latin America is testament to the adage that public sector fiscal reform is slow, often costly, but ultimately worth it.

DIVERSE DEMOGRAPHIC AND ECONOMIC PATTERNS

The region as a whole has performed well in the last decade owing to: high commodity prices (especially oil and copper) and sound macroeconomics; flexible exchange rates and inflation targeting by central banks; and fairly responsible fiscal policies (*Economist* 2006a, 54). Up to 2009, the region has had the lowest rate of inflation since the 1960s; a current account surplus 2003–05; reduced public debt as a percentage of GDP; and a fiscal deficit of only 1.7 percent of GDP in 2005. Growth has been the fastest since 1981 (5.9 percent), though this is predicted to fall to 3.8 percent (2006b, 91). While some countries such as Chile and Brazil are predicted to continuing growing in 2009, average GDP for the six major Latin American countries is expected to fall -1.1 percent (*Economist* 2009a). This GDP contraction will increase proportionately the amount of public spending necessary to deal with the global recession and financial sector collapse. As indicated in Table 6.1, even Chile with its extremely prudent fiscal policies will run an estimated fiscal deficit of -2.9 percent (after a string of surpluses culminating in +4.5 percent in 2008). The six large countries' (Argentina, Brazil, Chile, Colombia, Mexico, and Venezuela) fiscal balance will still be an affordable -1.1 percent of GDP (*Economist* 2009a). The major regional problem is enduring poverty and

TABLE 6.1. 2009 Projections of Fiscal Deficits as a Percentage of GDP

Country	Deficit	2008 OBI Rating
Argentina	-0.80%	56
Brazil	-3.80%	74
Chile	-2.90%	No Data
Uruguay	-2.30%	No Data
Colombia	-3.00%	60
Mexico	-2.00%	54
Bolivia	-2.50%	6
Peru	-1.80%	66
Costa Rica	-3.00%	45
Panama	-0.30%	No Data
Ecuador	-4.00%	38
Venezuela	-5.20%	35
El Salvador	-2.10%	37
Honduras	-2.00%	11
Guatemala	-1.90%	45
Nicaragua	-3.70%	18
Dominican Republic	-3.70%	11

Source: The Economist (2009), World Bank (2008); World Bank (2008) comes from the FY09 Unified Survey; OBI index scores range from 0–100 with 88 as the currently highest rated country (UK) and Ecuatorial Guinea as the lowest (0) www.openbudgetindex.org.

inequality. Latin American income distribution is more unequal than anyplace outside Africa (2006a, 57). Poverty rates (extreme and total) are falling but not very fast. Total poverty fell 1990–2005 from 49 percent to 40 percent and extreme poverty from 24 percent to 17 percent in the same period (2006a, 57).

Innovative and effective antipoverty programs have been developed such as Mexico's PROGRESA and Brazil's *Bolsa Familia,* which provide conditional cash transfers or monthly stipends to mothers in return for keeping their children enrolled in school and for taking them to regular health checks. The federal or central government provides the financing and local governments administer the programs, allocating benefits to those meeting national eligibility standards. Municipal governments in Brazil collect data on eligibility and compliance and payments are made by the federal government (*Economist* 2008a, 39). To control "leakage," each eligible beneficiary receives a debit card on which monthly benefits are added if mothers keep up with vaccination and school attendance requirements. About eleven million people receive this transfer in Brazil and it has dramatically improved health, school attendance, and economic growth in Northeast Brazil (the poorest part of the country) (2008a, 39). In Mexico, PROGRESA has reduced extreme poverty by 50 percent 1998–2004 despite only moderate economic growth in the same period. The Mexican *Opportunidades* program is a social assistance program predicated on conditional cash transfers (CCTs). Recipients are monitored rigorously to ensure that their children attend school and use health facilities regularly (*Economist* 2009b, 70). There is evidence that this incentive-based approach is also working in Colombia (2006a, 57) and will be shortly initiated by Peru, as well as in New York City.

A major constraint on Latin American public programs is state weakness—corrupt and bureaucratic civil services and judiciaries at the central level and poorly organized and managed intermediate levels of government. This has led to "leakages" of public expenditure for all programs and antipoverty programs in particular. For example, it is estimated that only twenty-nine cents of every dollar transferred by the Peruvian central government for its *Vaso de Leche* food for the poor program reaches its intended beneficiaries with milk products to provide protein and calcium. It targets children up to six years old, pregnant and nursing mothers, and secondarily children seven to thirteen, elderly, and tuberculosis sufferers (2006, 78). This lower-level institutional leakage of funds is partly the product of weak audit controls, which do not function well in the poorest urban and provincial municipalities (World Bank 2003, 9). The problem is a persistently unreformed state that afflicts most countries of Latin America. Weak and politicized budget planning and allocation systems are but symptoms of this public sector difficulty in planning and implementing good public policies.

Pressures from IMF/World Bank over the past several decades to reform Latin American public finances at the aggregate (strategic) level have paid off.

Even in the current economic crisis, most countries can still claim that their aggregate levels of spending are consistent with the core medium-term objectives of sustainable fiscal deficits and public debt ratios. Throughout the Latin American region over the past fifteen years, macroeconomic stability has held and inflation has been minimal. Nevertheless, there are three perennial challenges to this stability, which have so far not been serious. First, pressures to increase fiscal transfers for decentralization and populist measures (earmarks) are increasing and should be offset by improvements in local revenue collection. This is especially true for Peru, where more than 180 functions have been assigned to regional and local governments (World Bank 2003, 23). The fiscal implications of this assignment on macroeconomic stability could be severe if prior technical assistance programs to increase local revenue and fiscal management capacity to meet certification criteria are not effective. Before receiving functions or funds for them, the Peruvian *Ley Organica de Gobiernos Regionales* requires that municipal governments first have sufficient human resource, fiscal, and management capacity. Localities to receive functional and project responsibilities must first demonstrate capacity and be certified through a formal system of accreditation (CNP 2006, 57–60). This certification policy acts as a brake on potential loss of spending discipline from the fiscal decentralization effort.

Second, public capital investment expenditure is low and dropping for most of the Latin American region. Infrastructure investment has been wrongly considered a residual expenditure, one to be first sacrificed for adjustment and austerity purposes. This is very short-sighted and could well become a point of economic strangulation. The capacity of fixed capital (together with that of capital maintenance) to generate growth needed for revenue generation is often ignored by budget processes more interested in covering state salaries. Peru's capital expenditure ratio of 3 percent GDP is among the lowest in the region and it is declining (2003,31). The significance of these trends is that absence of infrastructure is a constraint to the region's development: 58 million people still lack access to treated water, 137 million lack sewerage services, fewer than 25 percent of main highways in Peru and Brazil can be classified as good (*Economist* 2006d, 53). While Chile has mobilized private funds through the capital markets to finance its infrastructure, most other countries of the region have decreased spending (e.g., Mexico 33 percent less in 2004 than 1994). Infrastructure spending for most Latin American countries has averaged less than 2 percent of GDP (2006d, 53). This means that the good economic performance noted above is more the product of export booms (oil, copper) and will eventually fall prey to clogged ports, poor railways and roads, and precarious electricity supplies. It also means that where commodity revenues have not been saved, decreasing prices will starve public investment to an even greater extent. For example, Chile fiscal rules required it to save a high proportion of copper revenues in its sovereign wealth fund when prices increase. Despite the need to spend for stimulus purposes now, Chile has the fiscal space to do so without jeopardizing debt sustainability (only 4 percent of GDP) (*Economist* 2009c, 40).

Third, the total size of state budgets continues to grow, driven mostly by wages (Peru's 39 percent was second-highest in the region). Overstaffing is evident in wage bills together with additional hidden wages under goods and services contracts. In the context of permanent staffing contracts and the civil law regulatory framework (noted in chapter 5), excess staffing increases budgetary rigidity, and by weakening adjustment possibilities, threatens macroeconomic stability. State modernization and reform programs, which begin with much fanfare and donor support, often ended up cutting very little from wage bills or rationalizing core state decision processes.

As in most comparative analyses, it is useful to subdivide regions into smaller blocs of countries. In the case of Latin America, one can distinguish three general blocs—high, medium, and poor performers. This allows stratification of countries along a range of high-low growth rates, income levels, service delivery quality, budget management, and (to a large extent) decentralization progress. While there are exceptions in some sectoral policy areas (e.g., health, education), the high performers are Argentina, Brazil, Chile, Uruguay, Colombia, and Mexico. The mid-level performers are represented by Bolivia, Peru, Costa Rica, Panama, Ecuador, and Venezuela. The poorer performers include the rest of Central America (El Salvador, Honduras, Guatemala, and Nicaragua), Haiti, and the Dominican Republic. As indicated in chapter 1, when comparing budget policy problems and solutions across regions, it is important first to ensure that the country performance level is roughly similar (e.g., Hungary with Argentina and not Haiti).

WIDESPREAD REGIME AND
POLITICAL CULTURE VARIATION

Political regimes are composed of state bureaucracies and political/economic leadership. Since this common kind of definition borders on being a meaningless generality, the analytic point is to use this to focus inquiry. For this region, the question is how the state actors link together and develop policies with particular ideological colorations, that is, those ranging from nonideological technocratic policies to the hard-left or hard-right state socialist/libertarian stateless privatization. Historically in Latin America, one can find examples of most of the worlds' possible regime types: totalitarian (Cuba), rightist military social welfare dictatorships (Peru 1968, Argentina 1950s), twenty-first century petro-socialist or populist authoritarian (Venezuela and Bolivia now), socialism (Chile 1972), pluralist, social democratic (Costa Rica, Uruguay, Chile now), corporatist/fascist (Brazil, Argentina, Chile 1980s), and populist regimes (Haiti). Other nuances can be filled in and may be invented in the future.

What this means is that, in contrast with much of the transitional and developing world, elections (and coups) produce changes, of not just leadership but ruling models and ideologies as well. This has,far-reaching implications for the economy and society, especially for any expectation that there will be an evolution to democracy. As noted by Linz and Stepan (1996, 13) democracy is a form of governance in the modern state. Variations in state capacity to perform basic functions such as territorial control, exercise legitimate use of force, allow civil and political society to exist (associations and electoral competition), and enforce rational-legal norms for law/order and economic purposes, constrain any program of transition to democracy. To the extent that a state exists and can perform most of these functions well, it is probably democratic. The Venezuelan (1970s-1980s) state performed these functions, then allowed them to lapse in the early 2000s. Venezuela is now governed by a hybrid populist regime headed rapidly toward state socialism under Hugo Chavez. Where state power is weak and power vacuums exist, parallel authority and political legitimacy structures often emerge, such as Mafias and NGOs, including religious organizations with their own agendas (e.g., Haiti). Where the state is weak, its functions can be easily perverted to perform entirely different ones than those intended—Venezuela's PDVSA state oil firm planning and financing health and housing programs. Weak state program coverage and institutional depth, combined with a large supply of poor people to mobilize, permit the rise of successful populist leaders. In countries such as Bolivia and Peru that contain massive amounts of poor, populist leaders are always either in charge or closely linked to the reins of power. At the other end, excessive accumulation of state power, either as state-driven coalitions of membership and political organizations (corporatist) can result in crypto-fascist or bureaucratic-authoritarian regimes (Brazil, Chile, Argentina, Uruguay in the late 1970s-early 1980s). Such regimes exercise softer control over individual and enterprise behavior than full totalitarian regimes (e.g., Cuba, Nicaragua in the 1980s). The well-known ingredients of passionate temperament, heat and high humidity, and a propensity for gaming behavior can be used as residual factors to explain the fact that regime change has occurred with rather high regularity in this region.

Despite the historical legacy of frequent regime changes, Latin America can also point to many democratic regimes governing for substantial periods of time. One could ask: If they are the apotheosis of development, why don't democratic regimes just emerge and persist? Many have written about the supposed teleological evolution to democracy from hierarchically controlled military regimes, and how the constraints imposed by this evolution could or would be removed (Linz and Stepan 1996). There are major constraints to such evolution. For instance, a common feature of Latin American states is a tight vertical command structure, which inhibits risk taking and innovation, especially in the civil service. In addition, civil code governing frameworks tends to encourage inaction and decision avoidance until precise orders are given—action only with authorization/approval (in contrast with U.S. action followed by asking for forgiveness). Action without explicit or implicit approval brings drastic consequences in famously opaque personnel systems that lack precise performance expectations or formal review processes. The institutional tendency is to require permission for each decision, meaning meetings, delays, and excessive processes. Given the large size of Latin American states, much of the work is focused on debating actions and approval requests. Note the similarity with another region having strong civil code influence: Central and Eastern Europe and the Former Soviet Union (chapter 5).

Formal management strictures are only part of the Latin American picture—the most visible part. The tight vertical command structure is full of holes and masks a lot of the informality by which decisions are often actually made. How bureaucratic structures/processes are changed by democratic transition from authoritarian regimes is an interesting question. Some would say, using the Eastern European experience, that they do not change much at all—unless entire ministries, functions, and structures are eliminated from the top. The officials and their minions often stay on, enforcing the same systems and procedures for such critical units as post offices, state railways, state oil companies, state telephone companies, and universities.

Frequently, regimes evolve finally to democracy in Latin America, only for the system to revert to military regime and/or special interest–dominated populism. Often the soft explanation of "political culture" is invoked at this point—the values and attitudes that affect political behavior. The values and attitudes are themselves the products of "myths, passions and irrationalities that in any age are central to decision-making" (Kaplan 2007, 80). Successful leaders have a knack for understanding what the cultural context means—for "seeing just what's out there." Unsuccessful leaders (or fiscal reformers) often have neither talent (Kaplan 2007, 82). It should come as no surprise to those who have worked in Latin America and perhaps read some of its fiction writers (see for example Vargas Llosa 1973) that centralization of state power together with deeply-rooted patronage (clientism) and patrimonial processes have impeded state reforms (Gasco 2005, 694). Digging slightly deeper, Gasco asks why there is little commitment to state reform and notes that the deeper causes of poor public performance relate to the "patrimonial dynamics of party politics" (2005, 695). These cultural features, centralization, patriomonialism/clientism, and resistance to delegation of authority to lower levels, are used to explain many of the distinct features of public sector governance and fiscal performance in Latin America. Again, note that they were also used to explain much of budgetary behavior in Eastern Europe (chapter 5).

Centralization in Latin America effectively means the culture of the strongman who fears delegation of power as a threat. It means strong families, groups, firms, but often weak states since governments are composed of coalitions of such strongman-led groups. It also means systems function as opaque intergroup, interfamily, or intertribal decision processes. They are informal and hard to discern or predict. Persistence of this centralized and fragmented governance pattern results in problems of institutional instability, informational opacity, weak mid-level management, distrust of subordinates, insufficient assignment of line management authority, and disconnected high-tech information systems to preserve tribal power and control. The frequently used term *informational asymmetry* takes on much more meaning in culturally centralized political economies. In Latin America, centralization explains instability and the oft-noted lethargy of processes. Fewer decisions mean less personal risk and more opportunities to keep one's head down in order to avoid higher-level disfavor. Centralization leads paradoxically to more systemic instability because it requires constant efforts to shore up control and play diversionary games to maintain power. Leaders specialize in theatrics, bombast, powerful oratory, heroic individual moves, and faked injuries (much like soccer or a round football game) to garner sympathy. Lethargy and corruption result as authority is maintained at the center, trust is withheld from most subordinates, and control is maintained by small cabals. Since this is untenable for any length of time, constant power plays occur, wasting time that could be spent on management and productive actions in most organizations including the state. Centralization and tight-knit clientism explain a lot of the fiscal instability (e.g., volatile fiscal transfer commitments to local governments; variable tax collections; gaming over ghost civil service slots; etc.) and lethargy (e.g., slow processes for permits and licenses that require constant "greasing" with bribes, gifts, or side payments).

Thus, centralized political culture helps explain why regimes change, and why there is such political and institutional instability. Others note the modern split between centralized ministries/agencies in a presidentially dominated bureaucracy and the expansion of decentralized and semiautonomous agencies. This describes the quest for centralization of power driven by cultural emphasis on personal pride, machismo, and dignity among Latin American men (Sondrol 2005, 523). This explanation, in turn, leads to other perhaps deeper, cultural theories. Political culture focuses on the macho autonomy games that perennially operate through centralized public sector institutions. That, in turn explains a good bit of the fiscal and political instability that leads to frequent regime changes and changes in regime type. It also explains an important part of why institutions often evolve and reform despite cultural constraints, then regress to previous patterns in endless cycles of political and personal gaming.

In a region with such distinct people, systems, practices, and habits, it is tempting always to use *political culture* as the core explanatory method. There can be little doubt to the visitor or long-term resident of this region that something is distinct. The question is whether it is a subset of something more generic, such as the "wealth" and "poverty" variables that produce the specific fiscal behavior described by Caiden and Wildavsky (1974). Political culture refers to values and attitudes that affect political and policy behavior. But this means individual and group values—which often behave differently than collective institutions. For example, voting rules on fiscal and tax issues have been promulgated here and elsewhere in Europe and in U.S. state and local governments, precisely to safe-guard against the imposition of taxes on individuals by small groups. To protect individuals, greater than simple majority voting approval rules are required (e.g., 66 percent) along with the requirement that elected officials (not appointed bureaucrats) do the imposing.

Despite the oversimplification fallacy (see Hirschman 1971), where behav-ioral features are so distinct (as in this region) it is sometimes useful to aggregate individual behaviors into organizational behavior and then take them apart again. With some variations, most observers come back with the same descriptions—whether they have lived there, worked with particular rich or poor families, or worked in generally rich or poor Latin countries. There are cultural features that can be ranged along the old spectrum of *traditional* to *modern* behavior (much crit-icized in the literature again as an oversimplification [see Chilcote and Edelstein 1974]), which varies across Latin America from poorer, less complex traditional states (and rural areas) to more cosmopolitan, modern and urban states (and urban areas). This should not be surprising. Table 6.2 describes the purported cultural features that may have explanatory value.

Such dichotomous cultural features above have been long discussed in the lit-erature and generally rejected as simplistic and incapable of linkage to any institu-

TABLE 6.2. Attributes of Latin American Political Culture

Traditional	Modern
Individual: Lack of focus, ease of distraction	Task-orientation
Individual: life as power game	Professionalism, authenticity and duty
Individual: Refusal or inability to defer gratification	Deferral of gratification
Individual: act only with precise rule justification-small print, narrow rule orientation;	Risk-taking, rule-interpretation mentality; product rather than process centered
Organizational/management: centralized, command and control; rigid hierarchy	Incentives and trade-offs; flat structures; decentralized operational responsibility
Organizational/management: legal job description; static evaluations	Accountability for performance; employee growth and development
Organizational: norms and procedures govern all actions; bureaucratic formalism and legal rigidity	Institutional and individual responsibility, authority and results

tional, policy, or budgetary outcomes. That critical assessment is generally correct. Nevertheless, the features remain for all to see, and our inability to empirically link them does not make them go away. The question of why these features exist and can be described has produced a rich literature. Why the negative effects often disappear so quickly when individual Latins move to more "advanced" or "modern" cultures is another question—this tendency is oft-noted as well (Naipaul 1974). Their effects are also debatable. Caiden and Wildavsky (1974) proposed wealth and predictability as the explanatory variables for comparative budgeting. The Latin American culture seems to engender instability, chaos, and lack of institutional redundancy (i.e., institutional poverty) that is a hallmark of poor countries.

For example, one might focus analysis on the oft-noted cultural absence of ability to defer gratification. If this is true, it could be nature or nurture. But this inability apparently exists across a wide range of countries (in a region with common language and religion, historical traditions). It is often observed that Latin Americans have a low "flash-point" for fiscal austerity reforms and react quickly and often energetically to deprivations. Another way of viewing this is that when the flash-point is reached, it is diffuse and distracted, leading to quick, often violent but superficial responses—support for populist political candidates, destruction of parts of town, demands for regime changes, etc. How does this cut across class lines? It may not cut across them at all, since these responses cannot explain how the rural poor endure daily deprivation for years without any resistance or rebellion at all! And occasionally, with proper leadership and guidance, locals can focus their attacks to precise targets as official price increases (milk and bread), which often brings street rioting and tire burnings (e.g., Panama 1976). Regimes can fall quickly after such ill-timed moves, often in feeble efforts to raise revenues in order to reduce budget deficits, satisfy donor conditions, and provide reasonable social safety nets for their people.

By contrast, Eastern Europeans, used to a permanent state of deprivation for decades, permitted austerity reforms in countries such as Poland to take place, with only a vague notion of possible better results in the future. Discipline born of deprivation allowed for a cultural gamble that paid off. While citizens have been more quiescent in Eastern Europe following the transition period of the 1990s, the mood has been changing in the last several years (2004 on) as consumer goods have been provided and now priced out of reach. Reserved, stoical behavior is diminishing and the culture is now becoming similar to Latin America, after exposure to the same set of incentives/disincentives or constraints and opportunities over time. Thus, the explanation of social and regime effects from low levels of deferral gratification is valid. But it would seem to apply anywhere that people are denied gratification, exposed to higher expectations and consumer and public goods, and then again denied basic commodities. Similar incentives/disincentives seem eventually to produce the same responses, other things being roughly equal (as they never are). To eliminate *other things*, one would have to eliminate such happenings as the vicious state police apparatus in Eastern Europe and those of the 1970s dirty-war period in Latin America.

Linking Regimes and Fiscal-Budget Policies

Is there a discernable link then between regime types and specific policies? Regimes should be thought of as composites of political and economic institutions that represent the principal governing sectors and produce policies. Given the rigid ethnic and social class distinctions in this region, the predominant institutional representatives are the military and industry allied with remnants of the Catholic Church and ruling landholder classes. Where populist leaders leverage the permanent bloc of poor into votes (as has been done for centuries here), the new regimes represent directly or indirectly this class—or rule in their name. Populist regime ideologies predictably are redistributionist and state socialist, with strong practical interests in public program financing through direct expenditures, fiscal transfers, debt, and radically progressive changes in the tax code. Populist programs have been financed historically by natural resource exports such as minerals and timber and now increasingly by petrodollars. These have been the major sources of financing for expanded redistributionist programs (e.g., Bolivia, Venezuela, and Ecuador in 2009). More pluralist regimes have less clear ideologies and focus on encouraging democratic pluralism (wide partisan representation of all societal interests as in Costa Rica) and distributional safety nets for the poor within the framework of sound fiscal policies and austerity packages where necessary (e.g., Costa Rica, Uruguay, Brazil, Chile).

More cynical observers of populist-leftist regimes suggest that they are obsolete, often representing illegitimate states, with no ideologies other than to remain in power. Russia fits this description now (Dempsey and Bennhold 2007, 6) in the FSU region. Little is known about how to eliminate poverty and large class differences in a short time, other than through forced expropriation and redistribution of resources (e.g., land reforms that have suddenly become popular again after a thirty-year absence from the policy agenda), which merely reduce its symptoms. Because of this unfortunate fact, populist regime policies are often ineffective. Similarly, bureaucratic-authoritarian or BA or corporatist-type regimes seek to protect industry and often enact import substitution industrialization (ISI) and high tariff policies, which end up being counterproductive. There are actually no examples of BA regimes at present in Latin America, but they can always return in this region of recycled policies and regimes. Democratic regimes have their own problems with endemic fiscal leakage and corruption. But they are at least more transparent than the other two types. The highest public expenditure levels/GDP and largest state growth has been achieved under BA and populist policies.

It has been observed that for fiscal policies to become a powerful tool for development (e.g., Peru), it is necessary to design an outcome-managed, consensus-built budgeting strategy (World Bank 2003, 14). What that means is that the regimes must allow a modern institutional infrastructure to be built and persist, that is, stability derived from modern systems and practices is required. This means that regimes and cultures must interact to allow this to happen—cultural practices must be leveraged to allow modern systems to function inside them. Forgetting that culture can be a constraint and also opportunity can be very expensive! Despite the context of endemic power games within regimes that weaken state performance, some regimes are better than others at this facilitation role.

It is no surprise that developing and implementing solid and sustainable fiscal policies requires considerable institutional capacity—and patience during implementation of reforms. Regardless of regime type, countries of this region rely on central institutions, such as MOFs, central banks, and tax authorities to perform budget and finance management tasks. Authority is centralized—and most would argue that at the strategic and macro level, it should be centralized in order to prevent diffusion of effort. That fiscal policy effectiveness requires solid institutional and systemic underpinning also means that reform can come from the bottom-up pressure as well as top-down. Improvements in microbudgetary systems (e.g., planning, accounting, budget implementation, and audit control) can have profound effects on macroplanning and results. The effects of institutional poverty and fiscal uncertainty make budgeting virtually impossible to perform well in this region and often ensure poor program performance. But these institutional effects can and have repeatedly been overcome and program results dramatically improved. Group influences or "cultures" can reinforce bad practices but they can be changed rather quickly by new institutional frameworks that require new "modern" incentives (often an individual or group gain for adopting a best practice). Lack of coordination, weakly defined roles (guardian versus spender) and lack of complex redundancy (i.e., back-up systems) are symptoms of very soluble public management problems. The problems do affect budgeting and program performance negatively, because they often persist from top-down inertia. The point is that public budgeting systems can operate as institutional change agents. Reform of budgeting and public sector practices that inhibit modern management can change cultures and improve performance. For instance, this worked in Ecuador for the microbudgetary process of budget implementation and it can work elsewhere in this region (Guess 1992). The reform chain can be reversed from macro to micro and best practices, with systemic improvements moving up the ladder to improve overall performance. In chapter 7, we will describe how this occurred with IFMS in Ecuador, with best practice moving from local government (Quito) to the national government.

The above discussion underscores how difficult it is to link regime types and fiscal practice or policy with any precision. The chain of decision making between

governance regimes and intervening variables that determine design and implementation of particular policies is long and affects analysis of causation. Any effort
to attribute policy results to regime types under these conditions becomes almost
meaningless. Nevertheless, some efforts have been made to link particular sectoral
policies and regime types, but further research is warranted. The three major types
of Latin American regimes that could be distinguished in the 1970s and 1980s
were: bureaucratic-authoritarian (BA), democratic, and populist. BA regimes were
technically more sophisticated authoritarian regimes in which the military took a
supporting role to civilian technocrats who were encouraged to combine state
and private resources to maximize production and ensure stability/security. They
were corporatist regimes, an offshoot of the fascist regimes in Europe that allowed
the private sector to produce and which supported it with public funds where
necessary (Collier 1979).

Comparing regime type and results has been useful by focusing on agro-
industrial policies (e.g., forestry) that can be associated directly with economic
development and employment. In the case of forestry in Latin America, BA
regimes focused on more advanced production forestry, especially the manufac-
ture of pulp/paper and secondary products such as furniture and building supplies. The forest resource was managed to maximize income and employment
opportunities as well as foreign investment and local contribution to GDP. Values
such as poverty reduction or environmental protection were important only so
long as they contributed to these policy ends. At the same time, regulation of the
tropical Amazonian forest resource was lax and corrupt under BA regimes, reflecting possibly technical ignorance of the production possibilities, indifference to the
opportunity cost of destroying a valuable natural resource, and corrupt clientistic
ties to large landowners in that region. By contrast, populist regimes of poorer,
less politically complex countries such as Honduras and Belize designed and
implemented statist policies. Belize followed its mercantilist tradition and continued to allow extraction of primary products with minimal local reprocessing but
with state protection. The industry remains weak and contributes little to development in Belize. Instead, Honduras nationalized the forest sector in the 1970s
and implemented import-export controls and a forest cooperative scheme
through its state enterprise (SOE) called COHDEFOR. This has not worked well
at all for consumers, wood industry exporters, furniture and goods manufacturers,
or forest landowners (Guess 1991). Democratic regimes such as Costa Rica (from
the 1980s) and Chile (in the late 1980s and early 1990s) initiated fiscal incentives
to encourage private growing to support private investments in forestry for pine
in both countries and preservation of tropical forest resources in Costa Rica
(Guess 1984).

Corporatist BA regimes seem to be able to marshal the resources of the pri-
vate/public sectors and focus them on narrower economic objectives. Populist
regimes have not been very effective at sustaining growth or development, despite

the rhetorical appeal of linking policies (including forestry) to equality, antipoverty, and anti-imperialism. The current mix of consolidated democratic regimes (including former BA states such as Argentina, Brazil, Uruguay, and Chile) now rely on a mix of tax subsidies, private incentives, supportive public expenditures, and enforcement of the tax code to achieve multiple objectives—social welfare, poverty reduction, and economic growth. What this suggests is that macrobudgeting and policymaking are more effectively performed at the center in BA regimes, less effectively performed at the center in populist regimes (as the state cannot deliver on its broad social promises), and more of a central-local, nongovernmental function for democratic regimes, which must combine macro and micro: central and departmental-local institutions (NGOs, LGUs, membership associations). Fiscal policymaking in democratic regimes seems to work best, as institutional flexibility and transparency is required to manage resources in the forest sector.

BUDGET INSTITUTIONS AND PRACTICES: ACCOMPLISHMENTS

Despite what has been said about the volatile cultures that produce repetitive regime and budget changes, the fiscal trends in Latin America have been extremely positive in the last decade. BA regimes have evolved into consolidated democratic states and this has stabilized the public finances. True, new populist regimes have emerged in which the public finances are out of control with potential risks for the future (Venezuela, Bolivia). But these kinds of extreme statist regime policies, wild rhetoric, and disastrous programmatic results have been seen before in this region. Even advanced countries like Argentina have suffered wild economic and political swings and return eventually to a normal, stable path of growth.

More importantly, habitually unstable states such as Ecuador, Peru, and Mexico have improved their fiscal stability. Differences between planned revenue estimates and actual collections and between planned and actual expenditures for the year have been narrowing in most countries. Even the poorer states of Central America, such as Honduras, Nicaragua, and Guatemala have improved—sounder policies, more stable finances, stronger currencies, and better balance sheets. Changes have been induced externally (often by donor austerity and with highly indebted poor country (HIPC) debt-relief programs) and institutionalized by successions of reformist local elites and political regimes over several decades. The institutional reality is that fiscal reform is always a slow process in any country. Unlike wars that are supposed to be won by next Christmas, fiscal reforms take years. Success often results from deliberate sequences of trial and error at the operational level. In the field, many fiscal aid workers report expensive, multiyear comedies of errors—but ultimately the fiscal systems (tax, customs, budget, accounting, treasury, MTEF, IFMS) are installed and work more or less as planned. Many fiscal reform projects depend on and are linked tightly to new IT systems performance—for information, sharing across government, and simplification of transactions. Given the poor record of e-governance and other information technology projects in government, the major successes in producing budget transparency and simplifying tax administration are significant (*Economist* 2008c, 6). Many of these successes have been in Latin America (e.g., Brazil, Peru, Chile, Mexico).

Macroeconomic controls over spending have also been installed and function well in most countries of the region. Overall inflation is low. This is almost amazing in the region that seems to have invented hyperinflation! At the sectoral or allocational level, budgeting has improved in areas such as health, education, and social services. Since 2000, for example, Peru has been implementing a successful countercyclical poverty-reduction program. Called the Protected Social Program (PSP), it is a social protection program that allocates guaranteed minimum amounts to poverty-related subsectors such as water/sanitation, transport, social and community assistance, health, and education (World Bank 2003, 57). While health and education programs still suffer from inefficiencies and lack of full coverage, the policy debate has narrowed considerably on how to improve institutions and maximize scarce budget resources in this country. Many of the ideas adopted for Peru were imported from successful comparative social programs elsewhere in the region, such as the *Oportunidades* program from Mexico (*Economist* 2009b, 70)—which is precisely the purpose of applied comparative fiscal research. For example, applied comparative studies of service performance in Brazil, Chile, Dominican Republic, Venezuela, and Uruguay indicate that how assignments of management and fiscal responsibilities are made to lower-tier officials in order to hold them accountable is critical to improving program performance (Savedoff 1998). Other comparative fiscal research points to the more microinstitutional reforms that are needed to improve results. This suggests that budget institutions and incentives for staff are critical—not just the introduction of more elaborate performance measures, forms, processes, and elegantly computerized systems.

Overall, at the management level (combining macrostrategic and micro-operational levels of budgeting), the trend is toward better fiscal control and linkage of expenditure to results measures. As will be indicated in chapter 7, installation of IFMS throughout the region has improved treasury accounting and control. There are fewer cash management and debt management surprises—though they still occur in the form of arrears, overborrowing, and operating deficits at the municipal level in Latin America. If there are decision system weaknesses in control (i.e., overspending, overcommitments), accounting and reporting systems likely predicted them in advance. The missing factor with all such systems is political will to act on the data. Someone or some institution must act on negative trend, share, or ratio information before it becomes a crisis. Because it is illogical to legally sanction honest mistakes, there are often imprecise penalties for failure to act on known fiscal risk information. Despite this conundrum for public sector management, fiscal transparency has increased as more budgets have been placed on the MOF Web sites and updated annually in Latin America (see for example fiscal condition information on Peru: www.mef.gob.pe). Transparency has also moved from a populist demand for unlimited data to the more focused need for standardized fiscal data (in GFS categories and in the four main budget formats) and relevant information (for decisions involving strategic policymaking, sectoral allocation, and program operations). Budget documentation has also improved—many budgets are reader-friendly and follow Government Finance Officer Association (GFOA) guidelines to serve as policy, operational, communications, and planning documents. NGOs such as the International Budget Partnership (IBP) (www.internationalbudget.org) regularly monitor fiscal trends and processes critically and attempt to link expenditures to particular country programs, such as antipoverty. As noted, IBP's recently updated Open Budget Index scores eighty-five countries on the basis of clarity, scope, availability of documents on public spending (IBP 2008). For Peru, the budget monitoring work of affiliate IBP group Grupo Propuesta Ciudadana (GPC) can be seen at: www.propuestaciudadana.org.pe.

That the region has improved in fiscal transparency is indicated by the fact that Brazil and Peru are ranked just below the United States and South Africa on IBP's "Open Budget Index" (*Economist* 2006c, 114) (see Table 6.1). Nearly nine years ago in 2000, the Peruvian MEF launched an economic transparency Web site that now provides citizens and civil society organizations with the tools to begin exercising controls over planned and actual expenditures related to social and decentralized programs (2003, 61). In addition, the rapid expansion of the *Sistema Integrada de Administraction Financiera* or SIAF (the Peruvian version of IFMS) throughout the government will allow full disclosure of defense and national security expenditures (unprecedented in Latin America) as well as expenditure/revenue trends and shares of subnational governments (2003, 61). This will produce whole-of-government fiscal accounting and reporting and ensure fiscal control (in principle) at all tiers of government and for all transactions of general government. In an indication of how far the region has progressed in fiscal transparency, Peru still has a lower transparency ranking than the other five Latin American countries surveyed, which include Mexico and Brazil (World Bank 2003, 62). This may be due in part to the fact that Peru and Guatemala are the only countries in the region in which line ministers are able to maintain cash accounts outside the treasury without daily transfer of balances—which threatens both transparency and fiscal discipline (Filc and Scartascini 2006, 168). But the trend is clear—budgeting and fiscal management systems are improving rapidly in this region.

Despite increased confidence in the validity, reliability, and transparency of fiscal data/information there are still accountability and responsibility problems. As in most countries, fiscal control problems still derive from the failure to actually use the better information for allocation decisions. That is, informational availability is not equal to actual use for decision making. Problems remain with the many advisory committees and groups that translate fiscal data into policy actions—cuts here, additions there, etc. If information is excluded by narrowing the range of critical opinions on the meaning and implications of data trends and shares, the process itself prevents sound policies from ever being formulated or implemented later. Incomplete budget analysis usually leads to big spending and revenue surprises and attempts to paste over them during implementation. Under such familiar conditions, budgets are made during implementation and "repetitive" budgeting (Caiden and Wildavsky 1974) becomes the norm—permanent fiscal instability. Exclusion of or indifference to budget analysis is an institutional problem that inhibits receptivity to fiscal and policy analysis in virtually all countries. Nevertheless, at the sectoral level (e.g., health rather than aggregate general government or general fund expenditures), there is much more emphasis on generation and use of activity statistics for allocation of funds according to performance—rather than recycling last year totals plus inflation to this year's line-item inputs. It is important to note that performance-program and economic classification budgets now complement each other at the national level and for many local governments in Latin America. Performance/line-item amounts can be and are "cross-walked" precisely across budget formats and used for allocation and control. In short, budget allocations have been increasingly based on program performance in this region. In addition, formula fiscal transfer programs, which used to be based purely on political influence, evolved to allocations based on static demographic and income data, and now often include an incentive component for performance. This is amazing fiscal reform progress! Still, election demagoguery and regime politics continues to play havoc with fiscal policy and program implementation. As indicated by recent events in Bolivia and Venezuela, the old instabilities are always still there, just below the surface.

REMAINING BUDGET AND FINANCE ISSUES

A number of budget process issues recur particularly frequently in Latin American countries. While accounting, budgeting, and planning subsystems have been modernized and function well, the institutional superstructure of the state performs less well and often operates as a constraint on improved fiscal performance. This section will review six major issues.

Fragmented State Budgetary Institutions

Budget institutions are sets of rules, procedures, and practices to guide preparation, approval, and implementation of budgets (Filc and Scartascini 2006, 158). Organizations consist of administrative units created by government, such as MOFs and ministries of education. Budget planning and execution in Latin America as elsewhere has historically been a shared function between ministries of planning and ministries of finance. Where the two can coordinate current and capital planning well, and have tight execution control systems (often supported by integrated financial management and accounting control systems), the institutional arrangement should ensure fiscal discipline. This means that controls produce intended results—cash flows, trends, shares, and rations. If budget planners estimate a 5.0 percent of GDP deficit and this amounts to eight billion dollars, the efficacy of controls can be gauged by whether the cash amount is exceeded and if so, whether areas of control weakness can be identified, for example, salaries, health, debt, etc.

Put another way, there should only be one organization charged with national fiscal planning and execution and one set of institutional rules. In most countries, this is not the way things work. In Brazil, for example, there are currently two rather well coordinated financial ministries and a supporting control system (SIAFI) (Petrei 1998, 237–38). But as recently as the early 1980s, Brazilian fiscal institutions planned and executed four separate annual budgets! The federal budget was approved or rejected in total by the Congress. The Social Security budget was prepared and approved by the executive. The public enterprise budget was prepared by a separate secretariat for both current and capital investments— which became a contingent liability of the treasury. The monetary budget was the product of a commercial bank (*Banco do Brasil*) with power to issue funds through a revolving account replenishable from the Central Bank. The Central Bank also had development bank duties, such as subsidized financing. Thus, among other problems, fiscal and monetary data/funds were coommingled, with monetary financing of budget obligations. The potential for fiscal damage by a system with four spending advocates that could dip into the treasury under the lenient gaze of a weak guardian was realized when the debt crisis occurred in 1982. Institutional consolidation finally took place with the Cruzado Plan in 1986 (Petrei, 235–36). Similar institutional dynamics and fiscal shenanigans have occurred elsewhere in this region and will likely recur, for instance, now in Venezuela.

In Peru, budget institutions are still fragmented and the fiscal guardian role remains weak. Budget formulation is performed in centralized fashion by MEF with little transparency. Amounts are known only ex post facto when registered in the SIAF system (World Bank 2003,44). Thus, the link between planning and budgeting is severed. There is no budget formulation module in SIAF as yet to link plans and execution or expenditures to service performance results (i.e., activity statistics translated into objects of expenditure totals). Since SIAF only registers current-year transactions, the impact of future obligations on current revenues and expenditures is not considered when developing the annual hard budget constraint. The guardian role is further diminished by use of various ad hoc institutional devices to commit budget funds in decentralized fashion. For example, even though SIAF is in place, it does not control the many transactions that take place through what are called: *encargos* or *anticipos*. These are ad hoc, off-budget methods of speeding the allocation of funds to the fifty thousand operational units (*unidades operativas*) (OUs) such as schools, health posts, and global sectors such as agriculture, transport, and defense (2003, 45). Fund transfers to and from these OUs are governed by informal bilateral institutional agreements (*convenios*). From a guardian perspective it might be surprising that there are no minimum requirements or norms for what constitutes OU status. As noted, line ministers can still maintain accounts outside the treasury single account system—adding to fiscal discipline problems. As often happens, what sounds like ignorance of modern fiscal systems design is more likely to be an example of the cultural propensity to play games and make a clever shot.

Latin American media stories are often replete with public corruption and fiscal scandals that are usually much less than reported. The advantage of a free and free-wheeling regional media is that stories get to the public quickly. The disadvantage is that they are often technically incomplete and intent on the sensational. What typically appears to be another fiscal control disaster or scandal revealing a major *leakage* of funds is often a rational response to the slow approval and transfer of funds to officials who need to execute their programs. This common problem of clogged budgetary releases is typically the product of a centralized control mentality that tries to control everything and ends up (1) controlling very little and (2) providing new corruption opportunities for bribery at each new control point (Bird 1982). To try and provide managerial maneuvering room or flexibility, MOUs or *convenios* are negotiated between ministries to facilitate approvals and targeted spending. Predictably, the MOUs often end up circumventing the controls without creating the necessary internal pressure to reform them. Archaic implementation control regulations and systems remain in place, overlaid by streamlined modern systems often transferred from commercial uses. As will be explained in chapter 7, SIAFs have been implemented in this region, and should speed results via real-time pay order approvals (eliminating corruption and waste opportunities). Yet, rigid and archaic state approval procedures often remain in place anyway to preserve state employment positions—vitiating the rationale for the expensive computerized system in the first place! What often happens is that computerized fiscal systems, as well as management information systems included as part of state modernization efforts, often reproduce the complexity and disorder of the state. Logically, state processes and structures should be reviewed and changed before installing new information systems, as part of a comprehensive financial re-engineering strategy. Since this would be disruptive and time consuming (possibly illegal or even unconstitutional), the easiest and fastest way is to develop a parallel IT system (which, consistent with civil law micromanagement tradition, also requires legal authorization). The operational premise is that while simplification, deregulation, and streamlining of fiscal and management processes should precede computerization (but usually cannot), instead, SIAFs will be installed first and act as incentive frameworks for eventual reform of the underlying fiscal systems. In short, as novel, high-tech systems paid for by international donors, SIAFs are installed before state processes are reformed. Though illogical, this sequence has, paradoxically, worked to stimulate broader state modernization.

Narrow Budgetary Coverage

If revenues and expenditures are registered off-budget and/or if their outlays are not controlled, problems of fiscal leakage arise. Off-budget registry of financial transactions is not a major problem if balances can be consolidated and trends analyzed regularly. U.S. local governments, for example, are effectively legalized collections of two types of funds: (1) *government* (special, general, debt service, capital project, and assessment funds) and (2) *proprietary* (enterprise and internal service) (Coe 1989,15). Entries for both revenues and expenditures are covered by Generally Accepted Accounting Practice (GAAP) rules (1989, 10–14). The balances and positions of these funds are transparent in budgetary accounts that are available publicly in interim and annual reports (or in real time now with IFMSs in operation in most cities and the central governments of advanced countries). Within this control and classification structure, short-term cash transactions are often not transparent—where special funds (e.g., water and sewage authorities) subsidize the general fund or vice versa. Thus, extrabudgetary funds (EBFs), or all government transactions that occur outside the normal budget process, should be *covered* by the general government budget and controllable. Budget coverage in Latin America has been historically narrow, that is, much has been excluded from the consolidated accounts.

For example, in Brazil, as noted, in the early 1980s there were effectively four off-budgets! (Petrei 1988, 235–36). In Peru, some EBFs have budget limits and regularly report to the SIAF as part of their budget envelope (*pliego*) or authorization. They are considered quasi-EBFs because they allow spending when funds are available and have their own commercial bank accounts (weakening control) (World Bank 2003, 50). Nevertheless, the trend in Peru and elsewhere in Latin America has been to increase budgetary coverage. With elimination of the housing EBF (6 percent of the total budget in 1999), Peruvian coverage increased to 82 percent in 2002 (2003, 50). While expansion of SIAF will take care of this problem, coverage currently excludes regulatory agencies, social funds, and local governments (2003, 48). Over time, they will be absorbed into SIAF. Such simple microbudgetary reforms bode well for macro fiscal discipline.

Budgetary Rigidity

In Latin America, budgets are difficult both to construct and to modify. In all countries, budget formulation is legalistic, form-driven, and revenue-constrained. As noted, fiscal managers in the United States and Commonwealth countries develop spending options and amounts based mostly on analyses of needs and results, not simply from laws and regulations. In Latin America, budget preparation is guided by laws and decrees (again the influence of the civil law system) rather than management analyses of how to meet needs for the coming budget year. In Honduras, for example, from July to August, the spending ministries (*secretarias*) develop program strategies (*lineamientos y estrategias*) to include in their proposals to the MOF (SEFIN) (*anteproyectos*). These are based in principle on both evaluations of activities (e.g., *1999 Informe Anual de las Actividades en Salud*) and operating plans for the year (*POAs*). In principle, ministries develop physical and financial goals (*metas físicos y financieros*) for each department/activity within the context of tentative ceilings provided by the budget department (DGP). Ministry and DGP advisors (*asesores*) review proposals and negotiate a final set of programs and objectives in August. Except for capital projects, plans are one-year only.

In practice, development of Honduran program strategies at the ministry level is driven by SEFIN revenue ceilings, GOH policy directives, and constitutional/legal earmarks of expenditures (e.g., 5 percent of gross receipts transferred to local governments—Decree 134-90 mandated direct expenditures for education, etc.). Most annual budget presentations are virtual replicas of past year expenditure plans with minor changes for inflation. Requests are not made on the basis of performance reports indicating needed changes in the composition of spending activities. An exception was the proposal and decision to contract out primary road maintenance by the *Secretaria de Obras Publicas y Transporte* in 1994. Honduras, like many governments, makes and analyzes current services budgets on the basis of line items. Proposed changes in social services investment levels are typically buried within the FHIS (health fund) budget or activities of other decentralized institutions. These are effectively off-budget and not within SEFIN scrutiny or part of the SISPU (public investment) computerized reporting system. For this reason, it is difficult to find a consolidated budget request that indicates the proposed use of total public sector resources (Guess 2000, 11).

In basic budget systems such as this, economic and cost analysis is largely replaced by formal legal review for compliance purposes. In the Honduran budget formulation phase, ministries should apply analytic techniques to assess the efficiency (cost-benefit) and effectiveness (value-for-money) of proposed expenditures. For example, proposed personnel expenditures could be related to workload programs and linked to programmed tasks to arrive at an aggregate budget. The ratio of personnel expenditures/total budget could be compared to countries of similar size in the Central American region. Proposed expenditure cutbacks could be reviewed by using a cost/job-eliminated methodology taking into account downstream personnel benefit and program performance costs. Specific budget line items such as road operations and maintenance often have their own methodologies to determine if expenditures are sufficient to maintain the value of capital stock. But cross-country comparisons based on them are useful for assessing expenditure performance. Comparative cost/patient day in health or cost/classroom hour or cost/student promotion data for primary education can usefully be employed to measure national program efficiency and effectiveness. These can be refined to link proposed allocations to necessary volumes to satisfy a particular sectoral norm, for example, ratio of expenditure volume required/ reduction of grade repetitions in primary school. Instead, Honduran ministries develop requests on budget worksheets provided by the MOF in (1) personal services, (2) operating expenditures, and (3) capital requests using inflation estimates and sectoral ceilings as guidelines. In Peru, as noted, the formulation phase is characterized by opacity and centralized control by the MEF. Ministries prepare requests but the actual approval of them is a behind-the-scenes and highly politicized process in which analysis plays only a small role (World Bank 2003, 51).

The capital budget process in Honduras also underscores the problem of rigidity in budget formulation that is typical of the Latin American region. Following presentation of ministry requests to SEFIN in late August, the SEFIN performs a legal analysis of requests by institution that covers both current and capital budgets (via *dictamenes*). This is a step required in many Latin American budget processes. The *dictamen* process is a formalistic-legal analysis in which recommended expenditure levels for a particular capital investment project do not follow directly from transparent cost-benefit reviews. This analytic mechanism has not changed in substance since the mid-1990s. The result is that palpably inefficient and cost-ineffective project proposals are often approved and funded because they are legal!

A related legal problem for formulation (in most regions, not just Latin America) is that most of the expenditures are fixed costs or mandated items. "Inertial" or legally mandated expenditures produce annual budgets that cannot easily be reallocated to meet changed priorities. Most expenditures in the Honduran budget are fixed or uncontrollable. In the United States, uncontrollable expenditures lock up about 75 percent of the annual federal budget (social security, interest on debt, medical care, pensions, public assistance, unemployment compensation, and farm price supports) (Axelrod 1988, 197). In Brazil it is 90 percent and Peru 86 percent (World Bank 2003, 51). These include earmarks for pet projects in home districts. Much of the rigidity in Latin America is due to mandated fiscal transfers to municipalities and the private sector (e.g., the Peruvian *vaso de leche* and *comedores populares* programs), wages, permanent contracts hidden as nonpersonal services, inertial payroll under prolonged investment projects, and misuse of contingency reserves (2003, 51). Thus, mandates are a major constraint to linking budgets with changing needs.

During implementation, a paradox exists between decentralized execution and legally constrained management. As noted, a cultural feature of the region is to delegate insufficient program management authority—to keep things centralized. Miffed ministry or local government managers then devise new games to go around these controls, producing new cracks in the fiscal control system. The control problem is worsened by delegation of some fiscal authority to NGOs. Even though EBF coverage has been increased in Latin America, the ability of off-budget operational units (*unidades operativas*) below the level of executing units to commit resources via *encargos* or *anticipos* remains high. This means that units outside IFMS controls can commit funds for which the treasury is later responsible through an implicit liability. Commitments remain out of control and increase operating deficits (a surprise if it is a cash system—a management error if it is accrual or commitments-based). At the same time, cash flows and budget modifications are tightly controlled—to the extent that line managers are constrained in what their programs can accomplish. Forty-three years ago, Gonzalo Martner noted the constraints imposed by Latin American legal systems on public budgeting and financial management (1967). Little has changed in the interim. More recently, Reid (1994) noted the prevalence of the rigid model of "top-down financial control" model that impedes management flexibility and keeps public sector institutions weak. These features are on display in a Latin American budget execution that spends but does not manage or control effectively.

Budgetary rigidity still prevails in Honduras. For example, while DGP quarterly cash flow forecasts are quite accurate, institutional and regulatory factors intervene to change planned versus actual ministry allotments. Budget modifications must often be made by departmental managers to make ends meet. This is as true for projects as for program or policy implementation. But transfer and reprogramming rules are rigid. In an attempt to maintain cash flows and preserve the validity of the approved budget, the rules constrain management abilities to shift resources quickly to meet new needs. That is the trade-off: control versus management discretion. Budget outturn data in Honduras indicate that many planned and unplanned modifications are occurring, none of which seem to affect the aggregate level of fiscal discipline (the current fiscal or operating balance). There are at least three types of modifications during execution: (1) congressionally approved packages of modification requests from ministries, (2) reprogramming by SEFIN in accord with changes in policy priority (not much evidence of this), and (3) diversions by the executive and/or congressional earmarks for pet projects (which probably occurs but for which there is no hard evidence). According to SEFIN, about 98 percent of the modification requests are due to cost estimation problems on existing or new projects and needed counterpart funds. The other 2 percent can be attributed to legislative projects added to the budget during the fiscal year.

The high levels of modification indicate that most budgeting is actually done during implementation. While not surprising for a poorer Latin American country, this vitiates the planning and formulation process and indicates that something is quite wrong. Attempted managerial adjustments are rational responses to the profound fiscal instability and institutional poverty in which Government of Honduras (GOH) officials work (Caiden and Wildavsky 1974). Despite failure to breach aggregate fiscal ceilings, the modifications and adjustments reflect fiscal instability during the year which weakens the efficiency and effectiveness of program delivery and operations. The problem of matching resources to needs by managers during budget execution affects allocational and operational efficiency. As noted, in FY 1999, the health ministry (SES) reported that they requested 460 modifications, which took about one and one-half months for approval by SEFIN. In FY 2000 this took even longer given the re-centralization of budget execution via the requirement of congressional approval (Guess 2000, 17).

Budget preparation and approval in Latin America is excessively formal and rule-literalist. Budget implementation is also formalistic. But as noted, institutional flexibility is created by informal adjustment mechanisms such as delegating commitment authority to multiple operating units that do not report to the IFMS (SIAF in Peru or SIAFI in Honduras). These and other fiscal countercontrol strategies work well when guardian roles are weak. Working against this informality and management discretion (and risk of losing fiscal control over balances) are internal and external controls. Not surprisingly, the expectation that controllers are always coming to inspect the accounts, adds to the formalism and increases small-print, heads-down reactions throughout the state to cover one's tracks. Latin America has a lengthy history of ex ante or preventive legal control derived from the legislative courts of accounts (*tribunales de cuentas*). During the 1500s colonial period, these courts reported and reviewed revenues and expenses of the governing viceroyalty to Spain from Lima, Mexico City, and Santa Fe de Bogota in Argentina. In the 1800s, budgets began to be prepared by executives and approved by parliaments (1822 in Argentina) (Petrei 1998, 212). Most *tribunales de cuentas* have evolved into external control units, or legislative audits (supreme audit institutions or SAIs) that no longer perform preventive control and concentrate on year-end audits and performance reviews. Internal controls and audit unit roles remained confused in many countries, as budget, accounting and auditing professionals all claimed the control function to be in their remit.

In many Latin American countries now, internal audit and review of internal controls is one function of the IFMS unit that governs the public finances (SIAF in Peru, SIGEN in Argentina, etc.) (Petrei 1998, 225). While the recent evolution of internal control away from ex ante approvals of each expenditure (to real time, batch transaction approvals) has reduced corruption opportunities and increased management accountability for performance (rather than form filling), administrative processes still need to be reformed. Line officials must often still go through approvals procedures outside IFMS to satisfy the many units in state government that are still performing some kind of internal control and inspection roles. This needs to be streamlined for state modernization and improved fiscal performance. For the future, efforts to computerize management and finances must be combined with efforts to reform underlying administrative processes.

Diffuse Budget Control

Despite all the institutional effort at internal and external control inspections and reviews, actual fiscal control is actually quite weak in many Latin American countries. Control procedures often succeed in increasing rigidity and inflexibility, making it harder to adjust for needed macroeconomic policy shifts in some cases. This is especially true of budget modification, transfer, and reprogramming regulations. Budgetary control problems can arise from three related sources. First, the government can have revenue/expenditure forecasting problems. It may lack the technical capacity to forecast or it may use an accurate methodology and then modify resulting estimates for political reasons, for example, inflating revenues to allow more expenditures, and/or deflating expenditures to satisfy donor programs and to allow for supplemental additions later. Second, accounting and reporting systems may not register and properly measure revenues and expenditures. The country may have excellent forecasting capabilities that are overwhelmed by the vagaries of cash accounting systems that prevent matching expenditures to resource consumption for each period (Finkler 2005, 49). Significant manipulation of operating balances are possible under a cash system, which will affect the validity of forecasting methods. That is, cash flows may exclude commitments; commitments might be made from off-budget institutions (as in Peru), and these will turn into registered outlays that produce unplanned deficits. But even the most basic budgetary accounting systems record encumbrances to prevent unplanned deficits. The problem for the analyst is to find out the level of total expected commitments so that expenditure forecasts are not rendered irrelevant. Third, internal controls may be weak, for example allowing pay order requests to be approved by someone with asset custody. This would permit the former to collude with the latter through such devices as issuance of phony invoices to pilfer funds. Internal audit systems may focus narrowly on legal compliance and miss the often creative and dynamic games that take place underneath the formal accounting and budgeting systems, especially in Latin America. For any or all of these reasons, fiscal indiscipline may prevail.

Worse still, in Latin America, it is frequently difficult to trace both direct outlays and indirect subsidies from the budget. Deliberate misclassification of expenditures can circumvent controls, since controllers are focused on laws/regulations. For example, classifying wages as nonpersonal services and including salaries in investment projects, avoids the problem of overspending appropriations approved for salaries and wages. Or, classification of routine maintenance as a capital expense is an old trick, made possible by often vague distinctions between major and minor maintenance. Subsidies, such as explicit support for food, oil, and crops, can be hidden in legally mandated transfer programs (a different object of expenditure). Implicit subsidies such as government loan guarantees (e.g., for student loan programs from commercial banks or for home mortgages) are also hard to detect until defaults occurs. These are obvious classification gimmicks and internal audit units must be vigilant to detect malfeasance by officials operating internal control systems. Typically there are few professional incentives for auditors to do this.

A related source of fiscal indiscipline is exercise of commitment authority by institutions with vague fiscal authority, for example, the fifty thousand operating units in Peru. In Colombia, in the late 1980s the MOF controlled payments via cash flow plans. This circumvented the overall fiscal management system as each ministry had its own authorized account. Ministries were able to overcommit funds regularly by breaching budget ceilings and creating a "fiscal lag." The ministries then reduced arrears and overcommitments by agreeing to finance current year accounts payable (i.e., overcommitments) with the next year's accounts receivable (i.e., appropriations). That future receivables would be reduced for current overcommitments was a sound plan. But doing that and creating a reserve fund for "reserves payable" (!) simply sanctioned more overcommitments and rolling deficits. That led to MOF cash rationing (cash limits) which has always been a crude, arbitrary, and across-the-board fiscal control mechanism (Petrei 1998, 287–88).

Some control problems are more serious than others. The common problem of seasonal or quarterly deficits is well known in most regions of the world. The timing of revenues and expenditures in the political business cycle is well known and almost universally accepted. Under these volatile circumstances, the tactic of ratcheting up year-end spending to take up the slack, and running up small surpluses in the first quarter to cover predictable commitments is common. In U.S local governments, the differential (or daily spread between revenue and expenditure balances) is financed by commercial banks via concentration accounts (See Mikesell 2007, ch. 16). However, this practice in Peru brought calls for tighter cash management (good idea!) and quarterly spending limits (bad idea!) by the

World Bank (2003, 52). In our view, adding quarterly limits could only increase system rigidity and encourage the creation of more ad hoc flexibility mechanisms that will only decrease overall control in the Latin American cultural context.

To ensure actual value for money, it is more important to control the fiscal leakage to intended programs. In Peru, roughly 60 percent of social safety net expenditures do not reach intended extreme poverty beneficiaries (2003, 91). Programs are implemented by hybrid intermediary organizations (quasi-government or NGOs) that transfer funds between municipalities and beneficiaries. These are committees of elected members, composed of local officials and beneficiaries. Funds are diverted by the committees for off-budget administrative costs, expenditures on noneligible products, in-kind deliveries to nonbeneficiaries, fees for overpriced items, and sheer corruption (2003, 71). The point is that in the name of democracy and decentralization, the local committees operate opaquely as self-styled representatives of the social safety net program's beneficiaries. This suggests that organizations closest to the people do not always allocate service benefits optimally (2003, 71). It also suggests that local governments with proper internal controls and audit units may be better at allocating funds than NGOs working in behalf of the intended clients of government programs. Paradoxically, centrally prepared budgets in a country considered one of the most centralized in Latin America, has permitted implementation of a core social program by decentralized, fragmented institutions that lack effective fiscal controls. For these reasons, the World Bank advocated a public expenditure tracking survey (PETS) to detect, analyze, and quantify leakages and delays in the transfer of public expenditure. PETS have been used in other regions (e.g., Africa) to successfully assess expenditure efficiency and to detect the sources of leakage problems (Stern et al. 2005, 190–92). In short, without basic fiscal controls, political decentralization is inconsistent with optimal responsiveness to local clients.

Weak Linkage to Fiscal Performance

The final step in any generic budget process should consist of feedback on physical program performance that is fed into next year's budget formulation phase. Lessons from review of the strengths and weaknesses of program design and implementation should be inserted into the debate on the size and composition of the next budget. Failure of budget institutions to do this allows recycling of mistakes into the next year, and encourages paying for them again. Even if program evaluation is performed, in most Latin American countries there are typically few incentives for changing the scope and composition of budgets based on formal analysis, for instance, flexible budgets linking service costs and different volumes. The reason is that honest efforts such as this may have perversely resulted in funding cuts or recomposition of departmental expenditures by higher authorities. At minimum, effective program evaluation depends on formulation of budgets using activity statistics by cost center within a performance format. Performance auditors may examine results using independent program data. In most OECD countries, budgets are formulated in performance terms and programs are evaluated independently as a check against gaming the measures and using fudged data. In regions such as Latin America, the need is for good performance/program budget systems that monitor and report implementation in financial and physical program data and then use those data to guide new allocations.

In this regard, Honduras is no different than most other poorer countries of this region. Overall budgets are not typically formulated in performance terms; instead, there may be an annex or two for sectoral programs containing activity statistics. Some municipal budgets tied to aid projects may have developed program budgets in the past. In most cases, little program or performance feedback actually occurs; if it does, the information may not used to reallocate resources for the next year. For example, the Honduran Management Planning and Evaluation Unit in MOF (*UPEG*) is responsible for both program results and management performance (Guess 2000, 24). While rather high-quality evaluations are performed by the spending ministries of their program performance in relation to norms and standards (e.g., health), UPEG and the rest of MOF focus on macrolevel concerns such as fiscal deficits, exchange rate policies, GDP, balance of payments, debt management, and exceptional programs such as the efforts to respond to the disastrous effects of Hurricane Mitch (see *Memoria 1998*).

Similarly, the *Contraloria-General* (CG) is responsible for the post-audit function and in many countries this includes program performance reviews. In Honduras, however, the audits are largely financial and compliance-oriented. Because of structural (lack of independence) and political obstacles (lack of budget resources), UPEG and the *Contraloria* do not focus on managerial and program effectiveness questions that would satisfy public demands for accountability. The CG also suffers from "goal displacement" in that its functions are a mixture of internal and external audit. In most Latin American countries, these functions have been separated institutionally to allow internal control and audit by the executive branch. For example, as noted by Petrei (1998, 225) internal control in Argentina is performed by the *Sindicatura General* (SIGEN) and includes financial (prior control through chiefs in each agency) as well as performance review activities. External control is performed by the *Auditoria General* (AGN), a dependency of the legislature that carries out ex-post control, financial and legal auditing. So far, at least, Honduras can learn few performance evaluation and budgeting lessons from the budget implementation experiences of other countries in the region.

The paradox is that in many Latin countries, sectoral ministries generate and use their own performance information—the information is just not analyzed very thoroughly or used for annual budget allocations by the MOF! As noted in chapter 5, this was true of sectoral ministries in the FSU countries as well. Since there was really no MOF or operating budget function in that period (it was simply accounting and reporting on progress of the state plan), there was no need to report or use such data. In Honduras, performance information is regularly collected and analyzed by sectoral ministries such as: health, education, and highways. The information is generated mainly for the POAs and *Evaluacion Annual* by SSP (MOF planning department) Region. While there are no national financial norms, for example, cost/student, there are physical input norms such as the thirty-five student/teacher ratio (again, similar to CEE/FSU practice). As is known, these measure resource inputs and not outputs. Demand estimates are also used to develop expenditure programs for patients and students by the respective ministries. Regional level units plan and allocate supplies (e.g., books) to schools on the basis of demand and enrollment figures. Thus, several basic measures of workload and resource inputs are used for planning budgets by the ministries. The SIAFI budget module even allows entry of performance data and statistics for budget execution which can then be used to develop the next year's request.

Output measures and statistics (e.g., number of graduates per student enrolled or cost per graduate) are still missing from the ministry level budgets and the Honduran SIAFI does not fully extend to that level of detail. Output/outcome measures are rarely used to allocate expenditures by ministries. Nor, within ministries, is there evidence that inputs are related to outputs in the form of expenditure reallocations or transfers during the year. SEFIN does not estimate, for example, the volume and costs of services required to meet health and educational needs in a comprehensive fashion. Despite the very poor program performance of sectoral services such as education and health (in unit cost efficiency and cost effectiveness of coverage), the FY 2000 composition of sectoral expenditures was roughly similar to that of FY 1999.

Again, there is no evidence in Honduras that SEFIN (or especially Congress) allocates resources on the basis of sectoral program performance. Despite the existence of POAs and rudimentary analysis by SEFIN's expenditure analysis unit, the budget is still developed only on the basis of inputs classified in line items. Local units of ministries, such as schools and clinics, solicit funds based on demand estimates; regional units provide them resources but physical inventory controls are weak. Local units also report piecemeal physical performance data (e.g., patients attended; student promotion, desertion, and graduation rates). Both SSP (planning) and SED (education ministry) central and regional units are relatively sophisticated at compiling performance statistics. SSP has been posting them into its SIGAF system since 1997; SED also generates physical performance information. But, in contrast with their counterparts in the CEE/FSU, many sectoral ministries in Latin American do not analyze costs and physical outputs/outcomes. Nor do they link allocations to past performance or future requirements to attain service objectives.

Without basic budget performance data it is practically impossible to program resources to meet client needs in such core areas as education and health. As noted, this is exacerbated by line-item (economic) classification of some wages/salaries as *Asignaciones Globales* . There are likely other uses of this category (hiding wage expenditures), which weakens overall expenditure programming and control. Without knowing the past levels of allocated funds to each sector or the performance attributable to these funds, future allocation decisions are difficult to make. Lacking this data, it is also difficult to cut back funds to maintain macroeconomic control (under frequent conditions of unplanned revenue shortage). Without efficiency and effectiveness data, across-the-board cuts taken by MOFs (either at the beginning of the year or as cash limits imposed during the year) effectively delegate the cuts to sectoral ministries and this may, perversely, reward inefficient programs and penalize efficient ones.

As in many countries of the Latin American region, the existing budget process in Honduras responds relatively well to aggregate fiscal discipline criteria, but not well to allocational or operational concerns in the face of widespread poverty and the need for a well-maintained infrastructure. Aggregate discipline is revealed by the fact that the fiscal deficit (overall fiscal balance) of Honduras for FY 2000 was only 3.5 percent of GDP. In FY 2008, the deficit was still low at 2.4 percent of GDP, reflecting consistent regional efforts on fiscal discipline. The forecasted 2010 deficit is 4.0 percent of GDP (EIU 2010, 11). The bulk of the consolidated deficit was attributable to public investment debt service payments and recurrent maintenance expenses. Sectoral public investment portfolios were often inconsistent with GOH policy priorities given large amounts of earmarked funds that diminished budgetary flexibility. Facilities maintenance in areas such as electricity (ENEE) was often deferred due to cumbersome parts acquisition procedures. Failure to maintain capital facilities and to provide sufficient resources for operations reduced the value of public investment to economic development, for example, poorly maintained roads failed to reduce transport costs and delivery time, which harmed the rural poor.

Local Government Fiscal and Management Autonomy: Decentralization

This is a region weighed down by a centralist colonial heritage—probably longer than any region discussed in this book. There has been a long tradition of resistance to delegation of authority to lower management levels within organizations and to lower-tier governments in countries of this region. A lot of this is due to the culture of centralization noted above—which is similar to that found in the CEE/FSU region. By the usual measures, historically, political and fiscal decentralization proceeded slowly in most countries of the Latin American region.

However, over the past twenty years, the region has made important progress, devolving resources and functions to lower-tier governments (Daughters and Harper 2006, 1). Triggered in most cases by the national democratic transitions of the 1980s, the reforms moved from political to fiscal. From creation of representative democracies at the local level (i.e., political decentralization), evidenced by direct local mayoral elections, reforms moved to the fiscal arena in many countries. Ironically, the same enthusiasm for fiscal and political devolution is now happening even in the more centralized UK, where local governments spend about 25 percent of total government expenditures but can count on only 10 percent of total financing from their own-source revenues (*Economist* 2007, 31). It is important to note that enthusiastic and well-thought-out programs of fiscal decentralization began in the CEE/FSU region in the 1990s and continue today, drawing many lessons from the longer Latin American experience with this phenomenon.

Some of the Latin American devolutions are surprising and suggest that democracy, political decentralization, and fiscal transparency may not be as tightly linked as previously thought. For example, the region's premier democracy, Costa Rica (since 1948), only authorized direct election of local mayors and separation of mayor and district council elections from national elections in 2002 (2006, Table 7.2). Even the transparency score of the Costa Rican budget is surprisingly low for this long-standing and well-functioning democracy, namely, slightly below Guatemala and just above Egypt and Turkey (IBP 2008, 7). And as noted in Peru, devolution of poverty program management to local representative committees paradoxically resulted in major fiscal leakage and failure of expenditures to perform as intended (World Bank 2003, 71). In short, the separate evolutionary paths of political and fiscal decentralization in Latin America can provide useful comparative lessons for other regions, especially Eastern Europe and the Former Soviet Union. This exchange of comparative lessons has already begun in earnest (see for example Grupo Propuesta Ciudadana 2006).

There are four major fiscal dimensions to decentralization: expenditure, revenue, transfers, and debt. Expenditure decentralization can be measured by such indicators as increased local total shares of national expenditures, assigned responsibilities for major services to local governments, and devolution of authority to local governments for program performance. There is wide regional variation in expenditure decentralization. Local governments in countries such as Argentina, Brazil, and Colombia spend nearly 50 percent of total national public expenditures. This puts them in the company of the world's most decentralized regimes, for instance, the United States, Canada, and Nordic European countries (2006, 6). In contrast with the federalist states of Argentina and Brazil, it should be noted that Colombia has a unitary regime—suggesting that regionalist traditions can still overcome centralist tendencies without the necessity of changing intergovernmental structures. Major fiscal decentralization has taken place in both unitary and federalist structures in this region. Other countries in Latin America have devolved significant expenditure authority: Mexico, Venezuela, Bolivia, Peru, and Ecuador range from 17.5 to 31.8 percent of total public expenditures controlled by subnational governments in 2002–03 (2006, 7). The lowest levels of expenditure decentralization can be found in Central America (Costa Rica, Panama, Honduras, Nicaragua, and Guatemala), Chile, and Uruguay (2006, 8). Countries of the region have also varied widely in expenditure assignments, that is, in the mix of delegated autonomy and responsibility for particular services. While the first wave of devolution included basic services and infrastructure such as urban transportation, the second wave included the more difficult services such as health, education, housing, and interurban roads (2006, 9). Much of the variation in expenditure decentralization can be traced to union opposition to decentralization of services and scarcity of resources to assign from central to lower tiers (2006, Table 7.5). Despite this opposition, sectoral decentralization has also moved ahead quickly, often on a trial and error or pilot basis in an attempt to achieve the best local service results.

In the revenue area, local own-source revenues have increased as shares of national revenues collected in many Latin countries. Own-source (as opposed to transfers, revenue sharing, or debt revenues) revenues are critical to decentralized governance. Often, transfers are misclassified as own-source despite the fact that they are centrally derived and conditional (i.e., often not under total local control). Without own-source funds, local governments are dependent on central transfers or other bases that are outside of their control. This means they are dependent on national tax bases and exercise minimal fiscal or political accountability for service performance. Maximization of reliance for service financing on own-source revenues increases local accountability for service benefits. Without local revenues, citizens have little interest in complaining to officials, since they lack any real authority to finance or implement services. The democratic link with voters depends on local officials that have fiscal authority and responsibility. Despite this well-known linkage, with the exception of Brazil, most Latin American countries have given only limited priority to assigning revenue bases to local governments. Central governments rely on centralized tax collections and share the proceeds with subnational governments via revenue sharing or transfers to finance local services. There is a wide range of revenue assignment levels in Latin America, from 32 percent of subnational collection of total national tax revenues in Brazil to only 8.6 percent in Chile and 1.9 percent in Colombia (2006, 15). Brazil actually has a subnational VAT, making it one of the most fiscally decentralized countries in the world (2006, 13). In other cases, such as Nicaragua, local governments may have assigned tax authority to set rates and collect various taxes and fees but lack own-source revenue bases on which to impose taxes. This is a clear mismatch of revenue authority and fiscal capacity.

In the fiscal transfer or grants area, most Latin American countries have co-participation or revenue-sharing schemes for intergovernmental finance. As is known, transfers to local governments should be provided on the basis of transparent formulae for equalization and/or program support. For transfers to be effective they should be transparent, predictable, and subject to an agreed formula that is nonnegotiable (Stren 2001, 109). For example, in Peru, public resources are distributed either by transfers to municipalities (e.g., *vaso de leche* program) or centrally allocated to branches of the central government, that is to say, deconcentrated (education) (World Bank 2003, 72). Transfer systems seek to reduce (1) vertical fiscal imbalances (between central and local tiers) and (2) horizontal fiscal imbalances (between regions). Among the more serious problems with central transfers are (1) formulae that are often opaque and grants that are really ad hoc or negotiated on a partisan or crony basis, (2) central governments that impose sectoral spending quotas which distort local services, and (3) volatile central transfers that increase the revenue instability of local governments while their expenditure obligations remain fixed (2006, 17). There is a slow trend in Latin America to increase the nondiscretionary amounts of central transfers and to try and make the criteria more transparent. Countries as diverse as Peru, El Salvador, and Ecuador have moved to modernize their transfer systems. This, however, does not increase local fiscal autonomy. It only makes their revenue sources more transparent and predictable.

Finally, local debt as a percentage of total public debt and local capital expenditures as a percentage of local expenditures have all increased in this region. This is in line with the decentralization goal of increasing local fiscal autonomy. Unfortunately, in Latin America there have also been major fiscal crises driven in large part by uncontrolled municipal borrowing. Fiscal crises in the mid-1990s in Brazil, Colombia, Ecuador, Peru, and Bolivia threatened macroeconomic stability in those countries (2006, 19). For example, in 2005, Argentinean subnational governments were responsible for 21 percent of the total consolidated national public debt of the country (2006, 31). While this sounds like positive fiscal autonomy, it also reflects uncontrolled borrowing—accrued debt from previous central government bailouts and special transfers to cover local fiscal shortfalls. Local borrowing behavior in such countries as Argentina contrasts with much more conservative indebtedness pressures from Eastern European governments in the same period— likely a reflection of a more reserved (or withdrawn) governmental political culture. In response, Latin American countries imposed several types of borrowing restrictions on local governments. Most governments (with pressure from rating agencies, such as Fitch and Standard and Poor's) introduced standardized fiscal performance benchmarks to allow monitoring and evaluation of local fiscal conditions and to register early warnings of any fiscal crisis (e.g., Brazil 1997 and 2000). Central governments imposed restrictions such as: (1) complete prohibitions of local borrowing, (2) borrowing conditioned on central nonobjection, (3) restriction to borrowing for infrastructure ("golden rule"), and (4) quantitative limits on amounts permitted to borrow (2006, 19). They also promulgated subnational debt restructuring laws to deal with accumulating liabilities (e.g., Colombia 1997 and 2003) and passed other laws that increased local fiscal disclosure (Mexico 2000) (Daughters and Harper 2006, Table 7.6).

Empirical and analytical discussions of fiscal decentralization need to cover at least two dimensions: (1) the degree of delegated fiscal autonomy and the link between proposed or actual fiscal autonomy, and (2) service performance. Most of the literature on this topic covers mainly the first dimension. Much of it covers the economic and institutional bases for revenue/expenditure assignments, the elements of legal/regulatory framework, the need for macroeconomic controls as a prior condition, and suggested sequences of decentralization for different country types.

The literature also covers sectoral decentralization, particularly health and education experiences. As noted in the above section on expenditure decentralization, good data exist on the level of range of this by service, but not on the link between mixtures of fiscal/management decentralization by service and actual performance. Countries such as Argentina, Brazil, Colombia, and Mexico (all large countries) decentralized education by the early 1990s (2006, 8). Other, smaller countries such as Costa Rica and Chile did not decentralize them but still provide efficient and effective levels of those services. This indicates that scale economies may work to keep some services centralized (or deconcentrated) and that this may be sufficient for good performance—despite the apparent absence of local democratic control. Besides the oft-discussed risk to macroeconomic stability and program effectiveness, the more important issue is how to design and assign the functions properly. Much has been written about the theory of assignments. Less is known empirically. In some cases, centralization of particular sectors may be preferable to decentralization or a mixture of functional responsibilities in order to maximize service benefits. Indonesia has discovered the major human costs of decentralizing responsibilities for disaster management to local authorities. Local governments are more responsible and accountable but with weaker central controls over shared functions such as this, competition between tiers of government can hamper program performance (Mydans 2007). The point is that, because of excessive spillovers and lack of correspondence between lower-tier service providers and their beneficiaries, some programs, such as disaster relief and social assistance, are decentralized but costly and ineffective. They should probably be deconcentrated from the center—unless special circumstances exist. This empirical notion is often masked in the ideological race to decentralize because of its assumed connection to democracy—when in some contexts it may lead instead to partition, fragmentation, and breakup of fragile national identities.

CONCLUSION

Latin American has made great strides in macroeconomic control of the public finances and in decentralization of political and fiscal authority to lower-tier governments. Many countries in this region have achieved these milestones despite widespread variation in demographics and income levels. They have also done this in spite of centralized political cultures that work against devolution and management accountability. Throughout the region, on the heels of donor-driven fiscal austerity programs and local policy achievements by a new breed of fiscal technocrat, budget institutions have made major improvements—in the last twenty years perhaps more than the previous 150 years. Improved fiscal planning, implementation, and control are evident from the sound fiscal positions of most countries in this region today. Public officials have greater technical capacity and better tools, such as IFMS to account for fiscal transactions which permit quick course corrections during the year. Budget coverage has widened substantially, and the fiscal transparency of its largest countries are a model for the rest of the world.

Problems remain at the management and operational levels. Centralized budget formulation processes remain indifferent to performance information. Services are inefficient and ineffective and this intensifies the poverty that permeates so much of this region. This poverty is often used as a resource by demagogues and populists to attain power on promises of massive spending to help the poor. As indicated by major financial leaks from some of Peru's antipoverty programs, lack of funds is often not the problem—despite its apparent causation. Expenditure control weaknesses remain at the management and operational levels and this, combined with rigid and uncontrollable (or fixed) budgets, perpetuates program inefficiencies and ineffectiveness. In order for budgeting to stimulate true development in this region, public financial management problems at the operational and management levels must be tackled next on the policy agenda.

7

BUDGET REFORM AND
DISSEMINATION OF INFORMATION

BACKGROUND ON REFORMS

This chapter extends the earlier discussion in chapter 5 and elsewhere in the book of budgeting and financial management systems reform. A common fallacy among practitioners and academics alike has been to equate the topic with progress toward achievement of only program or performance-type budgeting. In that "reform" has come to mean this kind of advanced budgeting in the minds of many people, it may have actually worked against the more needed budget reforms that can increase the efficacy of public expenditures. We often forget that the earliest reform efforts and many underway in developing and transitional countries related to accounting and reporting of government expenditures. Relating expenditures to actual program results beyond formal budget documents is considered science fiction by many practitioners. But the perception still exists that this is what the field is all about. Fundamental budget reform really means having budgets that cover all expenditure types and revenue sources, and getting expenditure classifications right so that they measure what is actually received in revenues and spent over the fiscal year. Not very exciting stuff but that is from where reforms must start.

In a historical and institutional sense, reforms are shaped by the problems and cultural values of the time and by the successes/failures of past reform efforts. Prior budget and policy commitments logically constrain future commitments (a major type of the "path dependency" noted in the institutional economics literature). More importantly, existing systems of law and the values they represent can predetermine the framework for reform. For example, the civil code system found in most transitional and developing countries places a high premium on rules and compliance with them before action can be permitted. If it isn't explicitly authorized, one must presume it to be prohibited under this pervasive cultural-legal system. This "state-centered dominance of public law" (Stillman 2002, 20, cited in Wright and Nemec) profoundly affects the behavior of public managers and especially budget managers and reformers. For fiscal managers in civil law–based countries, matters must be carefully planned and scripted by law or permission is withheld for budget modifications, for budget supplements, new programs, and even for the installation of new treasury and accounting systems. Since this is difficult to do in practice, the operational systems are plodding and lethargic. They are hard to change. They force managers in many cases either to do nothing or to circumvent the law. Only actions specifically authorized by law are permitted. By contrast, common law areas, such as the United States and Commonwealth countries operate from a different premise—laws derive from precedent and are driven by practice. Actions are presumed to be permitted unless explicitly prohibited. Budget formulation and execution is more of a matter of management discretion than legal compliance. There is more flexibility and discretion in budget formulation and management systems and this can encourage professionalism, innovation, and program entrepreneurship. Without sound fiscal controls, of course, it can and has encouraged misappropriation of funds and abuse of power.

Years ago, Schick distinguished control, management and planning reforms without implying any progression or evolution (Schick 1966). Early *control* reforms in the nineteenth century (United States) simply attempted to get accounting control of budgets and to add up the deficits—corruption was a big problem in the early days of modern state budgeting. The economic classification was a reform over previous systems that amounted to one large slush fund or "other" category for politicians to play with. As will be discussed further below, Nigeria used a homegrown classification system that allowed for large amounts of "slush" as recently as 2003. The U.S. 1971 "current services budget" was a reform to the concept of the baseline needed for annual preparation. For discretionary programs (not mandated by law, such as social security and other entitlements), MOFs and the U.S. OMB need estimates of inflation-adjusted line ministry budgets that include workload changes but ignore policy changes (Axelrod 1988, 36). They also require that departmental or ministry expenditure requests be calculated in nominal amounts (un-adjusted for inflation) that include at the line ministry level after policy changes. Before this reform, budget "bases" were variously defined as past year's planned budget (not approved!) or actual expenditures (when it takes about two years to audit yearly accounts!). This led to loss of control over the budget and the initial preparation and approval stages. In most places, the base became the past year's approved budget. MOFs also disallowed submission of real (inflation-adjusted) budgets from ministries. Allowing real requests meant that the treasury would pay for increased costs of service—not the ministries. When word gets out (as it did in Britain in the 1970s) that the treasury will pay for inflation adjustments anytime during the year, ministry incentives are to increase program expenditures (usually a worthy objective) and the treasury will absorb the resultant fiscal deficits. These perverse incentives led to major inflationary pressures in the British economy, as it would any other place.

Early-twentieth-century progressive reaction to the input orientation and incremental nature of budgetary analysis (leaving last year's base intact except for inflation and workload adjustments) led to reforms that would link expenditures to outputs and encourage analysis of results attained (cost/student; students graduated; service coverage of potential student population; cost/quality patient service day). These were reforms geared to *management* of programs and improved performance. Performance- or results-oriented budgeting required improved databases, development of activity statistics and staff analytic capabilities, and incentives to engage in service and program analysis. An important lesson learned from the attempt to link expenditures with outcomes or quality results (e.g., police budgets and safer streets, not just more officers on the beat) was that the major format reforms of the 1960s, such as PPBS, did not penetrate the routines of decision making (especially in legislatures) nor did they produce any major changes to allocations or results. Other less radical and more incremental changes such as performance, cost-center analysis, and zero-based or "decremental" budgeting did result in performance measurement and better linkage of funds with results.

Besides efforts to improve control and performance results or outputs (e.g., miles of paved roads; operating costs/passenger mile for bus service) and outcomes (e.g., percentage of coverage of a region by paved roads or public transit), other reforms sought to encourage forward budget *planning*. Working from new budget calendars that integrated current and capital expenditures over a four or five year period, these processes developed multiyear estimates of current and capital expenditures and linked them to economic assumptions to form a functioning hard budget constraint. As explained in chapter 3, the medium-term expenditure framework (MTEF), for example, encouraged changes in procedures to allow rolling forward of new estimates each year to include new assumptions, which required adjustments to the annual budget in order to meet deficit targets. This allowed forward planning and underscored the constraints under which present-year budgeting was taking place. If combined with public disclosure of revenue and expenditure projections, it reduced the ability of policymakers to deny these fiscal constraints when developing budgets.

Reforms of budget control, management, and planning systems have occurred in a context of dynamic tensions between macro budgetary forces that often tried to "guard" against overexpenditures or hold the line against institutional changes of any kind. The guardians work on the aggregate totals from top down. At the other end of the process is the spender or program advocate role. Occupants of this institutional role want more funding to achieve their stated ends: assist poor people, provide health and education, deliver more passenger miles of transit service, etc. These officials often could care less about centrally derived totals and budget ceilings. They like reforms that indicate the value of their work—unit costing, effectiveness measures, activity-based costing, multiyear budget commitments, and so on. They also like decentralized operational responsibility—having maximum flexibility and discretion to modify budgets including personnel expenditures. Whether national or local line officials, they rarely want to deal with strategic issues such as reducing budget deficits by making cutbacks.

The context of guardian-spender conflict is the budget process, which many argue should be reformed. In the quest for the genie of performance, we may have been distracted from the purpose of budgeting itself—which is the planning and control of public spending. The budget process is the one opportunity in the policy process to compare means and ends and to try and link the results of public expenditure with original plans. As many observers such as Posner (2009) have pointed out, this process is in need of repair in the United States. In contrast with the heady days of transferring lessons from the United States abroad, the practical situation now is that many successful budget process lessons from overseas can and should be applied in the United States.

DEFINITIONS AND TYPES OF BUDGET REFORM

"Reform" is one of the undefined terms in public sector and public budgeting literature. Previous chapters discussed a host of changes in five regions of the world (Europe, the United States, Latin America, Commonwealth Countries, and Central-Eastern Europe/Former Soviet Union). To round out our regional review of fiscal practices, reforms, and remaining issues, this chapter includes country examples from the African and Asian regions. Fiscal changes in these regions represented important reforms. The important question was: Were they successful?

One often assumes that any change, major or minor is a "reform" when, of course it might not be. A *reform* is a type of change that seeks to improve procedures and underlying practices in any of the major areas of public financial management. These are often *structural* in that they attempt to change more than one core financial management system, for example, budgeting, accounting, and procurement. But reforms can also be minor, *marginal* or incremental. These could focus on one core system, for instance, modification of the budget calendar. Modification of budget forms and formats are typically more marginal reforms than changes in analytic methods, databases, informational and allocation systems. The latter are typically structural-type reforms and take longer because they penetrate more deeply into institutional routines and repertoires. Thus, two distinctions should be made. First, one should distinguish between major and minor reforms. Second, one should distinguish those reforms that affect particular levels of budgetary decision making. It was noted that there are three levels of budget decision making: (1) aggregate discipline or control (e.g., macroeconomic plans and con-

TABLE 7.1. **Reforms of Budget Process Stages**

Preparation	*Approval*	*Execution/Control*	*Evaluation/Audit*
MTEF (e.g. UK, African countries)	Analytic Unit (e.g. CBO)	Integrated Financial Management Systems (IFMS) (e.g. Latin America)	Supreme Audit Institutions (SAIs) (e.g. U.S. GAO)
PPB/Program (e.g. US state-local governments)	Broad Line-Item Approval (eg New Zealand and some U.S. states)	Single Treasury Accounts	Budget Office Monitoring and Evaluation Units
Performance-Based	Legislative Analysis Units: Flexible Volume Budgeting and Service Costing	Accrual Accounting and Budgeting	Legislative Performance Audit Units (external audit)
CIP-Capital Plan/Budget (e.g. Romania)	Weighting and Scoring Models with community stakeholders; cost effectiveness and cost-benefit analyses	Independent Internal Audit Units (e.g. IGs)	Budget office investment monitoring and evaluation units
Current Services Budget (CSB)	Zero based budgeting analysis to examine cost/ consequences of service changes in real terms	Performance reporting	Departmental level annual fiscal and program performance reviews

trols, fiscal deficit limits), (2) strategic allocation and management (e.g., sector investment plans, MTEF), and (3) operational (e.g., road O&M management systems). Those reforms that affect two or three levels are more major (e.g., IFMS systems) and those that affect only one level or one core system are likely more minor (e.g., O&M system).

For example, budget reforms may target one or more phases of the process. This is evident from Table 7.1.

DIMENSIONS OF RECENT BUDGET SYSTEMS REFORM

Public financial management reforms (which may or may not include budget reform because budgeting is only one of its functions) can be identified at all decision levels and at all stages of the process. As suggested by previous chapters, public fiscal management has improved in most places of the world. Many reforms have been tried and some have been well institutionalized. Even in those regions beset by political and economic instability, public finance officials know most of the right lessons and practices. They just may not be able to apply them.

To get a better picture of what has been done in the reform area, we can distinguish four reform targets: (1) core fiscal foundations and databases, (2) budget formulation documents, information structures, and analysis, (3) budget management and implementation, and (4) actual legislative allocations and other measures of reform results. Countries in virtually all regions have put various reforms into place across these four categories. For example, they have improved or reformed systems of cash management through single treasury accounts (e.g., Eastern Europe). Many countries have improved audit and financial control procedures and practices (e.g., EU). Most countries have reduced the number of extrabudgetary accounts and eliminated loosely regulated and often superfluous public agencies (e.g., Latin America). Many countries have developed budget ceilings for both the aggregate budget and for line ministries to improve expenditure planning and control (e.g., Commonwealth). Legislated borrowing limits for subnational or local governments have taken place in many countries and are consistent with this trend (e.g., Latin America). Countries have also developed capital investment programs (often called PIPs) and integrated them with current budgets—to ensure that future maintenance is covered and debt service is paid on contracted loans. A few countries have tried "accrual budgeting," which links net worth accounting of assets to budgetary accounting systems (Petrei 1998, 358). But most countries limit themselves to partial accrual (imputing expenditures but not capital charges) or mixed accrual (expenditures on a commitments basis; revenues on a cash basis) to avoid politicization of data that is often weak and subjective. Most countries have improved the transparency of their budget documents from presentations of raw accounting data by legal budget codes and chapters to narrative descriptions of problems and program responses measured by activity statistics.

On the other side, there are countries that have not succeeded or even attempted these kinds of reforms. We noted the 2006 outcry against the Hungarian PM for lying about fiscal fundamentals, touching off riots and calls for his ouster. After almost a decade of fiscal reforms following the early 1990s transition, the ironic backlash is now against proper fiscal reform in much of the CEE region. After the Hungarian experience, the Ukrainian PM said publicly he would avoid fiscal reform to avoid setting off riots (Dempsey 2006). How can fiscal fundamentals be put back in shape without reforms that will touch off broad social unrest? The history of fiscal reform in Poland indicates that short-term sacrifice is required and must be tolerated in order to succeed. In other regions (and now parts of Eastern Europe itself), the public no longer wants to go through this and reacts violently at reform proposals, real reforms, and PMs who lie about the need for reform. Should the tenure of elected officials take precedence over the need for national fiscal reforms? What can be done about it?

By contrast, why have Commonwealth countries tried consistently to reform budget rules and processes (as noted in chapter 3)? What is the difference? Has it been failure to convince political regimes of any more tangible benefits in taking on reform risks? Has it been a perception that technical capacity was lacking? Was it inability to develop the right technical sequence for installation of reforms? Or was the "stall" a kind of institutional /legal legacy or "path dependency" that limited efforts on reform? Without knowing what determines reform successes, it is difficult to make the case to either civil servants or the public. Some African and Asian countries have opted for Medium-Term Expenditure Frameworks imported largely from Commonwealth countries (Peterson cited in Shah 2007). Others have installed performance-type systems only (Shah and Shen cited in Shah 2007). Still others have tried to do both at once. Most of these have been only partly successful. What determines the successes? Was it simple technical capacity? Or was it something in the political culture? Can that something be changed or is it constant? If it is the latter, this could limit the transferability of most budget reforms.

One almost predictable finding is that lack of basic capacities to develop an annual budget and to manage cash can strike a death knell to more complex reform programs. Such basic control capacities are virtually absent in countries such as Ghana, leading to in-year cash shortages (Andrew and Turkewitz 2005, 207). This dampens managerial support for more strategic and managerial reforms such as performance-based or accrual budgeting. For this reason, it was advocated in 2002 that Pakistan begin output-based reforms with input-performance measures using the existing economic classification and accounting database, for example, O&M expenditures as a percentage of total budget (Guess 2002). The premise was that this would generate demands for improved data and analysis that can rapidly provide both fiscal control and service performance improvements—normally associated with much more sophisticated and longer-term reforms.

FISCAL DATABASES

Classification and Coverage

Budget watchdogs and the public increasingly demand *transparency* of the public accounts. The response is often massive dumps of raw fiscal data onto Web sites that are of little use for analysis or decision making. For transparency to have meaning, information should be required that is relevant and standardized (*Economist* 2009). The terminology of public budgeting is often confusing and inconsistent and needs to be standardized along with budget formats and reporting categories. To a large extent, norms have been standardized and it is important that watchdogs and the public learn and apply them. Otherwise, calls for transparency will be met with more useless data, which only increases public frustration with the budget process. This increases public distrust in government and in fiscal reform.

To begin with, there can be no reform (however defined) unless budget expenses are first controlled. The government budget needs to cover comprehensively all major expenditures through use of a general fund and explain in notes what is exceptional, that is, off-budget funds. The question of what the budget should "cover" is not easily answered nor is practice as uniform as it should be. Resolution of this definitional issue is critical to cash flow and fiscal deficit measurement. The exact level of deficit (whether *primary*, meaning interest payments are excluded; *cash* deficit, meaning actual outlays and collected revenues; or *commitments* deficit, meaning cash receipts and accrued expenditures) (Schiavo-Campo and Tommasi 1999, 98–99) cannot be determined without a firm definition of basics such as: budget, revenue, and outlay. That is, the level of budget deficit will turn to a great extent on the scope of the budget and what is defined in the budget law as an "expenditure."

Historically, extrabudgetary funds (EBFs) have been a problem for budget discipline and analysis because they often carry their own money. Such funds are often earmarked from the budget (e.g., road funds, regional funds, energy funds) or derived from external sources (e.g., counterpart aid funds). Some EBFs are justified by their nature (e.g., social security). Social security payments should be integrated into the budget. If this is not possible, at least revenue sources, uses, and balances of social security payments should be annexed to the consolidated government financial report (Schiavo-Campo and Tommasi 1999, 47). The existence of other EBFs may be justifiably released from traditional appropriation management rules because such rules would limit the flexibility of budget management (e.g., road maintenance funds and departmental enterprises) (1999, 37–43). Disagreements remain on whether to include gross versus net expenditures in the budget. Gross calculations include expenditures, budget revenues, and revenues recovered by fees or sales. Netting governmental activities reduces the size of the budget but could impede analysis of costs of production by program or policy (1999, 47).

For transparency, it must be clear how well budgets cover measurement of "quasi-fiscal" activities, such as interest rate subsidies and payments for loss-making state enterprises (1999, 48). Including all of them as direct government expenditures for subsidies would definitely make the budget more transparent and improve targeting. These issues are well known by most fiscal analysts who know the games that governments can play to hide the size of their expenditures and their uses. The significance of transparent coverage and the need for wide budget scope was underscored in the United States. According to many experts, including

Meyers (2009, 217), the recent banking and financial crisis "arose in part because the government failed to accurately determine the scope of the budget—that is what's counted and what's properly excluded" (2009, 217). "The huge government sponsored housing and mortgage enterprises (GSEs) Fannie Mae and Freddie Mac avoided budget scrutiny despite the huge risks they were imposing on government" (2009, 217). The point is that implicit subsidies to government-sponsored entities should be included in the budget. In many countries, such as the United States, they have not been. Failure of basic budgetary reform rules such as appropriate scope and coverage jeopardize not only service delivery but also the stability of the international economy as well.

A related fiscal reform problem is the transparency of public debt figures. Private public partnerships (PPPs) for such large projects as roads are often kept in EBFs off-budget. Leases are also often kept off-budget, despite the fact that they, as well as PPPs, are explicit contingent liabilities of the government that the treasury must pay in the event of default or failure of lower-tier levels of government to pay them (1999, 48). In the case of lease-purchase agreements, local governments often acquire capital equipment and infrastructure via multiyear lease-purchase arrangements. Lessors (banks, equipment companies) "lease" capital to governmental units to avoid the agreement being classified as debt, since this affects future capacity to borrow and can threaten high local bond ratings (Vogt and Duven 1983, 65–66). U.S. local government leases typically include "nonappropriation clauses" to avoid their classification as debt. But this increases risks to lessors (lenders and investors) expecting to be paid for government infrastructure projects via annual appropriations. The problem with such arrangements is that in the event of default, an implicit liability is created at the next higher tier of government—meaning that the debt should have been transparent in the budget to begin with.

Local government budgets are typically more transparent. At the U.S. local government level, the many special funds such as enterprise funds (called proprietary funds) can be consolidated at any time to ascertain their fiscal position, to reveal levels of consolidated indebtedness and to ensure that overall fiscal balance targets are not breached. Automated accounting and reporting systems reveal cash flows and help pinpoint any problems in advance. If enterprise EBFs are opaque, for instance, it may make matters worse to include enterprise balances within general funds. This could hide the flow of subsidies to and from cities and their enterprises (Coe 1989, 17). Political leaders often use general funds to cover deficits in the water and sewer enterprise funds. If a city is in financial trouble during one quarter of the fiscal year, the flow could be reversed by the next quarter depending on personal contacts facilitating the right institutional arrangements. The "broad-based budget" in Latin America at the national level is an example of a successful budget reform that has increased coverage of all the major expenditures of "general government." (General government expenditures, as indicated, include those of: the central, regional, and local government units, together with social security and social assistance funds. It does not include "non-financial" or public financial institutions.) Many "reformed" budgets also include an estimate of contingent liabilities such as loan guarantees or subnational debt. These are important figures in that if there is a default by a larger local government debtor, the central treasury might have to make extra outlays. That would breach its planned fiscal deficit target and likely affect both its creditworthiness and ability to fund planned programs. In short, the objective of good budgetary coverage is to produce a comprehensive budget that consists of a transparent, timely, and accurate statement of the government's consolidated fiscal position.

Budget expenditures should also be classified for fiscal and programmatic accountability purposes. This means the government must know its cash position at any one time and be able to budget without fear of overexpenditure, either through miscalculation or reliance on simple cash accounting systems that exclude obligations accrued during the year via purchase orders issued and contracts signed. Payables and receivables will appear in the balance sheet accounts for almost any government. But they will not appear in the budgetary accounts unless it is a more modern cash system or at least modified accrual system (which reports commitments, encumbrances, or accrued expenditures, and possibly accrued revenues). Fiscal managers cannot make rational choices on the budget without having commitments information throughout the fiscal year. As simple as the problem sounds, some governments continue to use narrow cash systems and hold balances off budget. This creates major fiscal management surprises. At a more complex reform level, because of technical capacity and service measurement problems, most governments still have little idea of the efficiency and effectiveness of actual expenditures on health, education, agriculture, public works, etc. This is less surprising than the inability to define and control annual cash flows for basic objects of expenditure budgets. Outside reviewers, such as external auditors, credit rating agencies, and citizen budget monitoring groups (often NGOs) have to deal then with unconsolidated balances and hidden deficits or debt in many developing countries—particularly in Sub-Saharan Africa. The problem of fiscal "black holes" weakens arguments to provide more aid funds to poor governments to reduce poverty. But change is afoot on fiscal reform for even the African region.

In FY 2005, the Nigerian Bureau of Finance (BOF) introduced a new classification system based on best international standards and practices (Guess 2005). New forms, instructions, and explanatory manuals were prepared during the fiscal year and were ready for use in preparation of the FY 2005 budget. The purpose of this seemingly marginal reform was made to increase the transparency and precision of the government budget. As is known, the budget classification is the foundation of the entire public budgeting system. To improve expenditure targeting and control, the majority of countries have adopted the IMF's Government

Financial Statistics (GFS) classification system. GFS has become the worldwide standard for reporting on fiscal operations and is used in most countries throughout the world. It introduced a single set of standards for reporting government spending both by inputs and by function or sector. The GFS system classifies expenditures by (1) *economic* class for statistical and economic analysis, and (2) *function* for policy analysis purposes. Categorizing expenditures and revenues according to these two formats permits policymakers and the public to ascertain what has been purchased and paid for by government.

GFS also classifies expenditures by (3) *organizational unit* and (4) *programs.* The latter consist of a set of activities that pursue the same set of objectives. Program classifications have often been overly ambitious and have failed generally to correspond with the organizational structures of government (Schiavo-Campo and Tommasi 1999, 74). In that program classification rarely translate well into line items, the stage is set for conflict and distrust between the executive (that typically favor cost-effective performance norms and program rationality) and legislative branches (district constituents are politically best served by allocations of funds via line-item amounts). In an ideal world, the goal should be accountability for program-related expenditures in one place and facilitation of performance measurement and evaluation. Much has been written about the failures of program/performance budgeting (Axelrod 1988). But there are many successful examples of new budget formats that link performance outcomes with expenditures. These formats and databases have been institutionalized and in many cases the budget process becomes the major opportunity for policy and program analysis. Such successes illustrate that much more could be done here with proper leadership. For examples, see Milwaukee's *outcomes* budget: www.city.milwaukee.gov. Go to budget documents and review the 2007 Plan and Budget Summary as well as its capital investment budget (CIP).

The historical pattern of Nigerian budgeting mixed up expenditures in economic, organizational, and functional classifications (Guess 2005). Total expenditures were classified into three categories by (1) overhead, (2) personnel, and (3) capital. This simple classification system used for budget preparation and reporting was problematic in that it obscured the actual sources and uses of public funds. The threefold classification hindered policy formulation, budget analysis, accountability, and daily budget management. For example, nowhere in existing budget documents could policymakers (or other users) determine exactly what was spent on wages, purchases of goods and services, transfers, or subsidies (*subventions*). In addition, it was impossible to determine from existing budget documents how much of the budget was allocated to health, education, defense, agriculture, or any other function of government. This information is essential to monitor and evaluate program expenditures over time and to ascertain whether shifts from one function to another are necessary to achieve strategic policy priorities, such as poverty reduction.

The new GFS-consistent economic classification in Nigeria allows direct linkage of expenditures with the system of national accounts. In this system, wages and benefits are the components of value added from the government sector; and wages and salaries plus goods and services are the measurable components of government consumption. The new GFS-consistent functional classification allows reviewers to see how government expenditures are made according to the core functions of government. As indicated in the discussion and tables below, both economic and functional classification systems contain multiple subclassifications; budgets prepared and reported in each system can be translated or "crosswalked" across to the other.

Economic Classification
The following discussion reviews current practice and modification by the Nigerian MOF for FY 2005. Table 7.2 indicates the budget for a hypothetical ministry using the old classification system. As is evident, expenditures were mixed among economic, functional and organizational categories that impeded transparency and accountability.

Beginning in FY 2005, instead of using the three-category classification system, all current expenditures were assigned to the following groups:

1. Salaries
2. Benefits
3. Purchases of goods and nonpersonal services
4. Lending minus repayments
5. Transfers
6. Interest payments

Subgroups could be defined for use by individual budget entities, but no overall group classification was made to supplement this list. Examples of such subgroups are presented here.

1. Salaries
   i. Executive staff
   ii. Professional staff
   iii. Support staff
2. Benefits
   i. Health insurance scheme
   ii. Transportation to and from work
   iii. Meals for employees
3. Purchases of goods and non-personnel services
   i. Office supplies
   ii. Petrol

TABLE 7.2. Ministry X: Past Line-Item Budget

	Overhead Costs	
G	Travel and Transport	$10,401,120
G	Utility Service	$1,560,000
G	Telephone Service	$1,039,680
G	Stationary	$5,200,320
G	Mtc. of Furniture	$2,079,840
G	Mtc. of Veh. & Other Capital Assets	$6,240,480
G	Consultancy Service	$2,079,840
S	Contributions and Subventions	$259,680
G	Training & Staff Development	$3,120,000
G	Entertainment & Hospitality	$415,680
G	Miscellaneous Expenses	$9,321,120
S	Contribution to Foreign Bodies	$1,039,680
L	Motor Vehicle Advances	$2,079,480
G	International Travel and Transport	$2,880,000
G	Conferences and Workshops	$960,000
G	Rent of Office Accommodation	$576,000
G	Insurance of Govt. Assets	$960,000
	TOTAL	$50,212,920

Summary

W	Personnel Costs	$62,339,737
	Overhead Costs	$50,213,280
	TOTAL	$112,553,017

Key: W = Wages; G = Use of Goods and Services; S = Subsidies and Grants; L = Lending Less Repayments; I = Interest; K = Capital.

    iii. Telephone service
    iv. Maintenance services provided by a contractor
4. Lending minus repayments
    i. Loans to employees to purchase a bicycle
    ii. Loans to farmers for inputs
    iii. Loans to industry
5. Transfers and subsidies
    i. Subsidies to public enterprises
    ii. Grants to local governments
    iii. Subsidies to agriculture
6. Interest payments
    i. On foreign debt
    ii. On domestic debt

TABLE 7.3. Ministry X: New Economic Classification of Expenditures

W	Compensation of Employees	62,339,737	
G	Use of Goods and Services	46,834,080	
S	Subsidies and Grants	1,299,360	
L	Lending Minus Repayments	2,079,840	Note: Repayments not included
I	Interest Payments	0	Usually in the MOF budget only
K	Capital Spending	0	
	Purchases of Equipment	0	Capital budget data required
	Construction	0	
	Capital Transfers	0	
	TOTAL	112,553,017	

Items such as "maintenance of vehicles" or "maintenance of buildings" were clarified as to whether they referred to contracted maintenance services provided by an external contracting firm, or if salaries and other expenditures were used to provide maintenance services from the government's own resources.

Applying the new economic classification system to these same data yields more succinct and economically more meaningful information, as indicated in Table 7.3 for the same hypothetical Ministry X.

Using the new classification system indicated in Table 7.2, analysis can now be performed that should lead to improved budget formulation and linkage with expenditure results. For example, newly classified information indicates that about 50 percent of the budget is spent on personnel. Relevant analytical questions include: How many employees are there and is this an appropriate amount for ministry tasks? Staffing ratios from other countries and similar ministries can be used for comparison. Note that expenditures for goods and services are roughly 33 percent of the budget. How much of this was spent for maintenance and what results were achieved, for example in the area of roads, water and sewage systems? Finally, no funds were spent for capital. Is this appropriate? Could this reflect a measurement and misclassification problem where capital spending actually flows from current expense categories? Should less be spent on maintenance next year and more on capital? Analysts can use the new information (i.e., same data but differently classified) to formulate new questions that can lead to better expenditure results.

FUNCTIONAL CLASSIFICATION

There is still no functional classification of the Nigerian budget. In the Central Bank's Statistical Bulletin, there was an attempt to classify government spending by function into four categories: (1) administration, (2) economic services, (3) social and community services, and (4) transfers. But this classification is quite confusing. For instance, "transfers" is an economic classification item but does not reveal for what purposes they were made. In some cases, transfers are actually direct functional expenditures. Transfers made to hospitals to support operations should be classified as health spending; whereas transfers to universities should be classified as education spending. The same confusing classification was also used for the development budget (which should identify expenditures and revenues for locally financed programs and projects). Even with the Central Bank's functional classification it is not possible to determine how much of the development budget has been devoted to road construction, port development, school rehabilitation, or new clinics in rural areas.

Functional classification of expenditures allows the reviewer to see how government expenditures are made according to the functions of government. The UN classification of functions of government (COFOG) divides major service commitments into ten functions (Mikesell 2007, 243). The U.S. government uses eighteen budgetary functions (2007, 241–43). Functional classification includes all types of expenditure for a specific purpose, including transfers to households, purchase of goods and services, payment of salaries, such as for teachers and nurses, and construction of roads, and other infrastructure or facilities. Functional classification permits analysis of government outlays over time, that is, several fiscal years. For instance, with an appropriate functional classification it would be possible to track how much money is going to defense, health, education, or foreign aid. This allows the government, the National Assembly, and other users to assess the government's priorities and how they contribute to the development prospects of the nation.

COFOG (which is part of GFS) uses ten broad categories of functional expenditures. The categories and relevant subcategories should serve as a guide for Nigeria. Table 7.4 presents a preliminary attempt to classify recurrent expenditures in the 2002 Appropriations Act into these ten categories.

Using the recurrent amounts, the distribution of current government spending by function can be presented in graphic format as shown in Figure 7.1.

Figure 7.1 indicates that more than half of the 2002 appropriations were destined to the "general public services" function. This is effectively an *other* category! To be more useful, this function should be broken down further into subfunctions and categories. Figure 7.2 provides this breakdown.

TABLE 7.4. Functional Classification of Recurrent Expenditures

2002 Appropriation Act

Function	Total
Defense	$ 61,893,116,177
Economic Affairs	39,422,873,871
Education	59,994,441,815
Environmental protection	1,814,189,364
General public services	306,204,571,494
Health	29,749,752,701
Housing and community amenities	2,377,770,631
Public order and safety	66,772,320,554
Recreation, culture, and religion	5,494,484,644
Other	3,500,000,000
TOTAL	$ 577,223,521,251

FIGURE 7.1. Functional Classification of the Budget

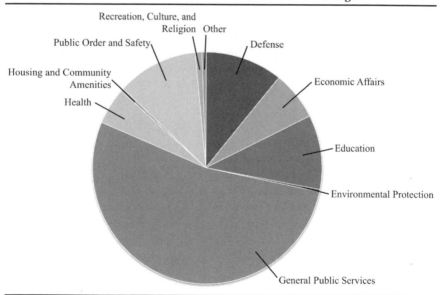

FIGURE 7.2. **Subfunctions of General Public Services**

Breakdown of General Public Services Expenditures

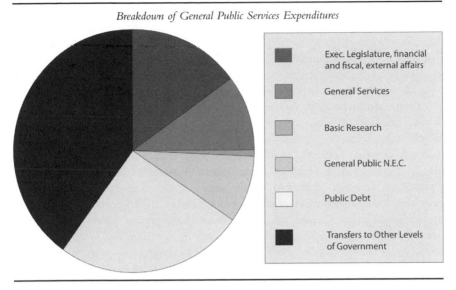

- Exec. Legislature, financial and fiscal, external affairs
- General Services
- Basic Research
- General Public N.E.C.
- Public Debt
- Transfers to Other Levels of Government

Computerized Financial Management Information Systems

Once data are classified properly, it is important that systems exist to process and consolidate them for meaningful decisions on such matters as cash flows, payment obligations for current items and capital projects, projected budgetary balances, and response to changes in revenue receipts.

An enormous amount of money has been spent worldwide on putting government services on line (e.g., licensing and permitting forms) via e-government and i-government systems. In many cases, the expensive computer systems have provided little improvements in public administration or how government organizations perform their work. In others, the projects fail altogether from design flaws, for example, the UK's $1billion project to merge two humdred criminal justice databases used by eighty thousand staff in the system (*Economist* 2008). While positive results from computerization in quality services have been hard to measure for the public services, reform projects in public financial management have generally produced good results (and also some spectacular failures).

An increasingly popular reform with international donors in all regions of the world has been introduction of automated financial management information systems (FMISs). These are known as integrated financial management systems (IFMSs) typically linked from a general ledger system to a treasury single account (which might be located in the central bank or ministry of finance). Such systems allow for tight control of budget implementation on a real-time, cash plus commitments basis. This also allows real-time consolidation of cash expenditures and expense commitments from ministries to be reconciled with bank balances. In that they cover the multiple functions of public financial management, they are structural reforms designed to increase macroeconomic and management control of public expenditures. In some cases, local government and subnational government units are included in the overall IFMS system design to provide a comprehensive picture of general government balances (*all-of-government accounting*). Where computerized accounting, reporting, and control systems have been installed, often in response to fiscal crises, expenditure management has been greatly improved. But many of these reform projects have not been properly designed or installed. Illustrated by the experiences of several Latin American countries, the problems have often been the institutional and capacity constraints for implementation—weak capacity of both the vendors/donors (who often oversell off-shelf products from the private sector) as well as the recipient or host country (whose institutions are fragmented and compete for parts of the FMIS work for them often to the detriment of the entire system).

As discussed more briefly in chapter 5, historically and presently, Latin America has suffered from undeveloped financial management systems. Typical problems and their consequences include:

- Failure to integrate payroll with accounting and budgeting entries leads to redundant payments and "ghost workers" (or paid no-shows) that drive up the costs of government. In many Latin American countries, payroll data is not shared with MOFs. Accounting and reporting systems are not linked to the personnel function, which includes the establishment roster and associated payroll system. This allows ghost workers to collect checks and, as personnel or *salary and wages* is usually a large item in the public budget, tends to drains the treasury. This is more than a technical problem with the core IFMS (which is typically the accounting, budgeting, and treasury functions) in that payroll and internal audit systems must function properly and be integrated with the overall core system for controls to work.
- Lack of integration of the procurement or acquisitions function and budgetary analysis of program options often allows cronyism to overprice government purchases. This can lead to arrears from governments that cannot pay penalties stipulated in supplier contracts as treasuries cannot find the tax revenues to cover inflated purchases.
- At a macropolitical level, structural disincentives have led to poor program results. For example, Latin American efforts to decentralize revenues and expenditures have been frustrated by failure to control

improper reprogramming of fiscal transfers from health and education supplies into salaries. Improperly designed and monitored fiscal transfer systems have led to increased funding for poor-performing schools—giving every incentive for low performance to school staff. Delegation of spending authority to the wrong level of government or type of organization for sectoral programs (school boards versus schools) can also siphon needed program funds from the intended beneficiaries (school programs and students).

• Failure to apportion counterpart funds (promised domestic budget contributions to donor programs) can lead to program delays and reduced country creditworthiness. In Bolivia, for example, while the Ministry of Planning signed an agreement with USAID for a small farmer program, the MOF was not instructed to program $14 million in counterpart funds (or perhaps instructed itself not to!). Either way, public credit data was not transparent, which diminished GOB accountability to both donors and local clients for programs such as this.

• Shared fiscal policy authority by the MOF and Ministry of Planning contribute to systemic weaknesses. This is a common governance design problem in many regions. Installation of IFMS alone cannot remedy institutional constraints to policymaking, that is, structural design problems. Moreover, as will be noted below, such problems impede the very design and installation of IFMSs in particular countries.

• Fiscal problems pointing to the need for IFMS installation are not unique to Latin America. Some of the best IFMS practices derive from New York City's fiscal crisis of 1975. In that case, the city could not determine the size of its debt and was unable to reconcile accounting and budgeting data with actual outlays. An IFMS was installed in 1977 linking accounting, budgeting, debt, payroll, and purchasing functions. Like other systems installed later in Latin America, this one enhanced budget management and control. The system signals on an exception basis major deviations in revenue collections and expenditures from plans and forecasts. It also tracks changes in budget implementation by agency, program, responsibility, or cost center (Axelrod 1988, 246). These are important fiscal policy tools for program management and evaluation without which cities and countries run high risks of having macroeconomic problems.

ECONOMIC GROWTH AND FISCAL MANAGEMENT
RATIONALE FOR IFMS

Given the similarity of fiscal problems in Latin America in the 1970s-80s, central administrations (MOFs, ministry finance departments, local government finance departments) needed to improve planning, budgeting, and expenditure controls.

Derived from U.S. state and local government practices dating back forty years, and applications of that experience to Latin America in the 1970s and early 1980s, IFMS offered a simple and proven model to plan and track expenditures with varying packages of incentives to perform these tasks. On paper, the new systems would include all fiscal data. Their operating assumption was that an empirical connection exists between improvements in fiscal transparency through improved data and governmental fiscal performance. Empirically, this has been validated. Studies such as Kopits and Craig (1998) listed a number of countries where a high degree of fiscal transparency was linked to greater fiscal discipline and a more robust economic performance. They also cited counterexamples where a lack of transparency was seen as a major contributor to poor economic performance.

In other words, improved fiscal data from each financial function led to its improved use in policymaking. Such studies support the need for financial management to accompany efforts to reform public policy systems. Costing and financing of policy proposals are as essential as evaluation of financial and program performance during implementation. This underscores the point that budgeting has become one of the chief political decision-making systems (Axelrod 1988, 1) As is known, the annual budget process is the one place where fiscal considerations of budget policy (such as its size, scope, and composition) are debated and analyzed (or should be). The better fiscal information that can be developed and shared, through such systems as IFMS, the better the results of fiscal policy and its associated fiscal implications for other policies such as health, education, and social assistance.

IFMS BASICS
In the academic literature and field reports of international donors, the idea of an IFMS reform is simple because it combines all major financial functions, and when extended includes most institutions of the state—linking financial management and state modernization efforts. Previous financial management reform efforts in the Latin American region concentrated on strengthening single functions, or an independent financial management system, through such efforts as budgeting and accounting reforms. This was appropriate in the early days of computerized management information systems. *Independent financial management systems* were less expensive to build, were modular in structure, had operational systems conforming to current financial procedures, and were flexible in that systems could be modified or discarded without damaging the other systems. But independent systems relied on manual inputs, could not integrate data from several sources, and were constrained by different coding arrangements (O'R.Hayes et al. 1982, 141). For expenditure planning and fiscal policymaking, independent systems allowed too many leaks in the entry and exit of fiscal data. Independent

fiscal systems also allowed costly delays and errors to occur when data were passed from unit to unit within government. MOFs and central banks could not really rely on these data to exercise control over their economies.

Under these conditions, it was recognized by consultants, international donors such as World Bank, and MOF officials that the simplest operational idea would be an *integrated* system composed of a single database that end users looked at from different points of view (budget reporting, analysis of budget execution, revenue collections, etc.). As noted, the operational theory was that improved linkage of fiscal and physical data on expenditures and revenues within the central government (and ultimately between tiers of government) would lead to better fiscal policymaking and better sectoral program results. IFMS offered advantages at both the central government (MOFs and ministries) as well as line offices of the ministries. At the center, IFMS would register and total up all transactions, which formed the basis of the daily cash position. For example, where modified accrual accounting systems existed, a contract commitment (purchase order, supplier invoice) would be registered in the accounts to prevent overbudgeting by MOF. MOF would then use the commitments data (i.e., contracts for the immediate purchase or future delivery of goods and services) and better revenue forecasts to manage cash and debt levels during the fiscal year. This linkage would smoothly integrate data transfer and use from budgeting, accounting, revenue, cash, and debt management systems. IFMS would clearly lead to better fiscal discipline at the strategic or macroeconomic level.

At the line management level, IFMS would decentralize operational responsibility for data entry. It can provide access to information by line managers at the appropriate level for decision making. In principle, line managers have access to all relevant data and can use it to make program adjustments that serve clients better. For example, urban transit department managers need to know costs/passenger mile in order to make allocational choices for improved service delivery. Hospital managers need to know costs/patient day and be able to compare them with other regional hospitals. Using IFMS, line managers enter data only once and it is stored in a central subaccount at the treasury. Managers can then use the IFMS data to make better operational-level decisions. IFMSs are also real time and thus eliminate redundant layers of approvals and multiple opportunities for delay/corruption. In short, IFMS links financial management component subsystems; it also links staff and line/center and periphery decision-making needs. It can improve overall public administration by identifying financial bottlenecks or wasted funds for particular services and programs.

The *core* IFMS system typically links the budget with the accounting subsystem. For this to occur the budgetary codes and chart of accounts have to be consistent—which they often are not. Transactions in cash and debt management are also included in the core system to ensure that the MOF or finance department knows its cash position and commitments (purchase orders, supplier invoices) with only minimal lags in reporting. Core functions are also called basic accounting functions and reporting. The *non-core* IFMS builds on the core base and typically includes other functions such as purchasing, payroll, and capital investment budgeting. These are called: (1) secondary and specialized functions and (2) advanced financial management functions.

IFMS is thus based on centralized accounting norms, uniform software, auditable transactions, and decentralized operational responsibility. Using standardized data gathered for relevant and predictable purposes, its underlying purpose is improved fiscal transparency. Data are entered in the field at the municipal level and at line ministry level by end users for budgeting, accounting, cash and debt management transactions. The data are then aggregated upward for use by program/policymakers to plan and allocate expenditures and to make course corrections during budget implementation. For government officials, the major advantage of the integrated system is that financial transaction data are posted only once. The computer automatically posts values to files maintained for various reporting purposes (cash management, debt management, program performance) (O'R.Hayes et al.1982, 133). This simplifies recording, eliminates unnecessary processing steps, and provides an audit trail that reduces inefficiency and opportunities for corruption. In principle, there is also a single bank account for the government in the MOF (treasury) which contains many linked subaccounts. This eliminates idle funds sitting in accounts on which interest could have been earned and allows for sensible government cash management during the fiscal year. Governments often have many bank accounts of which some are used to hide funds. Account fragmentation prevents valid analysis of the cash position and again, wastes interest-earning opportunities for the treasury in the process.

Installation of computerized management information systems in slow-moving bureaucracies anywhere is difficult—whether in OECD countries or transitional and developing countries. IT projects in the private sector suffer from the same problems. In its annual evaluation of IT projects, the Standish Group concluded that in 2004, only 29 percent of health care IT projects "succeeded," which was down from 34 percent in 2002. Cost overruns averaged 56 percent of original budgets and projects took an average of 84 percent more time than scheduled (*Economist* 2005a, 57; *Economist* 2005b, 63). In practice, the major problem with IFMS has been mainly in design and start-up of implementation. Wesberry (1989, 63) once noted that despite the conceptual popularity of integrating accounting and budgeting, "such integration never seems to work out." The major problem and lesson has been that design is an important determinant of implementation outcomes. In the case of the Kansas Financial Information System (KFIS), for example, lack of a thorough agency needs analysis resulted in inadequate specifications in the RFPs to vendors and overestimation of the skills of state employees assigned to the project (Ubokudom 1993, 66–67). In addition, shared responsibility for program implementation resulted in interorganizational conflicts. In the Kansas case, changing the initial goals by the state government (through modification of specifications) made it difficult to target resources for policy implementation. In other cases of implementation, failure of one subsystem causes failure of the entire system; often it causes organizational disruption and may also cause error propagation in data (O'R.Hayes et al. 1982, 133).

Many of these problems plagued earlier IFMS installations. Several years ago, installation of USAID's "New Management System" (NMS) was plagued by many of the problems typical to IFMS in Latin America, and to the New York City and KFIS experiences. In this case, AID did not designate technical responsibility to a prime contractor or technical unit within AID. AID hired multiple contractors to design and install separate subsystems in isolation. There was no single overall design to integrate the four subsystems (Ottaway 1998). The initial result was a hard to use system that often produced decision paralysis. More recently, AID has used the integrated system to eliminate the antiquated mishmash of computers inherited and now uses only two computer systems to process financial data. The data produced is more timely and accurate than the old system and the costs of design and installation have been about the same as those estimated for a nonintegrated system. In short, successful IFMS installations require a qualififed lead agency, sufficient time, and operational flexibility. Similarly, the New York City IFMS (1977) was plagued by vast overruns and design errors. With trial and error and more funds, the system finally became operational and now serves its original purposes of improved budget management and control (Axelrod 1988, 246). In other countries and cities, more flexible software and better computing technology have remedied most technical problems of IFMS installation. Lessons have been learned.

CORE VERSUS NONCORE SYSTEMS AND LEVELS OF INTEGRATION

At the design stage, one should also distinguish different levels of financial management systems integration. Full integration requires more time and funding than simple integration of core components. However, installation of only core components still leaves major parts of the fiscal management system open to abuse. For example, the typical IFMS core module for projects does not integrate payroll or purchasing (often considered non-core!), which allows ghost worker and contracting abuses and frauds to continue. In several cases, the concept of IFMS itself has been criticized for failure to achieve controls in non-core areas when in fact only a core system had been installed.

Political Transparency Problems

The major IFMS reform implementation problem in many jurisdictions now is political—that new transparent information systems recognizing fiscal responsibility threaten existing power relationships. MOFs and other central institutions prefer to hoard data and IFMSs really threaten this cozy arrangement. So, the political costs of IFMS systems can outweigh their aggregate benefits in improved reporting, more efficient data collection/processing, and better analytic capacity. The point is that it is often not the scientific or technical features of the system but rather misuse of the system in the wrong hands. This underscores the need for internal controls and audit as part of any fiscal management system.

It should be recognized that in IFMS implementation there are levels of integration and functions to be included in the system. Implementation constraints affect the velocity with which a finance management reform moves from independent to full integration over time—and the level of integration desired will vary by country and level of government. More advanced financial management systems include reforms of basic accounting, program budgeting, revenues, and reporting functions. Not all functions can be feasibly included in IFMSs in the immediate term. IFMSs typically move from basic accounting functions and reporting to advanced financial management functions. As noted, in the generic or "core" system, the IFMS software links the budget, accounting, cash, and debt management transactions of the spending ministries and other agencies into one system. In the United States, local governments have taken fifteen years in some cases to move from independent to fully-integrated core systems. In Australia, installation of the full IFMS took roughly that long. Because of political and technical constraints, linkage of "non-core" components (purchasing, payroll, investment budgeting) can take even longer.

Case Examples
Given the real implementation constraints experienced by first world countries, any cases in Latin America with fewer problems and in less time are important to document. In fact, there have been many IFMS successes:

- The first IFMS in this region was the administration and control system component (called SAFCO) of the Bolivian Public Financial Management Operation initiated in 1987 by World Bank (IDA). This consisted of budgeting, internal control, cash management, and audit subsystems linking the MOF with fifteen central ministries and other decentralized entities. As is common, the tax administration subsystem was initiated separately and not linked to the IFMS.
- Argentina's SIDIF system links budgeting with treasury and public credit operations. The budget is prepared through SIDIF, which allows expenditure programming on the basis of the needs of each spending unit. SIDIF allows monitoring of execution through comparison of targets with actual outlays. Additionally, different phases of expenditure are recorded through SIDIF, namely, commitment (*compromiso*), accrual (*devengado*), and payment (*pago*), and funds are transferred to creditors

using the banking system (Petrei 1998). SIDIF was based on the earlier SAFCO effort in Bolivia.

- Another early IFMS was Brazil's SIAFI, which links the accounts to budget programming. The treasury also uses SIAFI as the basis for cash management and release of funds to the operating units (Petrei 1998). Budget allocations are linked to the payments system to prevent overbudgeting and unplanned deficits. But the problem with even the most advanced systems, such as SIAFI and SIDIF, is that they are only information systems. They can reveal transparently that expenditure burdens or revenue assumptions are unsustainable. They cannot eliminate expenditure mandates and increase budget inflexibility caused by constitutional or political authority. They cannot alone force institutional change. Budget rigidity has been a major problem in Brazil that has contributed to hyperinflation. In the medium term, SIAFI information can lead decision makers to cut budgets and seek new revenue sources to avoid fiscal problems. But they have to take the risks of acting on that information. They have to act on the new information.

- Guatemala's SIAF system began installation in 1994 with World Bank funding. It now links data from budgeting with accounting, treasury, public credit, and public investment. Since 1994, SIAF has reduced the floating debt from between 1 and 1.3 million Quetzales annually to zero. It reduced the number of steps to approve purchase and pay orders from 130 to 12. The SIAF project moved to Phase II in 1998 with emphasis on installation of more non-core components.

- Nicaragua's SIGFA, financed by World Bank, began installation in 1995. It has linked the central government's budgeting, accounting, and debt functions and also moved to Phase II in 1998. SIGFA uses adapted software design from Argentina's SIDIF.

- Colombia's Comprehensive Financial Management Project was relatively unique in that it combined core and non-core elements in the first phase. The project included: tax administration, treasury, public credit, accounting, budgeting, auditing, macroeconomic programming, and public policy evaluation.

It may be a stretch to link IFMS reforms to improved macroeconomic performance. But the machinery of IFMS is designed to facilitate control over annual budgets, preventing unplanned deficits and accumulation of further debt. If this is a plausible link (and we think it is), the March 2008 fiscal balances of Argentina (surplus of 1.2 percent of GDP), Brazil (deficit of only -2.5 percent of GDP) and Colombia (deficit of only 1.3 percent of GDP) all demonstrate the macroeconomic value of IFMS reforms.

Municipal IFMS

Decentralization of IFMS has been a more recent occurrence. Part of the problem is that donors have operated from the premise that given lack of local capacity, central IFMS must precede installation of local IFMS. Thus, the evolutionary sequence for diffusion of IFMS reform has been: (1) MOF or spending ministries, (2) autonomous agencies, (3) state enterprises, and (4) state and local governments. Since few IFMS are fully functional at the central government level, only those countries with lengthy experience in IFMS have taken the next steps and gone local. For this reason, only Bolivia has devolved its SAFCO down to the subnational/local levels. In exceptional cases, such as Ecuador, IFMS successes at the local level (City of Quito) flowed upward and became the basis of national level improvements!

In short, the IFMS installation sequence can in practice work top-down or bottom-up. In the United States, many credit the early 1900s budget systems improvements by the NYC Bureau of Municipal Research with creation of the executive budget and program budgeting that later were adopted at the national level. (It should be noted the U.S. executive budget system which thrust responsibilities for coherent budget making on elected chief executives is almost twice as old as executive budgeting systems in most of Europe). The same bottom-up progression of reforms was evident in Ecuador. Ecuador promulgated the region's first IFMS law (1977) but it was not utilized. Quito took the initiative to develop SIGEF. In a twist, the same technical people worked at the national MOF to install an IFMS in the central government.

Similarly, such systems as SIDIF in Argentina are now being devolved to lower tiers of government. The "inter-operability" feature with more disaggregated local databases is being developed in Argentina and will be extended to all units that use the same programs. Other IFMSs are being developed for the state tier of government in Latin American federal systems. The most obvious examples are Brazil, Mexico, and Venezuela. Because of regime politicization in Venezuela since 2003, expenditure controls have been relaxed and cash flows both nationally and locally have become extremely opaque—IFMS data is generated but not used. The World Bank and IADB are moving ahead with plans to diffuse IFMSs to state and local governments throughout Latin America. At the microsystems level, IFMSs are often successful in generating consensus to delegate fiscal authority to line ministries, such as health and education, and for discretion of local governments to modify their budgets within set limits. This generates demands for information and encourages further decentralization of IFMS.

Conversely, some have argued that the failure of several countries to fully install IFMSs at the national level should slow further installation at the ministry, state enterprise, or local levels. For purposes of planning and allocating transfers and subsidies to units beyond the MOF and to lower tiers, they believe that integrated data is first needed at the central level. While this is a plausible position, the case of upward transfer of systems from SIGEF in Quito to the national government of Ecuador and the case of Guatemalan installation of SIAF first in spending ministries followed by MOF (because MOFs want to centralize the flow of information), reveal that central installation is probably not a precondition to IFMS success. Better returns to information should be evident to local authorities (e.g., increased fiscal transfers or expansion of borrowing authority) to encourage local reporting and participation in national IFMSs. Local governments need more incentives in the form of increased assignments of authority from the center for revenue generation and budget modification. Without this delegation of authority, local officials have few incentive to either increase local revenue mobilization or to report transactions into national IFMSs. This again is a structural problem that IFMS officials can explain but do nothing directly about.

IFMS LESSONS
Based on the above discussion of design and implementation experiences for IFMSs, at least five major lessons can be stated:

1. IFMS system specifications must be based on thorough needs assessments derived from agency operational problems,
2. Shared implementation responsibility does not work. A single, technically qualified unit or lead organization must oversee design and implementation,
3. Implementation is characterized by learning and trial and error. The system must be flexible to encourage and receive suggestions for change during implementation,
4. The IFMS cannot be installed all at once. IFMS typically distinguishes core (budget, account, cash, and debt management) from non-core (payroll, purchasing-contracting, decentralization). Some cases begin with non-core (based on their needs); others begin with accounting and budgeting. There is no one best way to sequence the installation of IFMSs, and,
5. System design affects implementation. Thus, administrative responsibility must be centralized for design (normative centralization) while operations must be flexible and decentralized.

BUDGET DOCUMENTS, INFORMATIONAL STRUCTURES, AND ANALYSIS

Budget reform has little sustainable value without supporting databases and proper classification of expenditures. At the same time, the notion of improving databases is not particularly compelling to politicians or the public. It is not a vote winner. Needed is a vehicle that translates reform into practical terms, linking all the talk about better fiscal data to tangible products that enable managers, the public, the media, and NGO watchdogs to ask better questions and link outlays with service results or lack thereof. Reformed budget documents can serve as a framework, an incentive structure for generation of new data (why collect better data if there is no place or step in the process to present analysis and recommendations in the policy agenda?) and an overall symbol of budget reform. On the other hand, too often budget reform has meant the reverse—flashy new modern program or performance budgeting documents and little supporting data, and few budget allocations actually based on it. A colleague at IMF responsible for Africa once noted that Nigeria had the finest looking state budget he had seen—and after viewing it we agreed. Unfortunately, all the numbers were totally "cooked."

Much of the success of budget reform depends on what kind of reform is intended and how that reform sits with the political culture of particular countries and regions. Those reformers who have ignored this linkage have done so at their peril—and there have been many, especially in the Balkans at the local government level.

Political Culture and Budgetary Change

As indicated in previous chapters, political culture affects institutional change and especially budget reforms. The general concept consists of the values and attitudes that affect administrative and political behavior (Inglehart 1988). But it really is what people do when no one is looking. It is can be recognized by such questions as: "You don't know the way things are done around here, do you?" This type of *outsider* screening test has been given to us in such diverse locations as: Jackson, MS, Karaganda, Kazakhstan, Shkoder, Albania, and San Pedro Sula, Honduras. It is an even more fitting litmus test in the Balkans. There are common features of the Balkan political culture that can be linked nicely to the mechanisms of administrative structure and policy that affect the success of budget reforms (Guess 2001). Centralization is a major feature of this region and it consists of three components: (1) revenue centralization, (2) state media control, and (3) assignments of insufficient or conflicting authority to manage programs. It can be argued that variation in these three components by country affects the level of centralization that, in turn, determines the likelihood of different types of budget systems reform. Utilization of the budget as a simple operations guide (the most basic reform) is perhaps most consistent with centralized political cultures. Official need for information remains at the basic technical-statistical level. Managers under central planning became adept at maneuvering and manipulating figures to attain ends and avoid responsibilities for failure. As well as or better than their Western counterparts, they knew how to use their budgets to control operations. In short, achieving this kind of reform would only be a marginal improvement since the information should already be available in local budgeting systems.

By contrast, existing political cultures in the Balkans (and elsewhere in the Former Soviet Union and Eastern European region) have not been amenable to use of budgets as more transparent communications devices with citizen groups or the media, or as opportunities for policy analysis or forward expenditure planning. The institutional requirements of these changes run up against the limits of political culture. For these purposes, municipalities would require greater autonomy, more tolerance of internal dissent, and greater freedom to use their own-source revenues. While these features of the political culture cannot be changed in the short term, municipal governments in countries such as Bulgaria that are roughly consistent with them achieved the greatest successes in budget reform. Focusing technical assistance and training on GFOA's four purposes of budgeting facilitates the evolution of budgeting systems beyond basic operational guides to the more complex and deeper roles of financial planning, public communications, and policy analysis. In this fashion, using four Balkan countries as test cases, it was noted how incremental changes in administrative systems has led to positive changes in the political culture that improved democracy and governance.

Political culture in this region (and most others) is a variable and can be changed. The trick is to determine those elements of a political culture that can genuinely deter reform program results and that either cannot be changed easily from those that are distinctive but which can be modified or built upon to achieve reforms in the short run. It is also easier to make marginal changes in cultural practices to accommodate incremental or minor reforms (e.g., the budget classification system) than major changes in the culture to accommodate structural fiscal reforms (e.g., IFMS). Incremental reallocation of rewards and requirements that already exist are critical to the success of budget reform. For example, with proper incentives, statistical reporting practices that served central ministries can be converted into useful analysis for budgeting and auditing. Passive line management can be turned into active program implementation by giving officials targets and enforcing existing expenditure controls. In this fashion, culture can be turned from a static obstacle into the dynamic foundation on which budget reforms can be built (Guess 2005, 222).

Western Budgetary Standards

Development of public budgeting systems is a slow process in any country. What must be avoided is any effort to impose a particular system on one country to which it may not be applicable. Eastern European countries are particularly sensitive to this in that so many consultants have been through since the transition period beginning in 1989, trying out their latest ideas on them. As the Hungarian tourist ad says, "The Ottomans stayed 600 years, the Soviets stayed 60 years, so you should stay 3 nights in a fine discount hotel by the Danube." Officials were forced to adopt many of the wrong systems but are often unable now to sort out who should stay, for how long, and what they have to offer to improve practices. Nevertheless, there are more or less common standards that can be applied as benchmarks to examine the progress of budget systems reform at the municipal level. These are as applicable in developing and transitional countries as in OECD countries (Guess 2007). It is suggested that the Government Finance Officer's Association's (GFOA) four standards (Miller 1984) also serve this normative purpose well. GFOA standards are not the only standards against which to gauge reform progress. For example, Premchand (1993) provided a number of alternative budgeting and expenditure control regimes. But the GFOA standards are clear, measurable, and to some extent tested. Estonian municipal officials found them very useful during our work there in 1995–96 and continue to use them as guides for budget reform progress. In this sense, the GFOA standards are nearly universal and not culture-bound.

First, the budget should be a *policy document*. It should describe and articulate policy changes as well as consequences for the status quo. The document should explain how major existing and new policies will be implemented. This is a tough standard to achieve in the Balkans because municipal governments have little control over most of their policies. Budget composition and tax rates are largely a function of central government directives. Municipalities are typically responsible for fees which provide only 1–5 percent of local budget financing. They often cannot set rates or collect taxes. Mandated service requirements in such sectors as health and education are largely financed by transfers from the center. This is particularly true in Bulgaria. Typically *compendia* of line items with little explanation, local or national budget documents reveal few of these major fiscal issues or problems faced by local policymakers.

Second, the budget should be an *operations guide*. It should provide data for comparison with past operations, include measures of performance and targets, and explain the relationship between capital and operating expenditures. Budgets in the Balkans have been mostly financial data and do little explaining. The financial data presented is typically limited to the budget year with no interyear comparisons of budget authority or outlays. The presumption is that all is legally spent and maximum efficiency and satisfaction are attained. Under central planning, the performance norm system provided physical indicators of targets for planners, for instance, five hundred bed/days/year will be provided by hospital x. But these were not related to costs or examined for efficiency-effectiveness. Service accountability flowed upward to the central ministries rather than downward to local citizens or groups. Capital and operating budget documents remained separate and are still not developed in an integrated planning process. There were no legislative audit institutions that conducted performance audits. The only question for auditors (i.e., control clerks) was whether all the funds were spent and could be accounted for through source documents. The budget still does not serve managers, mayors, or city councils as a decision guide to needed resource shifts that could improve service delivery or program performance.

Technical assistance inputs from the West have changed some of these practices. Many Bulgarian (and Polish) cities now have budget documents and databases that would be the envy of many U.S. cities. In Serbia, where technical assistance has been ongoing, budget preparation documents have been transformed from old standards that provided little operational guidance other than accounting and financial consistency with the state plan—to new performance and results documents based on accurate activity statistics. One of Yugoslavia's other former six republics, Macedonia, has also reformed its local budget documents and structures. Technical assistance applications to fashion the budget as an operations guide in Macedonia have largely been successful (Guess 1997). But without a sustained demand for the document to serve as operations guide, basic data may not continue to be collected. Without authority to prepare and execute their own budgets and to finance them, municipalities will have little continuing need for a comprehensive budget document that can guide expenditure performance. There are simply not enough incentives at this point to ensure sustainability of these important reforms.

Thus, as will be explained below with regional country examples, there have been significant changes in the budget structure toward performance measurement and analysis. As Thurmeier once noted (1994), it took Poland only a few years to accomplish in the mid 1990s what took the United States seventy-five years to accomplish in budget reform. Many national and local budgets now feature narrative budget messages, analyses of major budget issues, description of programmatic responses, activity statistics, and cross-walks of performance information from the economic classification for maximum fiscal and program accountability.

Third, the budget should be a *financial plan*. It should be a consolidated statement of all operations and financing activities. Extrabudgetary funds should be clearly defined and procedures indicated for reconciliation and consolidation of general and specific funds. From a defined base, the budget should explain revenue and expenditure projections for at least one year ahead. The financial condition of the city should also be forecasted and measured through trends in core ratios, such as per capita revenues. Debt management issues that affect future operations should be explained. This has been a hard standard to attain in the Balkans at this point. Funds are still not fully consolidated—many expenditures still remain off-budget. Projections and re-budgeting exercises are not explained. In practice, debt management is not a big municipal issue because there is little debt issuance. Planning under the old system was simply preparation of a plan by the ministry. It was not a forward estimate limited by resources or other transparently objective standards.

Planning was mainly a top-down politicized process unlinked to the budget. In Serbia and Macedonia, the cities are still mainly a collection of city enterprises that deliver service with minimal fiscal or programmatic control by the city administration. Weak reporting requirements mean that regulatory oversight is minimal. The "city" is but a small administrative operation that often is unaware of its own enterprise finances. Thus, there are many budgets and there is no single financial planning tool.

In transitional countries such as those in CEE/FSU and Brazil-Argentina, budget systems have moved from annual to multiannual frameworks. Current and capital budget calendars have been integrated and projections are made for current expenditures for three or four years beyond the current year. This allows future expenses to be programmed into current plans in order to develop a "hard budget constraint" that is consistent with both macroeconomic targets and microbudgetary needs. While legislative appropriations remain annual, the planning framework becomes multiannual. Multiyear budgeting has been used for many years in capital investment planning. This framework is now used in the form of capital improvements plans (CIPs) for local governments and public investment programs (PIPs) for national level governments. Both CIPs and PIPs now include the recurrent expenditure implications of capital investments and have started to include programmatic analysis as well. As indicated in chapter 5, since 2003, Romania has been a regional leader in installation of local CIPs, and these have been used to actually affect both current and capital budget allocations.

Fourth, the budget should be a *communications device*. The document should be understandable to the lay reader, and contain a transmittal letter from the mayor to the council outlining key policies and strategies with supporting fiscal data. The document should also explain assumptions underlying revenue and expenditure estimates. Some progress has been made here, especially in Albania (i.e., before the 1997 civil war following the collapse of the "pyramid schemes" and before the 1998 evacuation of U.S. aid organizations due to terrorist threats). However, the normal organizational communications function runs up against the secrecy feature of the Balkan political culture. Accounting and financial information flows upward and is sometimes shared horizontally, but rarely does it flow downward in other than a regulatory format. The media and press are state-controlled in most cases, meaning that publication of critical data—political, fiscal, economic, or social—is viewed often as subversion by the state. This has been especially true in Serbia and Montenegro (Smith 1998) as well as Albania (UNDP 1995), but far less so in Bulgaria. Thus, budget documents remain masses of financial data and laws without narrative explanation in the majority of cities. They rarely contain policy analyses of the successes and failures of existing programs. Central government budgets are not much different from corresponding localities in regard to their attainment of any GFOA standards.

BUDGET MANAGEMENT

As noted by Tommasi (2007, 279), "Budget execution is the phase when resources are used to implement policies incorporated in the budget." In his view, "A well-formulated budget can be poorly implemented, but a badly formulated budget cannot be executed well" (2007, 279). Budgetary reforms described above under database and management information systems should lead to more effective budget implementation. Better control systems improve implementation or budgeting in action. Such fiscal reforms should strengthen the control levers for: cash management and pre-audit systems, allotment and apportionment rules, and transfer authority (Axelrod 1988, 170). Better accounting and performance reporting provide data needed by managers to ensure proper control of deficits, better cash management, and maximization of allowable funding for service delivery. Stronger budget management systems and processes can provide the foundation for improved budgeting for policy and financial planning purposes. For example, implementation reforms from Western/OECD countries in the CEE/FSU region have been applied with good success in such countries as Ukraine. Still, many problems surface during the budget management stage, for instance, an excessive number of earmarks for particular expenditures and the management and operational problem of dealing with cash limits set by MOFs to achieve macro deficit targets. Budget managers have little control over rules and regulations imposed from above and can only allocate funds within these constraints as best they can. Analytic information derived from reforms should reveal the costs and consequences of alternative cutback strategies. This can serve line managers and allow them to make a more persuasive case to senior staff in order to balance program needs with fiscal limits.

Monitoring Budget Execution

The approved operating budget or allotment is a direct control device. Budgets in a narrow sense are effectively control devices. For example, Ukrainian Budget Code provisions clearly intend that expenditures not exceed approved budget amounts nor result in any significant deviations from its approved composition over the course of the year. This is the legal dimension of budgetary control, violation of which incurs penalties. Local financial managers need tools to monitor budget execution that serve the broad legal purpose of balance and control but at the same time provide them with the information they need to make sound fiscal decisions. The finance office needs information to plot rates of spending and take corrective measures such as revising work plans, reducing service objectives, or curtailing expenditures deemed not necessary to maintaining the most essential services. This is the management dimension of budgeting. There are many cases where the pressures of time caused by the realities of budget implementation place the legal compliance and management dimensions in conflict.

Line-Item Controls

Most governments focus on line items to control budget implementation, for example, salaries, maintenance, supplies, investments, etc. Fiscal managers tend to multiply controls over them and apply them down to the subchapter or functional (*spherical*) level. This inhibits managerial flexibility and converts the budget into a set of rigid categories that are very hard to modify. Such a rigid budgetary system, aka *fiscal fascism*, may work out to be a triumph for stabilization goals at the expense of programmatic need. For example, where inflation is a problem, countries often impose cash limit systems, effectively replacing the approved budget with monthly releases of authority—usually lower. The idea is to force spending agencies to deal with higher than planned inflation by cutting back their releases of funding authority on a monthly basis—sometimes weekly (Premchand 1993, 75). A problem with this control technique is that it, if supported by cash-only budgetary accounting systems, it often allows agencies to continue commitments of funds, creating higher deficits later. Conversely, reformers pushing for new classifications of expenditures by programs, subprograms, and activities as the units of control rather than objects of expenditure can actually weaken expenditure control as major outlays can easily be hidden or buried in broad program categories. For example, how can salaries and supplies can be controlled if such categories are buried in programs such as *human resource development* or *facilities* (Mikesell 2007, 213) How can outlays for *facility safety inspections* be identified and reduced by multiple organizations?

An innovative compromise method between narrow control and management discretion is now used by the Australian and New Zealand finance departments to control budget implementation. Their finance departments use broad line items classified into three large categories: current (e.g., salaries and maintenance), capital (i.e., public works), and other expenses (e.g., debt service). Finance managers in line departments are permitted to shift funds within the broad line items to achieve service performance targets negotiated between the department heads and the central MOF—operational responsibility is very decentralized. Conversely, reports on spending are made daily to the treasury and payments must be approved by the treasury—a very centralized control system. To facilitate effective budget implementation in order to achieve targeted outputs and outcomes, the focus of the reporting and control system is measurement of cash position as well as value for money. Decisions to shift funds from one larger category to another (e.g., current to capital) require approval of the MOF and parliamentary budget committee. For an explanation of New Zealand's budget and financial management system, see: www.treasury.govt.nz. Go to *budget process* and read: "Putting it All Together: An Explanatory Guide to the New Zealand Public Financial Management System."

Budget Modification

During the year, because of revenue shortfalls or unforeseen expenditures, budget adjustments are inevitable. Transfers of funds within or between line items in the same area (e.g., travel), reprogramming funds between larger chapters (e.g., maintenance to travel), or shifting funds to different programs altogether (e.g., health to education) are decisions permitted by budget modification rules in most countries. Most are contained in operating or implementing regulations that accompany the annual budget appropriations law and set specific limits and approval requirement, that is, no more than 5 percent of the total appropriation account. Other common prohibitions include: no shift of funds from wage or personal services to non-wage object classes; expenditure increases are prohibited for the total object class that increase overall expenditures—i.e., there must be an offsetting cutback; and transfers require legislative committee approval, etc.

To the extent that these adjustments modify the intent of the original appropriation, budgeting is being performed during execution rather than during the expenditure planning and preparation phase when it should be. This amounts to uncontrolled budget modification and should be limited by budgetary "guardians" or controllers. By contrast, in New Zealand line managers have maximum flexibility to transfer funds among "running costs" to meet negotiated performance targets. In some cases, funds can be moved ahead to the next fiscal year rather than returned to the treasury unspent. This is the extreme decentralized fiscal management model and is an example of controlled flexibility (as well as the "New Public Management" in action). This can be done only where strong internal and external controls over financial management are in place and the accounting and reporting systems provide commitments or accruals data for solid cash and program management.

At the other extreme, illustrated by Central Asia, budget adjustments are made excessively difficult in order to ensure compliance with the original plan. This short-circuits the management of service delivery function. Where strategic and macro considerations rigidly outweigh program needs, the stage is set for perpetuation of error, fraud, and waste. Such a disincentive framework also makes budgeting a mechanical and rigid exercise rather than an opportunity to deliver effective services driven by analysis of expenditure performance. Thus, governments need to balance controls over budget modification against legislative intent, the need for expenditure control, and the need for management flexibility. In the context of budget management, there are two types of intrabudget transfers: (1) policy and (2) nonpolicy. Policy shifts require funding reallocations and typically need legislative review and approval, for instance, from health to education or from primary to secondary education. Policy shifts are effectively new budgets made during implementation. Nonpolicy transfers involve shifts of funds to execute existing policy priorities differently. Where sufficient funds are absent to execute planned budget priorities, managers often attempt to shift funds, for example, from supplies to maintenance, or from wage to non-wage expenditures. Such decisions should be consistent with implementing regulations and not affect the overall balance of the group account (e.g., permitting a 5 percent shift up or down within specified categories without supervisory approval so long as the overall budget is not increased). The extent to which transfer authority can be provided should depend upon the capacity of the spending unit to report transactions and balances regularly and the need to ensure internal control of the funds. The budgetary accounting system should provide a running log of deviation from budget authorizations. Thus, spending units should also be capable of performing variance analyses on budgeted to actual funds. Beyond OECD countries, few spending departments seem to have authority or capability to perform variance analyses. This is due in part to the over-centralization of budget management processes.

Budget Reserves

Article 24 of the 2002 Ukrainian Budget Code provides authorization to establish a fund for contingency expenditures at the national level. Implied authority exists for establishment of reserve funds at the local level for the same amount specified in the article: no more than 1 percent of the general fund. In the United States, bond rating agencies view reserve funds favorably because they can ensure timely payment of debt service. Governments that fail to establish reserve funds or establish them and fail to maintain reserves receive lower bond ratings. For bond rating agencies, the rule of thumb for local governments is at least 5 percent of operating revenues.

Budget reserve funds provide a cushion against the vagaries of the economy and against the need to borrow funds short-term to finance operations. Reserve funds also serve as insurance against revenue fluctuations. They are known as: *rainy day funds* and *stabilization funds* and come in handy for creation of fiscal space to spend for emergencies such as economic stimulation in recessions (as now). They are an important management and fiscal control tool for budget execution—they provide flexibility as well as the predictability needed to implement the budget consistent with approved targets.

The advantage of creating a separate or special fund is that the purpose and procedures for using the resources can be defined by law. Most funds have the familiar purpose of fighting against revenue shortfalls. More comprehensive purposes include: *intercepting* fiscal transfers to establish equity for longer-term infrastructure borrowing, withholding appropriations to pay for debt service, and reprogramming funds as needed during the year. These policy-type funds have run afoul of legislatures which justifiably argue that the funds amount to appropriation decisions that are constitutionally reserved to legislatures—not the executive.

Treasury Management

Treasuries have a variety of functions ranging from cash management to budget execution. Often, treasury roles reflect local institutional histories and adjustments made through trial and error. Historically, the debate in the Ukraine on treasury functions reflects the failure to define boundaries between the budget and banking sectors under central planning. The central bank performed most budget execution functions and budget priorities were set by the ministry of planning. Budget financing and control of execution were not functions of either an MOF or treasury institution. They were largely accounting functions performed by the central bank.

A state-of-the-art treasury should facilitate cash management by implementing the budget effectively, controlling aggregate spending, and minimizing the cost of borrowing. It can only perform these functions if accounting and budgetary data can be reconciled quickly with bank balances for government agencies. If not, there are major opportunities for leakage and slippage that can produce fiscal surprises in the form of increased deficits and debt. For such treasury functions to be executed, the accounting system must register commitments—not just cash transactions. The difference is in the registration and matching of resource use to a period (e.g., quality patient days) versus only recording the value of goods and services acquired (e.g., personnel and supplies). Governments in New Zealand and Australia, for example, issue *forward commitments reports* containing information from the budgetary accounting system that facilitates treasury management. Treasury design and management is a complex topic and only the simplest elements will be presented here. The OECD distinguishes three treasury functions: (1) accounting-reporting, (2) cash-debt management, and (3) budget execution and financial planning.

For accounting-reporting purposes, the treasury should register all payments transactions in a single account in the central bank. The central bank should be able to consolidate the government position each day from balances in line ministry subsidiary accounts. As noted, computerized IFMSs assist in this task, which allows for sound macroeconomic control over budget implementation. An important question is whether payments should be made by the central treasury or the line ministries. Centralization of accounting and payment controls in the treasury is plausible from a macroeconomic control perspective. But there are at least three problems with payments centralization. It could: (1) overload the treasury with many small transaction decisions, (2) result in politicization of decisions as accounting and payments would be centralized in the same organization (a potential conflict of interest or failure of internal control), and (3) be inconsistent with fiscal decentralization programs of the government in which lower-tier units have payments authority.

Thus, it may be more useful to decentralize accounting to subsidiary accounts. Regional units of the treasury that exist in the FSU/CEE countries provide ceilings and clearances of local government payments (as before). But they would not have approval authority over the scope and purpose of the payments (this would be new). To prevent arrears and facilitate local budget implementation, regional treasuries would also perform monthly reconciliation of local unit cash deposits with bank statements. This was the arrangement before the transition when systems were largely cash based in the MOF but commitments were recorded at the spending ministry level for internal management purpose. This meant that cuts by the MOF ignored program problems in the form of inability to meet the physical norm targets (e.g., bed days, patient days, student/teacher ratios) on which budgets were formulated. Internal audit units in the local governments would control only for budget consistency and legality. The more decentralized approach makes the local unit responsible for internal management while the treasury maintains control of the cash (consistent with the principle of normative centralization and operational decentralization).

For the function of cash and debt management, the treasury needs to provide MOFs with cash and commitment data for the year in order to prepare a borrowing plan. Such mechanisms as an adjusted baseline plan are planning and monitoring tools that allow the budget department and the treasury to forecast cash flows. On a cash basis, this would reveal the timing of revenues and expenditures and prepare the treasury to receive the annual borrowing requirements of local units. The addition of commitments is another issue. The apportionment and allotment stages reveal planned use of budget appropriations. But they do not indicate timing of contractual payments for purchases and physical progress of public works. To improve budget planning and prevent major arrears from occurring, commitments can be divided between: permanent and nonpermanent. It is critical that cash limits developed by the treasury consistent with the cash plan of line ministries not interfere with needed commitments. Estimation of nonpermanent commitments can help.

In the Ukraine, the major roles and functions of the state treasury in budget execution are provided for in the Budget Code, articles 48–51. The code implies a larger role for Treasury in budget planning and this is the source of some friction between MINFIN, Treasury, and local governments. They are: (1) budget accounting and reporting, (2) budget "servicing" and cash management, (3) budget payments, and (4) budget supervision and oversight. There is still debate as to the operational meaning of these roles for local budget execution.

The first role is clear—accounting and reporting of budget transactions and registry into the single account. This ensures macroeconomic control of consolidated expenditures from all tiers of government—not just the central government. The aim is to move accounting from cash-based to commitments-based in order to record the stages of payment (i.e., appropriation, commitment, verification, payment) and includes purchasing transactions to provide timely and comprehensive statements of fiscal position. With the single treasury account, it becomes feasible (technically easy and nonintrusive to local managers) to report upward on a daily/ weekly basis. Thus, in most countries, the treasury accounting and reporting function is centralized.

The second role is also clear. In Ukraine, it is held that the treasury provides budget financing consistent with approved budgets to spending units and makes payments for purchasing transactions. This refers to both fiscal transfers and direct budget expenditures. There is speculation that "servicing and cash management" could also mean a banking-type role in which the treasury would provide short-term financing to fill budget gaps during the year. But the Budget Code does not include the treasury as a source of budget deficit financing. Other countries trying to legislate in the treasury area suffer from the same role confusion.

Short-term cash gaps in county or *oblast* budgets can be covered by loans from the banking system via revenue anticipation notes (RANs) and other instruments. As an interim measure while the commercial banking system tries to strengthen itself, the state treasury can fill this role via direct loans or even loan guarantees to oblasts. This can create problems with fiscal control and potential breaching of the wall between fiscal and monetary account and lead to hidden fiscal deficits (or "contingent liabilities"). But it can work as an interim device. The French treasury system includes banking as a normal role—local governments do not rely on commercial banks. Nevertheless, there should be a larger role for commercial banking in short-term cash management. As for longer-term treasury financing of local infrastructure projects, this would seem to be a matter for the MOF. It could authorize establishment of municipal development funds (which exist in many countries) that allocate credit on evaluation of municipal creditworthiness—neither of which have to be part of the treasury function or even the public sector at all.

The third role of paymaster is clear. Regional/*oblast* treasury units can feasibly make all payments consistent with the approved budget for wage and non-wage expenditures. At the local level, this would mean that regional or local units of the state treasury would make payments authorized by pay orders issued by the local governments. Requests for payment and approval should be to the extent possible *oblast* functions. In this fashion, centralized macroeconomic control would be preserved, as transactions would be recorded in the single account. Conversely, operational responsibility for initiating and approving pay orders could be decentralized to local fiscal officials.

The fourth role of budget supervision and oversight is less clear. The Ukrainian MOF supports the interpretation that local officials will determine their own budget priorities, and that *supervision* means review of reports on cash position to ensure consistency with planned budgets during execution. It does not have to mean micro-approval of purchase orders or invoices. These should remain the responsibility of local spending units and local officials. State treasury, by contrast, interprets the language to mean more direct control of budget formulation as well as execution. Since an important feature of fiscal decentralization is local determination of both budget composition and revenue-raising strategies, this interpretation of treasury responsibility is contrary to the intent of the budget code. Most national treasuries do not set budget priorities; that is an MOF or local finance department function. The strong, centralized French treasury model is an exception.

Comparative analysis can be used to clarify and define state treasury roles:

First, most treasuries conduct monitoring and oversight of budget implementation. While in some countries, treasuries are independent of the MOF, in Ukraine and most transitional countries the state treasury is a dependency of the MOF. MOFs typically supervise budget formulation and evaluation and utilize treasury institutions to monitor and report on budget execution activities. It is also a normative expectation that transactions will be reported on a commitments basis as well as cash, to strengthen budget control. Organizationally, federal systems have had problems consolidating lower-tier governmental transactions into single accounts on a timely basis. With the advance of computerized financial management information systems (FMISs), timely consolidation is no longer a technical problem. Most transactions are real-time and not affected by geographic distance. Thus, the Ukrainian treasury role of accounting for budget operations of local governments through its regional units can be strengthened.

Second, many treasuries facilitate the financing of central government recurrent and capital needs. Central treasuries perform direct banking functions, such as issuance of sovereign bonds, and indirect banking functions, such as guaranteeing loans of particular institutions to encourage commercial banks to make them. As is particularly evident in 2009 with the U.S. treasury purchasing bank stocks and other assets, injecting capital into firms and banks, and moving toward nationalization of commercial banks, treasuries perform these functions. In normal times, treasuries also perform banking functions to finance short-term gaps in budget execution at the national level. Depending on the country, either commercial banks with treasury accounts or state treasury units cover idle balances by paying overnight interest to local governments or charging interest on budget timing gaps as part of overdraft services. They also provide short-term notes to local governments in anticipation of regularly scheduled revenues from transfers or taxes. The U.S. treasury has no role in financing lower-tier budget execution—although federal loan guarantees do impact local banks and stimulate economic development. Government financing operations are largely the responsibility of state-local governments that have delegated much of that role to commercial banks. The French treasury provides short-term financing for gaps in local budget execution. International experience on this is varied and countries facing the issue of treasury system design such as the Ukrainian government need to decide how much of the banking function should be delegated to the commercial banking sector and other financing institutions.

Third, treasury power to authorize payments by lower-tier governments also varies internationally. The U.S. treasury has no role in authorizing payments by state or local governments. By contrast, regional units of the French treasury receive and approve pay order and purchase order requests of lower-tier governments (prefects and communes). The French system is much more centralized in regard to budget payments. Based on international experience, it would appear that fiscal decentralization is consistent with local approval of pay orders within the context of tight internal control and audit systems.

Fourth, few treasuries have direct influence in budget priority determination. MOFs typically determine these, and their counterparts at lower-tier governments do the same. In the United States, the OMB determines budget priorities and the treasury has no role except in credit and financing policies. The U.S. treasury has no role in lower-tier government budget priority determination. Nor would it appear that the French treasury influences lower-tier budget formulation. Its role is limited to budget implementation and financing. Based on international experience, the Ukrainian State Treasury should limit itself to budget implementation and leave formulation to MINFIN and local financial authorities.

Monitoring and Evaluation

An important role for any budget office is monitoring and evaluation. This should extend to both fiscal and physical performance indicators. Most offices are good at cash flow projections and reporting back to finance departments any changes in revenue forecasts or expenditure needs that will require changes in quarterly budget releases or setting cash limits. It is important for the mayor, council, and relevant departments to set service targets, for instance, daily household waste collection, and to monitor the progress toward that target. Monitoring can take the form of progress reports, surveys, or complaints received. This is the back end check on actual expenditure results—whether funds are being properly allocated to serve the public, or whether they simply cover employee salaries.

Capital project monitoring is more difficult and finance departments have had problems here. Some, such as in the city of Milwaukee reorganized to ensure that change order requests and financing decisions would be integrated with physical project progress reports. The institutional roles and incentives had to be changed before the M&E function could produce valid information for decision purposes (Milwaukee 2003, 5). In terms of managing projects (which is an important part of budget execution) success rates in on-time performance and meeting budget targets has not really improved in the past thirty years (*Economist* 2005b, 57). The problem of overly optimistic forecasts and weak audits has a lot to do with improper assignment of roles and responsibilities. Better IT and more elaborate GANTT charts are not enough to monitor project progress. If there are five project stages (initiation, planning, execution, control, and closure), the problem seem to lie when the stage of initiation (securing the bid through optimistic cost and revenue projections) and execution are separated. Implementers must tough it out under often impossible conditions that have been set for them by initiators. Overruns and delays are commonplace for large IFMS, road, stadium, and other infrastructure projects. Monitoring strictly recurrent expenditures is easier in that they are more predictable and few technicalities that change orders have to be reviewed by engineers, who often must translate the vagaries of soil and weather into construction costs.

Budget Compliance and Control

During the fiscal year and at its end, at least five sets of major institutions monitor compliance of local receipts and expenditures with approved apportionments and payments or outlays. Ukrainian practice is similar to that in the CEE/FSU region. First, the Ukrainian Budget Code provides for local verification of budgets approved, apportioned and implemented by the state administration. Second, the State Treasury, through its regional units, would also account for all revenues and expenditures of local budgets and monitor budget execution to ensure that payments comply with commitments and budget appropriations. This is the budget execution function of the treasury. Third, the Accounting Chamber verifies use of budget funds consistently with the State Budget Law. This is an external control function. Fourth, the State Control and Auditing Administration reviews compliance with accounting procedures and efficient use of resources by local units. This is the internal audit function. Finally, committees of the local *radas* (city councils) now serve as local *supreme audit institutions* and provide periodic and final postaudits on the status of budget execution.

Institutionally, it is not clear if the roles and responsibilities of each control unit have been defined. There may well be overlap and redundancies, which weaken the performance of these controls and can lead to multiple intrusions that constrain program management. For example, in Bulgaria internal audit functions are performed by the accounting department, meaning that there is no separate pre-audit for vouchers and purchase orders. This violates one of the principles of internal control that separates asset custody duties from payment approval authority. Without separation, the same person can authorize and approve pay orders and checks, a potential conflict of interest. Similarly, to minimize fraud, responsibility for cash receipts should be separated from record keeping. The distinguishing feature of audit compliance operations is that they are systematic—based on transparent norms. Earlier systems in developing and transitional economies functioned more as ad hoc *control corps* that responded to personal complaints and did not conduct audits on a systematic basis. Thus, it may be useful to distinguish three types of modern budget compliance controls:

INTERNAL CONTROLS

These are rules and systems that provide data to management for such basic transactions as purchasing and personnel. Internal controls are established in the accounting system but should not be enforced by the accounting department. Internal controls safeguard public assets and ensure the accuracy of financial statements. They allow managers and internal auditors to make decisions on valid and reliable fiscal data. In Ukraine, the Accounting Chamber has responsibility for establishing internal control systems.

INTERNAL AUDIT

This is a unit at the departmental level that independently appraises the internal control system. These are typically decentralized to the line level and are called *inspector generals* or IGs in the United States. They have three main functions. First, they pre-audit transactions or samples of transactions, such as purchase orders, invoices, and other types of payments. This tests the accounting system and its capacity to generate valid and reliable fiscal data. A common problem with this function is the tendency to turn it into a legal control function that requires multiple steps before transactions are approved by finance and budget officials. This process was common in Latin America and led to the very corruption that controls were designed to guard against. Second, internal audit units also investigate irregularities where financial control procedures are not followed or are not consistent with good practice. Third, internal audit units also evaluate the efficiency and effectiveness of governmental programs. The last function is typically the least emphasized—exceptions are the UK and Swedish National Audit Offices.

EXTERNAL POST-AUDIT

Most auditing is done prior to outlays to ensure the legality and sufficiency of expenditures with appropriations. Legislative audit units typically focus on post-expenditures and provide year-end reports of the budgetary accounts. In addition, these supreme audit institutions (SAIs) perform value for money audits similar to those performed by internal audit units—there may be overlapping investigations in some cases. Legislative performance audits contribute to analytic checks and balances that increase accountability to the public.

ALLOCATIONS AND OTHER REFORM RESULTS

An intriguing question has always been the actual impact of budget and financial management reforms. Those who have attempted to link output/outcome type reforms to expenditure allocations have been hard pressed. Efforts with early ZBB reforms were mostly inconclusive—analyses found that expenditure composition either changed only marginally or that the main benefit was that the council or legislature found out the costs and benefits of their programs and its alternatives (Schick 1978, 179). This was important in that few knew this before the reform. Others have noted that budget analyses and performance measurements produced major changes in recommendations for allocations that were later nullified or ignored by political leaders. In 2002, Aimee Franklin did some pathbreaking research comparing the impact of budget reforms in Arizona and Oklahoma on appropriations. Specifically, she examined how and why the legislative appropriations process was shifted from traditionally narrow line-item controls to broader allocations that provided more management incentives (2002). Others have noted that the success of performance budget–type reforms depends a lot on supply of information to different types of users. Virginia instituted a performance budget–type system starting in 1995. Hill and Andrews (2005, 265) found that the new system tried to take account of different users—citizens, managers, or policymakers. They considered the reform to change the culture and practice of budgeting and financial management to be generally successful (2005, 271).

However, these findings raise the trigger question often forgotten in the rush to reform: How do the new systems handle negative information? Negative performance information can threaten the governance process—especially for policymakers and even managers if their budgets end up being reduced for bad performance. They suggest five damage control strategies by policymakers: (1) keep it confidential, (2) discredit the information, (3) ignore it, (4) reinterpret the information, and (5) reduce its visibility by publishing it at a time when other more compelling stories dominate the headlines (2005, 268). The extent to which governments use negative information to push for positive reforms and better budget targeting depends on how capable the government is. While the state of Virginia (recognizably one of the leading performance-based budget reformers in the United States) can do a reasonably good job, one wonders how well Macedonia or Nigeria would handle similarly negative information and whether it would destroy even nascent performance budgeting reform efforts?

For accounting and control reforms, impacts are easier to measure, for example, improved cash management, improved budget balances, faster purchase order approvals, fewer steps in approving pay orders and other financial transactions with impliedly fewer opportunities for corruption, faster procurement, better facilities planning and budgeting from integrated calendars of capital-recurrent budgets, fewer ghost workers and greater correspondence between salary payments and establishment rosters. The impacts of such reforms have been confirmed repeatedly and thus the demand for continuing them is high. Other more diffuse reforms such as fiscal decentralization offer mostly promises of better service responsiveness and accountability without firm evidence of these actually occurring.

CONCLUSIONS AND LESSONS FOR REFORM

Budget reforms have taken many forms. They vary from input controls to output performance measurement, to improved control of budget execution. In terms of GFOA's four purposes, budget reformers typically attempt to move from operations guides to policy and financial plan documents depending on political support and analytic capacities. In some cases, countries apparently well on the way to performance budgeting have had to move back and strengthen input controls to improve fiscal discipline—before going forward again. Some lessons can be drawn from efforts at performance budget reforms (mainly at the formulation stage), based on comparative experience:

1. *Performance reforms cannot work in centralized context.* The case of Thailand in the late 1990s indicates that results budgeting cannot feasibly be implemented in a centralized context where inputs and outputs are determined by the MOF. Where MOF micromanages the line items during budget execution, this reduces agency responsibility, accountability, and any incentive it might have to proceed with output type reforms (Dixon 2005, 366). Line agencies under these circumstances had few incentives to increase capacity, leaving them weak and vulnerable to more micromanagement from the center in a vicious cycle.

2. *Fiscal reforms need to be linked to wider state reforms.* Block grants to local units on a pilot basis increase management flexibility and discretion and lead to greater service productivity. The case of Vietnam in 2000 indicates that block grant budgeting to give regional spending units more flexibility and discretion increased their service productivity. An important lesson is that where the central reform unit (e.g., MOF) has the confidence to flesh out local innovations, it may be better to proceed with pilot programs rather than full-scale roll-outs (Bartholomew, Lister, Mountfield, and Van Minh 2005, 337). Thus, the experimental approach to policy reform should be followed over a heavily scripted, rapid-fire roll-out of a uniform system.

3. *Fiscal reforms cannot do everything at once even in the medium term.* Tanzania has linked the major fiscal reform effort (MTEF) to the financing of its poverty reduction strategy (PRSP) and reforms of the central and local government (Ronsholt and Andrews 2005, 316). Successful fiscal reform will turn on the results of many sub-processes such as costing of services and performance budget allocations to the social sectors. Fiscal reforms should proceed incrementally and not overload local capacities, especially in the poor countries of sub-Saharan Africa.

4. Unlike transitional countries that have substantial statistical and data collection capabilities, developing countries have poorly paid and trained civil servants throughout their governments. To expect them suddenly to initiate fiscal reforms based on new ways of collecting data and reporting expenditures is unrealistic. Nevertheless, substantial donor funds have been spent on this unstated premise, with predictable results. In Pakistan (2000–02), it was recommended that new district (LGUs) governments should adopt a staged incremental approach to budget reform—moving from input-based performance measurement to outputs and outcomes much later. For example, with existing figures, officials would collect administrative expenditures/student or administrator/teacher ratios and expenditures—then proceed to analysis of student performance by school. As analytical capacities of officials improved, reforms could move from inputs to outputs and outcomes.

In the budget implementation and management area, major advances have been made in improved fiscal databases and computerized information systems—and these have improved governmental performance. Budget documents and analytic capacities have vastly improved around the world. There is wide understanding of practical changes taking place in both the West and OECD countries by practitioners in developing and transitional countries. There is also healthy skepticism based on knowledge of reforms that have failed. Improvements in budget management at the micro level have followed on the general effort to improve fiscal discipline at the strategic level in order to stabilize macroeconomic variables. In general, budget and financial management reforms are well known to budget practitioners around the globe. This reflects the influence of international donor missions, funded projects, and international consultants. The missing information for reformers that would move to next steps is, What determines successful implementation in different contexts? On this question, research is taking place and more is warranted.

Some of the major lessons from operational and budget execution reforms are:

5. *Budget management reforms begin with improved classification and coverage.* Pressures on transitional and developing country MOFs over the past fifteen years have dramatically improved budget comprehensiveness, fiscal transparency, and program accountability. Despite gains in most countries, one of the most notori-

ously corrupt and badly governed countries (Nigeria) has only recently developed an acceptable economic and functional classification of its state budget. Corruption and mismanagement has been allowed to flourish precisely because the classification system was absent. The conclusion is that structures determine budget rules. For decades, the U.S. state enterprises Fannie Mae and Freddie Mac have enjoyed privileged, off-budget budgetary positions, which allowed their profit maximization cultures to thrive. This was exploited by managers and ignored by regulators. Like SOEs everywhere, their contingent liabilities to the government must be made clear in regularly audited balance sheets and income statements. The next step for fiscal reform is to clarify the audit trails of internal controls and to strengthen internal audit institutions that can detect both misappropriation and excessive risk taking with public assets.

6. *Multiple lessons can be learned from design/installation of FMIS/ IFMS in Latin America.* First, IFMS system specifications must be based on thorough needs assessments derived from agency operational problems. Second, shared implementation responsibility does not work. A single, technically qualified unit must oversee design and implementation. Third, implementation of complex IT projects such as these must necessarily be characterized by learning and trial and error. The implementation system must be flexible to encourage and receive suggestions for change. Fourth, the IFMS cannot be installed all at once. IFMS typically distinguishes core (budget, account, cash, and debt management) from non-core (payroll, purchasing-contracting, decentralization). Some cases begin with non-core (based on their needs); others begin with accounting and budgeting. There is no one best way to sequence the installation of IFMSs. Fifth, system design affects implementation. Thus, administrative responsibility must be centralized for design (normative centralization) while operations must be flexible and decentralized.

7. *Incentives are needed to get official buy-in for any budget reforms.* There is no reason why officials should simply want to do a better job or be more rational today than yesterday. Often being rational involves more work—especially accounting and reporting. Thus, incentives in the form of quid pro quos need to be established. In Ecuador, the MOF permitted greater budget transfer authority during execution in exchange for better reporting. In Australia, line officials have significant authority to transfer funds and even shift some to future years in exchange for meeting program targets negotiated with the MOF. Line officials also have higher paid, shorter term employment contracts to encourage risk taking and performance.

8. *Ensure that technical capacity exists in agencies responsible for local reforms.* Concentrate on basic reforms first (as in lesson 5 above); initiate complex reforms later. Accrual budgeting and *New Public Management* creation of independent agencies and other modern concepts sound good. But reformers should be cautious until basics are in place—budget classifications, cash management systems, budget controls, good budget laws, and clear roles and responsibilities. Thailand

has tried to install the *philosopher's stone* of program/results focused budgeting many times since the 1980s (Dixon 2005, 356). In 2001–02, they introduced a *hurdles* approach in which conditional devolution for budget tracking and control would be allowed to six pilot line agencies that met internal audit, procurement management, and other standards. The goal was to reduce central BOB controls through line itemization and replace it with a value for money approach. This is similar to lesson 7 above in that positive incentives are applied to achieve program results. Unfortunately, BOB itself lacked technical capability to provide the assistance to line agencies, and there was no time limit for line agencies to upgrade their management standards (2005, 362).

8

CONCLUSION

Dissemination of Budget Lessons and Innovations

INTRODUCTION

This concluding chapter concentrates on two issues of comparative budgeting and finance. First, is it possible to move toward any kind of general theory of budgeting or are the differences between countries too great? That is, is there a framework or model that can be used to compare budget system design and installation internationally? Second, in this global age, to what extent can innovation and reform in one country be transferred and applied to another country? More specifically, what can the EU 8/10 countries learn from the rest of the EU about national and subnational budgeting and finance? What can the FSU countries learn from Commonwealth countries? Latin America from Eastern Europe? Eastern Europe from Latin America? The rest of the world from the United States? Related to this broad concern is the deeper question of how one country may be induced to listen to other countries for advice on how to improve fiscal systems. There are plenty of ignored examples out there crying out for application. How can country fiscal policymakers become *incentivized* to act in their country's best interest in particular cases?

USES AND ABUSES OF COMPARATIVE BUDGETING RESEARCH

Interest in comparative institutional and financial policy research is growing. In foreign policy, daily comparisons of planning and fiscal decision making for the conflicts in Iraq and Vietnam can be found. Health care provision and financing has become a problem in virtually all OECD countries and is once again on the national agenda in the United States for the new Obama administration. Solutions to the problem of providing health care to large, aging populations at reasonable cost to the state budget can be found in Canada and several U.S. states. The question is whether these systems are transferable across national boundaries and cultures. Given regional disparities and political differences, are they even transferable among U.S. states? Policy advisers seek comparative lessons on school choice, financing, and student performance from the UK. Is the institutional and financial lesson that a major hurricane, such as Katrina in New Orleans, is required to wipe out past practices before bad U.S. school systems can be radically reformed? (Waldman 2007, 89). Urban transportation systems across the world face the same constraints of reduced state funding, growing congestion and pollution, and increasing fuel prices. What solutions can be found from comparative planning, budgeting, and financing experiences? Why are the urban transport lessons from Toronto, Bern, or Washington, D.C., systems relevant or not for other locales? Decentralization of management responsibilities and financial authority for some social programs in Eastern Europe has worked well. In others, it has not. What explains the differences and how can comparative budgetary research offer better lessons for design and implementation of these and other programs?

These and other policy and budgeting issues come up daily. Unfortunately, analyses are often flawed, leading to questionable options and recommended solutions. Quah (2006, 940), for example, recently reviewed a book presenting a comparative analysis of the successes and failures of anticorruption strategies in different countries. Noting the "pitfalls of comparative analysis" when applied to countries in which there are enormous differences in size, population, and quality of governance indicators, he suggested that it is "difficult to draw valid comparisons among such disparate environments" (2006, 940). Nevertheless, the book was published and its conclusions are taken seriously by many who ignore (or perhaps do not recognize) this basic methodological weakness.

In the area of comparative budgeting we have argued through our framework in chapter 1 that more attention should be paid to the cultural and institutional settings and to the constraints on fiscal systems modification. One might consider this emphasis odd.. Wouldn't *soft* constraints such as culture affect the transfer of lessons for the larger policy issues (e.g., pollution and poverty)? It might be thought that the results of public budgeting systems and processes would be less tangible, and have less impact than failure of big policies such as anticorruption or air/water pollution. But periodic macro-collapses of the public finances and weakening of economies are often the result of bad policy, questionable program or project design, and weak implementation systems. The larger economic impact of microfailures such as budget classification and accounting systems are well known to professionals in this field and are not really a matter of debate (as anticorruption methods would be). Weak classification means weak baseline projections and loss of fiscal discipline with predictable effects on deficits, debts, and probably service results. This may be because the rules of fiscal classification and reporting are largely standardized. Fiscal analysts and budget watchdogs (e.g., International Budget Partnership with its Open Budget Index) typically know from a comparative international perspective how data should be recorded and reported. They also know how micro failures can lead to serious empirical consequences for the larger issues of economic growth and development. Nor are there any serious doubts about the criteria for functioning procurement, internal control, or accounting systems. They are well known. Similarly, the linkage between a deficit control rule and selection of a transparent measure of fiscal deficits is relatively straightforward. But how to modernize such fiscal systems under conditions of major political uncertainty is debatable. For such reasons, empirical works on comparative public budgeting are critical to policymaking and national development.

Rules of the public fiscal game, from accounting and reporting to deficit-control systems (e.g., benchmarking with soft and hard action triggers for exceeding them; Posner 2009, 237), to criteria for public fiscal transparency (i.e., standardized norms and relevant information requirements) are well known. For the most part, as indicated in this book, countries in most regions of the world have conformed to them, with corresponding advances in budget discipline, allocational certainty, operational stability, and fiscal sustainability. The same cannot be said for the private financial and banking sectors. Beginning around 2006, evidence increased of major gaps in internal transparency. Institutional actors from mortgage brokers, banks, insurance companies, and quasi-government housing enterprises interacted on the basis of their own rules, making high-risk bets derived from origination of subprime mortgages and expectations of high profitability from collateralized debt. The resulting destabilization of global finance generated major fiscal responses from governments in the United States, Latin America, and Commonwealth countries. They have responded to the limits of their fiscal space based on how prudently they managed their debts and deficits in periods of economic growth. Those that controlled and saved public resources, such as Chile, now have more space to finance stimulus packages with high multiyear deficit budgets.

From our review of comparative budgetary behavior, it is clear that (1) governments compile far more transparent fiscal data than private financial and nonfinancial firms, (2) the effect of rules for discipline and fiscal control (e.g., deficit triggers) in countries as diverse as the United States, Chile, and Switzerland are well known. These lessons are being transferred to countries such as the United States (mainly at the state level) to limit expenditures to sustainable levels of financing, (3) reform efforts have been well catalogued and an important lesson is that they should be built on existing systems using clear incentives and comparative examples that suggest they will likely work, and (4) given the depth of the current recession and banking sector collapse, public budgeting reform should attempt to expand MTEF-type efforts that link current expenditures with both public revenue constraints and expenditure needs, as well as their effects on economic growth and stabilization of the wider economy. It is apparent that relevant information to gauge the impact of alternative public subsidies, direct expenditures, loan guarantees, and investments in the banking and financial sector is at best weak and at worst irrelevant to decision making in a crisis. More empirical work in comparative budgeting systems and processes should be targeted to enhance economic growth and development.

REVIEW OF DISTINCT PRACTICES, SYSTEMS, AND METHODS

From our comparative and international review in the above seven chapters of global budget practices, we suggest that there are systems that can be transferred without major changes in the core values or attitudes of the political culture. These system possibilities are summarized in Table 8.1 below. The practices originated in their home regions, where they function properly, and they have been successfully transferred overseas. The problems addressed by these *developed country* practices and their overseas destinations are indicated in Table 8.2. While many systems and methods have also been unsuccessfully transferred, as we have seen, this is less from the distinctiveness of the system or practice than poorly designed and/or implemented reforms. The success of budgeting in Commonwealth countries to achieve fiscal discipline and planning objectives, for example, has been based to a large extent on effective use of MTEF planning frameworks. MTEFs have provided multiyear revenue and expenditure data by objects of expenditures and functions/programs and, in many cases, this has facilitated superb forward planning. MTEFs have contributed to control of aggregate deficits and funds for downstream payments of capital maintenance, debt service, and current service operations have been made available. At the same time, exports of MTEFs have had hit or miss success experiences. In countries as diverse as Armenia (far outside the cultural values and attitudes of Commonwealth political culture), MTEFs have been implemented with great fanfare (Poghosyan, cited in Guess 2007). There, it took about eight years of donor pressure and central government cooperation for the fiscal reform to be almost fully institutionalized (2007, 166–67). Multiyear fiscal plans, projections, and policy papers multiplied as the system was implemented. But changes in the composition of spending attributable to the multiyear analysis of needs and resources in other MTEF export locations have so far not been evident. Few allocational changes can be traced to this system. Cuts, where they have occurred, have followed traditional line-item, across-the-board decisions after standard adjustments for inflation. In Armenia, hard budget constraints have often been ignored and implementation of MTEF has been weakened by inclusion of performance budgeting requirements, for example, activity

TABLE 8.1. Comparative Budget System Reforms

Region	Reform	Purpose
US	Independent congressional review Budget as policy document High capacity budget and policy analysis institutions (e.g. OMB and CBO)	Planning and value for money (efficiency) Transparency and focused oversight Value for money
Commonwealth	MTEF Internal Audit Performance Line-Item (NZ/Australia)	Planning Control/Value For Money Management/Service- Performance
Eastern Europe/ FSU	Equalization Transfers Results Norm to Needs Based Allocations	Regional Equalization Management-Service Performance
Latin America	IFMS Supreme Audit Institutions (SAIs) Program/Performance	Control Control and Value for Money Value for Money
European Union	Macrobudgetary planning Cohesion and competitiveness grants	Strategic fiscal targeting Fiscal equalization

statistics, performance measures, and cost analysis. The temptation to add performance budgeting to MTEF in one large reform was overwhelming in Armenia as elsewhere. As noted in chapter 3, the result is often to weaken both reforms.

In addition, the success of budgeting in Commonwealth countries is due in large part to a long institutional tradition of financial reporting and auditing (derived from a culture that places a premium on precise accounting and legal behavior). This allows fiscal reform to move beyond budget structures and formats to the larger concerns of incentives for state modernization and improved public sector performance. Having sound internal audit systems that serve management program objectives permits devolution of discretion to mid- and lower-level public managers to shift funds and spend them to attain program purposes as they see fit. The normative control emphasis is enforced through post-expenditure in the context of tight reporting requirements. And the reports must be in both fiscal and physical service terms. Thus, internal audit and control serve *New Public Management* objectives of normative concentration/centralization and operational decentralization. This approach encourages decentralization of fiscal structures and increased local autonomy (of local governments, line ministries, and line managers) to achieve more expenditure efficiency and effectiveness. In the context of

MTEFs supported by strong reporting and auditing systems, both central programs (e.g., social assistance) and local programs (e.g., schools), function transparently and effectively. Thus, these two systems from Commonwealth countries should be considered by countries in other regions and limited to the purposes for which they were intended.

TOWARD APPLIED COMPARATIVE BUDGET THEORY

Our book offered a general comparative budgetary analysis framework. The intent is for practitioners and academics to use the multiple variables from the model in chapter 1 to generate applied comparative budgeting lessons. From that framework, it is evident that the budgetary institutions and political culture variables have the most descriptive and explanatory power for lesson generation. Since institutions and culture have always been softer analytic concepts, the important questions are (1) what elements of each are operationally most important, and (2) how should one use them to compare budget systems (and subsystems) performance? The practical purpose of engaging in comparative budgetary analysis is to improve technical support interventions. In an unpublished 2002 World Bank draft report on Armenia, a consultant catalogued approximately $200 million in fiscal reform projects from several international donors that she argued were a complete waste of money. Scarce time and funding is still wasted on interventions in other places that, as we have noted from previous chapters, often lack senior support, are culturally inconsistent with local practices and institutional capacities, and are technically infeasible or irrelevant to local needs. To avoid these kinds of design errors and to try and improve comparative budgetary research, we offer a three-stage analytical approach or model. The idea is that each stage contains a set of constraints that policymakers should recognize as trigger points for review, course correction, or possibly jettisoning the fiscal systems reform effort.

In the first stage, there must be *background support* from the political regime and local technical capacity to design and implement the reforms (Guess 2005, 221). Support can be provided by public statements and legal authorizations, for example, the Honduran SIAFI law. Technical capacity can be acquired for fiscal systems applications rapidly by training methods. The experience is that this capacity can be acquired so quickly and effectively that it may be a risk rather than a benefit! Some regimes fear that capacity building for the installation of new computerized accounting and budgeting systems, for example, will actually cause an outflow of capable civil servants seeking higher pay in the private sector. In the view of most, increased capacity of human resources and its transfer to other sectors should be considered as a developmental benefit to society (i.e., a positive externality).

In the second stage, the important issues of *culture and institutions* arise. In transitional and developing countries, there are serious constraints in the form of centralist values/cultures, lack of intermediary civil society organizations that can hold officials accountable, and weak institutional rule systems that cannot enforce universalist-type norms. While these exist more or less in most countries, all of them work against successful design, adaptation, and implementation of improved fiscal systems. Fortunately, culture and institutions are typically variables, not constants. Some cultural/institutional features are deeply embedded but malleable with the right efforts, at least in the medium term. New incentives, for example, can improve universal reporting practices (overcoming nepotism and tribalism), and activate line management interested in meeting service targets (overcoming job-for-life public service mentality). Fiscal reform programs need to recognize these constraints and build in systemic incentives that can modify cultural/institutional constraints. Fiscal/budget reforms are uniquely capable of doing this because they produce tangible systemic expectations and behavioral results.

An important definitional point for the second stage of comparative analysis should be reemphasized. Much of the fiscal systems and reform work described in this book is done in the name of improved *performance*. But the very notion of *performance* is a relative, culture-specific concept. It could mean rule compliance, obedience, protection of resources, or cooperation/overt conflict avoidance, etc., where these are the dominant societal (or just organizational) goals (Schiavo-Campo and Tommasi 1999, 11). Fiscal reformers should not necessarily expect the *modern* outputs or outcomes of efficiency and effectiveness at all. For example, achievement of performance improvements within different cultures may require less ambitious reforms than costly performance-program or activity based costing (ABC) systems. Failure to recognize this produces many surprises after spending vast amounts of funds for advanced computerized systems. Frequently, reformers find out that because there was really no demand for the new systems in the first place, there are no output or outcome performance improvements. This has often been the lesson of procurement systems reforms that span multiple organizational boundaries, often across widely different cultural regions of a country. The ordered goods somehow never arrive and more money than budgeted keeps disappearing from the accounts. In budgeting, it is often forgotten that *inputs* (often considered a worn-out concept along with the method of *incrementalism*) are still important concepts and methods. Relying on them for initial project design to gain experience with local staff can lead to major results improvements, for instance, encouraging input measurement and reporting of maintenance costs as a percentage of total expenditures. Over several fiscal year cycles, staff become adept at generation and analysis of input performance data and in many cases want to move toward output and outcomes data and information. The input performance system institutionalizes incentives and motivation for shifting to output and outcomes budgeting. As noted by Schiavo-Campo and Tommasi (1999, 67), the link between performance results and budget systems is often inferential and indirect rather than direct and automatic. The need is to integrate cultural constraints and build on them for improved operation of new fiscal systems and practices. That means that someone must know the lessons (i.e., how to recognize the constraints and opportunities of the local political culture) and how to work them into the design phase. The focus in this book has been on how to make budgeting and finance systems work around the world via the transfer of feasible lessons. Often, budgeting systems are imported off-shelf along with technical methods that merely gather dust in ministries of finance or line ministries. To avoid that, one must pay attention to the feasibility of the technical sequence consistent with cultural constraints.

Much has been written on institutions indicating the need to get cultural values and incentives right (North 1990, 137–38). Others have written about international budgeting sytem practices but leave out the cultural variable (Shah 2007). Unfortunately, not much has been written on the technical sequencing for actual installation of fiscal institutions. Therefore, fiscal system designers must in the third stage of comparative analysis, pay close attention to *technical design and sequencing installation* of the systems. For, despite the technically superficial coherence of fiscal management systems, little is known about the optimal sequencing for installation of such systems—because they are affected by the first two stages of constraints and those vary by and within country.

Here, it is important to standardize the technical activities for particular fiscal programs, such as fiscal decentralization or performance budgeting systems, so that they are similar across countries. This task is easier for fiscal systems, since most of the activities (e.g., control macroeconomic aggregates, strengthen internal controls, assign expenditure responsibilities, assign revenue responsibilities, and monitor revenue and expenditure assignment performance) are roughly the same. This means that while the activities are similar, the sequencing in local contexts is typically different. For this reason, further research should be focused on two important elements of technical sequencing.

First, as noted, the technical sequencing experiences for international fiscal systems installation vary and need to be researched. General empirical advice can be found. For example, it has been suggested that countries adopt a four-phase sequence for fiscal decentralization implementation: (1) ensure macroeconomic stability, (2) ensure economic efficiency, especially public expenditure control, (3) assign expenditure and revenue responsibilities to lower-tier governments, and (4) ensure regional horizontal balance (Guess, Loehr, and Martinez-Vazquez 1997, 39–42). But even this advice has proven to be too general. It is also evident that there are major differences in how particular countries implement their programs, for example, by assigning revenues and expenditures at the same time. The results of these local sequences need to be examined and compared (e.g., their impact on local fiscal autonomy). Similarly, one country may develop performance budgeting systems by first modifying their accounting codes, increasing capacity for activity-based statistical analysis, and then changing their budget format. Many countries follow this technical sequence. Other countries may use this sequence, but delay changing the codes and budget format until officials become familiar with generation of input-based budget performance measurement, for example, by calculating the changes in O&M expenditures/total expenditures in education. When this initial level of competence is reached, reformers then guide officials to the other technical tasks. Such has been the history of many successful country experiences with performance budgeting installation. Many countries that have adopted the more complicated first approach have not institutionalized the system and resultant budgets have not been used for analysis or actual allocation of funds by parliaments/legislatures. Thus, there is much to be learned from the variations in technical sequencing of countries installing fiscal and budgeting systems. Little research has been performed comparing these different technical sequences (Guess 2005).

Second, the success rates of fiscal systems installed under tough cultural and political conditions need to be researched. There is a growing comparative literature on how fiscal/budget systems were installed in difficult cultural and governance contexts. But it does not extend to the effects of culture and local institutions on design/installation of particular fiscal tools and methods (e.g., column three of Table 8.2 below). As indicated in that table, comparative budgetary analysis should begin with transitional and developing country needs and problems. At the same time, comparative analytical depth and knowledge generation for its own sake is elegant and edifying but ultimately not the purpose of our book. The cultural literature on area studies is also vast.

The question, then, is not where budget reforms and solutions have been successful—we know that most answers lie in OECD countries and exceptional local contexts, such as Brazil and Chile. For officials and elected reformers in transitional and developing countries, the question is, Where have reforms and improvements been successfully adapted in transitional and developing countries similar to ours? Then they can decide if the examples are of comparable utility to their own fiscal management work. As we have seen, there is often a perverse preference (out of jealousy or misguided patriotism) to ignore neighboring successes (e.g., successful Costa Rican health care financing is still ignored by Nicaragua and Honduras but was imported into Cuba thirty years ago!) and go for modern but irrelevant examples in poorer Latin countries (e.g., Argentina's IFMS by Nicaragua's MOF).

Nonetheless, based on the chapter reviews in this book, tips and suggestions can be offered on the receptivity of fiscal management systems to particular cultural contexts. At the policy level, reformers need to understand the constraints and opportunities of "change-prone" and "change-resistant" cultures (Harrison 2006, 97). One could provide examples of the former, such as Chile and Novgorod (Russia), and the latter, such as Nigeria and Honduras. But such classifications only beg the question of what caused the culture to become change prone or resistant? More importantly, would such a broad cultural classification work for all kinds of fiscal management systems? More sophisticated and complex fiscal management systems require more radical institutional, regulatory, and incentive changes than others. This suggests that the fiscal tool or method may have a hand in changing the underling culture to allow its own introduction. That is, the type of fiscal system may affect the underlying culture and produce the incentives needed to for their introduction (Guess 1992).

By this approach or chain of reasoning, the fiscal management system becomes the change agent. That is, it is not the culture as independent variable that causes the success or failure of systems installation. To gauge fiscal systems success potential, the system or method itself becomes almost as important as the culture. It was noted in chapter 5 that successful budgeting and financial systems installation (corresponding to the four types of GFOA budgets) in the Balkans depended largely on their systemic implications (Guess 2001). Those with more complexity (affecting staff-line relations, regulations, and wider networks of interorganizational relations) ran up against more of the local culture and could only be installed over the medium term. For example, changing the budget from a legal document to an *operational guide* for management that included appropriations-commitment, outlay balances, unit costs, and related figures did not really clash with the core features of the Balkan political culture. Since the political culture meant centralization and informational secrecy, this affected Balkan budgeting. The CEE/FSU culture also encompassed a strong work ethic (when *incentivized*) and clear and rigid (if often irrational) administrative systems. Under these conditions, it would be harder change the budget to be a *multiyear financial plan* (because this would require transparency about future intentions), a *policy document* (because this would require changes in organizational responsibility and turf as well as economic analysis—a relatively new concept since it is not law-driven), or a *communications device* (because of the continuing force of informational secrecy).

When targeting transitional and developing countries, an important lesson for fiscal modernizers is to start with operational changes and move up slowly to policy and communications reforms—letting new techniques drive institutional and management changes to ensure that they are used properly. Supplying new fiscal techniques without generating sufficient demand for them is a clear recipe for disaster or for, in the words of Allen Schick during a fiscal reform effort in Thailand, "a train wreck!" (World Bank 1999). In short, fiscal reformers should begin the three-stage process by assessing the quality of top-level political support, then review culture and institutions—What does the political culture mean and how change resistant is it? Then, as indicated, in the third stage, they should try and link the technical system and operational sequence with potential influences of culture. Little has been written on the last phase and it remains mostly an affair of trial and error Thus, more research is needed on fiscal systems installation in transitional and developing countries to see if they did or did not adapt developed-country best practice. If they did, what was the result and why? What does this suggest for other country governments that would want to adapt such systems and methods? Such analysis would reveal that further research and analysis needs to be done on the installation and impact of advanced-country fiscal systems in transitional and developing countries. More pre-post data and information on systems design and impact are needed.

Many of the budgetary systems and practices of the Latin America, Former Soviet and Eastern Europe, Commonwealth, European Union countries, and the United States have been discussed in this book. What follows is a list of the major public budgeting and financial management problems that have been tackled in OECD countries. Transitional and developing countries have adopted or adapted these solutions with varying degrees of success. The reasons for successful or unsuccessful systems transfer need to be researched using appropriate comparative methods. From Table 8.2 below, it should be evident that comparative research on the use and results of these systems in developing and transitional countries is in the early stages (despite a relatively vast literature) and needs to be stepped up by scholars, researchers, and the international donors that finance such projects. It is hoped that this book will contribute to the stimulation of such efforts.

TABLE 8.2. **Adaptation of Advanced Country Fiscal Management Systems**

Problem / Need	OECD / Developed Country Practice	Transitional / LDC Benchmark Use
Incomplete coverage: All revenues and expenditure data of general government are not in one document; nor is this data available, understandable or in relevant form as information for decision-making.	Transparent budget information, e.g. websites and budgets in brief	Peru; see work of International Budget Project, e.g. http://www.internation albudget.org/openbudgets/fullreport.pdf IMF Country Reports on Observance of Standards and Codes—Fiscal Transparency Module (ROSC)
Formalistic budgets: Budgets prepared based on some combination of revenue estimates, laws, physical norms and last year's base + inflation adjustments.	Modern analytical methods comparing cost/consequences used during budget formulation (general and sectoral)	Bulgarian, Romanian and Armenian LGUs. Sectoral financing of health, (Chile primary care performance transfers) education (Brazilian school cost and service performance transfers) and public transit (Brazilian performance transfers and integrated social services) (www.fazenda.gov.br)

TABLE 8.2. (continued)

Problem/Need	OECD/Developed Country Practice	Transitional/LDC Benchmark Use
Top-down budgeting: Current and capital expenditures planned and approved with minimal citizen or stakeholder inputs.	Citizen participation (general and sectoral)	Armenia (www.ichd.org), Brazil (Porto Alegre Popular Participation), Ukraine (health care spending budget watch: www.icps.com.ua)
Input budgeting: Budgets planned and implemented via inputs (salaries, supplies) rather than production of outputs (e.g. passenger miles of transit) or outcomes (e.g. reduction of congestion and pollution costs)	Results/Performance/ Program budgeting: Functional budgets (U.S.), envelope budgeting (Canada); Swedish performance incentive budget for departmental efficiency.	Few examples of successful installations where legislatures/city councils/ parliaments use performance analysis for allocations. Armenian LGUs have had some success. Some Brazilian LGUs have installed them. Many national governments have tried and partly or totally failed, e.g. Thailand, Ghana, Bolivia. In the mid to late 1960s, many Latin American countries adopted program budgets following the US example (e.g. Chile, Venezuela, Peru). Since that one largely failed, the Latin American ones did too. Research in Indonesia, Philippines and Pakistan suggests that LGU officials find other fiscal reforms more important and useful.
Lack of expenditure targeting and monitoring: Allocations not well-targeted to poor. Important especially in social services. Leakage of funds from pro-poverty programs during implementation.	Pro-Poor Budgeting Public poverty reduction consists of cash and non-cash benefits targeted to the poor and ultra-poor. Cash benefits include: means-tested social assistance payments, child allowances, unemployment compensation, and micro-grants and credits for business. Non-cash benefits include: health,	Peruvian poverty-mapping system; counter-cyclical protected poverty budget (PSPs); enhanced virtual poverty fund (Uganda). Others: Zambia, Mauritania, Mozambique, Tanzania and Honduras. See: Rocio Campos campos@cbpp.org

TABLE 8.2. (continued)

Problem/Need	OECD/Developed Country Practice	Transitional/LDC Benchmark Use
	education, rural roads, water-sewer systems, and urban transport subsidies.	
Inaccurate budget forecasts: Institutional weakness contributes to forecast error (US S&L +15 -25% caused by fiscal stress) Elections create pressure for over-estimation; until early 1990s, Colombian forecasts by law could not exceed PY amounts by 10% nor fall by more than 30%!	Revenue Forecasting Organizations and Methods: Use of countervailing institutional forecasts (US federal government—CBO v OMB); independent forecasts (Washington DC government); use of "rainy day funds" to cushion bad forecasts. Models: single-executive agency, council of outside forecasters, consensus forecasting.	Chile has oil and copper stabilization funds to break link between trade and fiscal (revenue) cycle; Nigeria has very opaque oil stabilization fund; Little comparative research on revenue forecasting accuracy has been done in transitional and developing countries.
No multi-year perspective: Budget plans are one-year only and ignore future consequences of O&M and debt service costs + future programmatic requirements.	Rolling multi-year expenditure planning leading to hard budget constraint/MTEF: Canadian PEMS; Australian and British MTEFs	Kenya, Uganda, Nigeria, Papua New Guinea, Peru (MABs combined with program and poverty reduction budgets).
Poor capital planning and financing: Capital improvements planning and financing systems are weak. Organizational responsibilities are confused/fragmented, and there is a lack of methods, systems and capacity to: assess capital needs, financial payback capacity, perform project analysis, rank project requests, and assess financing options.	Integrated capital planning and financing	Romanian LGUs and central government;

TABLE 8.2. (continued)

Problem/Need	OECD/Developed Country Practice	Transitional/LDC Benchmark Use
Bloated states and regulatory over-control: Excessive state resource absorption and bureaucratic controls (facilitating corruption and harming investment climate) strangle economic growth. In past, hyperinflation and currency collapse were not uncommon among developing countries.	Aggregate spending control and radical state modernization: British Treasury	Budgets are prepared with limits from formal macro-economic analyses. For this reason the budgets of most transitional and developing countries are under control and inflation is minimal. However, expectations are outpacing state capacities to deliver results without transforming/ downsizing themselves. State reforms have proceeded in countries like: Chile, Estonia, Czech Republic, which have produced increased savings that have been reprogrammed to needed services and infrastructure.
Fiscal deficit problems: Large and persistent fiscal deficits crowd out private investment and create inflationary pressures.	Fiscal deficit controls (driven by macroeconomic forecasts, caps, pay-go etc) control cash, commitments and primary types of deficits.	Most FSU/CEE and Latin American countries; exceptions indicate major socio-economic costs of failure to follow best practices in this area (e.g. Zimbabwe, Bolivia)
Minimal legislative input into budget approval or execution: Laws/constitutions limit legislative inputs in budget approval; in many cases they may not vary the composition or aggregate levels by % of amounts proposed by executive; parliaments have weak analytical units	Parliamentary/ Congressional budgeting: US Congress very powerful in budget process;	Parliamentary budget analysis and approval role is still quite weak. The Peruvian parliament has little influence over composition of expenditures in the approved budget or in ensuring reconciliation of planned v actual outlays during implementation.

TABLE 8.2. (continued)

Problem/Need	OECD/Developed Country Practice	Transitional/LDC Benchmark Use
Fragmented fiscal information: 15 yr ago, in the early days of computerized management information systems, Independent financial management systems were less expensive to build, modular in structure, had operational systems conforming to current financial procedures, and were flexible in that systems could be modified or discarded without damaging other systems. Independent systems relied on manual inputs, could not integrate data from several sources, and were constrained by different coding arrangements. For expenditure planning and fiscal policy-making, independent systems allowed too many leaks in the entry and exit of fiscal data. Independent fiscal systems perpetuated and multiplied costs, delays and errors when data was passed from unit to unit within government. MOFs and central banks could not rely on this data to exercise control over their economies.	Expenditure controls, single treasury accounts and IFMS: An integrated system is composed of a single data base which end users look at from different points of view (budget reports, analysis of budget execution, revenue collections etc). At the center, IFMS registers and totals all transactions which form the basis of the daily cash position. Where modified accrual accounting systems exist, a contract commitment (purchase order, supplier invoice) is registered in the accounts to prevent over-budgeting by MOF. MOF can then use commitments data and better revenue forecasts to manage cash and debt levels during the fiscal year. This linkage integrates data from: budgeting, accounting, revenue, cash and debt management systems. At the line level, an IFMS decentralizes operational responsibility for data entry. Hospital managers, for instance, need to know costs/patient days and be able to compare them with other regional hospitals. But line managers need to enter data only once and it is kept in a central subaccount at the Treasury (single treasury account). This eliminates layers of approvals, delays and corruption opportunities.	Most Latin American countries now use some form of IFMS, e.g. Honduras (SIAFI), Bolivia (SAFCO), Argentina (SIDIF), Brazil (SIAFI), Guatemala (SIAF), Peru (SIAF), and Nicaragua (SIGFA).

TABLE 8.2. (continued)

Problem/Need	OECD/Developed Country Practice	Transitional/LDC Benchmark Use
Fixed and rigid budgets: Budgets are rigid (made fixed and inertial by prior commitments) and cannot be changed easily during execution. If they are modified, it is often via cash limits or crude cuts and additions.	Flexible expenditure and program management systems (via such mechanisms as active allotments management; *virement* or *traspaso*).	Mexican analysis-based budget modification and use of allotment system to maximize program performance + fiscal discipline by Secretaria de Hacienda y Credito.
Lack of management controls: Internal Audit: Internal audit units are designed improperly and function to control for legal compliance only. They often report to the ministry finance office rather than a central audit officer (Comptroller-General). There may also be multiple units performing internal compliance control at cross-purposes to the confusion of auditees.	Independent ministry and LG Internal audit units, e.g. U.S. Office of Inspector General (OIG); Canadian Comptroller-General. Ensure that internal controls function within ministries and LGUs, and may perform value for money reviews of particular services and programs.	Brazil (Secretariat for Internal Control), Argentina (National Comptroller-General's Office; Argentina's National Accounting Office is the central organ for internal control;
External Audit and Control Units focus on administrative/legal compliance and financial balance issues; and preventive control (e.g. Latin American courts of accounts).	British NAO; U.S. GAO; Swedish Parliamentary Audit Office.	Supreme Audit Units (SAIs) report external audit findings to parliaments in Latin America and CEE on reconciliation of fiscal accounts and value-for-money performance 1` of particular services, e.g. Argentina AGN, Brazil Court of Accounts, Chilean Office of Comptroller General, Malaysian AG, and Chinese (PRC) NAO. Even AGN still focuses primarily on financial-administrative control and performs few studies or analyses of key issues, such as: control of public revenues,

TABLE 8.2. (continued)

Problem/Need	OECD/Developed Country Practice	Transitional/LDC Benchmark Use
		privatization performance, regulatory agency performance, or fiscal decentralization progress.
Weak program monitoring and evaluation. Ex post (retrospective) service performance is either not examined or analyses are made and not worked into next year's budget. Impacts of current expenditures and capital investments not thoroughly examined.	U.S. OMB—GAO reviews; NGO results and coverage analyses, e.g. Center for Budget and Policy Priorities (www.cbpp.org); Australian DOF provides TA and support to departments to conduct program evaluations;	Successful Public Expenditure Tracking and Evaluation Systems (PETS): Uganda, Peru; Quantitative Service Delivery Surveys (QSDs): El Salvador;
Local borrowing threatens macroeconomic stability: Local fiscal autonomy risk of over-commitment and lack of national controls. Problem in Latin America (Argentina, Brazil) less so in FSU/CEE countries.	National laws (restricting loan guarantees and bail-outs), whole-of government accounting systems (local-national balances consolidated daily); credit agency ratings (periodic financial condition reviews) largely control risks of local borrowing (e.g. US, CEE).	LG debt authority and borrowing controls put in place. In most of Latin America, central government authorization is now required (i.e. MOF) and there are restrictions both on the amounts borrowed (e.g. debt service cannot exceed 15% of past year's actual budget for Prague) and how it is used (i.e. infrastructure only). In some countries, such as Chile, subnational borrowing is still prohibited. There has been dramatic improvement in standardized fiscal performance condition analysis and benchmarking, both by rating agencies and by LGUs themselves in many regions (e.g. Brazil, Romania). Some countries now feature local fiscal stress early warning systems, insolvency matrices and bankruptcy provisions (e.g. Macedonia, Romania and Bulgaria).

NOTES

CHAPTER 1. COMPARATIVE BUDGETING

1. Before moving the budget issues in the regional cases, we should say a word about application of the comparative framework. In the current context of intensifying world development efforts, ending military conflicts, and solving all the world's policy problems, wild comparative statements have become commonplace. For example, Pakistan public finances are often compared to India, when the determining professionalism and strength of its state may be more like a middle range Latin American country, such as Peru or Ecuador. Comparison with India can result in misleading and irrelevant policy propositions. It is important that comparisons be valid—regardless of the type of analytic framework that is applied. Country development levels, budget systems and accounting practices, and governmental capacities should be similar. The objects of comparative analysis should be selected with similar backgrounds and analogous characteristics. This allows the analyst (1) to exercise control over these similarities in order to reduce the problem of multiple causation and (2) to explain why similar rules produce different results in identical contexts (Xavier 1998). It allows one to explain why similar systems can produce different results by focusing in on the particular elements of budget systems provided in our framework, e.g., budget execution, accounting and reporting systems, or political culture and regime support.

CHAPTER 2. BUDGETING IN THE UNITED STATES

1. The Senate switched back to Democratic control in 2001 after Senator James Jeffords of Vermont left the Republican Party to become an Independent caucusing with the Democrats. The 2002 elections restored a Republican majority in the Senate.

CHAPTER 3. COMMONWEALTH COUNTRIES

1. In a creative twist however, Vice President Richard Cheney asserted in 2006 that he was "co-independent," i.e., not accountable to either branch of government. At the same time, he claimed "executive privilege" from disclosing information that in his judgment might be "sensitive."

CHAPTER 5. CENTRAL AND EASTERN EUROPE AND THE FORMER SOVIET UNION

1. The question is why? One answer is that the Soviet Communist system was good at producing educated and trained people up to a certain limit. But beyond that level, according to Rudolf Bahro's *The Alternative*, cited in Hitchens (2009), the system forbade them to think, inquire, or use their initiative. While the system produced vast amounts of "surplus consciousness," "it could find no way of employing this energy except by squandering and dissipating and ultimately repressing it" (Hitchens 2009, 92). Since budget analysis requires critical challenges to accepted premises and figures, and generation of program and policy options often contrary to official lines, budget analysis was repressed along with other political kinds of activities. Analysis was restricted to recording entries in the accounting statements and controlling them for consistency with budgetary allocation laws.

2. As occurred with this system throughout the former Soviet Union, the norms generated incentives to overallocate resources to salaries and institutions which more or less worked in the context of free money and unlimited plenty produced by transfers from Moscow under the old system. The norms did not produce cost effectiveness or efficiency. Now the norms serve to lock in inefficiencies from the center. It is recognized that the norm system has outlived its usefulness in the context of scarce resources. The new normative method of calculating transfers should permit local governments to optimize the use of resources for health and other services. Decision-making authority and information will be shifted to the facility level for most transactions, allowing managers to combine resources for better service results. The short-term incentive is fiscal authority to allocate up to 10 percent of oblast consolidated revenues to smooth out budget disruptions. In addition, the Council of Ministers has adopted program budgeting for 2002 (i.e., budgeting according to tasks, goals, and measurable benchmarks as opposed to existing functions such as health). This should lead to forward expenditure programming on the basis of outcomes and use of performance data to allow monitoring and evaluation of expenditures.

References

Alesina, A., and R. Perotti. 1995. Fiscal expansions and adjustments in OECD countries. *Economic Policy* 10: 207–47.

Allan, B. 1994. Public expenditure management and budget law: Toward a framework for a budget law for economies in transition. *Discussion Paper K39, H61.* Washington, DC: International Monetary Fund.

Allen, R., and D. Tommasi. 2001. *Managing public expenditure: A reference book for transitional countries.* Paris: OECD.

Andrews, M., and J. Turkewitz. 2005. Introduction to symposium on budgeting and financial management reform implementation. *International Journal of Public Administration* 28: 203–11.

Annett, A. 2006. Reform in Europe: What went right? *Finance and Development* 43: 32–35.

———, and A. Jaeger. 2004. Europe's quest for fiscal discipline. *Finance and Development* (June 22–25).

———. 2005. Europe's quest for fiscal discipline. *Finance and Development* 42 (June 22–25).

Arakelyan, A. 2005. Public–private transit mix strands Yerevan's vulnerable. *Local Governance Brief:* 18–22.

Axelrod, D. 1988. *Budgeting for modern government.* New York: St. Martin's Press.

Bahl, R. 1995. Comparative federalism: Trends and issues in the United States, China, and Russia. In *Macroeconomic management and fiscal decentralization,* ed. J. Roy, 73–103. Washington, DC: World Bank.

Baumgartner, F. R., M. Foucault, and A. Francois. 2007. *Patterns of public budgeting in the French Fifth Republic: From hierarchical control to multi-level governance.* Paper presented at the annual meeting of the American Political Science Association, August 30-September 2, Chicago IL.

Berman, L. 1979. *The Office of Management and Budget and the presidency, 1921–1979.* Princeton: Princeton University Press.

Bernik, I. et al. 1997. Slovenian political culture: Paradoxes of democratization. In *Making a New Nation: The Formation of Slovenia,* ed. D. Fink-Hafner and J. Robbins, 56–82. Aldershot, UK: Dartmouth.

Binder, S. A. 2003. *Stalemate.* Washington, DC: Brookings Institution.

Bird, R. M. 1982 Budgeting in Colombia *Public Budgeting and Finance* 4, no. 3: 87–99.

Blond, P., and A. Pabst. 2006. Centrism that leads to decay. *International Herald Tribune,* 7.

Bokros, L. 2006. *The role of IFIs in economic reform.* Presentation at Central European University, October 19, Budapest, Hungary.

Burki, S. J., and G. Perry. 1998. *Beyond the Washington consensus: Institutions matter.* Washington, DC: World Bank.

Caiden, N. and A, Wildavsky. 1974. *Planning and budgeting in poor countries.* New York: John Wiley.

Calia, R. 2001. *Priority-setting models for public budgeting.* Chicago: Government Finance Officer's Association.

Chilcote, R. H. 1994. *Theories of comparative politics: The search for a paradigm reconsidered.* 2nd ed. New York: Westview Press.

Coe, C. K.. 1989. *Public financial management.* Englewood Cliffs, NJ: Prentice-Hall.

Collier, D. 1979. *The new authoritarianism in Latin America.* Princeton: Princeton University Press.

Committee on Appropriations, Subcommittee on HUD and Independent Offices, U.S. House of Representatives, *Hearings, National Aeronautics and Space Administration,* 94th Congress, 2nd session, February 18, 1976: 144.

Congressional Budget Office. 2007. *Budget options.* http://www.cbo.gov/doc. cfm?index=7821.

———. 2007. *The economic and budget outlook, 2008–2017.* http://www.cbo.gov/ doc.cfm?index=7731.

———. 2009. *The budget and economic outlook, 2009–2019.* http://www.cbo.gov/ doc.cfm?index=9957.

Conrad, K., and J. Gregg. 2009. A fiscal battle on two fronts. *The Washington Post,* January 15, A16.

Consejo Nacional de Descentralizacion. 2006. *El Modelo Peruano de descentralización.* Lima: CND, 57–60.

Cramm, L. et al.. 1999. *Developments in the European Union.* New York: St. Martin's Press.

Cutler, L. 1989. Now is the time for all good men. *William and Mary Law Review* 30: 391.

Dafflon, B., and S. Rossi. 1999. Public accounting fudges towards EMU: A first empirical survey and some public choice considerations. *Public Choice* 101: 59–84.

Daughters, R., and L. Harper. 2006. Fiscal and decentralization reforms. In *The state of state reform in Latin America,* ed. Eduardo Lora. Washington, DC: Inter-American Development Bank.

Davey, K. 2006. *Comments at local government and public service reform initiative, Budapest. In Fast track: Municipal fiscal reforming Central and Eastern Europe and the former Soviet Union,* ed. George M. Guess. Budapest: Local Government and Public Service Reform Initiative of the Open Society Institute.

Dempsey, J. 2006. Riots fail to force a resignation in Hungary. *International Herald Tribune*, 1.

———. 2006. Ukraine chief resists E.U. push for reforms: Kiev's priority is social stability he says. *International Herald Tribune*, 3.

———, and K. Bennhold. 2007. Energy sends Russia on a power trip, but in which direction? *International Herald Tribune*, 6.

Dixon, G. 2005. Thailand's quest for results-focused budgeting. *International Journal of Public Administration* 28: 203–11.

Dumitru, B. and R. Mihai. 2005. All public transport is not equal in Chisinau. *Local Governance Brief:* 13–17.

Ebel, R. and G. Peteri. 2007. Intergovernmental transfers. In *Kosovo decentralization briefing book,* ed. Robert Ebel and Gabor Peteri, 121–33. Budapest: Local Government and Public Services Reform Initiative.

The Economist. 2005. IT in the health care industry: The no-computer virus, April 30, 61–63.

———. 2005. Overdue and overbudget, over and over again, June 11, 57–58.

———. 2005. Peace, order, and rocky government: A survey of Canada," December 3.

———. 2006. Hungary's election: The re-election precedent, April 29.

———. 2006. Improving on the Latin rate of growth, May 20, 54–55.

———. 2006. Infrastructure in Latin America: Slow! Government obstacles ahead, June 17, 53–54.

———. 2006. Italy: Stormier weather ahead, September 16, 33–34.

———. 2006. When the victory spells defeat, October 6, 59–60.

———. 2006. Chile's schools: How to make them better, October 7, 60.

———. 2006. Italy's budget: Smoke and mirrors, October 7, 34–35.

———. 2006. National Health Service: Handing over control, October 14, 39–40.

———. 2006. Central and Eastern Europe: Shadows at Europe's heart, October 14, 30–34.

———. 2006. Ex-communist countries: Europe's fraying edge, October 14, 13–14.

———. 2006. Open budget index, October 28, 114.

———. 2006. The world in 2007.

———. 2006. *Pocket world in figures.* London: The Economist Ltd.

———. 2007. Trust the locals: Reasons to be hopeful that Britain will become less centralized, January 27, 31–32.

———. 2007. Austria: Sleeping with the enemy, November 22, 12.

———. 2008. Brazil: Happy families, February 9, 39–40.

———. 2008. In search of an insurance policy, February 16.

———. 2008. Economic and financial Indicators, February 16.

———. 2008. The electronic bureaucrat: Special report on technology and government, February 13, 18.

———. 2008. Special report on technology and government, February 16, 18.

———. 2008. Exxon's wrathful tiger takes on Hugo Chavez, February 16, 43–44.

———. 2008. Does Wall Street's meltdown show that financial globalization is part of the problem? September 27, 92.

———. 2008. Briefing: Money markets—blocked pipes, October 4, 73–75.

———. 2008. Public finances: Counting the costs, October 18, 65–66.

———. 2009. East European economies: To the barricades, January 24, 56–57.

———. 2009. Briefing: Global economic imbalances, January 24, 74–76.

———. 2009 Rescue efforts: Big government fights back, January 31, 79–80.

———. 2009. Open budget index, February 7, 86.

———. 2009. Anti-poverty programs: Quid pro quo, February 14, 70.

———. 2009. Chile's economy: Stimulating, February 21, 40.

———. 2009 Full disclosure: The case for transparency in financial markets is not clear-cut, February 21, 78.

———. 2009. Economic and financial indicators, February 28, 102.

———. 2009. The government's finances: Brave rhetoric, grim reality, February 28, 31–32.

———. 2010. Honduras Country Report. London: Economist Intelligence Unit EIU.

Edwards, G. C. III, A. Barrett, and J. Peake. 1997. The legislative impact of divided government. *American Journal of Political Science* 21: 545–63.

European Union. EU budget 2007. http://europa.eu/budget/finance/index.

———. EU budget at a glance. http://ec.europa.eu/budget.

———. EU Budget in detail. http://ec.europe.eu/budget/budget_detail.

———. The European Commission. http://europa.eu/institutions/inst/comm/index_en.htm.

———. The Treaty of Lisbon at a glance. http://europa.eu/lisbon.

Fenno, R. 1965. *The power of the purse.* Boston: Little Brown.

Ferrier, J. 2004. *Passing the buck: Congress, the budget, and deficits.* Lexington: University Press of Kentucky.

Filc, G., and C. Scartascini. 2006. Budgetary institutions. In *The state of state reform in Latin America,* ed. Eduardo Lora. Washington, DC: Inter-American Development Bank.

Finkler, S. A. 2005. *Financial management for public, health, and not-for-profit organizations,* 2nd ed. Upper Saddle River: Pearson-Prentice-Hall.

Fisher, L. 1978. *The Constitution between friends.* New York: St. Martins.

Franklin, A. L..2002. An examination of the impact of budget reform on Arizona and Oklahoma appropriations. *Public Budgeting and Finance* 22: 25–45.

Freire, M., and R. Stren, eds. 2001. *The challenge of urban governments: Policies and practices.* Washington, DC: World Bank Institute.

Fusfeld, D. R.. 1982. *The age of the economist.* Glenview, Ill: Scott, Foresman.

Grodzins, M. 1966. *The American system.* Chicago: Rand McNally.

Grupo Propuesta Ciudadana. 2006. *Democracia, Descentralizacion y Reforma Fiscal en America Latina y Europa del Este.* http://lgi.osi.hu/documents.php?m_id= 118&bid=1.

Guess, G. M. 1984. *Bureaucratic-authoritarianism and the forest sector in Latin America.* Austin: University of Texas, Institute for Latin American Studies Technical Paper 43.

————. 1988. Budgetary cutback and transit system performance: The case of MARTA, *Public Budgeting and Finance* 8, no. 1 (Spring): 58–68.

————. 1991. Poverty and profit in Central American forestry. *Public Administration and Development* 11: 573–89.

————. 1992. Centralization of expenditure controls in Latin America. *Public Administration Quarterly* 16, no. 3: 376–94.

————. 1997. Macedonian cities adopt results-oriented budgeting. *Partnership* 2, no. 1: 10. Washington, DC: World Bank.

————. 1997. Comparative government budgeting. In *Public budgeting and finance,* 4th ed., ed. R. Golembiewski and J. Rabin, 243–66. New York: Marcel Dekker.

————. 2000. *Honduras: Public expenditure management: The institutional dimension.* Washington, DC: The World Bank.

————. 2001. Decentralization and municipal budgeting in four Balkan states. *Journal of Public Budgeting, Accounting and Financial Management* 13, no. 3: 397–436.

————. 2001. *Issues and recommendations for pro-poverty budgeting in Kazakhstan.* Astana: Asian Development Bank. (unpublished report).

————. 2002. *Pakistan: Roadmap for installation of local integrated multiyear performance budgeting system.* Islamabad: Asian Development Bank.

————. 2005. Comparative decentralization lessons from Pakistan, Indonesia, and the Philippines. *Public Administration Review* 65: 217–31.

————. 2005. *Nigeria: FY 2004 preparation and submission and call circular.* Bethesda, MD: Development Alternatives, Inc.

————. 2007. Letter from Budapest: Liar liar. *The American Interest* 2: 121–25.

————, ed. 2007. *Fast track: Municipal financial management in Central and Eastern Europe and the Former Soviet Union.* Budapest: Central European University Press/ Local Government and Public Service Reform Initiative of the Open Society Institute.

————, ed. 2008. *Managing and financing urban public transport systems: An international perspective.* Budapest: Local Government and Public Service Reform Initiative of the Open Society Institute.

————, and K. Koford. 1984. Inflation and the federal budget deficit: Or blaming economic problems on a statistical mirage. *Policy Sciences* 17, no. 4: 385–402.

————, J. Martinez-Vazquez, and W. Loehr. 1997. *Fiscal decentralization: A methodology for case studies.* CAER Consulting Assistance on Economic Reform II: Discussion Papers, no. 3. Cambridge, MA: Harvard Institute for International Development.

————, and P. G. Farnham 2000. *Cases in public policy analysis.* 2nd ed. Washington, DC: Georgetown University Press.

————, and S. J. Sitko. 2004. Planning, budgeting, and health care performance in Ukraine. *International Journal of Public Administration* 27, no. 10: 767–98.

————, and C. Todor. 2005. Capital programming and budgeting: Comparative local government Perspectives. In *Encyclopedia of public administration and public policy*, ed. Jack Rabin. New York: Marcel Dekker.

Gyurcsany, F. 2006. Extracts from speech, delivered to MSZP Party, Closed Session, Balatonoszod.

Hallerberg, M. 2004. *Domestic budgets in a united Europe: Fiscal governance from the end of Bretton Woods to EMU.* Ithaca: Cornell University Press.

————, and J. Von Hagen. 1999. Electoral institutions, cabinet negotiations, and budget deficits within the European Union. In *Fiscal institutions and fiscal performance,* ed. J. Poterba and J. Von Hagen, 209–32. Chicago: University of Chicago Press.

Hambleton, R., and D. Sweeting. 2004. U.S.-style leadership for English local government? *Public Administration Review* 64, no. 4: 474–88.

Harrison, L. E. 1995. *Underdevelopment as a state of mind: The Latin American case.* Lanham, MD: University Press of America.

————. 2006. The culture club: Exploring the central liberal truth. *The National Interest* 83: 94–101.

Hibbs, D. 1977. Political parties and macroeconomic policy. *American Political Science Review* 71: 1467–87.

Higginson, M. 2006. Long-term instability seen unlikely. *Budapest Business Journal.* http://www.bbj.hu/main/news_17043_long-term%2Binstability%2Bseen%2Bunlikely.html.

Hill, H., and M. Andrews. 2005. Reforming budget ritual and budget practice: The case of performance management implementation in Virginia. *International Journal of Public Administration* 28: 255–73.

Hirschman, A. O. 1971. *A bias toward hope: Essays on development and Latin America.* New Haven: Yale University Press.

Hitchens, C. 2009. He's back: The current financial crisis and the enduring relevance of Marx. *The Atlantic* (April), 88–95.

Hoffman, D. 1996. Harsh history stymies civil society. *The Washington Post*, A1.

Hood, C. 2006. Gaming in Targetworld: The targets approach to managing British public services. *Public Administration Review* 66, no. 4: 515–21.

Inglehart, R. 1988. The renaissance of political culture. *American Political Science Review* 82: 1203–31.

Institut National de la Statistique et des Etudes Economiques. http://www.insee.fr/fr/indicateur/cnat_annu/base_2000/finances_publique/depenses_recettes.httm.

International Budget Partnership. 2008. Open budgets.transform lives. The open budget survey 2008. Washington, DC, International Budget Partnership of the Center for Budget and Policy Priorities.

International Monetary Fund. 2007. *Republic of Slovenia: Selected issues. IMF Country Report no. 07/182*. Washington, DC: International Monetary Fund.

———. 2007 (June). *Working Paper 07/182* .Washington, DC: International Monetary Fund.

Joint Committee on Taxation. 2008. *Revenue estimates of selected tax policies relating to the 2001 and 2003 tax cuts.* Washington, DC: U.S. Government Printing Office.

Kaplan, R. D..1998. The fulcrum of Europe. *The Atlantic Monthly,* 28–36.

———. 2007. A historian for our time. *The Atlantic Monthly* 299, 78–84.

Kasso, Z. 2006. Budgeting: Methods, process, and execution. In *Kosovo decentralization briefing book,* ed. R. Ebel and G. Peteri,. Budapest: Local Government and Public Service Reform Initiative (forthcoming).

Key, V.O. 1940. The lack of a budgetary theory. *American Political Science Review* 34: 1137–44.

Knapp, A., and V. Wright. 2001. *The government and politics of France.* 4th ed. London: Routledge.

Kopits, G., and J. Craig. 1998. *Transparency in government operations.* IMF Occasional Paper #158. Washington, DC: International Monetary Fund.

Laitin, D.D. 1995. The civic culture at 30. *American Political Science Review* 89: 168–73.

LeLoup, L. T. 1988. From microbudgeting to macrobudgeting: Transition in theory and practice. In *New Directions in Budget Theory,* ed. Irene Rubin, 19–42. Albany: State University of New York Press.

———. 1998. Budgeting in Hungary during the democratic transition. *Journal of Public Budgeting, Accounting and Financial Management* 10, no. 1: 90–120.

———. 2004. Parliamentary budgeting in Hungary and Slovenia. *Financijska Teorija I Praksa* 1: 49–74.

———. 2005. *Parties, rules, and the evolution of Congressional budgeting.* Columbus: Ohio State University Press.

———, B. L. Graham, and S. Barwick. 1987. Deficit politics and constitutional government: The impact of Gramm-Rudman-Hollings. *Public Budgeting and Finance* 7: 83–103.

————, B. Ferfila, and C. Herzog. 2000. Budgeting in Slovenia during the democratic transition: A comparative analysis. *Public Budgeting and Finance*: 63–92.

————, B. Ferfila, and C. Herzog. 2001. The Slovenian budget: A comparative perspective. *Review of Current Issues in Economics* 46: 273–98.

————, and B. Ferfila. 2001. Have parliaments influenced budget policy during democratization? *Public Administration (Javna Uprava)* 2: 183–212.

————, and B. Ferfila. 2002. Slovenia and the European Union. *Teorija in Praksa* 39: 646–53.

————, and B. Ferfila. 2003. Have parliaments influenced budget policy during democratization? A comparison of Hungary and Slovenia. *Journal of Transforming Economies and Societies* 10: 46–65.

Lienert, I. 2007. *British influence on Commonwealth budget systems: The case of the United Republic of Tanzania.* International Monetary Fund Working Paper #07/78. (April). 37 pp.

Lijphart, A., ed.. 1992. *Parliamentary versus presidential government.* Oxford: Oxford University Press.

Linz, J., and A. Stepan. 1996. *Problems of democratic transition and consolidation: Southern Europe, South America, and Post-communist Europe.* Baltimore: Johns Hopkins University Press.

Logan, M. 2006. Double boost for the PM's survival odds. *The Budapest Times* 3: 1.

Lopez Murphy, R. 1995. *Fiscal decentralization in Latin America.* Washington, DC: IADB.

Lora, E., ed. 2006. *The state of state reform in Latin America.* Washington, DC: IADB.

Lyden, F., and E. Miller. 1972. *Planning programming budgeting.* Chicago: Markham.

Martinez-Vazquez, J. 1994. Expenditures and expenditure assignment. In *Russia and the challenge of fiscal federalism,* ed. C. Wallich, 96–128. Washington, DC: World Bank.

————. 1995. Intergovernmental fiscal relations in Bulgaria. In *Decentralization of the socialist state: Intergovernmental finance in transition economies,* ed. R. M. Bird, R. D. Ebel, and C. Wallich, 183–223. Washington, DC: World Bank.

————, and J. Boex. 1995. Fiscal decentralization in the Baltic countries. *Proceedings of the National Tax Association.* San Diego.

Martner, G. 1967. *Planificacion y Presupuesto por Programa.* Mexico: Siglo Veintiuno.

Mayhew, D. 1991. *Divided we govern.* New Haven: Yale University Press.

McCubbins, M. 1991. Party governance and U.S. budget deficits: Divided government and fiscal stalemate. In *Politics and economics in the 1980s,* ed. A. Alesina and G. Carliner, 83–111. Chicago: University of Chicago Press.

Meyers, R. T. 2009. The "ball of confusion" in federal budgeting: A shadow agenda for deliberative reform of the budget process. *Public Administration Review* 69, no. 2 (March/April): 211–23.

Mikesell, J. L. 2007. Fiscal administration, analysis, and applications for the public sector. 7th ed. Belmont, CA: Thomson Wadsworth.

————, and D. R. Mullins. 2001. Reforming budget systems in countries of the former Soviet Union. *Public Administration Review* 61: 548–68.

Miller, G. 1984. GFOA's program of awards for distinguished budget presentation. *Governmental Finance* 13: 29–33.

Miller, T. 1996. *Fiscal federalism in theory and practice: The Philippines case.* Washington, DC: USAID/G/EG/EIR.

Milwaukee (Wisconsin). 2003. *City of Milwaukee 2003–2008 Capital Improvements Plan.* www.city.milwaukee.gov.

Mitric, S. 2003. *Urban transport in Belgrade: A policy note.* Washington, DC: World Bank.

Montgomery, L. 2009 As stimulus grows, so does task of closing whopping deficit. *The Washington Post,* February 15, AI.

————, and D. Eggen. 2008. Spending surge pushing deficit toward $1 trillion. *The Washington Post,* October 18, AI.

Morse, K and R. J. Struyk. 2006. *Policy analysis for effective development: Strengthening transition economies.* Boulder: Lynne Rienner.

Moynihan, D. P.. 2006. Managing for results in state government: Evaluating a decade of reform. *Public Administration Review* 66, no. 1: 77–89.

Mydans, S. 2007. Presentable disaster in Yakarta? Decentralization brings risk in dealing with new calamities. *International Herald Tribune,* 5.

Naipaul, V.S.. 1974. *India: A wounded civilization.* New York: Vintage.

North, D. C.. 1990. *Institutions, institutional change and economic performance.* New York: Cambridge University Press.

Nugent, N. 1999. *The government and politics of the European Union.* 4th ed. Durham: Duke University Press.

O'R. Hayes, F., D. A. Grossman, J. E. Mechling, J. S. Thomas, and S. Rosenbloom. 1982. *Linkages: Improving financial ,anagement in local government.* Washington, DC: Urban Institute.

Oatly, T. 1999. How constraining is mobile capital? The partisan hypothesis in an open economy. *American Journal of Political Science* 43: 1002–27.

Office of Management and Budget. 2008. *FY09 budget of the United States Government.* Washington, DC: U.S. Government Printing Office.

Organization for Economic Cooperation and Development. 1997. *OECD economic surveys: Slovenia.* Paris: Organization for Economic Cooperation and Development.

————. 2008. *2007 Edition, statistics on the member countries.* Washington, DC: OECD.

Ott, K., ed. 2006. *Making public finance public: Subnational budget watch in Croatia, Macedonia, and Ukraine.* Budapest: Open Society Institute, Local Government and Public Service Reform Initiative.

Ottaway, D. B..1998. AID struggles to recover from '96 computer fiasco. *The Washington Post,* November 3, A15.

Peterson, S. B. 2007. Automating public financial management in developing countries. In *Budgeting and budgetary institutions*, ed. A. Shah, 323–58. Washington, DC: World Bank.

Petrei, H. 1998. *Budget and control: Reforming the public sector in Latin America.* Washington, DC: Inter-American Development Bank.

Pierson, P. 2000. Increasing returns, path dependence, and the study of politics. *American Political Science Review* 94: 251–67.

Poghosyan, S. 2007. Community budget reforms in Armenia: Introducing a new outlook on budgeting. In *Fast track: Municipal fiscal reform in Central and Eastern Europe and the former Soviet Union,* ed. George M. Guess, 149–73. Budapest: Local Government and Public Service Reform Initiative of the Open Society Institute.

Posner, P. L. 2009. Budget process reform: Waiting for Godot. *Public Administration Review* 69, no. 2: 233–44.

Premchand, A. 1983. *Government budgeting and expenditure controls: Theory and practice.* Washington, DC: International Monetary Fund.

———. 1993. *Public expenditure management.* Washington, DC: International Monetary Fund.

———. 1999. Budgetary management in the United States and in Australia, New Zealand, and the United Kingdom. In *Handbook of government budgeting,* ed. R. T. Meyers, 82–115. San Francisco: Jossey-Bass.

Quah, J. S.. 2006. Curbing corruption: The elusive search for a cure. *Public Administration Review* 66, no. 6: 939–43.

Reid, G. 1994. *Modernization of the state in Ecuador.* Washington, DC: World Bank (draft).

Reinhorn, L. J. 2007. Butter mountains and wine lakes. *Economic Letters* 94: 197–201.

Republic of Slovenia. 2002. *Negotiations of the accession of the Republic of Slovenia to the European Union completed: Presentation and assessment of the financial package.* www.svez.gov.si/fileadmin/svez.gov.si.

———, Statistical Office. 2007. *Social cohesion indicators.* http://193.2.238.17/end/novica_prikazi.aspx?id=708.

Reuters Alertnet. 2006. *Costs for Iraq war approach record.* December 19.

Roubini, N., and J. Sachs. 1989. Political and economic determinants of budget deficits in the industrial democracies. *European Economic Review* 33: 903–33.

Roy, J. 1995. *Macroeconomic management and fiscal decentralization.* Washington, DC: EDI Seminar Series, World Bank.

Rubin, I. 1990. *The politics of public budgets.* Chatham, NJ: Chatham House.

Savage, J. D. 2005. *The politics of budgetary surveillance and the enforcement of Maastricht.* New York: Oxford University Press.

Savedoff, W. D., ed. 1998. *Organization matters: Agency problems in health and education in Latin America.* Washington, DC: IADB.

Schiavo-Campo, S., and D. Tommasi. 1999. *Managing government expenditure.* Manila: Asian Development Bank.

Schick, A. 1966. The road to PPB: The stages of budget reform. *Public Administration Review* 26: 243–58.

———. 1978. The road from ZBB. *Public Administration Review* 38: 177–80.

———. 1986. Macro-budgetary adaptations to fiscal stress in industrialized democracies. *Public Administration Review* 46, no. 2: 124–34.

———. 1999. *Opportunity, strategy, and tactics in reforming public management.* Paper presented at OECD Symposium, *Government and the future: Getting from here to there,* September 14–15, Paris, France.

Schneider, S. K. 2005. Administrative breakdowns in the governmental response to Hurricane Katrina. *Public Administration Review* 65, no. 5: 515–16.

Schopflin, G. 1991. The political traditions of Eastern Europe. In *Eastern Europe...Central Europe...Europe,* ed. S. R. Graubard, 59–94. Boulder: Westview Press.

Semjen, A. 1994. Some fiscal problems during economic transition in Hungary. In *Developing public finance in emerging market economies,* ed. K. Mizsei, 19–57. New York: Institute for East-West Studies.

Shah, A. 1994. *The reform of intergovernmental fiscal relations in developing and emerging market economies. Policy and Research Series* 23. Washington, DC: World Bank.

———, ed. 2007. *Budgeting and budgetary institutions.* Washington, DC: World Bank.

———, and C. Shen. 2007. A primer on performance budgeting. In *Budgeting and budgetary institutions,* ed. A. Shah, 137–78. Washington, DC: World Bank.

Shin, A. 2009. Crisis prompts calls to boost IMF reserves: Eastern Europe's struggles may test fund's capacity. *The Washington Post,* February 24, D1.

Siddiquee, N. A. 2005. Public accountability in Malaysia: Challenges and critical concerns. *International Journal of Public Administration* 28, no. 1–2: 107–29.

Siemiatycki, M. 2008. Seeking transportation for a livable city: The case of Vancouver, Canada. In *Managing and financing urban public transport systems: An international perspective,* ed. G. M. Guess. Budapest: Local Government and Public Service Reform Initiative of the Open Society Institute.

Smith, J. R. 1998. Montenegro appears closer to splitting off from Serbia. *The Washington Post,* November 27, A31.

Smith, R., and T. D. Lynch. 2004. *Public budgeting in America.* Upper Saddle River, NJ: Pearson/Prentice-Hall.

Somali, I. G. 1992. *Fancy footwork: Entrapment in and coping with the Nepali management model.* Katmandu.

Sondrol, P. 2005. The presidentialist tradition in Latin America. *International Journal of Public Administration* 28: 503–17.

Stern, N., J.-J. Dethier, and F. H. Rogers. 2005. *Growth and empowerment, Making development happen.* Cambridge: MIT Press.

Stillman, R. 2002. Preface. In *Public management in the Central and Eastern European transition: Concepts and cases,* ed. G. Wright and J. Nemec. Bratislava: Network of Institutes and Schools of Public Administration in Central and Eastern Europe.

Stockman, D. 1986. *The triumph of politics.* New York: Harper and Row.

Straussman, J. D. 1996. Ideals and reality in the evolution of fiscal reform in Central and Eastern Europe. *Public Budgeting and Finance* 16, no. 2: 79–95.

————, and K. Fabian. 1994. Local government finance in Hungary: Okun revisited. *Public Budgeting and Finance* 14, no. 4: 71–83.

Stren, R. 2001. Municipal and subnational financial management. In *The challenge of urban governments: Policies and practices,* ed. M. Freire and R. Stren, 107–11. Washington, DC: World Bank Institute.

Swianiewicz, P., ed. 2004. *Local government borrowing: Risks and rewards.* Budapest: Open Society Institute, Local Government and Public Service Reform Initiative.

Sylvers, E. 2006. Italy faces higher borrowing costs. *International Herald Tribune,* 11.

The Washington Post. 2008. The long term cost, September 28, B2.

Thurmeier, K. 1994. The evolution of local government in budgeting in Poland: From accounting to policy in a leap and a bound. *Public Budgeting and Finance* 14, no. 4: 84–98.

Tommasi, D. 2007. Budget execution. In *Budgeting and budgetary institutions,* ed. A. Shah, 279–322. Washington, DC: World Bank.

Tonko, A. 2007. Municipal budget reforms in Hungary: Have they made a difference?. In *Fast track: Municipal fiscal reform in Central and Eastern Europe and the former Soviet Union,* ed. G. M. Guess, 99–149. Budapest: Local Government and Public Service Reform Initiative of the Open Society Institute.

U. S. Census Bureau. 1976. *Historical statistics, Colonial times to 1970.* Washington, DC: U.S. Government Printing Office.

U.S. Advisory Commission on Intergovernmental Relations. 1983. *Intergovernmental Perspective* 9, no. 3: 24.

Ubokudom, S. 1993. The Kansas Financial Information System (KFIS): Policy design and policy failure. *Public Budgeting and Finance* 13, no. 3: 63–72.

United Nations Development Program. 1995. *Human development report: Albania 1995.* Tirana: UNDP.

Vargas Llosa, M. 1973. *Pantaleon y Las Visitadoras.* Madrid: Alfaguara.

Vasco, M. 2005. Exploring the e-governance gap in South America. *International Journal of Public Administration* 28: 683–703.

Vickland, S., and I. Nieuwenhuijs. 2005. Critical success factors for modernizing public financial management information systems in Bosnia and Herzegovina. *Public Administration and Development* 25: 95–103.

Vitrenko, Y., and A. Nagorna. 1999. *Health care policy.* Kyiv: World Bank.

Vogt, A. J. 2004. Chapter 4. *Capital budgeting and finance: A guide for local governments.* Washington, DC: International City/County Management Association.

Vogt, J. A., and D. R. Duven. 1983. *A guide to municipal leasing.* Chicago: Municipal Finance Officer's Association.

Von Hagen, J. 1999. *Budgeting institutions for aggregate fiscal discipline. ZEI Paper* B98-01. www.zei.de.

Waldman, A. 2007. Reading, writing, resurrection. *The Atlantic Monthly* 299, no, 1, 88–103.

Wallace, R. A.. 1960. *Congressional control of federal spending.* Detroit: Wayne State Press.

Wallich, C. I., ed. 1994. *Russia and the challenge of fiscal federalism.* Washington, DC: World Bank.

Weaver, K., and B. A. Rockman. 1993. Assessing the effects of institutions. In *Do institutions matter?,* ed. R. K. Weaver and B. A. Rockman, 1–41. Washington, DC: Brookings Institution.

Weitzman, B., D. Silver, and C. Brazill. 2006. Efforts to improve public policy and programs through practice: Experiences in 15 distressed American cities. *Public Administration Review* 66: 386–99.

Wesberry, J. 1989. Integrating accounting and budgeting systems. *Association of Government Accountants Journal.*

Whiteley, P. 1996. Review of *The Treasury and Whitehall: The Planning and Control of Public Expenditure: 1976–1993,* by C. Thain and M. White. American Political Science Review 90, no. 4: 945–46.

Whitlock, C. 2009. E.U. denies request for bailout of Eastern Europe. *The Washington Post,* A6.

Wildavsky, A. 1964. *The politics of the budgetary process.* Boston: Little Brown.

———. 1989. *Budgeting: A comparative theory of budgetary processes (revised edition).* New Brunswick, NJ: Transaction.

The World Bank. 1995. *Better urban services: Finding the right incentives.* Washington, DC: IBRD.

———. 1998. *Public expenditure management handbook.* Washington, DC: World Bank.

———. 1999. *Improving Public Expenditure Management.* Seminar, Bangkok, Thailand.

———. 2001. *Ukraine: Public expenditure and institutional review.* Washington, DC: IBRD.

———. 2003. *Restoring fiscal discipline for poverty reduction in Peru: A public expenditure review.* Washington, DC: IBRD.

———. 2004. *International Development Association country assistance strategy for Moldova.* Washington, DC: IBRD.

————. 2005. *Current issues in fiscal reform in Central Europe and the Baltic states 2005.* Washington, DC: IBRD.

————. 2006a. *Fiscal policy for growth and development: An interim report on transfer of resources to developing countries.* Washington, DC: IBRD.

————. 2006b. *World Bank EU8 quarterly economic report.* Washington, DC: IBRD.

Wright, G., and N. Juraj. 2002. *Public management in the Central and Eastern European transition: Concepts and cases.* Bratislava: Network of Institutes and Schools of Public Administration in Central and Eastern Europe.

Xavier, J. A.. 1998. Budget reform in Malaysia and Australia compared. *Public Budgeting and Finance* 18: 99–118.

INDEX